The Holocaust:
An Annotated
Bibliography
and Resource Guide

The Holocaust: An Annotated Bibliography and Resource Guide

Edited by
DAVID M. SZONYI

KTAV PUBLISHING HOUSE, INC.
for
THE NATIONAL JEWISH RESOURCE CENTER
New York

This work was made possible in part by a grant from the
National Endowment for the Humanities (EH-0362-79)

Library of Congress Cataloging in Publication Data

Main entry under title:

The Holocaust: an annotated bibliography and resource guide.

1. Holocaust, Jewish (1939-1945)—Bibliography.
I. Szonyi, David M. II. National Jewish Resource Center
III. B'nai B'rith. Anti-defamation League.
Z6374.H6H65   1985   [D810.J4]   016.94053'15'03924   84-26191
ISBN 0-88125-057-0
ISBN 0-88125-058-9 (pbk.)

MANUFACTURED IN THE UNITED STATES OF AMERICA

DEDICATED TO

THE MEMBERS OF THE BOARD OF ZACHOR:
HOLOCAUST RESOURCE CENTER
a project of the National Jewish Resource Center

- Exemplars of memory, commitment, passion
- Who remembered before it was fashionable to remember
- Who work to insure that the memory will never perish.

Irvin Frank . . . . .Tulsa, Oklahoma
Founding Chairman

Jeffrey M. Boyko . . . . .New York, New York
Chairman

Richard Bergman . . . . .Louisville, Kentucky

Dr. Sidney Busis . . . . .Pittsburgh, Pennsylvania

Steve & Susan Cummings . . . . .Westmont, Quebec

Profs. Alice & Roy Eckardt . . . . .Cooperburg, Pennsylvania

Prof. Henry Feingold . . . . .New York, New York

Warren Finn* . . . . .Houston, Texas

Rhoda Goldman . . . . .San Francisco, California

Sol Goldstein . . . . .Skokie, Illinois

Harry Guterman . . . . .Tulsa, Oklahoma

Paula Kaufman . . . . .San Antonio, Texas

Miles Lerman . . . . .Vineland, New Jersey

William Mayer . . . . .New York, New York

Benjamin Meed . . . . .New York, New York

Rev. John Pawlikowski . . . . .Chicago, Illinois

Sigmund Strochlitz . . . . .New London, Connecticut

Prof. David Weinberg . . . . .Toledo, Ohio

*deceased

Contents

Contributors

Harry James Cargas is Professor of Literature and Language, and Professor of Religion, at Webster College in St. Louis. A member of the United States Holocaust Memorial Council, he is the author of five books on the Holocaust.

Nama Frenkel is an independent film producer who recently worked on *Lights: A Chanukah Story*, and is currently writing a screenplay based on her experiences producing *Jewish Mothers*, a documentary on Boro Park, Brooklyn.

Mary T. Glynn is a Sister of Mercy who is a secondary-school teacher. She was Project Director of a study on the impact of Holocaust education on high school students which was published by the National Jewish Resource Center under a grant from the National Endowment for the Humanities. A member of the Advisory Committee for the New York State Holocaust Curriculum, she has been a consultant on education to the U.S. Holocaust Memorial Council.

Eric Goldman is Director of the Jewish Media Service/JWB and is the author of *Visions, Images and Dreams: Yiddish Film Past and Present* (UMI Press).

Rena Septee Goldman is an attorney practicing in New York. She has done extensive research on Jewish resistance in Auschwitz.

Irving Greenberg is founder and President of the National Jewish Resource Center and former Director of the U.S. Holocaust Memorial Council

Irene Heskes is a musicologist, writer, and lecturer who specializes in Jewish music as social history.

Jeffrey Hirschberg, who holds a Ph.D. in medieval literatures and linguistics, as well as an M.B.A., from the University of Wisconsin, has written widely on literature and language for a variety of scholarly publications. Until recently assistant editor of the *Dictionary of American Regional English*, he is currently an accountant with the firm of Daniel Joseph and Company in Buffalo.

Sara Leuchter, a historian/archivist with the State Historical Society of Wisconsin, is editor of its *Guide to Wisconsin Survivors of the Holocaust*.

Samuel Mozes is the Executive Director of the International Society for Yad Vashem and the American Society for Yad Vashem.

Judith Herschlag Muffs is Director of Research and Curriculum for the Anti-Defamation League of Bnai Brith. She has worked extensively on various aspects of Holocaust education and literature.

Bernard Postal was, until his death in 1982, one of America's most outstanding Jewish journalists, as well as the author of *American Jewish Landmarks* (Fleet Press).

David Roskies teaches Jewish literature at the Jewish Theological Seminary of America and is the author of *Against the Apocalypse: Responses to Catastrophe in Modern Jewish Culture* (Harvard University Press).

Bea Stadtler is a Holocaust educator and the author of many Jewish juvenile books.

*   *   *

David M. Szonyi is the former Assistant Director of ZACHOR: The Holocaust Resource Center/NJRC and the former Associate Director of the Radius Institute in New York. Currently a graduate student in casework at the Hunter College School of Social Work, he is the co-editor of *Living After the Holocaust: Reflections of the Post-War Generation in America* (Bloch).

Preface

IN THE PAST decade, there has been an extraordinary increase in popular awareness of, and interest in, the Holocaust.* This burgeoning of interest can be seen in part in popular culture. Recently, for example, a "docu-novel" on the Holocaust, Thomas Keneally's *Schindler's List*, has received wide acclaim, while a documentary film, *Genocide*, won an Academy Award, and the feature film *Sophie's Choice* stirred widespread interest.

In part too, study and commemoration of the Holocaust are a growing local phenomenon. Almost every major Jewish community has a Yom HaShoah (Holocaust Remembrance Day) commemoration.+ Hundreds, if not thousands, of churches observe the corresponding "Week of Remembrance," as do—on a civic or ecumenical basis—many cities, states, and even the U.S. government.

As a result, organizations such as ZACHOR: The Holocaust Resource Center are deluged with requests for information about books, films, music, speakers, and other resources on the Holocaust. This *Bibliography and Resource Guide*, which is funded in part by a grant from the National Endowment for the Humanities (EH-0362-79), represents the most comprehensive attempt to date to provide lists of resources for those interested in Holocaust education and commemoration.

Specifically, the thirteen sections of the *Guide* list resources on sites related to learning about or teaching the Holocaust, as well as programming and commemorations pertaining to it. There is also an essay on oral history, based on a model program in Wisconsin, as well as very brief suggestions for obtaining speakers on the Holocaust, and funding for programs.

This *Guide* clearly is not totally comprehensive or up-to-date; there are now so many new resources on the Holocaust that it will be

---

* The term "Holocaust" itself has aroused some controversy. In this work, it is used to refer to the murder of six million European Jews by the Nazis and their collaborators between 1933 and 1945.

+ Yom HaShoah occurs on the 27th of Nisan on the Hebrew calendar. Thus, its date on the Gregorian (civil) calendar varies from year to year. It always occurs five days after the end of Passover.

necessary periodically to update it. Indeed, the number of resources and other "data" which have recently become available are in part responsible for this *Guide* appearing several years later than was originally intended. Finally, this *Guide* could not have been produced without the help of dozens of people, to whom ZACHOR is most grateful. A special word of thanks is due to Judith Herschlag Muffs, Director of Research and Curriculum of the Anti-Defamation League of B'nai B'rith, who critiqued most of the sections of this work and offered numerous helpful suggestions which I have used. We are also indebted to the editors of individual sections, all of whom devoted many hours at very little, or no, renumeration. Tragically, one of these contributors, the veteran journalist Bernard Postal, died several months after completing his section on Holocaust-related sites and memorials.

Irving Greenberg, the National Jewish Resource Center's President, was a persistent and sensitive friend and "prodder" over the past months and years. Two former colleagues, Dr. Mary Glynn and Susan Grossman, also have been most helpful. I am also grateful to Joshua Samborn, the NJRC's former Executive Director, and to Joan Soskind, his assistant, for their help in late 1983 and early 1984. Miriam Craig and Dr. Hillel Levine of the U.S. Holocaust Memorial Council were instrumental in securing permission for use of the two commemorative services included in this work. Of the research assistants, proofreaders, and typists who have worked on this *Guide*, five in particular, Rena Septee, Patricia Scott, Miriam Husney, Denise Barricklow, and Carol Cancro, have put in many hours and played key roles in the production of this work.

ZACHOR expresses its appreciation to the National Endowment for the Humanities for helping to underwrite part of the cost of this project, and to present and former members of its staff, particularly Dr. Cynthia Wolloch, for their guidance and their patience.

Finally, I wish to thank Theodore Freedman of the Anti-Defamation League of B'nai B'rith for encouraging his organization to aid in making this publication possible.

In a work with as many listings as this one, there are bound to be some errors. Any mistakes in sections I have edited or co-edited are, of course, solely my responsibility.

ZACHOR welcomes any corrections or additional information for a later edition of this *Guide*. Please send pertinent information to:

Guide to Resources and Programming on the Holocaust—Update
ZACHOR: The Holocaust Resource Center
421-7 Avenue
New York, N.Y. 10001

David M. Szonyi

Section I-A
Scholarship, Memoirs, and Other Nonfiction on the Holocaust

by David Szonyi

The bibliography of nonfiction works on the Holocaust which follows is in part a "pooling" and updating of the recent bibliographies listed below. It does not purport to be comprehensive, for given the recent vast outpouring of scholarship and memoirs, such an effort would require several years to compile and would, in itself, consist of hundreds of pages.*

I have included a limited number of out-of-print books, on the assumption that serious students of the Holocaust have access to such works through local public or university libraries, or through interlibrary loans. (The growing use of microfilm, microfiche, and computer technology should also make works which are now out-of-print more accessible in the future.)

Most Holocaust bibliographies are limited to books, and so fail to inform researchers of the important essays which have appeared. I have combed through a dozen or so periodicals which either are entirely devoted to scholarship on the Holocaust or periodically include in-depth essays on it, and have listed a selected number from them.

An asterisk precedes the names of books which have been published in paperback editions; a plus sign (+) indicates books appropriate for younger readers (ages 15–18).

Finally, I wish to acknowledge with thanks the four other bibliographies on which I relied and—with the editor's permission in each case—whose annotations I sometimes used.

Harry James Cargas (ed.), *The Holocaust: An Annotated Bibliography* (Haverford, Pa.: Catholic Library Association, 1977).

---

* While no up-to-date comprehensive bibliography exists, two works by the late Jacob Robinson—*The Holocaust and After: Sources and Literature in English* (1973) and *Guide to Jewish History Under Nazi Impact* (1974)—are indispensable, as is Dr. Robinson and Yehuda Bauer's *Guide to Unpublished Materials on the Holocaust Period* (3 vols., 1970–75). For complete bibliographical listings on these, see Section I-A, Part 22 ("Bibliographies and Bibliographical Essays").

Sharon Joseph (ed.), *The Holocaust: An Annotated Bibliography* (Montreal: Canadian Jewish Congress, 1980).

Byron L. Sherwin and Susan G. Ament (eds.), *Encountering the Holocaust: An Interdisciplinary Survey* (Chicago: Impact Press, 1979). Each of the fourteen essays in this excellent anthology is followed by a bibliography. I relied on individual bibliographies by M. Cherif Bassiouni, Helen Fein, Jack Nusan Porter, Byron L. Sherwin, and David Weinberg.

Judith Herschlag Muffs (ed.), *The Holocaust in Books and Films: A Selected Annotated List* (New York: Anti-Defamation League of B'nai B'rith, 1981).

I am indebted to the editors listed, and to Theodore Freedman of the Anti-Defamation League Holocaust Center, for permission to utilize their bibliographies. Any errors are, of course, my sole responsibility.

ABBREVIATIONS

The following abbreviations have been used for periodicals (all are quarterlies, except where indicated):

AHR	*American Historical Association Review*
AJH	*American Jewish History*
AJHQ	*American Jewish Historical Quarterly*
CEH	*Central European History*
JCH	*Journal of Contemporary History*
JSS	*Jewish Social Studies*
LBI Yrbk	*Leo Baeck Institute Yearbook* (annual)
M&R	*Martyrdom and Resistance* (bimonthly)
Shoah	*Shoah: A Review of Holocaust Studies and Commemorations*
WLB	*Wiener Library Bulletin*
YVS	*Yad Vashem Studies* (annual)

1.

European Jewish Life
Before the Holocaust

A. General Works

Baron, Salo W. *From a Historian's Notebook: European Jewry Before and After Hitler.* New York: American Jewish Committee, 1962.

Based on a memorandum the eminent historian prepared when called to testify at the 1961 Eichmann trial; packed with statistics, this work deals mainly with European Jewry in the 1930s, including demographic changes, economic trends, emancipation, communal and intellectual life. It also discusses life under the Nazis and the effects of the Holocaust.

Edelstein, Alan. *An Unacknowledged Harmony: Philo-Semitism and the Survival of European Jewry.* Westport, Conn.: Greenwood Press, 1982.

As the title indicates, this is one of the few studies of the positive aspects of the Jewish-Christian relationship from the Middle Ages to the modern period.

Eitinger, S. "The Modern Period." In H. H. Ben Sasson (ed.), *A History of the Jewish People.* Cambridge, Mass.: Harvard University Press, 1977.

An excellent, succinct overview of Jewish history from the era of Emancipation to the Holocaust.

Glatzer, Nahum (ed.). "The Dynamics of Emancipation." In *The Judaic Tradition*, pp. 505–607. Boston: Beacon Press, 1969.

A good anthology on the making of the modern period in Jewish history.

Katz, Jacob. *Exclusiveness and Tolerance. New York: Schocken, 1982.

> A well-written, key overview of Jewish-Christian relations in the premodern era.

———. *Out of the Ghetto.* Cambridge, Mass.: Harvard University Press, 1979.

> A multifaceted view of European Jewry's modernization and emancipation in the eighteenth and nineteenth centuries.

Marcus, Jacob R. *The Jew in the Medieval World.* New York and Philadelphia: Meridian and Jewish Publication Society, 1960.

> By far the best one-volume anthology of medieval Jewish life— covers the fourth to the eighteenth century.

Mendes-Flohr, Paul, and Reinharz, Jehuda. *The Jew in the Modern World.* New York: Oxford University Press, 1980.

> A very good anthology of writings and documents on modern Jewish history.

Sachar, Howard. *The Course of Modern Jewish History.* New York: Dell pb., 1970.

> A very readable short history of the Jews from the Emancipation on.

B. Western and Central Europe

Bach, Hans. *The German Jews: A Synthesis of Judaism and Western Civilization, 1730–1930.* Teaneck, N.J.: Fairleigh Dickinson University Press, 1983.

> An almost 600-page anthology of writings by outstanding German Jews from Mendelssohn to Buber and Rosenzweig.

Gay, Peter. *Freud, Jews and Germans: Masters and Victims in Modernist Culture,* New York: Oxford University Press, 1978.

> Several essays on German Jews and German-Jewish life are included in this major work in intellectual history.

Hyman, Paula. *From Dreyfus to Vichy: The Remaking of French Jewry, 1906–1939.* New York: Columbia University Press, 1979.

> An incisive study of French Jewry's communal life in the generation before the Holocaust, with a special focus on the tensions and areas of cooperation between native Jews and immigrants.

Liptzin, Solomon. *Germany's Stepchildren.* Philadelphia: Jewish
    Publication Society, 1944.

> Short biographies of German Jews of the eighteenth to twentieth
> century.

Marrus, Michael. *The Politics of Assimilation: A Study of the French
    Jewish Community at the Time of the Dreyfus Affair.* New York:
    Oxford University Press, 1971.

> An important study that shows how the French-Jewish community
> refused to recognize the significance of the Dreyfus Affair for its
> own cherished beliefs in emancipation and assimilation.

Meyer, Michael A. *The Origins of the Modern Jew.* Detroit: Wayne
    State University Press, 1967.

> An excellent study of the early stages of Jewish emancipation in
> Germany, from the generation of Moses Mendelssohn to that of his
> grandchildren.

Niewyk, Donald L. *The Jews in Weimar Germany.* Baton Rouge, La.:
    Louisiana State University Press, 1980.

> The first major study of the various German-Jewish ideologies, and
> of German-Jewish relationships in the immediate pre-Holocaust
> period (1918–1933).

Noren, Catherine Hanf. *The Camera of My Family.* New York: Knopf,
    1977.

> A photographic history of several generations of German Jews, up
> to the author's family, with interesting prose passages.

Poppel, Steven M. *Zionism in Germany, 1897–1933.* Philadelphia:
    Jewish Publication Society, 1977.

> An interesting overview of German Zionism, and of its growing
> "radicalism."

Ragins, Sanford. *Jewish Responses to Anti-Semitism in Germany,
    1870–1914: A Study in the History of Ideas.* New York: Ktav, 1980.

> Analyzes the pattern of responses to Anti-Semitism employed by
> German Jews and why they responded as they did.

Reinharz, Jehuda. *Fatherland or Promised Land: The Dilemma of the
    German Jew, 1893–1914.* Ann Arbor: University of Michigan Press,
    1975.

Reinharz provides an excellent analysis of the different world views of German Zionists and of the partially assimilated, "defense"-oriented Jews active in the *Centralverein*.

Rozenblit, Marsha L. *The Jews of Vienna, 1867–1914: Assimilation and Identity*. Albany: State University of New York Press, 1984.

A fine study of demographic and socioeconomic patterns among the Jews from throughout the Austro-Hungarian Empire who poured into its capital in the half-century before World War I.

Schorsch, Ismar. *Jewish Reactions to German Anti-Semitism, 1870–1914*. New York: Columbia University Press, 1972.

Schorsch's thesis is that German-Jewish leaders grew to recognize the dangers of anti-Semitism in Germany before World War I and took effective action to counter it.

Weinberg, David H. *A Community on Trial: Jews of Paris in the 1930's*. Chicago: University of Chicago Press, 1977.

An analysis of Parisian Jewry as a case study of the attitudes and behavior of European Jewry on the eve of the Holocaust.

Note: A major source of scholarly articles on German-speaking Jewry is the *Leo Baeck Institute Yearbook* (27 volumes through 1983, 129 East 73rd Street, New York, N.Y. 10021).

C. Eastern Europe

Dawidowicz, Lucy. *The Golden Tradition: Jewish Life and Thought in Eastern Europe*. New York: Holt, Rinehart & Winston, 1967, and Boston: Beacon Press, 1968.

An anthology of primary source materials by East European Jewish writers and thinkers going up to the Holocaust.

Dobroszycki, Lucjan, and Kirschenblatt-Gimblett, Barbara. *Image Before My Eyes: A Photographic History of Jewish Life in Poland*. New York: Schocken, 1977.

This album of 300 photographs selected from over 10,000 housed at the YIVO Institute for Jewish Research gives us an eyewitness pictorial account of all aspects of Polish-Jewish life. It is beautiful, revealing, and moving.

Dubnow, Simon M. *A History of the Jews in Russia and Poland from the Earliest Times Until the Present Day*. 3 vols. in 2. New York: Ktav, 1975.

The reprint of a major history written near the turn of the century.

Duker, Abraham G. *Studies in Polish-Jewish History and Relations.* New York: Ktav, 1981.

Treats important aspects of Jewish life in a country that for many centuries was one of the main centers of European Jewry, including the Polish Great Emancipation of 1830 and the Jewish role in Poland's 1830 and 1863 revolts against Russia. Most of the essays are based on archival documents destroyed by the Nazis.

Heller, Celia S. **On the Edge of Destruction: The Jews of Poland Between the Two World Wars.* New York: Columbia University Press, 1977; Schocken pb., 1979.

An extensive historical and sociological discussion of the Polish-Jewish community in the 1920s and 1930s.

Howe, Irving, and Greenberg, Eliezer. *Voices from the Yiddish: Essays, Memoirs, Diaries.* Ann Arbor: University of Michigan Press, 1975.

An excellent introduction to East European Jewish life.

Klepfisz, Heszel. *Culture and Compassion: The Spirit of Polish Jewry from Hasidism to the Holocaust.* New York: Ktav, 1983.

A moving, spiritually powerful, and lyrical description of a world now gone; especially interesting is the picture of Jewish intellectual life in Warsaw and other urban centers in the 1920s and 1930s. The author served as a Jewish chaplain in the Free Polish Army during World War II.

Meltzer, Milton. + **The World of Our Fathers: The Jews of Eastern Europe.* New York: Farrar, Straus & Giroux, 1974; Dell, 1976.

A picture of East European Jews up to World War I, which incorporates excerpts from eyewitness accounts, diaries, songs, etc.

Mendelsohn, Ezra. *The Jews of East Central Europe Between the World Wars.* Bloomington: Indiana University Press, 1983.

A major study of the demographic, cultural, and socioeconomic changes of a number of major Jewish communities, as well as on the changes in Jewish-Gentile relations.

————. *Zionism in Poland: The Formative Years, 1915–1926.* New Haven, Conn., Yale University Press, 1982.

An important study on why Zionism gained a growing number of followers in the two and a half decades before the Holocaust; Mendelsohn also provides an incisive essay on the Jewish condition in the interwar period.

Mondry, Adele. *Wyszkowo: A Shtetl on the Bug River*. Translated by Moshe Spiegel. New York: Ktav, 1980.

A good account of the people, ups and downs of a Polish *shtetl* destroyed by the Nazis.

Roskies, Diane K., and Roskies, David G. +*The Shtetl Book*. New York: ADL and Ktav, 1975.

A colorful and interesting book about the Yiddish-speaking Jews in the villages (shtetls) of Eastern Europe, 1800–1914—their stories, songs, history, and problems; it makes heavy use of primary sources and contains many illustrations.

Schoenfeld, Joachim. *Shtetl Memoirs*. New York: Ktav, 1985.

A compelling description of Jewish life in Galicia, with special emphasis on the author's hometown, Sniatyn, from the turn of the century till the outbreak of World War II. Of special interest is the account of wartime service in the Austro-Hungarian army, the post–World War I pogroms, and anti-Semitism in the Polish Republic in the 1930s.

Shulman, Abraham (ed.). *The Old Country: The Lost World of East European Jews*. New York: Scribner's, 1974.

A photographic introduction to Eastern European Jewish life before the Holocaust.

Weinryb, Bernard. *The Jews of Poland*. Philadelphia: Jewish Publication Society, 1973.

A major, balanced, and well-documented study.

Note: A major source of articles on Eastern European Jewry is the *YIVO Annual* (18 volumes through 1982; 1048 Fifth Avenue, New York, N.Y. 10028).

2.

The Roots of the Holocaust

A. Anti-Semitism: General

*Anti-Semitism. Jerusalem: Keter Books, 1975, reprinted from the *Encyclopaedia Judaica*, 1975.

The book, taken from the *Encyclopaedia Judaica*, surveys the reasons for anti-Semitism and its history throughout the ages.

Baron, Salo W. "Changing Patterns in Anti-Semitism." *JSS* 38, no. 1 (Winter 1976): 5–38.

A history of anti-Semitism and the "reasons" behind it, by the preeminent American Jewish historian.

Langmuir, Gavin I. "Tradition, History and Prejudice." *JSS* 30, no. 3 (July 1968): 157–168.

On anti-Semitism as a factor in Jewish history.

Parkes, James W. *An Enemy of the People: Anti-Semitism*. New York: Penguin Books, 1945, and Chicago: Quadrangle, 1964.

A masterful one-volume history.

Poliakov, Leon. *The History of Anti-Semitism*. New York: Schocken, 1965.

The best in-depth historical study of anti-Semitism.

Talmon, J. C. "European History—Seedbed of the Holocaust." *Midstream* 19, no. 5 (May 1973): 3–25.

An excellent short summary of the thread of anti-Semitism which runs through European history.

Tractenberg, Joshua. *The Devil and the Jews: The Medieval Conception of the Jew and Its Relation to Modern Anti-Semitism.* New Haven: Yale University Press, 1943; Philadelphia: Jewish Publication Society pb., 1983.

A thorough study of the demonization of the Jew during the Middle Ages.

Zisenwine, David, and Rossel, Seymour (eds.). +Anti-Semitism in Europe: Sources of the Holocaust. New York: Behrman House, 1976.

Among the topics covered are the Dreyfus case, Hitler's anti-Semitism, and the war crime trials. A discussion guide is included.

B. The Context of Jewish-Christian Relations and Christian Anti-Semitism

Davies, Alan T. *Anti-Semitism and the Christian Mind.* New York: Herder & Herder, 1969.

A probing, thoughtful study of the nature and evolution of Christian attitudes toward Jews.

Ecclestone, Alan. *The Night Sky of the Lord.* New York, Schocken, 1982.

An Anglican priest, the author probes the Christian roots of anti-Semitism in terms of both theology and a pattern of rejection throughout history.

Eckardt, A. Roy. *Elder and Younger Brothers.* New York: Scribner's, 1967; Schocken pb., 1973.

A profoundly intelligent study of the Christian-Jewish encounter before and after the Holocaust.

Flannery, Edward H. *The Anguish of the Jews.* New York: Macmillan, 1965.

A priest's history of anti-Semitism from pre-Christian times through the Holocaust.

Hay Malcolm. *Thy Brother's Blood.* New York: Hart, 1975 (published originally as *Europe and the Jews*) and Boston: Beacon Press, 1962; Freedom Library/ADL, 1982.

The roots of Christian anti-Semitism.

Heer, Friedrich. *God's First Love.* New York: Weybright & Talley, 1970.

A survey of Christian, particularly Catholic, anti-Semitism, by a major European thinker.

Isaac, Jules. *The Teaching of Contempt.* New York: Holt, Rinehart & Winston, 1964.

Perhaps the best study to date of Christian anti-Semitism as expressed in the New Testament and the early Church Fathers.

Luther, Martin. "The Jews and Their Lies." In *The Christian Society,* vol. 4 of *Luther's Works,* edited by Franklin Sherman. 47 vols. Philadelphia: Fortress Press, 1971.

Luther's most vitriolic anti-Semitic essay, calling for the razing of Jewish homes, burning of synagogues, and accusing the Jews of "diabolical, blasphemous and horrible sins."

Parkes, James. *The Conflict of the Church and the Synagogue.* New York: Hermon, 1974 (rep.), and Atheneum, 1969.

A study in the origins of anti-Semitism, and of the long history of Christian polemics and laws against Judaism.

Ruether, Rosemary. *Faith and Fratricide: The Theological Roots of Anti-Semitism.* New York: Seabury, 1974.

A leading Protestant theologian examines why the Jews, as "older brothers" to the Christians, came to be hated by them.

Schoeps, Hans-Joachim. *The Jewish-Christian Argument: Theologies in Conflict.* New York: Holt, Rinehart & Winston, 1964.

On Jewish-Christian polemics from the medieval to the modern period.

Tillich, Paul. "The Jewish Question: Christian and German Problem." *JSS* 33, no. 4 (October 1971): 253–271.

The parallels between the German and Jewish characters and the divergence between the Christian and Jewish faiths are outlined and discussed by the seminal Protestant philosopher.

Williamson, Clark A. *Has God Rejected His People? Anti-Judaism in the Christian Church.* New York: Abbeville Press, 1983.

Williamson provides a succinct history of Christian anti-Semitism with a focus on the modern period. He often uses strong words, as in "Hitler and Bonhoeffer were united in seeking a world without Jews. One would extinguish them physically; the other would convert them—eliminate them religiously."

C. Anti-Semitism: Modern Racial and National

Arendt, Hannah. "From the Dreyfus Affair to France Today." *JSS* 4, no. 3 (July 1942): 195–240.

> A history of modern French Jewry 1894–1942, with a special focus on French anti-Semitism.

Bernstein, Herman. *The Truth About the Protocols of Zion.* Introduction by Norman Cohn. New York: Ktav, 1971.

> The full story of the notorious fabrication of the *Protocols* by anti-Semites; includes translations of all the relevant evidence, including the complete text of the *Protocols*.

Byrnes, Robert. *Anti-Semitism in Modern France.* New York: Howard Fertig, 1969.

> A thorough, straightforward history of modern French anti-Semitism.

Cohn, Norman. **Warrant for Genocide: The Myth of the Jewish World Conspiracy and the Protocols of the Elders of Zion.* New York: Harper & Row, 1967; Chico, Calif.: Scholars Press pb., 1981.

> Traces how the myth of a Jewish world conspiracy inspired a whole series of forgeries which influenced the minds of Hitler and his followers.

Hertzberg, Arthur. **The French Enlightenment and the Jews.* New York: Columbia University Press, 1968; Schocken pb., 1970.

> The best study to date on the Enlightenment's often jaundiced view of the Jews, and the philosophes' distinction between the Jew as an individual and the Jewish nation.

Katz, Jacob. **From Prejudice to Destruction: Anti-Semitism, 1900–1933.* Cambridge, Mass.: Harvard University Press, 1980; pb., 1982.

> A magisterial, fascinating history of modern anti-Semitism.

Pinson, Koppel (ed.). *Essays on Anti-Semitism.* New York: Conference on Jewish Social Science, 1966.

> An excellent anthology on modern anti-Semitism in many European countries.

Poliakov, Leon. *The Aryan Myth: A History of Racist and Nationalist Ideas in Europe.* New York: Basic Books, 1971.

> A fine interdisciplinary study of the eighteenth- and nineteenth-century myth of an Aryan superman.

Pulzer, Peter. *The Rise of Political Anti-Semitism in Germany and Austria*. New York: Wiley, 1964.

A study of the politicization of anti-Semitism in Central Europe at the end of the nineteenth century.

Rotenstreich, Nathan. *The Recurring Pattern: Studies in Anti-Judaism in Modern Thought*. London: Weidenfeld & Nicholson, 1963.

The distinguished Hebrew University philosopher looks at the strand of reductionist and anti-Semitic thought in modern European intellectual history from Kant to Toynbee.

Szajkowski, Zosa. *An Illustrated Sourcebook of Russian Anti-Semitism, 1881–1978*. 2 vols., New York: Ktav, 1980.

An excellent reference work covering 1881–1978 and including over 500 photographs and other documents, as well as broadsides, poems, sermons, and other liturgical materials.

Tal, Uriol. *Christians and Jews in Germany: Religion, Politics and Ideology in the Second Reich, 1870–1914*. Ithaca, N.Y.: Cornell University Press, 1975.

The major study to date on the persistence of Christian anti-Semitism in the period between the establishment of the German Empire and World War I.

———. *Religious and Anti-Religious Roots of Modern Anti-Semitism*. LBI Memorial Lecture no. 14. New York: Leo Baeck Institute, 1971.

On the strands of Christian and pagan anti-Semitism.

D. Totalitarianism, Fascism, and Racism

Arendt, Hannah. **The Origins of Totalitarianism*. Cleveland and New York: World, 1958; rev. ed., New York: Harcourt, Brace, 1966.

An analysis of the bases of both Nazi and Stalinist totalitarianism; the three sections of the volume, *Anti-Semitism, Imperialism*, and *Totalitarianism*, have been published separately as paperbacks by Harcourt, Brace.

Field, Geoffrey. *Evangelist of Race: The Germanic Vision of Houston Stewart Chamberlain*. New York: Columbia University Press, 1981.

An analysis of the most influential exponent of the cult of Aryanism.

Friedrich, Carl (ed.). **Totalitarianism*. New York: Universal Library; Grosset & Dunlap pb., 1964.

Includes a number of seminal essays on totalitarianism, including Waldemar Gurian's "Totalitarianism as Political Religion."

Mosse, George L. *Toward the Final Solution: A History of European Facism*. New York: Howard Fertig, 1978.

A succinct, very readable account of the intellectual, cultural, and political roots and evolution of modern racism.

———. *The Nationalization of the Masses*. New York: Howard Fertig, 1975.

An excellent study of the growth of nationalism as a secular religion, with its own rituals and symbols.

Nolte, Ernst. *The Three Faces of Fascism*. New York: Holt, Rinehart & Winston, 1966; New American Library pb., 1969.

An examination of Nazism in the context of the two other fascist movements—that of Mussolini and that of the *Action française*.

Talmon, J. L. *The Origins of Totalitarian Democracy*. New York: Praeger, 1960.

Talmon's provocative thesis is that modern totalitarianism has its origins in the Enlightenment's doctrine of the "popular cult."

Weiss, John (ed.). *Nazis and Fascists in Europe 1918–1945*. Chicago: Quadrangle Books, 1969.

An excellent anthology providing a comparative look at anti-Semitism in Western and Eastern Europe.

E. Psychoanalytic Interpretations of Anti-Semitism, Totalitarianism, and Prejudice

Adorno, Theodore W., et al. *The Authoritarian Personality*. New York: Harper & Row, 1950.

The classic scientific study of the roots of the fascist mind.

Braatz, Werner E. "The Volkisch Ideology and Anti-Semitism in Germany." *YIVO Annual* 15 (1974): 166–187.

Fromm, Erich. *Escape from Freedom*. New York: Holt, Rinehart & Winston, 1941; Avon pb., 1971.

Fromm's thesis is that those who cannot stand the "insecurity of freedom" seek refuge in totalitarian ideologies and leaders.

Kren, George, and Rappoport, Leon. *The Holocaust and the Crisis of Human Behavior*. New York: Holmes & Meier, 1980.

A psychohistorical explanation of the Holocaust that focuses equally on killers and victims.

Luel, Steven, and Marcus, Paul (eds.). *Psychoanalytic Reflections on the Holocaust: Selected Essays.* New York: Ktav, 1984.

Articles by leading psychoanalytic authorities on anti-Semitism, the Nazi mentality, etc.

Milgram, Stanley. *Obedience to Authority.* New York: Harper & Row, 1973.

A controversial study which maintains that most people would seriously harm others rather than disobey authority.

Sartre, Jean-Paul. *Anti-Semite and Jew.* New York: Schocken, 1965; 1976.

Sartre provides psychological analyses of the marginal Jew and the anti-Semite in this most readable, if controversial work. He concludes that "anti-Semitism is not a Jewish problem; it is our problem."

Simmel, Ernst. *Anti-Semitism: A Social Disease.* New York: International Universities Press, 1946.

A classical study of anti-Semitism as manifested by the alienated man.

F. Modern Germany

Epstein, Klaus. *The Genesis of German Conservatism.* Princeton, N.J.: Princeton University Press, 1966.

A first-rate study of German conservative thought and politics, and how it sometimes resisted, sometimes gave in to, anti-Semitic tendencies.

Halborn, Hajo. *A History of Modern Germany, 1840–1945.* New York: Knopf, 1969.

A fine one-volume history of modern Germany.

Kohn, Hans. *The Mind of Germany: The Education of a Nation.* New York: Scribner's, 1958.

An excellent intellectual history of modern Germany with a special focus on the history of modern nationalism.

Lorant, Stefan. *Sieg Heil!* New York: Norton, 1974.

An illustrated history of Germany from Bismarck to Hitler.

Massing, Paul. *Rehearsal for Destruction: A Study of Political Anti-Semitism in Imperial Germany.* New York: Harper, 1949.

> The focus shifted from religious to racial and nationalist anti-Semitism in the nineteenth century. This is an excellent political history of one of the first manifestations of this new anti-Semitism.

Meinecke, Friedrich. *The German Catastrophe.* New York: Peter Smith, 1963; and Boston: Beacon pb., 1963.

> Reflections and recollections on the German roots of Nazism by one of the leading German historians.

Meyer, Michael. "Great Debate on Anti-Semitism—Jewish Reaction to New Hostility in Germany, 1879–1881." *LBI Yrbk* 11 (1966): 137–170.

Mosse, George L. *The Crisis of German Ideology.* New York: Grosset & Dunlap, 1964, and Universal Library, 1964; Schocken pb., 1981.

> A comprehensive survey of the ideological roots of Nazism, tracing its growth from the early nineteenth century, with special emphasis on education and youth activities; see in particular chap. 7, "The Jews," and chap. 17, "The Anti-Jewish Resolution."

Pinson, Koppel. *Modern Germany: Its History and Civilization.* New York: Macmillan, 1957.

> This comprehensive, informative history is balanced in terms of political, social, and cultural dimensions.

Stern, Fritz. *The Crisis of German Ideology.* New York: Grosset & Dunlap, 1964.

> On the intellectual origins of the Third Reich, particularly in terms of a reaction to modernity and a search for *Volkisch* roots.

———. *The Politics of Cultural Despair.* Berkeley and Los Angeles: University of California Press, 1961.

> A masterful study of three major turn-of-the-century *Volkisch* thinkers.

Viereck, Peter. *Metapolitics.* New York: Knopf, 1941 and Capricorn, 1961.

> A valuable examination of the roots of the Nazi mind, from Luther to Hitler.

Volkov, Shulamit. "Anti-Semitism as a Cultural Code—Reflections on the History and Historiography of Anti-Semitism in Imperial Germany." *LBI Yrbk* 23 (1978): 25–46.

G. Germany: The Weimar Republic (1918–1933)

Braatz, Werner F. "Two Neo-Conservative Myths in Germany, 1919–1932: The 'Third Reich' and the 'New State'." *Journal of the History of Ideas* 32 (October 1971): 569–584.

A detailed analysis of the intellectual reaction to the Versailles treaty and the sometimes chaotic nature of Weimar democracy.

Fromm, Eric. *The Working Class in Weimar Germany: A Psychological and Sociological Study.* Cambridge, Mass.: Harvard University Press, 1984.

A study of the relationship between character structure and political activism/orientation in the Weimar Republic, Fromm's work is key to understanding the psychosocial roots of Nazism's success among the German people.

Hamburger, Ernest. *Jews, Democracy and Weimar Germany.* LBI Memorial Lecture no. 16. New York: Leo Baeck Institute, 1973.

Mosse, George L. *Germans and Jews: The Right, the Left, and the Search for a "Third Force" in Pre-Nazi Germany.* New York: Howard Fertig; Grosset and Dunlap pb., 1970.

A collection of essays that probes the intellectual roots of German totalitarianism, the Jewish response, and the attempts at a German-Jewish dialogue.

Pachter, Henry. *Weimar Etudes.* New York: Columbia University Press, 1982.

A series of essays that blend memoir, social history, and cultural criticism.

Paucker, Arnold. "Jewish Defense Against Nazism in the Weimar Republic." *WLB* 26, nos. 26–27 (1972): 21–31.

Reck-Malleczewen, Fritz P. *Diary of a Man in Despair.* Translated by Paul Rubins. New York: Macmillan, 1970.

A remarkable journal of the last years of the Weimar Republic and the early Nazi years.

Showalter, Dennis. *Little Man, What Now? "Der Stuermer" in the Weimar Republic.* Hamden, Conn.: Shoe String Press, 1982.

A study of Julius Streicher's rabidly anti-Semitic newspaper in its early days—whom it appealed to and why.

Stochura, Peter D. *Nazi Youth in the Weimar Republic.* Santa Barbara, Cailf.: Clio, 1975.

How the young were incorporated into the Nazi program.

H. Genocide: Theories and "Practice"

Charney, Israel. **How Can We Commit the Unthinkable? Genocide: The Human Cancer.* New York: Hearst Books, 1983.

A thoughtful, challenging psychosocial study of the roots of the genocidal impulse.

Horowitz, Irving Louis. *Taking Lives: Genocide and State Power.* New Brunswick, N.J.: Transaction Books, 1981.

On the role of the totalitarian state in organizing and administering campaigns of genocide.

Kuper, Leo. *Genocide: Its Political Use in the Twentieth Century.* New Haven, Conn.: Yale University Press, 1982.

On the possibilities for genocide inherent in modern technology and big-power rivalry.

Porter, Jack Nusan. **Genocide and Human Rights: A Global Anthology.* Washington, D.C.: University Press of America, 1982.

A major anthology providing both a theoretical understanding of genocide and a study of genocide against the Jews, gypsies, and homosexuals during the Holocaust as well as against many other peoples.

3.

The Nazis, Hitler, and the Response of the German People

A. The Nazis' Road to Power, 1920–1933

Abel, Theodore. *The Nazi Movement: Why Hitler Came to Power.* New York: Atherton Press, 1966.

A fine study of the rise of the Nazi movement based on 600 autobiographies of Nazis.

Allen, William Sheridan (ed.). *The Infancy of Nazism: The Memoirs of Ex-Gauleiter Albert Krebs, 1923–1933.* New York: New Viewpoints, 1976.

The edited version of the memoirs of a local Nazi leader in the decade leading to the *Machtergreifung* (seizure of power).

———. **The Nazi Seizure of Power.* Chicago: Quadrangle, 1965; New York: New Viewpoints, 1966; Franklin Watts, 1983.

Here is the experience of a single German town during the period of Hitler's rise, 1930–1935.

Baum, Rainer. *Holocaust and the German Elite: Genocide and National Suicide in Germany.* New York: Rowman & Littlefield, 1981.

Baum suggests three sources in German society for the Holocaust: conflicted attitudes toward social values, status insecurity resulting from rapid industrialization, and social disunity.

Gordon, Harold J. **Hitler and the Beer Hall Putsch.* Princeton, N.J.: Princeton University Press, 1972.

On the rise of the dictator, with detailed background on the 1923 Putsch attempt.

Halborn, Hajo (ed.). *Republic to Reich*. New York: Vintage pb., 1972.

An excellent anthology, taken from articles in the *Vierteljahrsheft für Zeitgeschichte*, on Germany's transition to Nazism, 1932–1934.

Hamilton, Richard F. *Who Voted for Hitler?* Princeton, N.J.: Princeton University Press, 1983.

In this lengthy and detailed study, Hamilton examines a series of elections in fourteen German cities, and finds that the Nazis' electoral success generally was tied to the class level of a given city, with the party receiving the greatest support among the wealthiest classes.

Hanser, Richard. *Putsch: How Hitler Made Revolution*. New York: Peter Wyden, 1970.

A very readable study of how Hitler maneuvered his way into power.

Lane, Barbara Miller, and Leila J. Rupp (eds.). *Nazi Ideology Before 1933: A Documentation*. Austin: University of Texas Press, 1978.

Political writings of Eckart, Rosenberg, Goebbels, Himmler, Strasser, and Darre before the National Socialists came to power.

Pool, James, and Pool, Suzanne. *Who Financed Hitler: The Secret Funding of Hitler's Rise to Power, 1919–1933*. New York: Dial Press, 1978.

Who really funded Hitler's rise to power? This well-written study provides some concrete answers.

Pridham, Geoffrey. *Hitler's Rise to Power: The Nazi Movement in Bavaria*. London: Hart-Davis MacGibbon, 1973.

One of the very few book-length studies of Nazism in one German region.

B. Nazism and the Third Reich: General Histories or Studies

Aycoberry, Pierre. *The Nazi Question*. Translated from the French by Robert Hurley. New York: Pantheon pb., 1981.

An essay on the various historical interpretations of National Socialism from its origin in 1922 through 1975.

Beaumont, Maurice; Fried, John H. E.; and Vermeil, Edmond (eds.). *The Third Reich*. New York: Praeger, 1955.

A large volume published in cooperation with UNESCO and the International Council for Philosophy and Humanistic Studies, this work contains important chapters on anti-Semitism, racialism, and SS troops in Germany.

Bessel, Richard. *Political Violence and the Rise of Nazism: The Storm Troopers in Eastern Germany*. New Haven: Yale University Press, 1984.

A close look at SA activities east of the Oder-Neisse line during Nazism's formative period. Examines the motivations and political uses of Nazi violence.

Bracher, Karl Dietrich. *The German Dictatorship*. Translated from the German by Jean Steinberg, with an introduction by Peter Gay. New York: Praeger, 1970.

On the origins, structure, and effects of National Socialism—one of the best studies to date of Nazism.

Gilford, Henry. *The Reichstag Fire, February, 1933*. New York: Franklin Watts, 1973.

A study on the event whose perpetrators may have been the Nazis rather than the Communist who was accused, and which led to the *Gleichschaltung*, or "leveling," of the Nazis' enemies.

Grunfeld, Frederic Y. *The Hitler File: A Social History of Germany and the Nazis, 1918–1945*. New York: Random House, 1974.

Essentially a pictorial review with over 750 black-and-white and 48 pages of color illustrations of posters, cartoons, photos, and art.

Grunberger, Richard. *The Twelve Year Reich: A Social History, 1933–45*. New York: Holt, Rinehart & Winston, 1971.

A narrative based on original, contemporary materials covering education, sports, the arts, beauty, family life, Nazi speech and humor.

Kater, Michael H. *The Nazi Party: A Social Profile of Members and Leaders, 1919–1945*. Cambridge, Mass.: Harvard University Press, 1983.

What kind of people joined the Nazi party? What kind became its leaders? How did the party's composition change? This major work in social history deals with these questions.

Neumann, Franz. *Behemoth: The Structure and Practice of National Socialism*. New York: Harper & Row, 1966.

A remarkable early study, first published in 1942, on the Nazi party and the nature of Nazi totalitarianism.

Neumann, Robert. *The Pictorial History of the Third Reich*. New York: Bantam, 1968.

A "different" kind of history with a strong emotional impact.

Noakes, Jeremy, and Pridham, Geoffrey. *Documents on Nazism, 1919–1945*. New York: Viking, 1975.

A strong anthology, using both German and non-German sources.

Orlow, Dietrich. *The History of the Nazi Party, 1933–1945*. Pittsburgh: University of Pittsburgh Press, 1973.

A good one-volume history of the party during its years in power.

Raab, Earl. + *The Anatomy of Nazism*. New York: ADL. 1961.

A basic description of the components of Nazism—brief historical background, life under Nazism, Nazi philosophy and techniques, with 20 pages of illustrations—generally useful for high school students.

Remak, Joachim (ed). *The Nazi Years*. New York: Prentice-Hall, 1969.

A collection of very short documents and speeches which gives the flavor of an era but seems somewhat disjointed in approach, although it is particularly accessible for high school or college students.

Schoenbaum, David. *Hitler's Social Revolution*. Garden City, N.Y.: Doubleday, 1966; Norton, 1980.

Perhaps the best study of the impact of Nazism on German society, particularly the class structure.

Shirer, William L. *Berlin Diary*. New York: Knopf, 1941; Penguin pb., 1979.

The journal of William Shirer, a foreign correspondent with access to Hitler, written with the sole purpose of chronicling the demise of Europe under the power of Hitler. The diary dates from 1934–1941.

———. *The Nightmare Years, 1930–1940*. Boston: Little, Brown, 1984.

A long, fascinating memoir of the last years of the Weimar Republic and the first seven years of the Third Reich, by the noted journalist and historian.

────. *The Rise and Fall of the Third Reich*. New York: Simon & Schuster, 1960; Fawcett-World pb., 1972.

> Perhaps the most comprehensive book covering the history of Nazi Germany—both an excellent record of an era and a good biography of Adolf Hitler.

Snell, John L. (ed.). *The Nazi Revolution: Germany's Guilt or Germany's Fate*. Lexington, Mass.: Heath, 1959.

> Examines the complex question of whether all Germans are collectively responsible for what happened during the Holocaust years— the author quotes extensively from a variety of sources.

Snyder, Louis L. *The Encyclopedia of the Third Reich*. New York: McGraw-Hill, 1976.

> A 338-page guide with a massive bibliography.

Speer, Albert. *Infiltration: The SS and German Armament*. New York: Macmillan, 1981.

> On the SS and the armaments industry, the Speer-Himmler rivalry, and aspects of the Final Solution.

────. *Inside the Third Reich*. New York: Macmillan, 1970; Avon pb., 1974.

> An account of evil days by one who helped make them so, Hitler's personal architect.

Toland, John. *The Last Hundred Days*. New York: Random House, 1966.

> On Germany's Götterdämmerung in the winter and spring of 1945.

Vogt, Hannah. *The Burden of Guilt: A Short History of Germany, 1914–45*. New York: Oxford University Press, 1964.

> Translated from a text directed to high school students in Germany today, this book hides none of the horrors of the Third Reich, and exhorts students to face the reality of the past and to accept responsibility for the future.

C. Adolph Hitler and His Policies

Binion, Rudolf. *Hitler Among the Germans*. New York: Elsevier, 1976.

> A study, based in part on mass psychology, of why Hitler was so enthusiastically received by the German people.

Bullock, Alan. *Hitler: A Study in Tyranny. New York: Harper & Row, 1964.

A fine historical and psychological portrayal of the dictator—it says little about the Final Solution, however.

Fest, Joachim. *Adolph Hitler. New York: Harcourt, Brace, Jovanovich, 1974: Vintage pb., 1978.

A better than adequate biography, particularly useful for tracing the roots of Hitler's beliefs, but containing little about the Holocaust.

Haffner, Sebastian. *The Meaning of Hitler. Translated by Ewald Osers. Cambridge, Mass.: Harvard University Press, 1983.

An important interpretative work showing why, in the context of German history and political culture, Hitler was able to achieve power.

Hitler, Adolf. *Mein Kampf. Boston: Houghton Mifflin, 1943.

Mein Kampf, written when Hitler was in prison in 1923–1924 after the failure of the Beer Hall Putsch, is crucial to understanding his world view.

Jackel, Eberhard. Hitler's Weltanschauung. Wesleyan, Conn.: Wesleyan University Press, 1972.

A book on Hitler's "world view," subtitled "A Blueprint for Power."

Jones, J. Sydney. Hitler in Vienna, 1907–1913: Clues to the Future. New York: Stein & Day, 1982.

An excellent study of the young Hitler.

Kubizek, August. The Young Hitler I Knew. Translated from the German by E. V. Anderson, with an introduction by H. R. Trevor-Roper. Boston: Houghton Mifflin, 1955.

A memoir of Hitler by one of his boyhood friends.

Langer, Walter. *The Mind of Adolf Hitler: The Secret War-Time Report. New York: Signet pb., 1973.

A study commissioned by the OSS during World War II, which seems to explain Nazi policy in terms of Hitler's psychological delusions; the work suffers from a rigid Freudianism and a general sloppiness reflecting the haste with which it was written.

Maser, Werner (ed.). *Hitler's Letters and Notes.* New York: Harper & Row, 1974.

Important insights on Hitler can be gleaned from these, his informal and personal writings.

Rauschning, Hermann. *The Voice of Destruction.* New York: Putnam, 1940.

A series of conversations with Hitler, by a perceptive former Nazi.

Rich, Norman. **Hitler's War Aims: The Establishment of the New Order.* New York: Norton, 1974.

An extensive discussion of the roles of Jew-hatred, anti-Bolshevism, and expansionism in Hitler's policies.

Snyder, Louis L. + **Hitler and Nazism.* New York: Bantam, 1971.

Primarily for students, this book explains how Hitler shaped the Nazi movement in his own image.

Syberberg, Hans-Jurgen. **Hitler: A Film from Germany.* New York: Farrar, Straus & Giroux, 1982.

A multidimensional look at Hitler, through meditations on Western civilization, the modern world, and the nature of art as well as of the Nazi Führer.

Toland, John. **Adolph Hitler.* 2 vols. New York: Doubleday, 1976: Ballantine pb., 1977.

Based on, among other things, 250 interviews with people who knew Hitler; this is an extensive, very readable biography.

Trevor-Roper, H. R. **The Last Days of Hitler.* New York: Macmillan, 1947.

A detailed look, based on many interviews and written sources, at Hitler's final months.

————. (ed.). *Hitler's Secret Conversations.* Translated by Norman Cameron and R. H. Stevens. New York: Octagon Books, 1972.

A record of Hitler's conversations from 1941 to 1944, with a fine introductory essay by H. R. Trevor-Roper on Hitler's mind.

Waite, Robert G. L. (ed.). **Hitler and Nazi Germany.* New York: Holt, Rinehart & Winston, 1969.

An interesting anthology of articles and documents.

————. *The Psychopathic God.* New York: Basic Books, 1977; New American Library pb., 1978.

A powerful dissection of Hitler's psyche, and a very significant contribution to the scholarly literature on Hitler.

D. Other Leading Nazis

Arad, Yitzhak. "Alfred Rosenberg and 'Final Solution' in the Occupied Soviet Territories." YVS 13 (1979): 263–286.

Bytwerk, Randall. *Julius Streicher: A Biography.* New York: Stein & Day, 1982.

The very major biography in English by the publisher of *Der Stürmer.*

Comer, Clarke. *Eichmann: The Man and His Crimes.* New York: Ballantine, 1980.

The depressing story of one of humanity's most infamous murderers.

Fest, Joachim C. *The Face of the Third Reich.* New York: Pantheon, 1970.

Equally skilled as a historian and a writer, Fest provides a series of portraits of Nazi leaders.

Goebbels, Joseph. *Final Entries 1945: The Diaries of Joseph Goebbels.* Edited and introduced by Hugh Trevor-Roper. New York: Putnam, 1978.

Worth reading both for Trevor-Roper's introduction and for evidence of the erratic nature of Goebbels's thinking during the war's final months.

————. *The Goebbels Diaries.* Westport, Conn.: Greenwood Press, n.d. (reprint of 1948 edition).

The diaries of Hitler's Propaganda Minister, who was both obsequious to Hitler and highly competitive with other Nazi leaders.

Loewenberg, Peter. "The Unsuccessful Adolescence of Heinrich Himmler." AHR 76, no. 3 (June 1971): 612–642.

A fascinating psychohistorical case study.

Miale, Florence, and Seltzer, Michael. *The Nuremberg Mind.* New York: Quadrangle, 1975.

Nineteen essays on the psychology of the Nazi leaders, based in part on Rorschach and other psychological tests taken shortly after the Nuremberg trials.

Moczarski, Kazimierz. *Conversations with an Executioner.* Englewood Cliffs, N.J.: Prentice-Hall, 1981.

A portrait of Jürgen Stroop, the liquidator of the Warsaw Ghetto, by a man who shared a cell with him in a Polish prison in 1981.

Rosenberg, Alfred. *Race and Race History, and Other Essays.* Edited by R. Pois. New York: Harper & Row, 1971.

Writings of Nazi Germany's leading racial theorist.

Sereny, Gita. **Into That Darkness.* New York: McGraw-Hill, 1974; Vintage pb., 1982.

Franz Stangl helped massacre 900,000 Jews. He and others talked about his work to the author, who provides readers with a rare look into a mass murderer's mind.

Smith, Bradley. *Heinrich Himmler.* Stanford, Calif.: Hoover Institution Press, 1971.

Smith's book concerns "A Nazi in the Making 1900–1926."

Speer, Albert. **Spandau.* New York: Macmillan, 1976; Pocket Books, 1977.

From the diaries of one of Hitler's accomplices, who while imprisoned reflects on war crimes perpetrated by him and others but never admits his own guilt.

Wistrich, Robert. *Who's Who in Nazi Germany.* New York: Macmillan, 1982.

Short (less than 500-word) but informative biographies of 350 prominent people in the Third Reich.

E. Nazi Ideology, Culture, Education, and Youth

Baird, Jay W. *The Mythical World of Nazi War Propaganda, 1939–1945.* Minneapolis: University of Minnesota, 1974.

A revealing look at how the Nazis saw their enemies, including the "Bolsheviks" and the Jews.

Blackburn, Gilmer W. *Education in the Third Reich: Race and History in Nazi Textbooks.* Albany: State University of New York Press, 1984.

A fine study of how youth was molded—by means of education, propaganda, and peer pressure—to conform to the ideology of a fascist state with a racial ideal.

Bleuel, Hans Peter. *Sex and Society in Nazi Germany.* New York: Lippincott, 1973.

Includes important material on the Nazi persecution of homosexuals.

Blumenthal, Nachman. "On the Nazi Vocabulary." *YVS* 1 (1957): 49–66.

———. "From the Nazi Vocabulary." *YVS* 6 (1967): 82–120.

Both articles are important contributions to an understanding of "Nazi-Deutsch" (Nazi-German).

Esh, Shaul. "Words & Their Meaning: 25 Examples of Nazi-Idiom." *YVS* 5 (1963): 133–168.

A detailed essay on the Nazis' use of euphemisms and other perversions of language.

Fromm, Erich. "The Psychology of Nazism." In *Escape From Freedom,* pp. 207–239. New York: Holt, Rinehart & Winston, 1961.

On Nazism's penchant for fervent nationalistic appeals and manipulation of crowds.

Hinz, Berthold. *Art in the Third Reich.* New York: Pantheon Books, 1980.

The most amply illustrated English-language book to date on Nazi art; it includes good sections on the opposition to the Nazis and the 1937 exhibit of "decadent" art.

Hull, David. *Film in the Third Reich.* Los Angeles: University of California Press, 1969.

A solid academic study of the Nazi use of film for propaganda and for diversion.

Kamenetsky, Christa. *Children's Literature in Nazi Germany: The Cultural Policy of National Socialism.* Athens: Ohio University Press, 1984.

How children's literature was affected by Nazi cultural policy throughout the twelve years of the Third Reich.

Kinser, Bill, and Aleinman, Neil (eds.). *The Dream That Was No More a Dream.* New York: Harper Colophon, 1969.

A remarkable collection of cartoons, paintings, photographs, film clips, and other graphics from the Nazi period that reflect the escapist nature of Nazi ideology; unfortunately, the prefatory essay is poorly written and often confusing.

Kracauer, Siegfried. *From Caligari to Hitler: A Psychological History of the German Film.* Princeton, N.J.: Princeton University Press, 1947.

A study of the German film, especially the Nazi use of film as a propaganda instrument—see the chapter, "The Holocaust and the Film Arts."

Loewenberg, Peter. "The Psychohistorical Roots of the Nazi Youth Cohort." *AHR* 76 (December 1971): 1457–1502.

On the roots of the Nazi youth movements in previous antimodernist movements.

Mann, Erika. *School for Barbarians,* New York: Modern Age Books, 1938.

On how Nazi Germany's educational system was perverted for totalitarian ends.

Mayer, Milton (ed.). *They Thought They Were Free: The Germans, 1933–1945.* Chicago: University of Chicago Press, 1955.

A first-rate, varied collection of writings that represent a distillation of Nazi culture.

Mosse, George L. (ed.). *Nazi Culture: Intellectual, Cultural and Social Life in the Third Reich.* New York: Grosset & Dunlap, 1968.

Following an excellent introduction, this illustrated anthology includes a Nazi child's prayer, a section of a novel by Goebbels, a children's story picturing Hitler as a friend of the young, material on the Gestapo, and the case of a pro-Jewish Christian minister.

Richter, Hans Peter. *I Was There.* New York: Holt, Rinehart & Winston, 1972; Dell pb., 1973.

An interesting memoir of daily life in Germany and especially of growing up in the youth movement.

Weinreich, Max. *Hitler's Professors.* New York: YIVO Institute, 1946.

On the Nazis who collaborated in Hitler's anti-Semitic "science."

F. Nazi Policy Toward the Jews

Adam, Uwe Dietrich. "Persecution of the Jews, Bureaucracy and Authority in the Totalitarian State." *LBI Yrbk* 23 (1978): 139–150.

> The leading German historian of the Nazi bureaucracy, Adam examines the uneven nature of the bureaucratic persecution and, ultimately, genocide against the Jews.

Goldhagen, Erich. "Pragmatism, Function and Belief in Nazi Anti-Semitism." *Midstream* 18 (December 1972): 52–62.

> Goldhagen argues that while one part of the German mind pursued scientific reason, another sank into primitive magic.

Reichmann, Eva. *Hostages of Civilization: The Sources of National Socialist Anti-Semitism.* Westport, Conn.: Greenwood Press, 1970.

> An excellent early study of the political and intellectual origins of Nazi anti-Semitism.

World Committee for the Victims of Fascism. *Brown Book of the Hitler Terror.* New York: Knopf, 1933.

> This important early volume deals not only with Jews but with all victims of the Nazi terror during its first year.

G. The "Implementation" of the Holocaust: The SS, Gestapo, and Others

Borkin, Joseph. *The Crime and Punishment of I. G. Farben.* New York: Free Press, 1978; Dell pb., 1978; Pocket pb., 1981.

> Borkin's history of the huge German chemical concern, which he investigated for two decades for a Senate committee and for the Nuremberg judges, includes important chapters on "IG Auschwitz" and on the surprisingly light punishments the key sixteen criminals received.

Browning, Christopher. *The Final Solution and the German Foreign Office.* New York: Holmes & Meier, 1979.

> Browning has meticulously researched how the objectives of German foreign policy and the Final Solution were coordinated by looking at the records of the Jewish Affairs Section of the German Foreign Office.

Crankshaw, Edward. *The Gestapo: Instrument of Tyranny.* New York: Viking, 1956.

The chilling story of one of the most notorious institutions in human history.

Delarue, Jacques. *The Gestapo: A History of Horror.* New York: Morrow, 1964.

This solid history contains a quite good, if by now somewhat dated, bibliography.

Dicks, Henry V. *Licensed Mass Murder: A Socio-Psychological Study of Some SS Killers.* New York: Basic Books, 1972.

A balanced look at the social pathology, and the normalcy, of some SS killers.

Grunberger, Richard. *Hitler's SS.* New York: Delacorte; Dell pb., 1971.

This book explains the origins of the SS, the psychological motivation of members, and details of SS practices. While the book may be flawed for classroom use, for it lacks an overall conceptual approach, it could be helpful to individual students. It also contains useful illustrations.

Höhne, Heinz. *The Order of the Death's Head Division.* New York: Coward, McCann & Geoghegan, 1970.

A first-rate history of the SS, which draws upon personal accounts of members of the Death's-Head Division.

Krausnick, Helmut; Bucheim, Hans; Broszat, Martin; and Jacobsen, Hans-Adolf. *Anatomy of the SS-State.* Introduction by Elizabeth Wiskerman. New York: Walter & Co., 1968; Chicago: Paladin/ Academy Chicago pb., 1984.

Four first-rate presentations originally prepared as background for the series of trials by the Auschwitz criminals: "The Persecution of the Jews" by Krausnick, "Two Analyses of the SS" by Hans Bucheim, and "History of the Concentration Camps" by Martin Broszat.

Manvell, Roger. *SS and Gestapo.* New York: Ballantine, 1969.

A brisk, short history of the Nazi forces specializing in torture and murder.

Reitlinger, Gerald. *The SS: Alibi of a Nation, 1922–45.* New York: Viking, 1957; Englewood Cliffs, N.J.: Prentice-Hall, 1981.

One of the best histories of the SS.

H. The German Occupation of Europe, 1939–1945

Lemkin, Raphael. *Axis Rule in Occupied Europe*. Washington, D.C.:
Carnegie Endowment for International Peace, 1944.

> In this detailed pioneering brief, Lemkin introduced the word
> "genocide" into Western discourse. He also dealt with the laws of
> occupation, the nature of the German occupation of various coun-
> tries, and proposals for redress.

Stein, George. *The Waffen SS*. Ithaca, N.Y.: Cornell University Press,
1970.

> A scholarly account of Hitler's unique guard at war.

I. The German People's Response to Hitler and the Nazis

Beradt, Charlotte. *The Third Reich of Dreams*. New York: Quadrangle,
1968.

> The record of dreams by citizens of the Third Reich—many of the
> dreams show the "perversion" of their minds.

Gordon, Sarah. *Hitler, Jews and the German Question*. Princeton, N.J.:
Princeton University Press, 1984.

> A far-reaching study of German attitudes towards Jews before and
> during the Holocaust; looks closely at what Germans knew about
> the Holocaust, which segments of the German people attempted to
> rescue Jews, when they did so, and why.

Henry, Frances. *Visitors and Neighbors: A Small Town in Germany
Remembered*. South Hadley, Mass.: Bergin & Garvey/International
Publisher's Group, 1984.

> On life in a German village, particularly relations between Jews
> and Christians, before and during the Third Reich.

Kempowski, Walter. *Did You Ever See Hitler?* New York: Avon, 1973.

> Questions asked of today's Germans about their impressions of
> Hitler.

Stokes, Lawrence D. "The German People and the Destruction of the
European Jews." *CEH* 6, no. 2 (June 1973): 167–192.

> One of the very few studies available that judiciously looks at what
> the German people knew, and when they knew it, concerning the
> Final Solution.

Switzer, Ellen. *How Democracy Failed*. New York: Atheneum, 1975.

An excellent book by a German-born writer who went back to interview people her own age who remember their teenage years under Nazism and what effect it had on their families and their own lives—a good, personalized account of the history of the period, with 24 pages of photographs.

Vogel, Traugott. *Under the SS Shadow*. New York: Bantam, 1978.

The true story of a member of the Hitler Youth who lived in the shadow of the past and fought to overcome it.

Von Staden, Wendelgard. *Darkness Over the Valley: Growing Up in Nazi Germany*. New York: Ticknor & Field, 1981; Penguin pb., 1982.

A memoir of growing up near a concentration camp by a woman whose mother, Irmgard von Neurath, helped POW's and Jewish prisoners.

4.

Germany's Jewish Policies, and the Jews' Responses, 1933–1939

A. German Policy Toward the Jews

Adam, Uwe D. "An Overall Plan for Anti-Jewish Legislation in the Third Reich." *YVS* 11 (1976): 33–55.

Adam examines the shifting "strategies" for "dealing with the Jews," which were influenced by bureaucratic in-fighting, economic, political and foreign policy considerations.

Browning, Christopher R. "Referat Deutschland, Jewish Policy and the German Foreign Office, 1933–1940." *YVS* 12 (1977): 37–74.

Carmon, Arye. "The Impact of the Nazi Racial Decrees on the University of Heidelberg: A Case Study," YVS 11 (1976): 131–163.

Friedman, Philip. "The Lublin Reservation and the Madagascar Plan (Two Aspects of Nazi Jewish Policy During the Second World War)." YIVO Annual 8 (1953): 151–177.

> Friedman has written the best essay to date on Nazi plans to "resettle" the Jews of Europe without resorting to genocide.

Schleunes, Karl A. The Twisted Road To Auschwitz. Champaign, Ill.: University of Illinois Press, 1970.

> Schleunes documents the complex and inconsistent nature of Nazi policy toward German Jews from 1933 to 1939 in this important study.

Thalmann, Rita, and Emmanuel Feinermann. *Crystal Night. New York: Coward, McCann & Geoghegan, 1974; Holocaust Library, 1980.

> On the night of November 9–10, 1938, organized Nazi terror against Jews erupted all over Germany. Using contemporary documents, Thalmann and Feinermann also examine the planning and implementation of the national pogrom, as well as the responses of a number of major powers to Crystal Night.

B. The Jewish Communal Response to Nazi Policies

Baker, Leonard. Days of Sorrow and Pain: Leo Baeck and Berlin Jews. New York: Macmillan, 1978.

> A prize-winning biography of the leader of German Jews during the Nazi period—it includes an interesting chapter on his controversial role in the Theresienstadt concentration camp.

Baldwin, Peter M. "Zionist and Non-Zionist Jews in the Last Years before the Nazi Regime." LBI Yrbk 27 (1982): 87–108.

Ball-Kaduri, K. Y. "The Central Jewish Organization in Berlin During the Pogrom of November, 1938." YVS 3 (1959): 261–282.

———. "The National Representation of Jews in Germany—Obstacles and Accomplishments at Its Establishment." YVS 2 (1958): 159–178.

Black, Edwin. *Transfer Agreement.* New York: Macmillan, 1984

> The first major account of the 1933 agreement between the German government and the Jewish Agency for Palestine which provided that, in exchange for an end to the boycott of German goods abroad, a significant number (ultimately, 60,000) of German Jews would be allowed to emigrate to Palestine.

Boas, Jacob. "Germany or Diaspora? German Jewry's Shifting Perceptions in the Nazi Era (1933–1938)." *LBI Yrbk* 27 (1982): 109–128.

Esh, Shaul. "Between Discrimination and Extermination." *YVS* 2 (1958): 79–94.

————. "The Establishment of the 'Reichsvereinigung der Juden in Deutschland' and Its Main Activities." *YVS* 7 (1968): 19–38.

> On the National Association of German Jews.

Gruenwald, M. "The Beginning of the Reichsvertretung." *LBI Yrbk* 1 (1956): 57–67.

Margaliot, Abraham. "The Dispute over the Leadership of German Jewry (1933–1938)." *YVS* 10 (1974): 129–148.

————. "The Reaction of the Jewish Public in Germany to the Nuremberg Laws." *YVS* 12 (1977): 78–108.

Szanto, A., "Economic Aid in the Nazi Era." *LBI Yrbk* 4 (1959): 208–219.

> On welfare and other aspects of German Jewish communal aid during the Nazi period.

Wischnitzer, Mark. "Jewish Emigration from Germany, 1933–1938." *JSS* 2, no. 1 (January 1940): 23–44.

C. Other Aspects of Jewish Life and Culture

Colodner, Solomon. "Jewish Education Under National Socialism." *YVS* 3 (1959): 161–186.

Edelheim-Muehsam, M. "The Jewish Press in Germany." *LBI Yrbk* 1 (1956): 163–176.

————. "Reaction of the Jewish Press to the Nazi Challenge." *LBI Yrbk* 5 (1960): 330–337.

> Edelheim-Muehsam surveys the whole range of Jewish press, including the papers of the *Centralvereinigung* (Main Association of German Jews) and the Zionists.

Freeder, H. "A Jewish Theatre Under the Swastika." *LBI Yrbk* 1 (1956): 142–162.

Friedland, Fritz. "Trials and Tribulations of Education in Nazi Germany." *LBI Yrbk* 3 (1958): 187–201.

> Among other issues, Friedlander examines the growth of non-Orthodox Jewish schools, the persecution of the Jewish children in public schools, and their ultimate exclusion from those schools.

Fuchs, Richard. "The Hochshule für Die Wissenschaft des Judentums in the Period of the Nazi Rule." *LBI Yrbk* 12 (1967): 3–31.

Gaertner, H. "Problems of Jewish Schools in Germany During the Hitler Regime." *LBI Yrbk* 1 (1956): 3–31.

Simon, Ernst. "Jewish Adult Education in Nazi Germany as Spiritual Resistance." *LBI Yrbk* 1 (1956): 68–104.

> In this lengthy, fascinating essay, Simon records the renaissance in adult Jewish learning between 1933 and 1939, and especially the efforts of such intellectual and spiritual leaders as Martin Buber and Leo Baeck.

Stahl, Rudolph. "Vocational Training of Jews in Nazi Germany, 1933–1938." *JSS* 1, no. 2. (April 1939): 169–199.

Strauss, Herbert A. "Jewish Emigration from Germany: Nazi Policies and Jewish Responses (I)." *LBI Yrbk* 25 (1980): 313–361.

5.

The Holocaust—General Studies and Colloquia

Bauer, Yehuda, *A History of the Holocaust*, New York: Franklin Watts, 1982

The distinguished Israeli historian has produced an exemplary history of the Holocaust. He devotes about a quarter of the 380-page study to the background of Nazism, and to Jewish life before the Holocaust. He also looks at such thorny historical questions as "Was rescue by negotiation possible?" and analyzes the theological and other implication of the Holocaust

Braham, Randolph L. (ed.). *Contemporary Views on the Holocaust* and *Perspectives on the Holocaust*. Hingham, Mass.: Kluwer/Nijhoff Publishing, 1984.

These two volumes consist of lectures and special studies presented at the Institute for Holocaust Studies at the Graduate Center of the City University of New York from 1981 to 1983.

Colloquium on the Holocaust. Philadelphia: Dropsie University Press, 1973.

A collection of lectures given at an interfaith colloquium exploring the roots and implications of the Holocaust; contributors include A. Roy Eckardt and John Cardinal Krol.

Dawidowicz, Lucy S. *The War Against the Jews, 1933–1945*. New York: Holt, Rinehart & Winston, 1975; Bantam pb., 1976.

The author shows how the German military hierarchy was more concerned with exterminating Jews than with pursuing World War II. This very well written book is one of the best single volumes on the history of the Holocaust, although it deals inadequately with the Holocaust outside of Poland.

Fein, Helen. *Accounting for Genocide. New York: Free Press, 1979; Chicago: University of Chicago Press, pb. 1983.

A detailed sociological study of the nature of genocide, country by country, during the Holocaust, as well as an analysis of how differences in national culture and history affected the Final Solution.

Friedlander, Henry, and Milton, Sybil (eds.). The Holocaust: Ideology, Bureaucracy and Genocide—The San Jose Papers. Millwood, N.Y.: Kraus International Publications, 1980.

An important, well-edited interdisciplinary anthology featuring essays by Raul Hilberg, Henry Feingold, Franklin Littell, and Lucjan Dobroszicki among others—it covers various aspects of Nazism in the context of World War II.

Friedman, Philip. Roads to Extinction. Edited by Ada Jun Friedman, introduction by Salo W. Baron. Philadelphia: Jewish Publication Society, 1980.

A remarkable collection of twenty-three essays by the late, distinguished historian of the Holocaust.

Gilbert, Martin. *The Macmillan Atlas of the Holocaust. New York: Macmillan, 1982; De Capo Press, 1984.

With over 300 maps, narrative, and photographs, this is a key reference work.

Grobman, Alex, and Landes, Daniel (eds.). Genocide: Critical Issues of the Holocaust. Chappaqua, N.Y.: Rossel Books, 1983.

This anthology of forty short studies on various aspects of the Holocaust is not only a fine companion to the film Genocide but an excellent introduction to the subject.

Gutman, Yisrael, and Rothkirchen, Livia (eds.). The Catastrophe of European Jewry. Jerusalem: Yad Vashem, 1976.

With twenty-five essays by leading scholars, this is perhaps the best anthology of articles about the Holocaust in existence. It contains sections entitled "Antecedents," "History," and "Reflections," as well as a detailed "Chronological Table of Events, 1933–1945."

Hilberg, Raul. *The Destruction of the European Jews. New York: Quadrangle, 1961, 1967; Harper & Row pb., 1979; Holmes & Meier expanded edition, 1983. (The 1967 edition has minor changes and a new postscript; the 1983 edition, published in three volumes, includes about 15% new material.)

This pioneering study is based on the entire unindexed collection of Nuremberg documents and materials in the Federal Records Center in Virginia, where Dr. Hilberg was a member of the War Documentation Project. It contains valuable information and references found nowhere else. Hilberg focuses largely on the Nazi machinery of destruction, about which he writes comprehensively. However, he deals inadequately with the Jewish responses.

*Holocaust. Jerusalem: Keter pb., 1974.

A comprehensive history of the Holocaust, based on the materials in the Encyclopaedia Judaica.

Levin, Nora. *The Holocaust: The Destruction of European Jewry, 1933–1945. New York: Schocken, 1973

A major history which attempts to write from the inside, with emphasis on the "failure" of German Jewry, the "dilemma" of the Jewish Councils, and resistance.

Poliakov, Leon. *Harvest of Hate. Syracuse, N.Y.: Syracuse University Press, 1954; Westport, Conn.: Greenwood, 1971; New York: Holocaust Library, 1979.

On the Nazi program for the annihilation of Europe's Jews—a detailed early study which includes good sections on "Pillage and Enslavement of the Jews" and on "Nazi Plans for the 'Inferior Peoples.' "

Rabinowitz, Dorothy. *About the Holocaust: What We Know and How We Know It. New York: Institute of Human Relations Press of the American Jewish Committee, 1979.

A well-written, booklet-length history.

+ *The Record: Persecution: Past and Present. New York: Anti-Defamation League of B'nai B'rith, 1979.

This short, tabloid-style deals with persecution today and includes a brief comparison with the Vietnamese boat people.

Schoenberner, Gerhard. *The Yellow Star: The Persecution of the Jews in Europe, 1933–1945. New York: Bantam, 1979.

A brief and extensively illustrated account of the persecution of European Jewry; this work, originally published in Germany in 1960, combines official and personal documents.

Sherwin, Byron, and Ament, Susan (eds.). *Encountering the Holocaust: An Interdisciplinary Study.* Chicago: Impact Press, 1979.

An invaluable anthology which covers the causes, nature, and implications of the Holocaust; *Encountering the Holocaust* will be particularly useful for college courses and for those preparing to teach the Holocaust.

Szajkowski, Zosa. *An Illustrated Sourcebook on the Holocaust.* 3 vols. New York: Ktav, 1979.

An available reference work with hundreds of illustrations.

Wiesel, Elie, et al. *Dimensions of the Holocaust: Lectures at Northwestern University.* Evanston, Ill.: Northwestern University Press, 1977.

The edited transcripts of four lectures given at Northwestern by leading scholars and writers in 1977.

World Jewish Congress et al. *The Black Book: The Nazi Crime Against the Jewish People.* New York: Nexus Press, 1982.

A long-overdue reprint of the 1946 anthology which provided a history of Nazism and served as a well-documented "brief" on the Nazi crimes against humanity.

Yad Vashem. *Black Book of Localities Whose Jewish Population Was Exterminated by the Nazis.* Jerusalem: Yad Vashem, 1965.

A guide to shtetls whose Jewish populations were utterly eliminated by the Holocaust.

6.

The Holocaust—Anthologies of First-Person Accounts, Documents, and Other Writings

Arad, Yitzhak; Gutman, Yisrael; and Margaliot, Abraham (eds). *Documents on the Holocaust*. Jerusalem and New York: Yad Vashem and Ktav, 1982.

A 500-page anthology of primary documents, most reproduced in full, on the destruction of the Jews in Germany, Austria, Poland, and the USSR.

Chartock, Roselle, and Spender, Jack. + *Society on Trial: The Holocaust Years*. Bantam, 1978.

A comprehensive anthology designed specifically for social·studies, English, and history classrooms. A teacher's guide by Erika Hess Merems is available.

Dawidowicz, Lucy S. (ed.). *A Holocaust Reader*. New York: Behrman House, 1976.

Accompanied by a valuable introduction to each section by the editor, this collection of documents is one of the finest single gatherings of its kind. Included are the words of both the persecutors and the victims, making for a realistic, balanced perspective.

Eisenberg, Azriel. *Witness to the Holocaust: Personal and Eyewitness Accounts of the Holocaust, Resistance and Rebirth*. New York: Pilgrim Press, 1981; pb., 1983.

From the beginnings of the Third Reich, through book burnings, Kristallnacht, the Evian Conference, the ghettos, partisans, the liberation and after—a remarkable anthology.

———. *The Lost Generation: Children in the Holocaust.* New York: Pilgrim Press, 1982.

Contains over 100 eyewitness accounts of the fate of children during the Holocaust—an excellent work for high school and college courses.

Friedlander, Albert H. *Out of the Whirlwind.* New York: Union of American Hebrew Congregations, 1968; Schocken pb., 1976.

This anthology includes particularly strong sections on the Nazi persecution of the Jews to 1939, and reflections on implications of the Holocaust.

Glatstein, Jacob; Knox, Israel; and Margoshes, Samuel (eds.). *Anthology of Holocaust Literature.* Philadelphia: Jewish Society; New York: Atheneum, 1972.

An outstanding compilation because it contains much material from lesser-known writers who are survivors and eyewitnesses.

Haas, Gerda. *These Do I Remember: Fragments from the Holocaust.* Freeport, Maine: Cumberland Press, 1983.

An anthology of several memoirs and diaries, including an autobiographical account by the author—with photographs, maps, and a glossary.

Hilberg, Raul (ed.). *Documents of Destruction, 1935–1945.* New York: Quadrangle, 1971; Franklin Watts pb., 1973.

English translations of original documents which nicely complement Hilberg's extremely valuable volume, *The Destruction of European Jews.*

Klausner, Carla C., and Schultz, Joseph P. *From Destruction to Rebirth: The Holocaust and the State of Israel.* Washington, D.C.: University Press of America, 1978.

One of the only anthologies that covers both turning points in twentieth-century Jewish history.

Korman, Gerd. *Hunter and Hunted: The Human History of the Holocaust.* New York: Viking Press, 1973; Delta pb., 1974.

A short, but useful anthology on the Holocaust from the viewpoint of both executioners and victims.

Mendelsohn, John (ed.), and Detwiler, Donald S. (advisory ed.). *The Holocaust: Selected Documents.* 18 vols. New York: Garland Publishing Co., 1982.

> The eighteen volumes, which consist of facsimile reproductions of documents on the Holocaust, consist of the following subjects: (1) Legalizing the Holocaust: The Early Phase, 1933–1939; (2) Legalizing the Holocaust: The Later Phase, 1939–1943; (3) The Crystal Night Pogrom; (4) Propaganda and Aryanization, (1938–1944); (5) Jewish Emigration from 1933 to the Evian Conference of 1938; (6) Jewish Emigration 1938 to 1940, Rublee Negotiations and Intergovernmental Committee; (7) Jewish Emigration: The *S.S. St. Louis* Affair and other Cases; (8) Deportation of the Jews to the East; Stettin, 1940 to Hungary, 1944; (9) Medical Experiments on Jewish Inmates of Concentration Camps; (10) The *Einsatzgruppen* or Murder Commandos; (11) The Wannsee Protocol and a 1944 Report on Auschwitz; (12) The "Final Solution" in the Extermination Camps and the Aftermath; (13) The Judicial System and the Jews in Nazi Germany; (14) Relief and Rescue of Jews from Nazi Oppression, 1943–1945; (15) Relief in Hungary and the Failure of the Joel Brand Mission; (16) Rescue to Switzerland: The Mussy and Saly Mayer Affairs; (17) Punishing the Perpetrators of the Holocaust: The Brandt, Pohl and Ohlendorf Cases; (18) Punishing the Perpetrators of the Holocaust: The Ohlendorf and Von Weizaecker Cases.

Roiter, Howard. *Voices from the Holocaust.* New York: William Frederick Press, 1975

> True accounts of the personal experiences during the Holocaust years of survivors who now reside in Montreal.

Strauss, Walter (ed.). *Signs of Life: Jews from Wuerttemberg; Reports for the Period after 1933 in Letters and Descriptions.* New York: Ktav, 1982.

> A unique collection of first-person accounts by almost 500 Wuerttemberg Jews, describing life under the Nazi terror and their struggles to build new lives in other countries.

Trunk, Isaiah. **Jewish Responses to Nazi Persecution.* New York: Stein & Day, 1980; Scarborough pb, 1981.

> A collection of sixty-two accounts by survivors, many recorded in the first few years after the Holocaust.

7.

Jewish Life in the Ghettos, in Shtetls, and in Hiding; Judenräte (Jewish Councils) and Religious Issues During the Holocaust

A. Memoirs, Diaries, Photographs, and Drawings

Berg, Mary. *The Warsaw Ghetto*. Edited by S. L. Schneiderman. New York: L. B. Fisher, 1945.

> One of the first extended accounts of the establishment and destruction of the Warsaw Ghetto, written by a non-Jewish woman who began keeping her diary at age sixteen.

Brand, Sandra. *Between Two Worlds*. New York: Shengold, 1983.

> The story of the struggle of the daughter of Hasidic parents to be accepted as a person, set in the context of the Nazi, and later the Russian, invasion of Poland.

David, Janina. *A Square of Sky* and *A Touch of Earth*. New York: Penguin Books, 1981.

> A two-volume memoir about coming of age during the Holocaust (the author was nine when the Nazis invaded Poland), both inside and outside the Warsaw Ghetto.

Ferderbar-Salz, Bertha. *And the Sun Kept Shining.* New York: Holocaust Library, 1980.

A finely written memoir of the Holocaust covering life in Cracow and in the death and concentration camps.

Grossman, Mendel. *With a Camera in the Ghetto.* Edited by Zvi Szner and Alexander Sened. New York: Schocken, 1977.

A collection of photographs from the Lodz Ghetto.

Hahn, Lili. *White Flags of Surrender.* Washington, D.C.: Robert B. Lucey, 1974.

This is the autobiography of a non-Jewish woman whose father was Aryan and whose mother was Jewish by descent. Her experiences are recorded in the form of a diary. Among the events recorded are her mother's escape, in part through her daughter's sexual bribery of a Gestapo officer.

Hersh, Gizelle, and Mann, Peggy. *"Gizelle, Save the Children!"* New York: Everett House, 1980.

Gizelle Hersh was sixteen when, with her three younger sisters, she was separated from her parents at Auschwitz. This is her story before, during, and after the death camp nightmare.

Hirshaut, Julien. *Jewish Martyrs of Pawiak.* New York: Holocaust Library, 1983.

An engrossing memoir of the torture-ridden Warsaw prison in which the Nazi and Ukrainian guards killed over 8,000 Jews, and from which the author miraculously escaped.

Kaplan, Chaim. A. *The Scroll of Agony (reprinted in paperback as *The Warsaw Diary of Chaim Kaplan).* Edited by Abraham Katsh and Chaim A. Kaplan. New York: Macmillan, 1965; Collier pb., 1981.

This remarkable diary, covering the period from September 1, 1939 to August 1942, was written by a Polish Hebrew teacher who perished not long after. The new (1982) paperback edition includes a recently discovered section of the diary covering the period April 4, 1941 to May 2, 1942.

Katznelson, Yitzhak. *Vittel Diary.* Edited by Myer Cohen. Israel: Kibbutz Lohamei Haghettaot, 1972.

This extraordinary diary covers the period from May 22 to September 16, 1943 in a small Polish city.

Korczak, Janusz. *Ghetto Diary. New York: Holocaust Library, 1978; pb., 1981.

> Korczak was a pediatrician, writer, educator, charismatic leader, and apostle of child welfare. During his last year as head of an orphanage of 200 children in the Warsaw Ghetto, he refused offers of personal rescue and insisted on accompanying his charges to their murder at Treblinka. The diary of those last years is shattering and inspiring, showing why Korczak has become a legendary symbol of selfless sacrifice and of the highest human values. The diary is enhanced by Aaron Zeitlin's long, fascinating biographical essay.

Kuper, Jack. *Child of the Holocaust. Garden City, N.Y.: Doubleday, 1968.

> A personal account of a young boy in Nazi-occupied Poland during World War II.

Kwinta, Chava. I'm Still Living. Toronto: Simon & Pierre, 1974.

> The memoir of a woman who as a young girl and then a teenager came of age in the Sosnowiecz Ghetto in Poland.

Meras, I. Stalemate. New York: Lyle Stuart, 1980.

> An account of the Vilna Ghetto.

Minco, Marga. *Bitter Herbs. New York: Oxford University Press, 1960.

> A memoir of a Dutch-Jewish childhood during the dangerous years.

Neshamit, Sarah. The Children of Mapu Street. Translated from the Hebrew by David S. Segal. Israel: Beit Lohamei Haghettaot and Kibbutz Hameuchad Publishing House, 1979.

> Life during the Second World War as told by children growing up in Nazi Germany and occupied Europe.

Ringelblum, Emmanuel. *Notes from the Warsaw Ghetto. New York: McGraw-Hill, 1958; Schocken pb., 1974.

> The remarkable day-by-day account of Warsaw Ghetto life by one of the most noted historians of the Holocaust period.

Rochman, Leyb. *The Pit and the Trap. New York: Holocaust Library, 1983.

> A classic memoir of the Holocaust in a Polish shtetl—an extraordinary work.

Rubenstein, Erna F. *The Survivor in Us All: A Memoir of the Holocaust.* Hamden, Conn.: Archon Books, 1984.

About four girls who helped each other through the Holocaust years.

Rubinowicz, Dawid. *The Diary of Dawid Rubinowicz.* Translated by Derek Bowman. Edmonds, Wash.: Creative Options, 1982.

A diary which covers the almost three years from the occupation of Poland (September 1939), when Rubinowicz was twelve, until the author's deportation to Auschwitz, from which he never returned.

Rudashevski, Yitzhak. *The Diary of the Vilna Ghetto: June, 1941–April, 1943.* Translated by Percy Matenko. Israel: Kibbutz Lohamei Haghettaot, 1972.

This diary of a fourteen-year-old boy gives unusual insights into the cultural life of the Vilna Ghetto. It includes a good introduction and notes by the translator.

Shulman, Abraham. *The Case of Hotel Polski.* New York: Holocaust Library, 1981.

The story of how the Nazis, in the late spring of 1943, lured survivors of the Warsaw Ghetto to a hotel on the Aryan side, promising them freedom and offering most death.

Wolfe [née Glicenstein], Jacqueline. *"Take Care of Josette."* New York: Franklin Watts, 1981.

A memoir of life in occupied France; the author was fourteen when her parents were deported to Auschwitz, and writes of her and her four-year-old sister Josette's struggle for survival.

Zeimian, Joseph. *The Cigarette Sellers of Three Crosses Square.* London: Vallentine, Mitchell, 1970; Minneapolis: Lerner, 1967; New York: Avon pb., 1977.

The true story of a group of Jewish children who managed to escape from the Warsaw Ghetto in 1942 and survived in the non-Jewish section of the city.

Zyskind, Sara. *Stolen Years.* Minneapolis: Lerner, 1981.

A memoir spanning the author's life from 1939 to 1945 (ages 11–17), including ghetto life, losing her parents, Auschwitz, and emigration to Palestine.

B. Scholarly and Other Works on Ghetto Life

Arad, Yitzhak. *Ghetto in Flames: The Struggle and Destruction of the Jews in Vilna in the Holocaust.* Jerusalem and New York: Yad Vashem and Anti-Defamation League, 1980; New York: Holocaust Library, 1982.

A model history of Jewish life, resistance, and destruction in one of Eastern Europe's largest Jewish cities.

Blumenthal, Nachman. "Magical Thinking Among the Jews During the Nazi Occupation." YVS 5 (1963): 221–236.

Fass, Moshe. "Theatrical Activities in the Polish Ghettos During the Years 1939–1942." JSS 38, no. 1 (Winter 1976): 54–72.

Friedman, Philip. *Martyrs and Fighters: The Epic of the Warsaw Ghetto.* New York: Praeger, 1954.

An account of the daily lives of Jews in the ghetto from the beginning of World War II to the last day of the uprising.

———. "The Jewish Ghetto of the Nazi Era." JSS 16, no. 1 (January 1954): 61–68.

A truly authoritative, documented account.

Gringauz, Samuel. "The Ghetto as an Experiment of Jewish Social Organization." JSS 11, no. 1 (January 1949): 3–20.

Gutman, Yisrael. *The Jews in Warsaw, 1939–1943: Ghetto, Underground, Revolt.* Bloomington: Indiana University Press, 1983.

Drawing extensively on Jewish materials in Hebrew and Yiddish, Gutman provides a detailed history of the Warsaw Ghetto.

Hershkovitch, Bendet. "The Ghetto in Litzmannstadt (Lodz)." YIVO Annual 5 (1950): 85–122.

Katz, Alfred. *Poland's Ghettos at War.* New York: Twayne, 1970.

An in-depth treatment of the establishment and functioning of the ghettos, including the resistance efforts.

Kermish, Joseph. "The Land of Israel in the Life of the Ghetto as Reflected in the Illegal Warsaw Ghetto Press." YVS 5 (1963): 105–132.

———. "On the Underground Press in the Warsaw Ghetto." YVS 1 (1957): 85–124.

———. "Emmanuel Ringelblum's Notes Hitherto Unpublished." YVS 7 (1968): 173–184.

Klibanski, Bronia. "The Underground Archives of the Bialystok Ghetto (Founded by Mersik and Tenenbaum)." YVS 2 (1958): 295–330.

Okczakowa, Hanna. *Mister Doctor: The Life of Janusz Korczak.* London: Peter Davies, 1965.

A detailed biography of Janusz Korczak which draws upon his memoirs and numerous works, as well as the author's personal knowledge of him.

Schneider, Gertrude. *Journey into Terror: Story of the Riga Ghetto.* New York: Ark House, 1980.

A good study, and one of the only English-language accounts, of the Holocaust in Latvia.

Trunk, Isaiah. "Epidemics and Mortality in the Warsaw Ghetto, 1939–1942." *YIVO Annual* 8 (1953): 82–122.

———. "Religious, Educational and Cultural Problems in Eastern European Ghettos Under German Occupation." *YIVO Annual* 14 (1969): 159–195.

An article written on the basis of Trunk's meticulous research and with his usual balanced approach.

———. "Why Was There No Armed Resistance Against Nazism in the Lodz Ghetto." *JSS* 43, nos. 3–4 (Summer–Fall 1981): 329–344.

Winick, Myron (ed.). *Hunger Disease: Studies by Jewish Physicians in the Warsaw Ghetto.* New York: John Wiley, 1979.

A group of doctors in the Warsaw Ghetto, themselves condemned to die of the diseases they were suffering, undertook a careful medical investigation of the clinical, metabolic, and pathological consequences of hunger and starvation. This book is a translation from the Polish of a manuscript smuggled out of the ghetto.

C. On the Judenräte (Jewish Councils), Jewish Police, and Other Jewish Leadership

Bloom, Solomon F. "Toward the Ghetto Dictator." *JSS* 12, no. 1 (January 1950): 73–78.

As Bloom insists, no figure in recent history has played a more tragic role than the leaders of ghettos under German occupation. Here he tries to understand their activities.

———. "Dictator of the Lodz Ghetto." *Commentary* 7 (February 1949): 111–122.

Includes the strange story of the Lodz Judenrat head, Mordechai Chaim Rumkowski.

Braham, Randolph. "The Role of the Jewish Council in Hungary: A Tentative Assessment." YVS 10 (1974): 69–110.

Czerniakow, Adam. *The Warsaw Diary of Adam Czerniakow: Prelude to Doom. Edited by Raul Hilberg, Stanislaw Staron, and Josef Kermisz. New York: Stein & Day, 1979; Scarborough pb., 1982.

For nearly three years Adam Czerniakow was the chairman of the Warsaw Judenrat. Thus his secret journal is not only the testimony of an unbearable personal burden, but principally the documentary of the terminal agony of the living-dying city-within-a-city that was the Warsaw Ghetto before its half-million people were annihilated. Adam Czerniakow killed himself on July 23, 1942.

Friedman, Phillip. "Aspects of the Jewish Communal Crisis in the Period of the Nazi Regime in Germany, Austria and Czechoslovakia." In Essays on Jewish Life and Thought Presented in Honor of Salo Wittmayer Baron, pp. 199–230. New York: Columbia University Press, 1959.

———. "Two Saviors Who Failed." Commentary 26, no. 6 (December 1958): 179–191.

About two Judenrat leaders who attempted a "rescue through work" strategy.

Glicksman, William. "Daily Record Sheet of the Jewish Police (District I) in the Czestochowa Ghetto (1941–1942)." YVS 6 (1967): 331–358.

Gutman, Yisrael, and Haft, Cynthia. Patterns of Jewish Leadership in Nazi Europe. Jerusalem: Yad Vashem, 1979.

A remarkable anthology of scholarly papers on the Judenräte (Jewish Councils), and other kinds of Jewish leadership during the Holocaust.

Trunk, Isaiah. *Judenrat: The Jewish Councils in Eastern Europe Under Nazi Occupation. Translated by Jacob Robinson. New York: Stein & Day, 1977.

The meticulously researched story of the Jewish Councils in Eastern Europe under the Nazi occupation; this is a brilliant work which won a National Book Award in history.

Tushnet, Leonard. The Pavements of Hell. New York: St. Martin's, 1972.

An attempt to try and understand the actions of three leaders of the Jewish Councils in Nazi-occupied Europe, *The Pavements of Hell* deals with why these men acted as they did.

Weiss, Aharon. "Jewish Leadership in Occupied Poland—Postures and Attitudes." *YVS* 12 (1977): 335–366.

D. Jews in Hiding or Otherwise Protected

Boehm, Eric H. (ed.). *We Survived*. New Haven, Conn.: Yale University Press, 1949.

Stories of persons hidden and hunted in Nazi Germany.

Brand, Sandra. *I Dared to Live*. New York: Shengold, 1978.

A memoir of escape to and existence in the Aryan side of Warsaw.

Feld, Marilla. *I Chose to Live*. New York: Manor Books, 1979.

The author worked three years in the home of an SA member by hiding her identity as a Jew.

Frank, Anne. **The Diary of a Young Girl*. New York: Pocket Books, 1965.

The famous account of a Dutch Jewish girl's ordeal in hiding, *The Diary* captures both the physical claustrophobia of hiding and a sensitive adolescent's hopes for the future.

Friedlander, Saul. **When Memory Comes*. New York: Farrar, Straus & Giroux, 1978; Avon pb., 1980.

A remarkable memoir by the Israeli historian about coming of age in a Catholic convent during the Holocaust.

Friedman, Ina R. + **Escape Or Die*. Reading, Mass.: Addison-Wesley, 1982.

Twelve portraits of Jews and non-Jews who, as children, survived the Holocaust.

Gabor, Georgia M. *My Destiny*. Alahambra, Calif.: Borden Publishing Co., 1982.

The memoirs of a Hungarian survivor of the Holocaust, with information about her experiences, her numerous escapes from the Nazis and Soviets, her existence in various DP camps, and her efforts to survive in the United States.

Gardus, Luba Krugman. *The Death Train: A Personal Account of a Holocaust Survivor.* New York: National Council on Art in Jewish Life and Holocaust Library, 1979.

Includes the artist-author's moving drawings.

Koehn, Ilse. **Mischling: Second Degree.* New York: William Morrow, 1977; Bantam pb., 1978.

Ilse Koehn's account of her adolescence in Nazi Germany universalizes the experience of young people bewildered, uprooted, and traumatized by war. Her story has an ironic twist in that, under the 1935 Nuremberg Laws, she was a *Mischling,* the "mixed" offspring of a union between a German and a Jew, a fact of which she remained ignorant until after the war.

Lind, Jakov. *Counting My Steps.* New York: Macmillan, 1969.

This autobiography of the Austrian-Jewish writer recounts his years of hiding and fleeing from the Nazis.

Rosen, Donia. +*The Forest, My Friend.* Translated by Mordecai S. Chertoff. New York: World Federation of Bergen-Belsen Associations, 1971.

The experiences of a six-year-old Jewish girl in the western Ukraine under German occupation, and how she survived in the woods.

Rubenstein, Donna. *I Am the Only Survivor of Krasnostav.* New York: Shengold, 1983.

A memoir of the only survivor of the Nazi massacre of a pogrom, who went on to live out the war years under a Christian identity.

Shapiro, Eda. "The Reminiscences of Ukter Kugler—The 'Mr. Kraler' of Anne Frank's Diary." YVS 13 (1979): 353–386.

Starhopf, Adam. **There Is Always Time to Die.* New York: Holocaust Library, 1981.

A memoir of a family—the author, his wife, and their two-year-old child—"passing" as Gentiles in the Aryan part of Warsaw during the Holocaust.

Tec, Nehamia. *Dry Tears: Story of a Lost Childhood.* New York: Everett House, 1982.

The memoir of a Polish-Jewish girl passing as a Catholic.

E. Religious Issues

Berkovits, Eliezer. *With God in Hell.* New York: Hebrew Publishing Co., 1979.

A moving account of many cases of spiritual resistance and dignity during the Holocaust.

Eliach, Yaffa. **Hasidic Tales of the Holocaust.* New York: Oxford University Press, 1982; Avon pb., 1983.

A fascinating anthology of tales and legends on the Holocaust from various Hasidic communities, all of which affirm traditional faith in the face of inhuman persecution.

Flinker, Moshe. *Young Moshe's Diary: The Spiritual Torment of a Jewish Boy in Nazi Europe.* New York: Board of Jewish Education, 1965, 1975.

Moshe Flinker died in Auschwitz, leaving behind this profound testament of his intellectual maturity and perception in dealing with disturbing moral dilemmas. A devoutly Orthodox Jew, the sixteen-year-old Moshe confronted the eternal problem of reconciling Jewish suffering with divine justice. His deep faith and identification with the afflictions of his fellow Jews are reflected in his poetic writing, which portrays a rare passion and commitment to God and Israel.

Goldberg, Izaak. *The Miracles Versus Tyranny.* New York: Philosophical Library, 1978.

Stories, many apocryphal, of religious resistance and miraculous escapes—or personal vindications.

Guttman, Alexander. "Humane Insights of the Rabbis, Particularly with Respect to the Holocaust." *Hebrew Union College Annual* 46 (1975): 433–455.

The response to the Holocaust in Jewish literature.

Oshry, Ephraim. *Responsa from the Holocaust.* Brookline, Mass.: Judaica Press/Israel Bookshop, 1984.

A halakhic authority in Kovno, Lithuania, during the Holocaust, when the normal canons of proper Jewish behavior often seemed inadequate to the exigencies of life under the Nazis, Oshry responded with scholarship, sensitivity, and compassion to the numerous legal and ethical questions posed to him. This volume is an abridgment of his five-volume *She'eilos Utshuvos Mima'amkim.*

Rosenbaum, Irving J. *The Holocaust and Halakhah.* New York: Ktav, 1976.

A study of the determined efforts to conform to halakhic norms during the Holocaust (Halakhah is Jewish law and pertains to all spheres of life).

Schneider, Pesach. "The Holocaust and Kiddush HaShem in Hassidic Thought." *Tradition* 13 (Spring 1972): 88–105.

Zimmels, H. J. *The Echo of the Nazi Holocaust in Rabbinic Literature.* New York: Ktav, 1976.

An exhaustive compilation of religious responsa which reflect upon the nature of spiritual resistance among Orthodox Jews.

Zuker, Simon. *The Unconquerable Spirit: Vignettes of the Jewish Religious Spirit the Nazis Could Not Destroy.* Translated by Gertrude Hirschler. Brooklyn, N.Y.: Zachor Institute/Mesorah Publications, 1980.

True and apocryphal stories of Jews who maintained their spiritual faith and dignity during the Holocaust.

8.

The Final Solution in the Concentration Camps, Among the Einsatzgruppen, and on Death Marches

A. Einsatzgruppen ("Mobile Killing Units"), Concentration Camps, and Slave Labor Memoirs and Accounts

Berkowitz, Sarah. *Where Are My Brothers?* New York: Helios Books, 1965.

> A personal memoir of Bergen-Belsen.

Bor, Josef. **Terezin Requiem.* Translated by Edith Pargeter. New York: Knopf, 1963; Avon pb., 1978.

> A memoir based on a famous incident at Theresienstadt in which inmates sang Verdi's "Requiem" shortly before being transported to their deaths.

Buber, Margarete. *Under Two Dictators.* London: V. Gollancz, 1949.

> A gripping memoir of life in both Nazi and Soviet concentration camps.

D'Harcourt, Pierre. *The Real Enemy.* New York: Scribner's, 1967.

> A Christian who was imprisoned in concentration camps provides insights into his camp experience and into the spirit it took to survive.

Edelstein, Dov. *Worlds Torn Asunder.* New York: Ktav, 1984.

> The author, a pious Hasidic youth from the town of Szatmár in Hungary, was sent to Auschwitz at the age of seventeen. A moving, religiously sensitive, and exceptionally well written account of life in the camp.

Geve, Thomas. *Youth in Chains.* Jerusalem: Rubin Maas, 1982.

> A memoir of the author's youth in concentration camps.

Glicksman, W. "Social Differentiation in the German Concentration Camps." *YIVO Annual* 8 (1953): 123–150.

Graebe, Herman F. "Testimony of Herman F. Graebe, Given in Israel." *YVS* 6 (1967): 283–314.

> The extraordinary eyewitness account of an Einsatzgruppen killing.

Grosman, Ladislav. "Memories of My Service in a Labor Battalion." *YVS* 14 (1981): 287–302.

Kantor, Alfred. **The Book of Alfred Kantor.* New York: McGraw-Hill, 1971.

> The drawings and commentaries of Kantor, who was an inmate of three concentration camps, are here gathered, giving a profound visual impression of Jewish life in the Holocaust period.

Katz, Joseph. *One Who Came Back: The Diary of a Jewish Survivor.* New York: Bergen-Belsen Memorial Press, 1973.

> Katz was fifteen when Hitler came to power; by the war's end, he had lived through ghettos, concentration and death camps, and a death march.

Klein, Gerda. **All But My Life.* New York: Hill & Wang, 1957.

> An autobiographical account of a woman who became a slave laborer.

Lorant, Stefan. *I Was Hitler's Prisoner: A Diary.* New York: Putnam, 1935.

> A memoir of concentration camp life by a noted popular historian.

Maurel, Micheline. *An Ordinary Camp.* New York: Simon & Schuster, 1958.

> An account of daily life in Neubrandburg concentration camp.

Mechanicus, Phillip. *Waiting for Death: A Diary.* New York: Marion Boyars/Scribner's, 1983.

Reprinted after many years out of print, this is the diary of a year in Westerbork, the Dutch "transit camp"; it was written by a Dutch-Jewish journalist who perished in Auschwitz.

Michel, Jean, with Nuoera, Louis. *Dora.* Translated by Jennifer Kidd. New York: Holt, Rinehart & Winston, 1980.

Dora was a German slave labor camp.

Michelson, Frida. *I Survived Rumbuli.* New York: Schocken Books, 1981.

A memoir by one of the two survivors of the Riga Ghetto.

Oberski, Jona. **Childhood.* Translated by Ralph Manheim. New York: Doubleday, 1983; Plume Books/New American Library, 1984.

A brief, remarkable, partially fictional memoir, written in lyrically sparse prose, covering early boyhood in Holland before the war, life under Nazi occupation, in a transit and then a concentration camp, and, finally, the first days after liberation.

Sandberg, Moshe. *My Long Year in the Hungarian Labor Service and in the Nazi Camps.* Jerusalem: Yad Vashem, 1968.

One of the relatively few memoirs of forced labor—and a significant contribution to the history of the Holocaust in Hungary.

Schoenfeld, Joachim. *Holocaust Memoirs.* New York: Ktav, 1984.

A survivor's moving account of what it was like in the Lwów Ghetto and the nearby Janowska concentration camp. Also includes brief accounts by various relatives of the author's about their own wartime experiences in Poland and Russia, some in camps, some in hiding, some victimized by Soviet anti-Semitism.

Schwarberg, Guenther. *Murders at Bullenhauser Dam: The S.S. Doctor and the Children.* Bloomington: Indiana University Press, 1984.

On the murder in April 1945 of twenty Jewish children, ages five to twelve, tortured by SS doctor Kurt Heissmeyer, who then had them killed so as to "cover his tracks."

Selzer, Michael. *Deliverance Day: The Last Hours of Dachau.* New York: Lippincott, 1978.

A solid journalistic account of the last days of the infamous concentration camp, as seen from the perspectives of the Germans, the Jewish and other prisoners, and the liberating American army.

Smith, Marcus J. *The Harrowing Hell: Dachau. Albequerque: University of New Mexico Press, 1972.

A scholarly look at the structure of Dachau, and at its many kinds of torture.

Weinstock, Earl, and Wilner, Herbert. The Seven Years. New York: Dutton, 1959.

Reminiscences of a childhood and youth in a concentration camp.

Wiechert, Ernst. The Forests of the Dead. New York: Greenberg, 1947.

A thinly veiled autobiographical account of the concentration camp experience by a non-Jewish German writer.

B. Death Camps and Death Marches—Memoirs and Accounts

Bezwinska, Jadwiga (ed.). Amidst a Nightmare of Crime: Manuscripts of Members of the Sonderkommando. Translated by Krystyna Michalck. Auschwitz: State Museum of Oswiecim, 1973.

A remarkable anthology taken from the diaries of the Sonderkommando, or crematoria workers, most of whom were themselves gassed after about three months of their ghastly work.

Birnbaum, Halina. Hope Is the Last to Die. New York: Twayne, 1971.

A personal documentation of the Nazi terror by a Polish survivor of Auschwitz, Majdanek, and other camps.

Breitowicz, Jacob. Through Hell to Life. New York: Shengold, 1983.

How a couple and their child survived the Holocaust.

Cohen, Elie A. The Abyss. New York: Norton, 1973.

Because he was a doctor, this (Dutch) Jewish man had skills which allowed him to survive at Auschwitz, although his young family did not. He tells his somber story as a confession.

Delbo, Charlotte. *None of Us Will Return. Boston: Beacon, 1978.

Delbo, a member of the French Resistance who was caught and brought to Auschwitz in 1942, remembers camp life in this remarkable, at times almost lyrical, memoir.

———. "Phantoms, My Companions" and "Phantoms My Faithful Ones." Massachusetts Review 12 (Winter 1971): 10–30 and 14 (Spring 1973): 310–315.

Donat, Alexander. *The Holocaust Kingdom: A Memoir. New York: Holt, Rinehart & Winston, 1965; Holocaust Library pb., 1978.

An extraordinary, detailed memoir of surviving death and labor camps.

———— (ed.). *The Death Camp at Treblinka*. New York: Holocaust Library, 1980.

Treblinka became the graveyard for Warsaw Jews as well as for Jews from other European countries. More than one million men, women, and children died there. On August 2, 1943, the thousand prisoners left alive rebelled, setting fire to the death factory. Two hundred broke through, although only fifty survived to tell the story. This book consists mainly of the unadorned testimony of survivors, most of which appears for the first time in English.

Dribben, Judith Strick. +*A Girl Called Judith Strick*. New York: Cowles, 1970.

The autobiographical account of a woman who survived the underground, the Gestapo, prison, and Auschwitz.

Eck, Nathan. "The March of Death from Serbia to Hungary (September 1944) and the Slaughter of Cservenka." YVS 2 (1958): 255–294.

Eisner, Jack. *The Survivor*. New York: William Morrow, 1980; Bantam pb., 1982.

A dramatic memoir of resistance and survival by the founder of the Warsaw Ghetto Resistance Organization.

Fenelon, Fania. *Playing For Time*. New York: Atheneum, 1977; Berkeley Press pb., 1977.

This is a personal narrative told by a member of the female orchestra of the Auschwitz concentration camp. The book serves as an excellent document on the spiritual resistance and is written with tact, warmth, and insight.

Gray, Martin, with Gallow, Max. *For Those I Loved*. Translated from the French by Anthony White, foreword by David D. Duncan. Boston: Little, Brown, 1972.

A memoir of the death camps, liberation, and the post-Holocaust years.

Haas, Albert. *The Doctor and the Damned*. New York: St. Martin's Press, 1984.

The memoir of a French-Hungarian doctor who served in the French underground, was caught by the Nazis, and was deported to Auschwitz, where he was forced to practice medicine. (His captors did not know he was Jewish.)

Hart, Kitty. *Return to Auschwitz*, New York: Atheneum, 1982.

> The basis for a TV documentary, this memoir describes life in the Lublin Ghetto, slave labor, and eighteen months in the most dreaded of all concentration camps.

Heimler, Eugene. *Concentration Camp* (orig. title, *Night of Mist*). New York: Pyramid Books, 1961; Vanguard, 1969; Westport, Conn.: Greenwood, 1978.

> Heimler writes with the intensity of a man who sees himself as a messenger from the dead, as one who has to report unbearable truths, in a taut, moving account.

Hellman, Peter (text). *The Auschwitz Album*. New York: Random House, 1981.

> An album of 180 photographs of one group of Hungarian Jews arriving at Auschwitz in 1944; it was apparently compiled by a German officer and found by a survivor.

Hoess, Rudolf. *Commandant of Auschwitz*. Cleveland and New York: World, 1960; New York: Popular Library pb., 1961.

> Hoess admits to being responsible for killing 2,000,000 people. His autobiographical account adds a personal dimension to our understanding of the evils of the period.

Jackson, Livia E. Bitton. *Elli: Coming of Age in the Holocaust*. New York: Times Books, 1980; Harper & Row pb., 1983.

> An account of an adolescent's incarceration in Auschwitz and the first months of liberation.

Kessel, Sim. *Hanged at Auschwitz*. New York: Stein & Day, 1972.

> A remarkable autobiographical memoir by a man who experienced many brushes with extinction.

Kieler, Wieslaw. *Anus Mundi: 1,500 Days in Auschwitz/Birkenau*. New York: Times Books/Harper & Row, 1980.

> The vivid account of a non-Jewish political prisoner, now a Polish film director, of the most terrible death camp.

Koestler, Arthur. *Scum of the Earth*. New York: Macmillan, 1968.

> An aptly titled book about the concentration camps and those who worked in them.

Kohner, Hannah, and Kohner, Walter. *Hannah and Walter: A Love Story*. New York: Random House, 1984.

About a couple who fell in love, were in separate concentration camps during the Holocaust, and survived to find one another in an accidental reunion.

Leitner, Isabella. *Fragments of Isabella: A Memoir of Auschwitz.* Edited by A. Leitner. New York: Crowell, 1978; Dell pb., 1980.

A series of vignettes about Auschwitz, and the now-exuberant, now-haunted memoirs of a survivor.

Lengyel, Olga. *Five Chimneys,* New York: Ziff-Davis, 1947.

A particularly gripping memoir of Auschwitz.

Levi, Primo. *Survival in Auschwitz: The Nazi Assault on Humanity* (orig. title, *If This Be a Man*). New York: Orion, 1959; Collier pb., 1973.

A beautifully written account of one man's strategy for survival.

Lewinska, Pelagia. *Twenty Months at Auschwitz.* New York: Lyle Stuart, 1968.

An extraordinary memoir that deserves to be back in print, and in a paperback edition.

Mitscherlich, Alexander, and Mielke, Fred. *Doctors of Infamy.* New York: H. Schuman, 1949.

The horror of Nazi medical crimes.

Muller, Filip. *Eyewitness Auschwitz: Three Years in the Gas Chambers at Auschwitz.* New York: Stein & Day, 1979; pb., 1980.

Muller came to Auschwitz with one of the earliest transports from Slovakia in April 1942 and began working in the gassing installations and crematoria in May. He was still alive when the gassings ceased in November 1944. By a sheer stroke of luck he survived. The author is neither a historian nor a psychologist, but a vital source on the depths of man's inhumanity to man in the twentieth century.

Naumann, Bernd. *Auschwitz.* New York: Praeger, 1966.

Contains much testimony and relevant documentation on Auschwitz, in part based on the Frankfurt trials of those accused of war crimes.

Nyiszli, Miklos. *Auschwitz: An Eyewitness Account.* New York: Frederick Fell, 1960; Crest, 1973; Fawcett pb., 1977.

A doctor's eyewitness account of the infamous medical experiments, including those of Josef Mengele.

Rawicz, Piotr. *Blood From the Sky. Translated from the French by Peter Wiles. New York: Harcourt, Brace & World, 1964.

The narrator records the various stepping stones on the road to extinction, the frantic activity of the doomed, and their pathetic hopes and illusions.

Shapell, Nathan. *Witness to Truth.* New York: McKay, 1974.

A survivor of Auschwitz tells his personal story.

Szmaglewska, Seweryna. *Smoke Over Auschwitz.* New York: Holt, Rinehart & Winston, 1947.

A personal narrative about Birkenau.

Vrba, Rudolf, and Bestie, Alan. *I Cannot Forgive. New York: Grove Press, 1964.

The story of Dr. Vrba's sufferings during two years in Auschwitz. Vrba was one of two key escapees from Auschwitz whose testimony alerted the West to the reality of the death camps.

Wells, Leon W. *The Death Brigade (orig. title, *The Janowska Road*). New York: Macmillan, 1963; Holocaust Library, 1978.

Dr. Wells, a physicist and inventor, recounts his experience as a young Jew in Lwow, Poland. He was a member of the Death Brigade, the group of Jews who were forced by Germans to obliterate traces of mass executions of inmates at the Janowska concentration camp by burning their bodies.

Wiesel, Elie. *Night. New York: Hill & Wang, 1960; Avon pb., 1972.

This powerful memoir recounts the author's years in concentration camps and the loss of his family, together with the moral dilemma regarding religious faith and conviction.

C. Post-Holocaust Studies About Death and Life in the Camps

Bettelheim, Bruno. *The Informed Heart: Autonomy in a Mass Age. New York: Avon pb., 1971.

A very controversial book that discusses the victims' psychological responses to their fate.

Cohen, Elie A. *Human Behavior in the Concentration Camp. New York: Norton, 1953; Universal Library pb.

A psychological perspective by a survivor of Auschwitz and Mauthausen.

Des Pres, Terrence. *The Survivor. New York: Oxford University Press, 1976; Pocket Books pb., 1978.

"An Anatomy of Life in the Death Camps" is the subtitle of this brilliant book, which focuses on the psychology of survival in German and Russian concentration camps.

Elkins, Stanley. *Slavery. New York: Universal Library, 1963.

See especially the discussion of slavery in Nazi concentration camps and its relationship to other kinds of slavery, pp.103–115.

Feig, Konnilyn G. *Hitler's Death Camps: The Sanity of Madness. New York: Holmes & Meier, 1981.

An excellent, very well documented, interdisciplinary account of each of the major concentration and death camps.

Ferencz, Benjamin. *Less Than Slaves. Cambridge, Mass.: Harvard University Press, 1980; pb., 1982

This post-Holocaust documentation tells the story of Jewish labor conscripted by the major German industrial concerns during World War II. It also recounts the usually futile attempts of the former slave laborers to collect reparations after the Holocaust.

Karas, Joza. "The Use of Music as a Means of Education in Terezin." Shoah 1, no. 2 (Fall 1978): 8–9.

Kogan, Eugen. *The Theory and Practice of Hell. New York: Octagon, 1972; Berkley-Medium pb., 1958.

A detailed and moving account of the SS and concentration camp system.

Kraus, Ota, and Kulka, Erick. The Death Factory: Documents on Auschwitz. Oxford and London: Oxford University Press, 1966; New York: Pergamon, 1966.

An impressive and important anthology on the largest and most infamous concentration camp.

Paweczynska, Anna. *Values and Violence in Auschwitz: A Sociological Analysis. Berkeley and Los Angeles: University of California Press, 1979; pb., 1980.

What social and cultural factors influenced behavior in Auschwitz? This book explores that question.

Rousset, David. *The Other Kingdom*. Translated with an introduction by Ramon Guthrie. New York: Reynal & Hitchcock, 1947.

This early post-Holocaust memoir is one of the most powerful presentations of the concentration camp universe.

Tenenbaum, Joseph. "Auschwitz in Retrospect." *JSS* 15, nos. 3–4 (July–October 1953): 203–236.

An important overview of Auschwitz—its history, "administration," and massive slave labor camps.

———. "The Einsatzgruppen." *JSS* 17, no. 1 (January 1955): 43–64.

A documented essay on the activities of the SS execution squads in occupied Russia.

9.

The Holocaust in Various Countries

A. Austria

Fischer, Eric. "Seven Viennese Jewish Families: From the Ghetto to the Holocaust and Beyond." *JSS* 42, nos. 3–4 (Summer–Fall 1980): 345–360.

Karlbach, Oscar. "The Liquidation of the Jewish Community in Vienna." *JSS* 2, no. 3 (July 1940): 255–278.

Maas, Walter B. *Austria Under Nazi Rule, 1938–1945*. New York: Frederick Ungar, 1978.

A factual account of Austria, 1938–1945.

Pauley, Bruce F. *Hitler and the Forgotten Nazis: A History of Austrian National Socialism.* Chapel Hill: University of North Carolina Press, 1981.

A well-documented history of Austrian Nazism up to the 1938 *Anschluss* (incorporation of Austria into Germany).

B. Bulgaria

Chary, Frederich B. *The Bulgarian Jews and the Final Solution.* Pittsburgh: University of Pittsburgh Press, 1972.

Chary covers anti-Semitic legislation, deportations, and much else, and analyzes why Bulgarian leaders did much to prevent the deportation of Bulgaria's native Jews in this excellent history.

C. Croatia

Jelinek, Yeshayahu. "The Holocaust of Croatian Jewry: A Few Reflections." *Shoah* 1, no. 4 (Summer 1979): 20–23.

Paris, Edmond. *Genocide in Satellite Croatia, 1941–1945.* Chicago: American Institute for Baltic Affairs, n.d.

This comprehensive work deals with both the Jewish and non-Jewish victims of the Nazi slaughter in Croatia.

D. Czechoslovakia

Rothkirchen, Livia. "Czech Attitudes Towards the Jews During the Nazi Regime." *YVS* 13 (1979): 287–320.

A thoughtful essay by perhaps the leading scholar of Czech Jewry during the Holocaust; it captures the differences between the treatment of Jews in Bohemia and Moravia, on the one hand, and in Slovakia on the other.

———. "The Czechoslovak Government-in-Exile; Jewish and Palestinian Aspects in the Light of the Documents." *YVS* 9 (1973): 157–200.

———. "The Defiant Few: Jews and the Czech 'Inside Front' (1938–1942)." *YVS* 14 (1981): 35–88.

E. Denmark

Bertelsen, Aage. *October '43.* New York: Putnam, 1954.

An account of the rescue of Danish Jews by one of the organizers of that rescue.

Flender, Harold. *Rescue in Denmark*. New York: Simon & Schuster, 1963; Holocaust Library pb., 1981.

An exciting, detailed rendering of the rescue of the Danish Jews.

Werstein, Irving. *That Denmark Might Live*. Philadephia: Marcus Smith, 1967.

A short but well-written history of the Danish rescue.

Yahil, Leni. *The Rescue of Danish Jewry*. Philadelphia: Jewish Publication Society, 1969.

A closely researched volume illustrating the clash between Nazi anti-Semitism and Danish democracy—this is by far the best book on the background of the Danish rescue.

F. France and North Africa

Abitbol, Michel. "Waiting for Vichy: Europeans and Jews in North Africa on the Eve of World War II." YVS 14 (1981): 139–166.

Bower, Tom. *Klaus Barbie: The Butcher of Lyons*. New York: Pantheon, 1983.

The first biography of the notorious Gestapo head in Lyons who, after the war, was used by the Americans as a paid informer. With American help, he escaped to Bolivia before being extradited to France in 1983 to stand trial.

Cohen, Yerahmiel. "French Jewry's Dilemma on the Orientation of Its Leadership (From Polemics to Conciliation: 1942–1944)." YVS 14 (1981): 167–204.

———. "A Jewish Leader in Vichy France, 1940–1943: The Diary of Raymond-Raoul Lambert." JSS 43, nos. 3–4 (Summer–Fall 1981): 291–310.

Klarsfeld, Serge. *Memorial to the Jews Deported From France, 1942–1944*. New York: Beate Klarsfeld Foundation, 1983.

A meticulously assembled list of names of the over 75,000 French Jews deported in the eighty-seven convoys between March 1942 and August 1944, with important notes, and sometimes documents, on each convoy.

Levy, Claude, and Tillard, Paul. *Betrayal at the Vel d'Hviv*. New York: Hill & Wang, 1969.

A popular rendering of the roundup and deportation of Parisian Jews in July 1942.

Marrus, Michael R., and Paxton, Robert O. *Vichy France and the Jews.* New York: Basic Books, 1981; Schocken pb., 1983.

The 1982 National Jewish Book Award winner for a work on the Holocaust: superbly researched and clearly written, this history of the Holocaust in France sets the record straight on both French collaboration in, and resistance to, the Final Solution.

Paxton, Robert O. *Vichy France: Old Guard, New Guard.* Princeton, N.J.: Princeton University Press, 1966.

A fine study of patterns of collaborationist leadership in German-occupied France.

Poliakov, Leon. "A Conflict Between the German Army and Secret Police Over Bombings of Paris Synagogues." *JSS* 16, no. 3 (July 1954): 253–266.

On an intra-German dispute over anti-Semitic terrorism in Paris in October 1941.

Sinder, Henri. "Lights and Shades of Jewish Life in France, 1940–1942." *JSS* 5, no. 4 (October 1943): 367–382.

On the legal position of Jews in occupied France.

Szajkowski, Zosa. *Analytical Franco-Jewish Gazetteer, 1934–1945.* New York: Ktav, 1966.

A collection of decrees and articles on French Jewry.

———. "The French Central Jewish Consistory During the Second World War." *YVS* 3 (1959): 187–202.

———. "Glimpses in the History of Jews in Occupied France." *YVS* 2 (1958): 133–158.

A series of vignettes of Jewish life in occupied France.

———. *Jews and the French Foreign Legion.* New York: Ktav, 1975.

An almost unknown chapter of Holocaust history: the deportation and internment as forced laborers in North African concentration camps of Jewish refugees who had voluntarily served in the French armed forces against the Germans until the fall of France in 1940. Based in part on the author's personal experiences.

———. "The Organization of the 'UGIF' in Nazi-Occupied France." *JSS* 9, no. 3 (July 1947): 239–256.

On the French equivalent of the *Judenrat*.

G. Germany

Ball-Kaduri, K. J. "Berlin Is Purged of Its Jews: The Jews in Berlin in the Year 1943." YVS 5 (1963): 271–316.

Blau, Bruno. "The Jewish Population of Germany, 1939–1945." JSS 12, no. 2 (April 1950): 161– 172.

A sociological analysis of German Jewry on the eve of the Holocaust—and how it was affected by the catastrophe.

———. "The Last Days of German Jewry in the Third Reich." YIVO Annual 8 (1953): 197–204.

Cahman, Werner. "The Decline of the Munich Jewish Community." JSS 3, no. 3 (July 1941): 285–300.

Conway, John S. "The Last Letters of the Brandt-Meyer Family From Berlin." YVS 11 (1976): 91–130.

Gross, Leonard. *The Last Jews in Berlin. New York: Simon & Schuster, 1982; Bantam pb., 1983.

A compelling account of the few thousand Jews who hid in the capital of the Third Reich during the Holocaust.

H. Greece

Matkovski, Aleksander. "The Destruction of Macedonian Jewry in 1943." YVS 3 (1959): 203–258.

Roth, Cecil. "The Last Days of Jewish Salonica." Commentary 10 (July 1950): 49–55.

On the deportation of the Jews from the oldest Sephardic community.

Sevillas, Errikos. Athens—Auschwitz. Port Jefferson, N.Y.: Cadmus Press, 1984.

A memoir of life in Athens during the Holocaust and of deportation to Auschwitz.

Vasileva, Nadejda S. "On the Catastrophe of the Thracian Jews." YVS 3 (1959): 295–302.

I. Hungary

Braham, Randolph L. The Destruction of Hungarian Jewry. 2 vols. New York: World Federation of Hungarian Jews, 1963.

A documentary account of what befell Hungarian Jews, containing a comprehensive list of documents with synopses in English.

————— (ed.). *Genocide and Retribution*. Higham, Mass.: Kluwer/Nijhoff, 1984.

The complete "judgment" of the 1946 Romanian People's Tribunal.

—————. *Hungarian-Jewish Studies*. New York: World Federation of Hungarian Jews, 1966–73.

Annual anthologies, all of which contain at least some information on the Holocaust.

—————. *The Politics of Genocide: The Holocaust in Hungary*. 2 vols. New York: Columbia University Press, 1980.

The definitive work on the Holocaust in Hungary, and a model history of the Holocaust in one country; Braham includes an excellent introductory section on Hungarian Jewry and thoroughly documents every phase of the Holocaust in Hungary.

Gutman, Y.; Vago, Bela; and Rothkirchen, Livia. *Hungarian Jewish Leadership During the Holocaust*. Jerusalem: Yad Vashem, 1976.

This exhaustively researched book examines Jewish leadership during the five different political phases Hungary underwent during the Holocaust, and delves into the community's evolving strategies for survival.

Handler, Andrew (ed.). *The Holocaust in Hungary: An Anthology of Jewish Response*. University, Ala.: University of Alabama Press, 1982.

An anthology taken from newspaper accounts, articles, diaries, letters, and documents; Part I deals with the Holocaust itself, while Part II concerns efforts at postwar reconstruction and efforts to remember.

Levai, Jeno. "The Hungarian Deportations in the Light of the Eichmann Trial." *YVS* 5 (1963): 69–104.

Nagy-Talavera, Nicholas. *The Green Shirts and Others: A History of Fascism in Hungary and Rumania*. Stanford, Calif.: Stanford University Press, 1970.

Includes the Holocaust years.

Vago, Bela. "Budapest Jewry in the Summer of 1944—Otto Komoly's Diaries." *YVS* 8 (1970): 81–106.

J. Italy

Katz, Robert. *Black Sabbath*. New York: Macmillan, 1969.

> A popular version of the deportation of Jews from Rome in October 1943; Katz's journalistic account is marred by his pseudo-Marxist attack upon "rich" Jews for allegedly saving their own lives at the expenses of the Jewish masses.

———. *Death in Rome*. New York: Macmillan, 1967.

> The history of the *razzia* (roundup for deportation) of Rome's Jews in March 1944.

Ledeen, Michael A. "The Evolution of Italian Fascist Anti-Semitism." *JSS* 37, no. 1 (January 1975): 3–17.

———. "Italian Jews and Fascism." *Judaism* 18 (1969): 272–288.

Michaelis, Meir. *Mussolini and the Jews: German-Italian Relations and the Jewish Question in Italy, 1922–1945*. New York: Oxford University Press, 1978.

> In this fine scholarly study, Michaelis demonstrates Mussolini's relatively "tolerant" attitude toward the Jews until 1937—and the attempts by many Italian officials to sabotage the Final Solution thereafter.

Poliakov, Leon. "Mussolini and the Extermination of the Jews." *JSS* 11, no. 3 (July 1949): 249–258.

Starr, Joshua. "Italy's Anti-Semites." *JSS* 1, no. 1 (January 1939): 105–124.

Stigliani, Nicholas A., and Marzotto, Antonette. "Fascist Anti-Semitism and the Italian Jews." *WLB* 28, nos. 35–36 (1975): 41–49.

Waagenar, Sam. *The Pope's Jews*. LaSalle, Ill.: Open Court, 1974.

> On the Jews of Rome and the ambivalent attitude of the Pope toward rescuing them.

K. The Netherlands

De Jong, Louis. "The Netherlands and Auschwitz." *YVS* 7 (1968): 39–56.

Presser, Jacob. *The Destruction of the Dutch Jews*. New York: Dutton, 1965.

> A detailed account, part-history, part-memoir, of the life and death of Dutch Jews under Nazi occupation.

L. Poland

Apenszlak, Jacob (ed.). *The Black Book of Polish Jewry*. New York: American Federation of Polish Jews and Roy Publishers, 1943.

> Compiled during the war from scattered reports, this is one of the first accounts of the Holocaust. It was sponsored by, among others, Eleanor Roosevelt and Albert Einstein.

Arad, Yitzhak. "Concentration of Refugees in Vilna on the Eve of the Holocaust." *YVS* 9 (1973): 201–214.

Eisenbach, Artur. "Operation Reinhard—Mass Extermination of the Jewish Population in Poland." *Polish Western Affairs* 3, no. 1 (1962): 80–124.

Falstein, Louis (ed.). *The Martyrdom of Jewish Physicians in Poland*. New York: Exposition Press, 1964.

> An important anthology of first-person accounts of the persecution of Jewish doctors in ghettos and death camps.

Franek-Osmecki, Kazimierz; Lichten, Joseph C.; and Raczynski, Edward. "The Polish Government in Exile and the Jewish Tragedy During World War II." *WLB* 29, nos. 37–38 (1976): 62–66.

Kranitz-Sanders, Lillian. *Twelve Who Survived: An Oral History of the Jews of Lodz, Poland, 1930–1954*. New York: Irvington Publishers, 1984.

> A look at Lodz Jewry before, during, and after the Holocaust, based on extensive interviews with twelve survivors now living in Kansas City.

Ringelblum, Emmanuel, *Polish-Jewish Relations During the Second World War*. Edited by J. Kermish and S. Krakowski. Jerusalem: Yad Vashem, 1974; New York: Howard Fertig, 1976.

> Written during the Holocaust, this account covers the multifaceted, almost always problematic relations between Poles and Jews, including the war against the Nazis, and Polish and Jewish resistance movements.

Wynot, Edward D., Jr. "A Necessary Cruelty: The Emergence of Official Anti-Semitism in Poland, 1936–1949." *AHR* 76, no. 4 (October 1971): 1035–1059.

M. Romania

Braham, Randolph L. (ed.). *Genocide and Retribution*. Hingham, Mass.: Kluwer/Nijhoff, 1984.

An edited version of the 1946 "judgment" of a Romanian people's tribunal on the killing of Jews in northern Transylvania (then part of Hungary) during the Holocaust.

Dorian, Emil S. *The Quality of Witness: A Romanian Diary, 1937–1944*. Edited by Marguerite Dorian and translated by Mara Soleanu Vamos; introduction by Michael Stanislawski. Philadelphia: Jewish Publication Society, 1982.

The day-to-day diary of a Romanian writer and physician—a fascinating account of the Holocaust in Romania and the very "mixed" record of the various governments in Bucharest.

Lavi, Theodore. "Documents on the Struggle of Rumanian Jewry for Its Rights During the Second World War, Part One." YVS 4 (1960): 261–316.

Safran, Alexander. "The Rulers of Fascist Rumania Whom I Had to Deal With." YVS 6 (1967): 175–180.

An account by the former chief rabbi of Romania.

N. Scandinavia

Yahil, Leni. "Scandinavian Rescue of Prisoners." YVS 6 (1967): 181–220.

O. Sephardic Jews

Avni, Haim. "Spanish Nationals in Greece and Their Fate During the Holocaust." YVS 8 (1970): 31–69.

On the special case of Sephardic Jews in Greece and how Spain attempted to rescue some of them

Jarabulus, Jeannie. "The Forgotten Victims." M&R 6, no. 1 (September–October 1979): 10.

On the persecution of Sephardic Jews and Jews from Islamic countries.

Note: See also the section on "Spain" (Sec. 14-I).

P. USSR

Ainsztein, Reuben. "Jewish Tragedy and Heroism in Soviet War Literature." JSS 23, no. 2 (April 1961): 67–84.

Arad, Yitzhak. "The 'Final Solution' in Lithuania in the Light of German Documentation." YVS 11 (1976): 234–272.

Bingel, Oberleutnant [Lieutenant] Erwin. "The Extermination of Two Ukrainian Jewish Communities—Testimony of a German Army Officer." *YVS* 3 (1959): 303–322.

Ehrenburg, Ilya, and Grossman, Vasily. *The Black Book.* New York: Holocaust Library, 1981.

Prepared in 1946, and removed from the press at Stalin's orders, this is an extensive anthology of documents on the Holocaust in Russia.

Friedman, Philip. "Ukrainian-Jewish Relations During the Nazi Occupation." *YIVO Annual* 7 (1958–1959): 259–296.

By far the best essay on the subject; Friedman correlates Ukrainian anti-Semitism and Ukrainian nationalism.

Gilboa, Y. A. *The Black Years of Soviet Jewry, 1939–1953.* Boston: Little, Brown, 1971.

Gilboa deals mainly with the bitter final years of Stalin's rule, 1948–1953, but includes information material on the Jewish Anti-Fascist Committee and other aspects of the Holocaust years.

———. "Jewish Literature in the Soviet Union During the Holocaust Period to 1948." *YVS* 4 (1960): 97–98.

Levin, Dov. "Estonian Jews in the USSR (1941–1945): Research Based on Survivors' Testimony." *YVS* 11 (1976): 273–297.

Litan, Dora. "The Destruction of the Jews of Odessa in the Light of Rumanian Documents." *YVS* 6 (1967): 135–154.

Pinchuk, Ben-Cion. "Soviet Media on the Fate of Jews in Nazi-Occupied Territory (1939–1941)." *YVS* 11 (1976): 221–233.

Redlich, Shimon. *Propaganda and Nationalism in Wartime Russia.* New York, Columbia University Press, 1983.

Redlich examines the USSR's policies as they affected the Jews, as well as Jewish responses to Soviet war propaganda and the complex relationship of Soviet policy and Jewish nationalism.

Schwarz, Solomon. *The Jews in the Soviet Union.* New York: Arno Press, 1951, 1972.

The book covers the complete history of anti-Semitism in the USSR. The entire second part emphasizes anti-Semitism before Hitler, during the Nazi occupation, and after.

10.
Jewish Resistance and Rescue

A. Armed Jewish Resistance—General Studies and Accounts

Ainsztein, Reuben. *Jewish Resistance in Nazi-Occupied Eastern Europe*. New York: Barnes & Noble, 1975.

> The definitive work to date on Jewish resistance in Eastern Europe; it includes a good background section on the history of Jewish resistance and a long section on the Warsaw Ghetto revolt.

Ariel, Joseph. "Jewish Self-Defense and Resistance in France During World War II." YVS 6 (1967): 221–250.

Bauer, Yehuda. *They Chose Life*. New York: American Jewish Committee, 1973.

> This illustrated pamphlet of 64 pages, based on a series of lectures, outlines Jewish resistance during the Holocaust.

Cholowski, Shalom. *Soldiers from the Ghetto*. Cranbury, N.J.: A. S. Barnes, 1981.

> An account of Jewish partisans in eastern Poland, and of their struggles not only against the Nazis but also against hostile Russian, Polish, and Ukrainian partisans.

Kabeli, Issa. "The Resistance of the Greek Jews." YIVO Annual 8 (1953): 281–288.

Krakowski, Schmuel. *War of the Doomed: Jewish Armed Resistance in Poland, 1942–1944*. New York: Holmes & Meier, 1983.

> Based on primary sources from almost 500 fighters, this book traces the efforts of Jewish partisans in Poland against both the Nazis and anti-Semitic Polish partisans.

Latour, Anny. *The Jewish Resistance in France (1940–1944).* New York: Holocaust Library, 1981.

A good narrative history of the French-Jewish resistance by one of its active members.

Levin, Dov. *Lithuanian Jewry's Armed Resistance to the Nazis.* New York: Holmes & Meier, 1983.

A major, well-researched study of Jewish partisans, and their links with the Soviet army, in one of the most important areas of Jewish resistance.

Nir, Akiva. *Paths in a Ring of Fire.* New York: American Zionist Youth Foundation, 1972.

Four stories of Jews in the resistance movements in Czechoslavakia during the Holocaust—with an outline for discussion and an annotated bibliography prepared by Eric Tucker.

Nirenstein, Albert. *A Tower from the Enemy: Contributions to a History of Jewish Resistance in Poland.* New York: Orion Press, 1959.

Most of the book concentrates on the Warsaw Ghetto Revolt, but Nirenstein also deals with resistance in other ghettos and concentration camps.

Porter, Jack Nusan (ed.). *Jewish Partisans: A Documentary of Jewish Resistance in the Soviet Union During World War II.* 2 vols. Washington, D.C.: University Press of America, 1982.

Volume I deals with resistance from the perspective of non-Jewish Russian, Polish, and Ukrainian army and partisan officers; Volume II consists of (1) selections from among forty-four eyewitness accounts gathered by Israeli journalist Binyamin West, and (2) material that deals with partisans belonging to the editor's family and friends.

Shabbetai, A. *As Sheep to the Slaughter.* New York: World Association of Bergen-Belsen Survivors, 1963.

A booklet intended to discredit the myth of Jewish cowardice.

Steinberg, Lucien. *Not as a Lamb: The Jews Against Hitler.* Translated by Marion Hunter. Farnborough: Saxon House, 1974.

A good overview of Jewish resistance during the Holocaust.

Suhl, Yuri. *They Fought Back.* New York: Crown, 1967: Schocken, 1967, 1975.

A Jewish resistance group was formed in nearly every ghetto and camp. These thirty-four essays, which deal with Jewish resistance in Germany, in the ghettos and death camps, and among the partisans, definitively establish that fact.

Temchin, Michael. *Witch Doctor: Memoirs of a Partisan. New York: Holocaust Library, 1983.

The memoirs of the legendary "witch doctor" called Zmakor, who, after escaping from a train bound for Sobibor, fought with a group of partisans in Poland.

Tenenbaum, Joseph. *Underground.* New York: Philosophical Library, 1952.

A history of Polish Jews under Nazi occupation, with emphasis on Jewish resistance.

Yad Vashem. *Jewish Resistance during the Holocaust.* Jerusalem: Yad Vashem, 1971.

Proceedings of a five-day 1968 conference held in Israel which highlights the complexity of research into the Jewish response; of particular significance is the paper by Levi Yahil, which discusses the need to evaluate both internal and external conditions affecting the nature of Jewish resistance during the Holocaust.

B. Jewish Resistance in the Third Reich, 1939–1945

Eschwege, Helmut. "Resistance of German Jews against the Nazi Regime." *LBI Yrbk* 15 (1970): 143–182.

On the Baum Group and other heroic acts of resistance.

Paucker, Arnold. "Notes on Resistance." *LBI Yrbk* 16 (1971): 239–248.

C. The Warsaw Ghetto and Other Ghetto Revolts

Barkai, Meyer (ed.). *The Fighting Ghettos.* Philadelphia: Lippincott, 1962, New York: Tower Publications, 1962.

A collection of brief eyewitness accounts of Jewish resistance activities by resistance fighters themselves; includes materials on the ghettos, the camps, the resistance in the woods.

Borzykowski, Tuvia. *Between Tumbling Walls.* Israel: Kibbutz Lohamei Haghettaot (Ghetto Fighters' House), 1972.

A first-hand account of the Warsaw Ghetto uprising by one of the active participants in the Jewish Combat Organization.

Edelman, Marek. *The Ghetto Fighters*. New York: American Representation of the Jewish Workers' Union of Poland, 1946.

Edelman was one of the key leaders of the revolt.

Goldstein, Bernard. *The Stars Bear Witness*. New York: Viking, 1949.

The personal narrative of one of the few to survive the Warsaw Ghetto uprising.

Goldstein, Charles. *The Bunker*. Philadelphia: Jewish Publication Society, 1970; New York: Atheneum, 1973.

How seven Jews tried to survive underground beneath the Warsaw Ghetto.

Grunszpan, Roman. *The Uprising of the Death Box of Warsaw*. New York: Vantage Press, 1978.

A documentary book about Jewish and Christian lives under Nazi rule in the Warsaw Ghetto and in the non-Jewish areas of Warsaw.

Gutman, Yisrael. "The Genesis of the Resistance in the Warsaw Ghetto." YVS 9 (1973): 29–70.

Kurzman, Dan. *The Bravest Battle*. New York: Putnam, 1976; Pinnacle Books, 1980.

A vivid journalistic account of the twenty-eight days of the Warsaw Ghetto uprising; includes photographs.

Lubetkin, Zivia. *In the Days of Destruction and Revolt*. Translated by Shai Tubin, edited by Yehiel Yanui. Tel Aviv: Hakibbutz Hameuchad Publishing House and Ghetto Fighters' House Publishers in cooperation with Am Oved Publishers, 1981.

An informative and moving account by a resident of the Warsaw Ghetto.

Mark, Ber. *Uprising in the Warsaw Ghetto*. New York: Schocken, 1975, 1976.

A superb account of the uprising.

Meed, Vladka. *On Both Sides of the Wall: Memoirs from the Warsaw Ghetto*. New York: Holocaust Library, 1979.

A remarkable personal account of the author's experience as a courier for the Jewish resistance movement in the Warsaw Ghetto.

Stroop, Jurgen. *The Stroop Report: The Jewish Quarter of Warsaw Is No More!* Translated and annotated by Sybil Milton, introduction by Andrzej Wirth. New York: Pantheon, 1980.

The Warsaw Ghetto Revolt as discussed in the official report of the German commander—contains rare photographs.

Zuckerman, Yitzhak. "From the Warsaw Ghetto." Commentary 60 (December 1975): 62–69.

Written in 1944, this is an account of the origins and development of the Warsaw resistance movement.

D. Resistance in the Concentration and Death Camps

Garlinski, Josef. *Fighting Auschwitz. New York: Fawcett, 1971.

The resistance movement in the camps, compiled from diaries and records.

Halivni, Tzipora Hager. "The Birkenau Revolt: The Poles Prevent a Timely Insurrection." JSS 41, no. 2 (Spring 1979): 123–154.

Novitch, Miriam. *Sobibor: Martyrdom and Revolt. New York: Holocaust Library, 1980.

Novitch bases her carefully constructed account of the 1943 Sobibor revolt on the testimony of all the available witnesses.

Perl, Gisella. I Was a Doctor at Auschwitz. New York: International Universities Press, 1948.

A unique view of what went on in a death camp by a doctor who performed abortions on over 300 pregnant women in order to save their lives.

Rashke, Richard. Escape from Sobibor. Boston, Houghton Mifflin, 1982.

Based on meticulous research, this is a study of the eighteen Jews who survived the October 18, 1943, breakout from the "forgotten" death camp.

E. Jewish Partisans

Arad, Yitzhak. *Partisan: From the Valley of Death to Mount Zion. New York: Holocaust Library pb., 1978.

Isaac Rudnicki was thirteen years old when the Germans overran Warsaw. He escaped into the woods and became a partisan. After the war, he traveled to Palestine via the underground route and became involved in the Palmach. A new, vertiginous military career started that raised Rudnicki, now Isaac Arad, to the rank of brigadier. After his retirement he became director of Yad Vashem in Jerusalem.

Bar-On, Zwi. "The Jews in the Soviet Partisan Movement." YVS **4** (1960): 167–190.

Eckman, Lester, and Lazar, Chaim. *The Jewish Resistance: The History of the Jewish Partisans in Lithuania and White Russia under Nazi Occupation, 1940–45.* New York: Shengold, 1977.

A frustratingly brief but otherwise strong history of the different Jewish partisan movements in perhaps the largest area of partisan activity; Eckman and Lazar do a particularly good job of explaining the tensions between the Jewish partisans and the Red Army, which tried to subsume them.

Gruber, Samuel. *I Chose Life.* Edited by Gertrude Hirschler. New York: Shengold, 1978.

An autobiography of a Jewish partisan fighter.

Kahanowitz, Moshe. "Why No Separate Jewish Partisan Movement Was Established During World War II." YVS **1** (1957): 153–168.

Kahn, Leo. *No Time to Mourn.* Vancouver: Laurelton, 1979.

The story of Jewish partisan fighters.

Kohn, Nathan, and Roiter, Howard. **A Voice from the Forest.* New York: Holocaust Library, 1980.

The memoirs of Kohn, a small-town matchmaker from a religious family who became a partisan fighter in the Volhynian forests.

Kowalski, Isaac. **A Secret Press in Nazi Europe: The Story of a Jewish United Partisan Organization.* New York: Shengold, 1969; 1978.

The only book-length history of the various "illegal" Jewish newspapers, and other Jewish publications.

Senesh, Hannah. **Hannah Senesh: Her Life and Diary.* New York: Schocken, 1972.

Hannah Senesh's diary, as well as accounts of her by those who knew this Hungarian-born Israeli who parachuted into Yugoslavia in an attempt to save Jewish lives, was captured, and died under torture without revealing the names of her compatriots.

Syrkin, Marie. + **Blessed Is the Match.* Philadelphia: Jewish Publication Society, 1947; 1978.

An account of Jewish resistance in many nations, with a special section on Hannah Senesh.

F. Jews in National Resistance Movements and Anti-German Armies

Ainsztein, Reuben. "The War Record of Soviet Jewry." *JSS* 28, no. 1
   (January 1966): 3–24.

Ehrlich, Blake. *Resistance: France 1940–1945.* Boston: Little, Brown,
   1965.

   Contains valuable material on the Jewish role in the French resistance.

Gutman, Yisrael. "Jews in General Anders' Army in the Soviet Union."
   YVS 12 (1977): 231–296.

Kulka, Eric (ed.). *Collection of Testimonies and Documents on the
   Participation of Czechoslovak Jews in the Second World War.*
   Jerusalem: Yad Vashem, 1976.

Michel, Henri. "Jewish Resistance and the European Resistance Movement." *YVS* 7 (1968): 7–16.

Mushat, Marian (ed.). *Jewish Soldiers in the War Against the Nazis.*
   Jerusalem: Yad Vashem, 1972.

   This is the only major anthology concerning Jews in the armies
   resisting the Nazis.

Rose, Leesha. *The Tulips Are Red.* New York: A. S. Barnes, 1978.

   The memoir of a Dutch-Jewish high school graduate who joins the
   Dutch resistance after escaping deportation.

G. Rescue Efforts

Adler-Rudel, S. "A Chronicle of Rescue Efforts." *LBI Yrbk* 11 (1966):
   213–241.

Bauer, Yehuda. "Rescue Operations Through Vilna." *YVS* 9 (1973):
   215–224.

Biss, Andreas. *A Million Jews to Save.* New York: A. S. Barnes, 1975.

   On the negotiations between Joel Brand and Eichmann, in which it
   was proposed to exchange Jews for trucks.

Brand, Joel. *Desperate Mission.* New York: Criterion Books, 1958;
   Grove pb.

   Joel Brand's own account of his 1944 attempted negotiations with
   Adolf Eichmann to ransom almost 1 million Hungarian Jews condemned to death in exchange for 10,000 trucks and other war
   goods.

Eck, Nathan. "The Rescue of Jews with the Aid of Passports and Citizenship Papers of Latin American States." YVS 1 (1957): 125–152.

Eliav, Arie. +Voyage of the "Ulua". New York: Funk & Wagnalls, 1969.

How 800 young Jewish women were rescued from the Nazis.

Friedenson, Joseph, and Kranzler, David. The Heroine of Rescue: The Incredible Story of Recha Sternbuch. Brooklyn, N.Y.: Mesorah Publications, 1984.

The exploits of an Orthodox Jew in Switzerland and her husband who, through daring, persistence, and self-sacrifice, were directly or indirectly responsible for saving thousands of lives during the Holocaust.

Gutman, Yisrael, and Zuroff, Efraim (eds.). Rescue Attempts During the Holocaust. Jerusalem: Yad Vashem, 1979.

These twenty-one articles cover many countries, their leaders and institutions. They document the heroic and not-so-heroic attempts at rescue and provide the answers to many disturbing questions.

Kluger, Ruth, and Peggy Mann. +*The Last Escape: The Launching of the Largest Secret Rescue Movement of All Times. New York: Doubleday, 1973; Los Angeles: Pinnacle, 1978.

The true story of the illegal immigration movement and its efforts to rescue Jews from Europe moves across the Balkans to Istanbul and creates a vivid picture of life in that period.

Kranzler, David, and Gertrude Hirschler (eds.). *Solomon Schoenfeld: His Page in History. New York: Judaica Press, 1982.

Justifiably impatient with other rescue efforts, Dr. Schoenfeld launched a one-person effort to snatch thousands of European Jews out of the jaws of death and bring them to England.

Papanek, Ernst, with Edward Linn. Out of the Fire. New York: Morrow, 1975.

An account of Dr. Papanek's work to save Jewish children from Nazi extermination, this book is both inspiring and sad. The author conveys the guilt of many survivors who questioned why they, rather than others, lived.

Vago, Bela. "Political and Diplomatic Activities for the Rescue of the Jews of Northern Transylvania." YVS 6 (1967): 155–174.

11.

The Protestant and Roman Catholic Churches and the Holocaust

A. The German Church Struggle

Barth, Karl. *The German Church Conflict*. Richmond: John Knox Press, 1965.

An overview by one of the leading Protestant theologians of the twentieth century.

Bentley, James. "British and German High Churchmen in the Struggle Against Hitler." *Journal of Ecclesiastical History* 23 (July 1972): 223–249.

Bethge, Eberhard. **Dietrich Bonhoeffer*. New York: Harper & Row, 1970, 1977.

The best biography to date of the anti-Nazi Protestant theologian, written by one of his closest associates.

Bonhoeffer, Dietrich. **Letters and Papers from Prison*. New York: Macmillan, 1962.

A poignant anthology of Bonhoeffer's writings before he was executed at Flossenberg Prison in April 1945.

Bosanquet, Mary. *The Life and Death of Dietrich Bonhoeffer*. New York: Harper & Row, 1968.

While not as strong as Bethge's, this is a well-researched, useful biography.

Cochrane, Arther C. "Barmen Revisited." *Christianity and Crisis* 33 (December 24, 1973): 267–273.

Goddard, Donald. *The Last Days of Dietrich Bonhoeffer.* New York: Harper & Row, 1976.

On Bonhoeffer's life and writings in the days before he was killed by the Nazis.

Gollwitzer, Helmust; Kuhn, Kathe; and Schneider, Reinhold (eds.). *Dying We Live.* New York: Pantheon, 1956.

The last words of some of the martyrs and victims of the Holocaust, including Dietrich Bonhoeffer, Sister Teresa Benedicta, Father Alfred Delp, and some fifty others.

Gutteridge, Richard. *The German Evangelical Church and the Jews, 1879–1950.* Oxford: Blackwell, 1976.

Gutteridge's work is key to understanding the split in the Evangelical Church vis-à-vis the Nazis. It begins during the first years of modern Germany, and at a time of a sharp upswing in anti-Semitism.

Helmreich, E. C. "The Nature and Structure of the Confessing Church in Germany Under Hitler." *Journal of Church and State* 12 (Autumn 1970): 405–420.

Littell, Franklin H. *The German Phoenix.* New York: Doubleday, 1960.

A history of the German Protestant Church's resistance to Hitler, by the leading American historian on the subject.

———— and Locke, Hubert G. (eds.). *The German Church Struggle and the Holocaust.* Detroit: Wayne State University Press, 1974.

Essays by Elie Wiesel, Gordon Zahn, Eberhard Bethge, Michael Ryan, and others, covering many aspects of this topic, beautifully synthesized by Littell's opening essay.

Lorit, S. C. *The Last Days of Maximilian Kolbe.* New York: New City Press, 1968.

A moving look at Kolbe's last weeks.

McFarland, Charles S. *I Was in Prison: The Suppressed Letters of Imprisoned German Pastors.* New York: Fleming H. Revell, 1939.

A fine anthology which demonstrates the courage of a select number of pastors in the prewar period.

Ritter, Gerhard. *The German Resistance: Carl Goerdeler's Struggle Against Tyranny.* Translated and abridged by R. T. Clark. London: Allen & Unwin, 1958.

The only major study of one of the Christian leaders of the German resistance.

Robertson, Edwin H. *Dietrich Bonhoeffer.* Richmond: John Knox Press, 1966.

A thorough, compelling biography.

Snoek, Johan M. *The Gray Book: A Collection of Protests Against Anti-Semitism and Persecution of Jews Issued by Non–Roman Catholic Church and Church Leaders During Hitler's Rule.* Assen: Van Gorcum, 1969.

One of the few major documentations of Christian acts of resistance and solidarity, with a fine introduction by Uriel Tal.

Stein, Leo. *I Was in Hell With Niemoeller.* New York: Fleming H. Revell, 1942.

A memoir portraying Niemoeller's defiant courage in a concentration camp, by one who knew him there.

Tiefel, Hans. "Use and Misuse of Luther During the German Church Struggle." *Lutheran Quarterly* 25 (November 1973): 395–411.

See also the response by Lowell C. Greene, "The Political Ethos of Luther" and "Lutherism: A Reply to the Polemics of Hans Tiefel," *Lutheran Quarterly* 26 (August 1974): 330–335.

von Oppen, Beate Ruhm. *Religion and Resistance to Nazism.* Princeton, N.J.: Center of International Affairs, Woodrow Wilson School, 1971.

A brief, fine study of the religious roots, and varieties of religious resistance to the Nazis.

Zabel, James A. *Nazism and the Pastors: A Study of Three Deutsche Christian Groups.* Missoula, Mont.: Scholar's Press, 1976.

Zerner, Ruth. "Dietrich Bonhoeffer and the Jews." *JSS* 37, nos. 3–4 (Summer–Fall 1975): 235–250.

———. "Germany's Confessing Church Leaders and the Jews in the 1930's: A Comment." *Centerpoint* 4, no. 1 (Fall 1980): 101–111.

B. Christian Europe, Nazi Germany, and the Jews

Robertson, Edwin H. *Christians Against Hitler.* London: SCM Press, 1962.

The best of several postwar studies of Christian resistance to Hitler throughout Europe.

Tennyson, Hallam. "Protestant Heroine of Auschwitz." *Jewish Digest* 18 (December 1972): 50–52.

Reprinted from *The Listener* (London), this article briefly recounts Dr. Adelaide Hautral's refusal to cooperate with the Nazis.

C. The Roman Catholic Church, Pope Pius XII, and Individual Catholics

Capri, Daniel. "The Catholic Church and Italian Jewry under the Fascists (to the Death of Pius XI)." *YVS* 4 (1960): 43–56.

On the pre-Holocaust history of Catholic-Jewish relations in Italy.

Cochrane, Arthur C. (ed.). Special section on *The Deputy. Christianity and Crisis,* March 30, 1964, pp. 44–54.

Falconi, Carlo. *The Silence of Pius XII.* Boston: Little, Brown, 1970.

A well-documented study of the Pope's failure to speak out on behalf of European Jewry.

Friedlander, Saul. *Pius XII and the Third Reich.* New York: Knopf, 1966.

A critical view with extensive documentation on Pius's silence about Jewish suffering; Friedlander notes that Pius's long period in Germany before he became Pope, and his stronger antipathy to communism than fascism, made him overly hesitant in speaking up on the Jews' behalf.

Helmreich, Ernst Christian. *The German Churches Under Hitler: Background to Struggle.* Detroit: Wayne State University, 1978.

This scholarly work focuses particularly on the largely "accommodationist" position undertaken by the German Catholic Church.

Kubovy, Aryeh. "The Silence of Pope Pius XII and the Beginning of the 'Jewish Document.' " *YVS* 6 (1967): 7–26.

Leboucher, Ferrante. *Incredible Mission.* New York: Doubleday, 1969.

A French Capuchin priest, Père Marie-Benoît, risked much to forge documents and otherwise help Jews during the Holocaust, as recounted in this book.

Levai, Eugene ["Jeno"]. *Hungarian Jewry and the Papacy: Pope Pius Did Not Remain Silent*. London: Sands & Co., 1968.

This volume documents Pius XII's intercessions with the Nazis on behalf of Hungarian Jews in the spring and summer of 1944. It includes 135 documents and photographs.

Lewy, Guenter. *The Catholic Church and Nazi Germany*. New York: McGraw-Hill, 1964; Holt, Rinehart & Winston, 1974.

The best scholarly volume to date on this topic.

Morley, John F. *Vatican Diplomacy and the Jews During the Holocaust, 1939–1943*. New York: Ktav, 1980.

Using recently-made-available Vatican archives, Morley has written the most balanced history to date of Pius XII's and the Vatican's role during the first four years of the Holocaust.

Ramati, Alexander. *The Assisi Underground: The Priest Who Rescued Jews*. New York: Stein & Day, 1978.

The moving story of Father Rufino Niccaci, an Italian priest who, along with his fellow Franciscans, sheltered and protected over 300 Jews from the Nazis in the town of Assisi.

Rhodes, Anthony. *The Vatican in the Age of Dictators*. New York: Holt, Rinehart & Winston, 1973.

Responding to Hochhuth's accusation in *The Deputy*, Rhodes explores the nuances of Pius XII's attitude toward the Jews of occupied Europe.

Rothkirchen, Livia. "Vatican Policy and the 'Jewish Problem' in 'Independent' Slovakia (1939–1945)." *YVS* 6 (1967): 27–54.

Treece, Patricia. *A Man for Others: Maximilian Kolbe, Saint of Auschwitz*. San Francisco: Harper & Row, 1982.

A short biography of the controversial Polish priest who volunteered at Auschwitz to die in place of a condemned prisoner.

Walker, Lawrence D. *Hitler Youth and Catholic Youth*. Washington, D.C.: Catholic University of America Press, 1971.

A solid study of the competing youth movements.

Zahn, Gordon C. *German Catholics and Hitler's Wars. New York: Sheed & Ward, 1962.

The most thorough study of the areas of cooperation, and the pockets of resistance.

———. *In Solitary Witness. New York: Irvington, 1964; Boston: Beacon, 1970.

The biography of Franz Jaggerstatter, an Austrian Catholic peasant who chose death rather than serve as a soldier in Hitler's army.

12.

Non-Jews Who Resisted the Nazis or Assisted Jews

A. The German Resistance to Hitler

Deutsch, Harold C. *The Conspiracy Against Hitler in the Twilight War.* Minneapolis: University of Minnesota Press, 1968.

This is the first detailed account in English of the German anti-Nazi plot of September 1939–May 1940, a conspiracy which involved the services of Pope Pius XII as an intermediary. It offers an intensive study of the role of the Pope in this conspiracy.

Fitzgibbon, Constantine. *20 July.* New York: Norton, 1956.

On the attempt to assassinate Hitler on July 20, 1944.

Friedlander, Saul. *Kurt Gerstein: The Ambiguity of Good.* New York: Knopf, 1969.

An account of the mysterious SS officer who provided Zyklon B for the operation of the gas chambers in the death camps, and who offered information on the camps to the West.

Friedman, Philip. "Was There an 'Other Germany' During the Nazi Period?" *YIVO Annual* 10 (1955): 82–127.

Gallin, Mary Alice. *Ethical and Religious, Factors in the German Resistance to Hitler.* Washington, D.C.: Catholic University of America Press, 1955.

An excellent analysis of what motivated the various German resistance movements, with particular emphasis on the different kinds of religiously motivated and anti-authoritarian resistance.

Graml, Hermann, et al. *The German Resistance to Hitler.* Introduction by F. L. Carsten. Berkeley: University of California Press, 1970.

A major, well-documented history of the German resistance.

Hanser, Richard. *A Noble Treason.* New York: Putnam, 1979.

This is the first major history in English of the "White Rose," an anti-Nazi student movement in Munich.

Hoffmann, Peter. *The History of the German Resistance, 1933–1945.* Cambridge, Mass.: M.I.T. Press, 1978.

A massive history of the German resistance to Hitler, with special emphasis on the group which attempted to assassinate Hitler on July 20, 1944.

Joffroy, Pierre. *A Spy for God: The Ordeal of Kurt Gerstein.* New York: Grosset & Dunlap, 1975.

The ordeal of Kurt Gerstein, the true story of a just man, an SS officer who defied Hitler's Final Solution.

Keneally, Thomas. *Schindler's List.* New York: Simon & Schuster, 1982.

A "novelistic nonfiction account" of Oskar Schindler, a German entrepreneur and former Abwehr agent whose phony concentration camp saved over a thousand Jews in Czechoslovakia.

Kramer, Arnold. "Germans Against Hitler: The Thaelmann Brigade." *JCH* 4, no. 2 (April 1969): 85–95.

Leuner, H. D. *When Compassion Was a Crime: Germany's Silent Heroes, 1933–1945.* London: Oswald Wolff, 1966.

The stories of Germans who acted out of human compassion to save the racially persecuted.

Manville, Roger, and Fraenkel, Heinrich. *The Canaris Conspiracy: The Secret Resistance to Hitler in the German Army.* New York: David McKay, 1969.

On the ongoing "war" between the Nazi party and segments of the German army and intelligence.

———. *The Men Who Tried to Kill Hitler.* New York: Coward, McCann & Geoghegan, 1964.

A collective biography of the conspirators in the July 20, 1944 plot.

Schlabrendorff, Fabian von. *The Secret War Against Hitler.* New York: Pitman Publishing Corp., 1965.

On the resistance to Hitler by one of the leaders of the July 20, 1944 assassination attempt.

Scholl, Inge. *Students Against Tyranny: The Resistance of the White Rose, Munich, 1942–1943.* rev. ed. Middletown, Conn.: Wesleyan University Press, 1970.

Deals with the Munich student resistance of 1942–1943, focusing on specific student dissenters and their writings, including primary source documents.

Zassenhaus, Hiltgunt. *Walls: Resisting the Third Reich—One Woman's Story.* Boston: Beacon Press, 1976.

An autobiography by a woman who now practices medicine in the United States, whose resistance acts against the Third Reich have become legendary—a fine adventure story, emotional and inspirational.

Zeller, Eberhard. *The Flame of Freedom: The German Struggle Against Hitler.* Translated from the German by R. P. Heller and D. Masters. Coral Gables, Fla.: University of Miami Press, 1969.

An overview which distinguishes different ideologies and motivations among various anti-Hitler conspirators.

B. Resistance Elsewhere in Occupied Europe

Anger, Per. *With Raoul Wallenberg in Budapest.* Translated from the Swedish by David Mel Paul and Margarita Paul. New York: Holocaust Library, 1981, pb., 1982.

The only major study of Wallenberg by someone who worked closely with him in Budapest during the war years.

Bartoszewski, Wladyslaw, and Lewin, Zofia (eds.). *The Samaritans.* New York: Twayne, 1970.

> An account of Poles who risked their lives to save Jews from destruction. Some of the heroes were laborers and farmers, others were clergy, professionals, and artists.

Bierman, John. *Righteous Gentile.* New York: Viking Press, 1981.

> A very well written biography of Raoul Wallenberg which focuses almost entirely on the war years and the evidence that Wallenberg may still be alive.

Friedman, Philip. *Their Brothers' Keepers.* New York: Crown, 1957; Holocaust Library, 1978.

> A brief history of individuals and groups who hid and otherwise aided Jews during the Holocaust.

Hallie, Philip. *Lest Innocent Blood Be Shed.* New York: Harper & Row, 1980.

> The story of Le Chambon, a French Protestant village which acted as a refuge center for Jews during World War II.

Hellman, Peter. *Avenue of the Righteous.* New York: Atheneum, 1980; Bantam pb., 1981.

> A series of portraits of righteous Gentiles who hid or otherwise saved Jews during the Holocaust, and who have been honored at Yad Vashem.

Horbach, Michael. *Out of the Night.* New York: Frederick Fell, 1967.

> On the rescue of Jews by Germans, based on interviews by a German journalist.

Iranek-Osmecki, Kazimierz. *He Who Saves One Life.* New York: Crown, 1971.

> Perhaps the definitive volume on Poles who saved Jews during the Holocaust.

Karski, Jan [pseud. of Jan Kulczynski]. *Story of a Secret State.* Boston: Houghton Mifflin, 1944.

> The memoir of the heroic Polish courier who informed the West about the Holocaust.

Kersten, Felix. *The Kersten Memoirs, 1940–1945.* New York: Macmillan, 1957.

Memoirs by the Swedish doctor who was active in trying to save Jewish lives at the end of World War II.

Lester, Eleanore. *Wallenberg: The Man in the Iron Web.* Introduction by Simon Wiesenthal. Englewood Cliffs, N.J.: Prentice-Hall, 1982.

An excellent, readable biography of Wallenberg the man, his extraordinary daring in the Budapest of 1944, the details of his capture by the Soviets, and the clues concerning his possible survival in a Soviet prison.

Lowrie, Donald. *The Hunted Children.* New York: Norton, 1963.

One story of the relief organizations' efforts to save the children of France is told. The author weaved the story together based on his personal experience and writings (letters, notes) of the time.

Marton, Kati. *Wallenberg.* New York: Random House, 1982.

A very readable, short account of the heroic activities of the Swedish diplomat in Budapest during the Holocaust.

Nowak, Jan. *Courier from Warsaw.* Foreword by Zbigniew Brzezinski. Detroit: Wayne State University Press, 1982.

A gripping, detailed account of the Polish underground during the Holocaust—written by one of its leaders, and a man who tried to help the Jews.

Rings, Werner. *Life with the Enemy: Collaboration and Resistance in Hitler's Europe.* New York: Doubleday, 1982.

The virtue of this study is that it looks at the thin line between collaboration and resistance, and that it examines both in Western and Eastern Europe alike.

Rosenfeld, Harvey. *Raoul Wallenberg: Angel of Rescue.* Buffalo, N.Y.: Prometheus Books, 1982.

A biography based on extensive research on Wallenberg and interviews with people who knew him.

Sim, Kevin. *Women at War: Five Heroines Who Defied the Nazis and Survived.* New York: William Morrow, 1982.

Portraits of four non-Jewish women and one Jewish woman who, through intelligence work, rescuing Jews or Scandinavians, giving birth to twins (in the Gestapo headquarters in Warsaw), or surviving Auschwitz through courage and a triumph of will, emerged from the Holocaust as anti-Nazi heroines.

Werbell, Frederich E., and Clarke, Thurston. *Lost Hero: The Mystery of Raoul Wallenberg*. New York: McGraw Hill, 1982.

> One of the two or three best Wallenberg biographies, *Lost Hero* focuses on the Swedish diplomat's last days in Budapest, his arrest, and the circumstances around his disappearance in Russia.

13.

The United States, American Jewry, and the Holocaust

A. The American Government and Military

Bauer, Yehuda. "When Did They Know?" *Midstream* 14, no. 4 (April 1968): 51–59.

> On how American Jewish leaders and the American government came to know of the Holocaust.

Compten, James V. *The Swastika and the Eagle: Hitler, The United States, and the Origins of World War II*. Boston: Houghton Mifflin, 1967.

> The context of American-German diplomacy on the eve of World War II.

Druks, Herbert. *The Failure to Rescue*. New York: Robert Speller, 1978.

> A history of American policy toward the persecuted Jews of Europe, 1939–1945.

Etzold, Thomas H. "An American Jew in Germany: The Death of Helmut Hirsch." *JSS* 35, no. 2 (April 1973): 125–140.

Feingold, Henry. *The Politics of Rescue: The Roosevelt Administration and the Holocaust.* New Brunswick, N.J.: Rutgers University Press, 1970; New York, Holocaust Library, 1981.

This is a very well researched, convincing documentation that the Roosevelt administration did little to rescue Jews during the Holocaust. See also Feingold's "Roosevelt and the Holocaust," *Judaism* 28 (Summer 1969): 259–276, and "Why FDR Failed to Meet the Challenge of the Holocaust," *Jewish Digest* 17 (March 1972): 25–31, for excerpts.

———. "Who Shall Bear Guilt for the Holocaust: The Human Dilemma." *AJHQ* 68, no. 3 (March 1979): 261–282.

A fascinating essay on an American and Western versus a more "Judeocentric" perspective on the Holocaust.

Friedman, Saul S. *No Haven for the Oppressed.* Detroit: Wayne State University Press, 1973.

The story of U.S. policy toward Jewish refugees, 1930–1945.

Gellman, Irwin F. "The St. Louis Tragedy." *AJHQ* 61, no. 2 (December 1971): 144–156.

Gottlieb, Moshe. "The Berlin Riots of 1935 and Their Repercussions in America." *AJHQ* 59, no. 3 (March 1970): 302–330.

Hirschmann, Ira. *Caution to the Winds.* New York: David McKay, 1962.

Hirschmann played a key role in rescuing Jews as the War Refugee Board's representative in Istanbul. This memoir relates some of these remarkable exploits.

Hochwald, Jack. "The U.S. Army T-Forces: Documenting the Holocaust." *AJH* 70, no. 3 (March 1981): 379–380.

Mashberg, Michael. "American Diplomacy and the Jewish Refugee, 1938–1939." *YIVO Annual* 15 (1974): 339–365.

———. "Documents Concerning the American State Department and Stateless European Jews, 1942–1944." *JSS* 39, nos. 1–2 (Winter–Spring 1977): 163–181.

Morse, Arthur D. *While Six Million Died.* New York: Random House, 1967; Hart pb., 1975; Viking, 1967.

Subtitled "A Chronicle of American Apathy," Morse's book examines both the apathy and callousness of the U.S. State Department toward the desperate plight of European Jewry.

Pinsker, Sanford, and Fischel, Jack (eds.). *Holocaust Studies Annual I: America and the Holocaust.* Greenwood, Fla.: Penkevill Publishing Co., 1983.

A 200-page scholars' anthology on four topics; responses of American intellectuals to the Holocaust, possibilities of resettling refugees, rescue efforts, and the responses of the communal leadership at the 1943 American Jewish Conference.

Rubin, Barry. "Ambassador Lawrence A. Steinhardt: The Peril of a Jewish Diplomat, 1940–1945." *AJH* 70, no. 3 (March 1981): 331–346.

Shafir, Shlomo. "American Diplomats in Berlin (1933–1939) and Their Attitude to the Nazi Persecution of the Jews." *YVS* 9 (1973): 71–104.

———. "George S. Messersmith: An Anti-Nazi Diplomat's View of the German Jewish Crisis." *JSS* 35, no. 1 (January 1973): 32–41.

Spear, Sheldon. "The United States and the Persecution of the Jews in Germany, 1933–1939." *JSS* 30, no. 4 (October 1968): 215–242.

Szajkowski, Zosa. "Relief for German Jewry: Problems of American Involvement." *AJHQ* 62, no. 2 (December 1972): 111–145.

Thomas, Gordon, and Witts, Max Morgan. **Voyage of the Damned.* New York: Stein & Day, 1974; Fawcett pb., 1975.

An hour-by-hour reconstruction of the "St. Louis Affair"—on the German luxury liner that sailed from Hamburg to Cuba in May 1939, and was refused entry by Cuba and other nations, including the United States. This fascinating book focuses on corruption, manipulation, and indifference.

Wilson, John P. "Calton J. H. Hayes, Spain, and the Refugee Crises, 1942–1945." *AJHQ* 62, no. 2 (December 1972): 99–110.

Wyman, David. *Paper Walls: America and the Refugee Crisis, 1938–1941.* Amherst: University of Massachusetts Press, 1969.

Wyman describes factors which influenced Congress and the Roosevelt administration, and is critical of both.

———. "Why Auschwitz Was Never Bombed." *Commentary* 56, no. 5 (May 1978): 37–47.

Wyman demolishes the argument that it would have been strategically impossible for the Allies to have bombed Auschwitz in this major essay on a gnawing topic.

B. The American Public, Business, and the Press

Bedford, Henry F. *From Versailles to Nuremberg: The American Encounter with the Nazis.* New York: Macmillan, 1969.

The reaction of the American people to the rise of the Nazi party and their feelings after the war.

Diamond, Sander A. *The Nazi Movement in the United States, 1924–1941.* Ithaca, N.Y.: Cornell University Press, 1974.

A well-documented, clearly written account of the rise and fall of American Nazism.

Gnizi, Haim. "American Interfaith Cooperation on Behalf of Refugees from Nazism, 1933–45." *AJH* 70, no. 3 (March 1981): 347–361.

———. "American Non-Sectarian Refugee Relief Organizations (1933–1945)." *YVS* 11 (1976): 164–220.

Gottlieb, Moshe R. *American Anti-Nazi Resistance, 1933–1941: An Historical Analysis.* New York: Ktav, 1982.

A thorough account of American movements to resist the Nazis.

Norden, Margaret K. "American Editorial Response to the Rise of Adolf Hitler: A Preliminary Consideration." *AJHQ* 59, no. 3 (March 1970): 290–301.

Peck, Sarah E. "The Campaign for an American Response to the Nazi Holocaust, 1943–1945." *JCH* 15, no. 2 (April 1980): 367–400.

Singer, David G. "The Prelude to Nazism: The German-American Press and the Jews, 1919–1933." *AJHQ* 66, no. 3 (March 1977): 417–470.

Strong, Donald S. *Organized Anti-Semitism in America: The Rise of Group Prejudice During the Decade 1930–1940.* Washington, D.C.: American Council on Public Affairs, 1941.

An important book on understanding the American context of anti-Semitism in the decade before the Holocaust.

Tenenbaum, Joseph. "The Anti-Nazi Boycott Movement in the United States." *YVS* 3 (1959): 141–160.

C. American Protestants and Catholics

Ross, Robert W. *So It Was True: The American Protestant Press and the Persecution of the Jews.* Minneapolis: University of Minnesota Press, 1980.

A comprehensive survey of how the American Protestant press—both national papers, such as the *Christian Century*, and denominational papers, such as the *American Baptist*—reported on the Holocaust.

Wentz, Frederick K. "American Protestant Journals and the Nazi Religious Assault." *Church History* 23 (1954): 321–338.

———. "American Catholic Periodicals React to Nazism." *Church History* 31 (1963): 400–420.

D. The American Jewish Community

Agar, Herbert. *The Saving Remnant. New York: Viking, 1962.

A history of the American Jewish Joint Distribution Committee which includes important information on the Joint's vital work during the Holocaust.

Bauer, Yehuda. *American Jews and the Holocaust: The American Joint Distribution Committee.* Detroit: Wayne State University Press, 1981.

This volume, a sequel to Bauer's *My Brother's Keeper*, is a lengthy, (500-page) and definitive history of the Joint's efforts to assist and save Jews during the Holocaust, including its role in the negotiations with Eichmann, Wisliceny, and Himmler.

Brody, David. "American Jewry, The Refugees and Immigration Restriction (1932–1942)." *AJH* 44, no. 4 (June 1956): 219–247.

Cohen, Naomi. *Not Free to Desist: The American Jewish Committee, 1906–1966.* Philadelphia: Jewish Publication Society, 1972.

Contains an all-too-brief analysis of what the AJ Committee—perhaps American Jewry's most prestigious organization—did and did not do on behalf of European Jewry.

Falk, Gerhard. "The Role of American Jewry in the Death of Their Brethren." *M&R* 4, no. 4 (November–June 1978): 11.

Gottlieb, Moshe. "The Anti-Nazi Boycott Movement in the United States: An Ideological and Sociological Appreciation." *JSS* 35, nos. 3–4 (July–October 1973): 198–227.

———. "The First of April Boycott and the American Jewish Community." *AJHQ* 57, no. 4 (June 1968): 516–556.

———. "In the Shadow of War: The American Anti-Nazi Boycott Movement in 1939–1941." *AJHQ* 62, no. 2 (December 1972): 146–161.

Grobman, Alex. "What Did They Know? The American Jewish Press and the Holocaust, 1 September 1939–17 December 1942." *AJHQ* 68, no. 3 (March 1979): 327–352.

————. "The Warsaw Ghetto Uprising in the American Jewish Press." *WLB* 29, nos. 37–38 (1976): 53–61.

Layen, Frederick A. "The Response of the American Jewish Committee to the Crisis of German Jewry, 1933–1939." *AJHQ* 58, no. 3 (March 1979): 283–304.

Penkower, Monty Noam. "In Dramatic Dissent: The Bergson Boys." *AJH* 70, no. 3 (March 1981): 281–309.

On Peter Bergson and the activities of the Emergency Committee to Save the Jews of Europe.

Szajkowski, Zosa. "The Attitude of American Jews to Refugees from Germany in the 1930's." *AJHQ* 61, no. 2 (December 1971): 101–143.

————. "Budgeting American Jewish Overseas Relief (1919–1939)." *AJHQ* 59, no. 1 (September 1969): 83–138.

————. "A Note on the American Jewish Struggle Against Nazism and Communism in the 1930's." *AJHQ* 59, no. 3 (March 1970): 272–289.

————. "Private and Organized American Jewish Overseas Relief (1914–1938)." *AJHQ* 57, no. 1 (September 1967): 52–136, and 57, no. 2 (December 1967): 191–253.

————. "Private American Jewish Overseas Relief (1919–1938): Problems and Attempted Solutions." *AJHQ* 57, no. 3 (March 1968): 285–352.

————. " 'Reconstruction' versus 'Palliative Relief' in American Jewish Overseas Work (1919–1939)." *JSS* 32, no. 1 (January 1970): 14–42, and 32, no. 2 (April 1970): 111–147.

The last part of this major essay on the *Kass* (Jewish credit cooperatives in Europe) and the various goals and disagreements of American Jewish relief organizations concerns the Holocaust years.

Zuroff, Efraim. "Rescue Priority and Fund Raising as Issues during the Holocaust: A Case Study of the Relations Between the Vaad Hatzala and the Joint, 1939–1941." *AJHQ* 68, no. 3 (March 1979): 305–326.

On the Orthodox relief organization and its sometimes harmonious, sometimes conflict-ridden, relation with the American Jewish Joint Distribution Committee.

E. The Holocaust and American Life Today

Jick, Leon A. "The Holocaust: Its Use and Abuse within the American Public." *YVS* 14 (1981): 303–318.

Lindecker, Clifford L. *The Swastika and the Eagle: Neo-Nazism in America Today.* New York: A and W Publishers, 1982.

On the personalities and complex motivations of today's neo-Nazis.

14.

Other Countries and the Holocaust; World Jewry and the Holocaust

A. The Allies

Conway, J. S. "Between Apprehension and Indifference: Allied Attitudes to the Destruction of Hungarian Jewry." *WLB* 27, nos. 30–34 (1973–74): 37–48.

Gilbert, Martin. **Auschwitz and Allies.* New York: Holt, Rinehart & Winston, 1981; pb., 1982.

Thoroughly documented and well-written, this is the definitive work to date on why the Allies did not intervene in any large-scaled, planned way on behalf of European Jewry.

Laqueur, Walter. *The Terrible Secret: Suppression of the Truth About the Holocaust. Boston: Little, Brown, 1981; New York: Penguin, 1982.

> After a remarkable bit of historical detective work, Laqueur finally reveals what was known about the Holocaust in the West, particularly in the United States, and when.

Penkower, Monty Noam. The Jews Were Expendable: Free World Diplomacy and the Holocaust. Urbana and Chicago: University of Illinois Press, 1983.

> Nine important, well-documented essays on the United States, Great Britain, the Red Cross, and the Holocaust, as well as on the Patria affair, and on several rescue attempts.

B. The Arabs

Friedman, S. "Arab Complicity in the Holocaust." Jewish Frontier 43 (April 1975): 9–15.

> An unusual subject, one of the few treatments of this topic.

C. Canada

Abella, Irving, and Harold Troper. None Is Too Many. New York: Random House, 1983.

> The first book-length history of Canada's restrictive immigration policy toward the Jews during the Holocaust.

Betcherman, Lita-Rose. The Swastika and the Maple Leaf: Fascist Movements in the Thirties. Toronto: Fitzhenry & Whiteside, 1975.

> Includes important material on Canadian anti-Semitism and pro-Nazism.

D. Great Britain

Barnes, James J. "Mein Kampf in Britain: 1930–1939." WLB 27, no. 32 (1974): 2–10.

Fox, John P. "Great Britain and the German Jews, 1933." WLB 26, no. 26–27 (1972): 40–46.

Sharf, Andrew. The British Press and the Jews Under Nazi Rule. Oxford: Oxford University Press, 1964.

Sharf deals not only with how the British press "covered"—and failed to cover—the Nazi persecution of the Jews and the Final Solution, but also how such reporting was affected by British policies.

Sherman, A. J. *Island Refuge: Britain and Refugees from the Third Reich, 1933–1939*. Berkeley: University of California Press, 1973.

Sherman hypothesizes that Britain had a more magnanimous policy toward Jewish refugees than did the United States.

Sompolinsky, Meier. "Anglo-Jewish Leadership and the British Government: Attempts at Rescue 1944–1945." *YVS* 13 (1979): 211–248.

Stein, Joshua B. "Britain and the Jews of Danzig: 1938–1939." *WLB* 32, nos. 49–50 (1979): 29–33.

Wasserstein, Bernard. *Great Britain and the Jews of Europe, 1939–1945*. New York: Oxford University Press, 1979.

Using archival sources from throughout the world, Wasserstein explores the policy of the British toward the Jewish problem during World War II. He examines reasons for the near total ban on Jewish refugee immigration to Britain during the war, the restrictive immigration policy on Palestine, the internment and deportation of aliens in Britain, the abortive Bermuda Conference on Refugees in 1943, the failure to aid Jewish resistance in Europe, and the rejection of a plan to bomb Auschwitz. What emerges is a study of lamentable bureaucratic complacency, inhumanity, and blindness to the reality of the Jewish catastrophe in Europe.

Yahil, Leni. "Select British Documents on the Illegal Immigration to Palestine, 1939–40." *YVS* 10 (1974): 241–276.

E. International Organizations

Silberschein (L.R.), A. "Rescue Efforts with the Assistance of International Organizations—Documents from the Archives of Dr. A. Silberschein (L.R.)." *YVS* 8 (1970): 69–80.

F. Japan

Kranzler, David. *Japanese, Nazis and the Jews: The Jewish Refugee Community of Shanghai, 1938–1945*. New York: Yeshiva University Press, 1979.

The story of the 18,000 German and Polish Jews who found a haven from Hitler in Japanese-occupied Shanghai in World War II; cutting across conventional historiographic divisions, this study uncovers aspects of Japanese conditions in wartime China and, above all, the Holocaust experience and the life and social structure of Jews in wartime Shanghai.

Michale, Donald. "The Nazi Party in the Far East, 1931–1945." *JCH* 12, no. 2 (April 1977): 291–313.

Tokayer, Marvin, and Swartz, Mary. *The Fugu Plan.* New York: Paddington Press, 1979; Dell pb., 1981 (as *Desperate Voyagers*).

Why did Japan protect thousands of Jews after Pearl Harbor? The answer lies in a complex scheme devised by the Japanese government to prevent war with the United States. *The Fugu Plan* is the story of a group of European Jews, their journey across Stalinist Russia, their life in Japan, and their eventual survival in an Asian ghetto.

G. Palestine

Bauer, Yehuda. *From Diplomacy to Resistance: A History of Jewish Palestine, 1939–1945.* New York: Atheneum, 1973.

A fine chronology of Jewish life and resistance in Palestine which emphasizes the impact of the Holocaust.

Gelber, Yoav. "Palestinian POW's in German Captivity." *YVS* 14 (1981): 89–138.

Katzburg, Nathaniel. "European Jewry and the Palestine Question: Appraisals and Predictions." *YVS* 13 (1979): 249–262.

H. Scandinavia

Valentin, Hugo. "Rescue and Relief Acting in Behalf of Jewish Victims of Nazism in Scandinavia." *YIVO Annual* 8 (1953): 224–251.

I. Spain

Avni, Haim. *Spain, the Jews and Franco.* Translated by Emanuel Shimoni. Philadelphia: Jewish Publication Society, 1980.

Meticulously researched, this is the definitive study of Franco's complex—if largely protective—policies toward the Jews during the Holocaust.

Lipschitz, Chaim U. *Franco, Spain, the Jews, and the Holocaust.* New York: Ktav, 1983.

Thorough account of Spain's Jewish policy during World War II, with an analysis of Franco's possible motives for saving upwards of 45,000 Jews from the Nazi gas chambers.

Robinson, Nehemiah. *The Spain of Franco and Its Policies Towards the Jews.* New York: World Jewish Congress, 1953.

One of the only studies of Franco's attitude toward the Jews.

J. Switzerland

Haessler, Alfred. *The Lifeboat Is Full.* New York: Funk & Wagnalls, 1969.

The only full-length study on Switzerland's vacillating policies toward Jewish refugees.

"Swiss Jews in Occupied Europe." *WLB* 18, no. 4 (October 1964): 54.

"Swiss Refugee Policy, 1933–45." *WLB* 12, nos. 1–2 (1958): 13.

"Swiss Rescue Efforts in 1944." *WLB* 16, no. 2 (April 1962): 32.

K. World Jewry

Gelber, Yoav. "Zionist Policy and the Fate of European Jewry (1939–1942)." *YVS* 13 (1979): 169–210.

———. "The Jewish Anti-Nazi Boycott." *WLB* 14, no. 1 (1960): 14–15.

Penkower, Monty Noam. "The World Jewish Congress Confronts the International Red Cross During the Holocaust." *JSS* 41, nos. 3–4 (Summer–Fall 1979): 229–256.

Sagi, Nanna, and Lowe, Malcome. "Research Report: Pre-War Reactions to Nazi Anti-Jewish Policies in the Jewish Press." *YVS* 13 (1979): 387–408.

15.

Jewish Refugees, 1933–1948

A. Exodus From Germany, International Attempts to Assist Refugees, and the German Response, 1933–1939

Adler-Rudel, S. "The Evian Conference on the Refugee Question." *LBI Yrbk* 8 (1968): 235–276.

Katz, Shlomo. "Public Opinion in Western Europe and the Evian Conference of July 1938." *YVS* 9 (1973): 105–132.

Mann, Peggy. *Prelude to Holocaust*. New York: American Jewish Congress, 1978.

This reprint of an article which originally appeared in the *Washington Post* concerns the 1938 Evian Conference and its failure to adopt a coordinated policy on behalf of Europe's Jews.

Prinz, Artur. "The Role of the Gestapo in Obstructing and Promoting Jewish Emigration." *YVS* 2 (1958): 205–218.

Rosenstock, W. "Exodus 1933–1939—A Survey of Jewish Emigration from Germany." *LBI Yrbk* 1 (1956): 373–392.

Wischnitzer, Mark. "Jewish Emigration from Germany 1933–1938." *JSS* 2, no. 1 (January 1948): 23–44.

B. General Studies and Accounts

Bentwich, Norman. *The Rescue and Achievement of Refugee Scholars: The Story of Displaced Scholars and Scientists, 1933–1952.* The Hague: Martinus Nijhoff, 1953.

A good account of the special efforts made to save and to find appropriate homes for gifted refugee intellectuals.

Pincus, Chasia. +*Come from the Four Winds*. New York: Herzl Press, 1970.

On children fleeing the Holocaust.

Proudfoot, Malcolm J. *European Refugees: 1939–52: A Study in Forced Population Movement*. London: Faber & Faber, 1957.

A detailed, general study encompassing Jews and non-Jews.

Segal, Lore. +*Other People's Houses*. New York: Harcourt, Brace, 1964; New American Library, 1973.

Nine months after Hitler entered Austria, a ten-year-old Jewish girl with a cardboard label marked 152 strung on a shoelace around her neck boarded a train in Vienna that was to take several hundred children west to safety. Lore reached England, and for seven years she lived in other people's houses. Her story includes an account of her coming of age in England, the Dominican Republic, and ultimately the United States.

Tartakower, Arieh. "The Jewish Refugees: A Sociological Survey." *JSS* 4, no. 4 (October 1942): 311–348.

A detailed sociological study, focusing largely on German Jewish refugees.

Wischnitzer, Mark. *To Dwell in Safety: The Story of Jewish Migration Since 1800*. Philadelphia: Jewish Publication Society, 1949.

A general study on Jewish migration which includes a description of Jewish emigration from Europe before, during, and after the Holocaust.

C. Refugees to and in Great Britain

Bentwich, Norman. *They Found Refuge*. London: Cresset Press, 1956.

A compelling account of British Jewry's work for the victims of Nazi oppression.

"Refugee Doctors in Britain." *WLB* 19, no. 2 (April 1965): 27.

D. Refugees in Europe and USSR

Diamant, Zanvel. "Jewish Refugees on the French Riviera." *YIVO Annual* 8 (1953): 264–280.

Hautzig, Esther. +*The Endless Steppe: Growing Up in Siberia*. New York: Crowell, 1968.

Esther Hautzig was one of thousands of young Jews evacuated from the parts of the USSR occupied by the Germans to Siberia. This is her gripping account of her often precarious existence there.

Michman, Dan. "The Committee for Jewish Refugees in Holland (1933–1940)." *YVS* 14 (1981): 205–232.

Pinchuk, Ben Cion. "Jewish Refugees in Soviet Poland 1939–1941." *JSS* 40, no. 2 (Spring 1978): 141–158.

Rothkirchen, Livia. "Hungary—An Asylum for the Refugees of Europe." *YVS* 7 (1968): 127–146.

E. Refugees to and in Palestine

Avriel, Elad. *Open the Gates!* New York: Random House, 1975.

On the "illegal" immigration of Holocaust survivors to Israel by one of the leaders of that effort.

Bauer, Yehuda. *Flight and Rescue: Brichah; The Organized Escape of the Jewish Survivors of Eastern Europe, 1944–1948.* New York: Random House, 1970.

This is a fully documented, detailed history of the mass movement of 300,000 Jewish survivors by a Palestine-based underground organization.

Carpi, Daniel. "The Diplomatic Negotiations over the Transfer of Jewish Children from Croatia to Turkey and Palestine in 1943." *YVS* 12 (1977): 109–124.

Freier, Recha. *Let the Children Come.* London: Weidenfeld & Nicholson, 1961.

A memoir by the co-founder of Youth Aliyah of its largely successful efforts to bring thousands of Jewish children to Palestine.

Gershon, Karen (ed.). *We Came as Children: A Collective Autobiography.* New York: Harcourt, 1966.

Short memoirs by Jewish children who came to Palestine as part of Youth Aliyah or the "illegal" immigration.

Kimche, Jon, and Kimche, David. *The Secret Roads: The Illegal Migration of a People, 1938–1948.* London: Secker & Warburg, 1951.

A general, well-written description of Zionist efforts to rescue Jews from Europe and transport them to Palestine.

Steiner, Eric Gershon. **The Story of the "Patria."* New York: Holocaust Library, 1982.

On the doomed refugee ship blown up in November 1941, with the loss of 257 lives.

Worman, Curt, D. "German Jews in Israel—Their Cultural Situation Since 1933." *LBI Yrbk* 15 (1970): 73–106.

F. Refugees in the United States

Dinnerstein, Leonard. *America and the Survivors of the Holocaust.* New York: Columbia University Press, 1982.

A carefully researched study of America's neglect of Holocaust survivors at the end of, and after, the Holocaust.

———. "The U.S. Army and the Jews: Policies Toward the Displaced Persons After World War II." *AJHQ* 68, no. 3 (March 1979): 353–366.

Gruber, Ruth. **Haven.* New York: Coward-McCann, 1983; New American Library pb., 1984.

A journalistic report on the 1,000 refugees who, in 1944, were invited to the United States as "guests" of the American government, and who were interned in a camp in Oswego, N.Y. A special assistant to the Secretary of the Interior, Gruber accompanied and spent considerable time with them.

Heilbut, Anthony. *Exiled in Paradise: German Refugee Artists and Intellectuals in America from the 1930's to the Present.* New York: Viking, 1983.

From Thomas Mann to Albert Einstein, to Kurt Weill and Lotte Lenya—a fascinating study of the German writers, artists, musicians, performers, and thinkers who came to America during the Nazi years.

Planner, Helmut F. *Exile in New York: German and Austrian Writers After 1933.* Detroit: Wayne State University Press, 1983.

Planner draws upon varied sources—autobiographies, letters, archives, and autobiographic fiction—to recreate the exiles' milieu in New York and elsewhere.

Taylor, John Russell. *Strangers in Paradise: The Hollywood Emigres 1933–1950.* New York: Holt, Rinehart & Winston, 1983.

A major group of German intellectuals, actors, and directors—both Jewish and non-German—settled in Hollywood after Hitler came to power. Taylor has produced a very readable study of this group.

G. Refugees in Latin America

Hirschberg, Alfred. "The Economic Adjustment of Jewish Refugees in Sao Paulo." *JSS* 7, no. 1 (January 1945): 31–40.

Neumann, Gerhardt. "German Jews in Colombia." *JSS* 3, no. 4 (October 1941): 387–398.

Wischnitzer, Mark. "The Historical Background of the Settlement of Jewish Refugees in Santo Domingo." *JSS* 4, no. 1 (January 1942): 42–58.

Why the Dominican Republic allowed a relatively high number of Jewish refugees to emigrate there during the Holocaust.

H. Refugees in China and Japan

Dicker, Herman. *Wanderers and Settlers: A Century of Jewish Life in China and Japan.* New York: Twayne, 1962.

The last part of this history deals with Jewish refugees before and during the Holocaust.

Gruenberger, Felix. "The Jewish Refugees in Shanghai." *JSS* 12, no. 4 (October 1950): 329–348.

A good, short memoir by a doctor who was part of the Shanghai refugee community.

Kranzler, David. "Restrictions Against German-Jewish Refugee Immigration to Shanghai in 1939." *JSS* 36, no. 1 (January 1974): 40–60.

Kranzler, David. *Japanese, Nazis and the Jews: The Jewish Refugee Community of Shanghai, 1938–1945.* New York: Yeshiva University Press, 1979.

Mars, Alvin. "A Note on the Jewish Refugees in Shanghai." *JSS* 31, no. 4 (October 1969): 286–291.

16.

War Crime Trials, Reparations, the Search for Suspected Nazi Criminals, and Denazification

A. The Nuremberg Trials Against Major Nazi War Criminals, Their Legal Basis, and Reflections on the Trials

Benton, W. E., and Grimm, G. *Nuremberg: German Views of the War Trials*. Dallas: Southern Methodist University Press, 1955.

A detailed look at the education of a people to the crimes of their leaders—and the resistance to that education.

Bernstein, Victor, H. *The Holocaust: Final Judgement*. New York: Bobbs-Merrill, 1980.

Analysis of the Nuremberg trials by journalists who covered the tribunal.

Biddiss, Michael. "The Nuremberg Trial: Two Exercises in Judgement." *JCH* 16, no. 3 (July 1981): 597–615.

Bosch, William J. *Judgement on Nuremberg*. Chapel Hill: University of North Carolina Press, 1970.

An examination of American attitudes toward the German war crime trials.

Conot, Robert E. *Justice at Nuremberg. New York: Harper & Row, 1983; Carroll & Graf pb.

A very extensive, behind-the-scenes look at the eleven-month trial, based on interviews, memoirs, letters, and testimony.

Davidson, Eugene. *The Trial of the Germans. New York: Macmillan, 1966, pb. 1972.

A long, fascinating account of the main Nuremberg trials of, among others, Goering, Bormann, Speer, and Von Papen.

Gilbert, G. M. *Nuremberg Diary. New York: Farrar, Straus & Giroux, 1947; New York: Signet, 1961.

As prison psychologist of the Nuremberg jail, the author had an unique perspective on Speer, Goering, Hess, and the crimes of many others. His viewpoint is shared here in almost anecdotal fashion, which considerably illuminates the Nuremberg trial.

Harris, Whitney R. *Tyranny on Trial*. Dallas: Southern Methodist University Press, 1954.

A presentation and analysis of the evidence at the Nuremberg trials.

International Military Tribunal. *Trial of the Major War Criminals Before the International Military Tribunal, Nuremberg, in November 1945–October 1946. Record of the Trial*. 42 vols. Nuremberg, 1947–49.

The official transcript of the trial—indispensable to any student not only of the Nuremberg trials but of the Holocaust in general.

Jackson, Robert. *The Nuremberg Case*. New York: Knopf, 1947.

This account by one of the chief U.S. judges includes the full text of the London Charter which mandated the trial.

Kahn, Leo. *Nuremberg Trials. New York: Ballantine, 1972.

Kahn's book gives a brief historical background of the trials and details the charges and evidence. It is excellent for understanding the historical nature of the trials. This somewhat conceptually difficult work discusses questions of responsibility and the trials' implications.

Mushkat, Marion. "The Concept 'Crime Against the Jewish People' in the Light of International Law." *YVS* 5 (1963): 237–254.

Neave, Airey. Nuremberg: *A Personal Record of the Trial of the Nazi War Criminals in 1945–1946*. London: Hodder & Stoughton, 1978.

A memoir by a member of the British prosecuting team at Nuremberg.

Robinson, Jacob, and Sachs, Henry. *The Holocaust: The Nuremberg Evidence, Part I: Digest, Index and Chronological Tables*. New York: YIVO, 1976.

A very useful anthology of the evidence presented at the Nuremberg trial.

Smith, Bradley. **Reaching Judgment at Nuremberg*. New York: Basic Books, 1976, New American Library, 1979.

In telling how the Nazi war criminals were brought to trial, Smith links the complex legal issues with postwar international politics in a clear, thorough study.

————. *The Road to Nuremberg*. New York: Basic Books, 1981.

A companion volume to the author's *Reaching Judgment at Nuremberg*—on how the Nuremberg trials came to be despite the bitter opposition of some American and British critics who wanted to destroy the German economy or shoot Nazi war criminals.

Taylor, Telford. **Nürnberg and Vietnam: An American Tragedy*. Chicago: Quadrangle Books, 1970; New York: Vintage Paperback, 1971.

A detailed controversial exploration of the legal implications of the Nuremberg trials for America in light of the Vietnam War—by the chief U.S. prosecutor in Nuremberg.

U.S. Chief of Counsel for Prosecution of Axis Criminality. *Nazi Conspiracy and Aggression*. 8 vols., 2 supp. vols., Washington, D.C.: U.S. Government Printing Office, 1946–48.

An extensive summary of the Nuremberg evidence, and an explanation of how the verdicts were arrived at.

Woetzel, R. *The Nuremberg Trials in International Law*. New York: Praeger, 1960.

A thorough analysis of the trials' basis in, and implications for, international law.

Note: There has been a large number of articles on the legal dimensions and repercussions of the Nuremberg trials in various law journals. Many are listed in the bibliography following M. Cherit Bassiouni's "International Law and the Holocaust" in *Encountering the Holocaust: An Interdisciplinary Survey*, edited by Byron L. Sherwin and Susan G. Ament, pp. 182–188. Chicago: Impact Press, 1979.

B. The Eichmann Trial and Reflections Thereon

Arendt, Hannah. *Eichmann in Jerusalem.* New York: Viking Compass, 1965.

Reportage on the Eichmann trial which is considered very controversial because of the author's theories about the behavior of the Jewish victims of the Nazis; yet Arendt's portrait of Eichmann is fascinating, and her theory that he exemplified the "banality of evil" is persuasively argued.

Bergman, Shmuel H. "Can Transgression Have an Agent? On the Moral-Judicial Problem of the Eichmann Trial." *YVS* 5 (1963): 7–16.

Eichmann, Adolf. *The Attorney-General of the Government of Israel v. Adolf, the Son of Adolf Karl Eichmann.* Minutes of session, Israel: Office of the Attorney General, 1961.

The transcript of the trial.

Glock, Charles; Selznick, Gertrude; and Spaeth, Joe. *The Apathetic Minority.* New York: Harper & Row, 1966.

A study of the public responses to the Eichmann trial.

Harel, Isser. *The House on Garibaldi Street.* New York: Viking Press, 1975, and Bantam pb., 1976.

A full account of the fifteen-year quest to capture Adolf Eichmann in hiding in Argentina, and bring him to trial in Israel; the author is a former head of the Israeli secret service.

Hausner, Gideon. *Justice in Jerusalem.* New York: Harper & Row, 1966; Holocaust Library, 1977.

A volume by the prosecuting attorney on the capture of Eichmann in Argentina and his trial in Israel, with a detailed presentation of the evidence which comprises a history of much of the Holocaust.

Pearlman, Moshe. *The Capture and Trial of Adolf Eichmann.* New York: Simon & Schuster. 1963.

Robinson, Jacob. *And the Crooked Shall be Made Straight*. New York: Macmillan, 1965.

> A critical reply to Hannah Arendt's *Eichmann in Jerusalem*, refuting many of her claims concerning Jewish conduct during the Holocaust.

Rosenberg, Harold. "The Trial and Eichmann." *Commentary* 32, no. 5 (November 1961): 369–381.

Rotenstreich, Nathan. "The Individual and Personal Responsibility." *YVS* 5 (1963): 17–34.

> An essay on the historical school of law and Eichmann.

von Lang, Jochen (ed.). **Eichmann Interrogated*. Translated by Ralph Manheim, afterword by Avner W. Less. New York: Farrar, Straus & Giroux, 1983; Vintage Books, 1984.

> A distillation of the more than 275 hours of Eichmann's interrogation by the Israeli police between May 1960 and April 1961.

Wiesel, Elie. "Eichmann and the Unheard Testimony." *Commentary* 32, no. 6 (December 1961): 510–516.

Zeigler, Henry (ed.). **The Case Against Adolf Eichmann*. New York: Signet, 1960.

> An anthology of articles and documents on the Eichmann case.

C. Other Trials of Nazi War Criminals in the 1960s and 1970s

Bonhoeffer, Emmi. *Auschwitz Trials: Letters from an Eyewitness*. Translated by Ursula Stechow. Richmond: John Knox Press, 1967.

> Reflections on the Auschwitz trials by Bonhoeffer's widow.

Germany, Federal Republic of. *The Prosecution Since 1945 of National Socialist Crimes by Public Prosecutors and Courts in the Territory of the Federal Republic of Germany*. Dusseldorf: Federal Ministry of Justice, 1962.

> A list and summary of West German prosecutions of Nazi war criminals.

Helendhall, F. "Nazi Spoilation and German Restitution—The Work of the United Restitution Office." *LBI Yrbk* 10 (1965): 204–226.

McPherson, Malcolm. *The Blood of His Servants*. New York: Time Books, 1964.

A well-researched, compellingly written account of the over-three-decades-long effort to track down, gather evidence against, and convict the Dutch war criminal Pieter Menten, who was responsible for the murder of almost all the Jews in a small Polish town, including an ex-friend and business partner.

Rucherl, Adalbert. *The Investigation of Nazi Crimes, 1945–1978.* Translated by C. F. Wuller. Fort Lauderdale, Fla.: Derek Prince Publications, 1979; Hamden Conn.: Shoe String Press, 1980.

A detailed chronicle of the investigation and prosecution of Nazi crimes, especially by the Federal Republic of Germany.

Weiss, Peter. *The Investigation.* New York: Atheneum, 1966.

A documentary play dealing with the question of guilt and responsibility; Weiss bases it on the testimony from the war crimes trial in Frankfurt, 1964–1965.

D. Denazification

Bower, Tom. *The Pledge Betrayed.* New York: Doubleday, 1981.

This is the first book-length story of how the Allies slowed, and ultimately dropped, the process of denazification to rebuild postwar Germany.

Tent, James F. *Mission on the Rhine: "Reeducation" and Denazification in American-Occupied Germany.* Chicago: University of Chicago Press, 1982.

An extensive study of America's complex—and, at best, ambivalent—attitude toward the denazification process.

E. On the Search for Suspected Nazi Criminals

Allen, Charles R., and Saidel-Wolke, Rochelle. *Nazi War Criminals in America: Facts . . . Action.* Albany, N.Y.: Charles R. Allen, Jr., 1981.

On the identity of over fifty Nazi war criminals and collaborators in the United States and on the status of legal action against them.

Blum, Howard. *Wanted: The Search for Nazis in America.* New York: Quadrangle Press, 1977, and Fawcett, 1978.

An exposé of Nazi war criminals living in this country with semiofficial protection; apparently, the American government is doing little to prosecute the murderers, and its half-hearted attempts are met by powerful, organized legal countermoves.

Elkins, Michael. *Forged in Fury. New York: Ballantine, 1971.

> Stories of Jews, survivors of the Holocaust now living in Israel, who formed a secret organization whose goal was to take vengeance upon the killers of Jews.

Klarsfeld, Beate. *Wherever They May Be.* New York: Vanguard, 1975.

> Born a German Christian on the eve of World War II, and married to a French Jew, Beate Klarsfeld relates the story of a Christian German woman in hunting Nazi war criminals. Her work earned her Israel's Medal of Courage.

Wiesenthal, Simon. *The Murders Among Us. Edited by Joseph Wechsberg. New York: McGraw-Hill, 1967, and Bantam pb., 1973.

> Memoirs of the Vienna-based Nazi-hunter whose painstaking research and perseverance have brought a number of war criminals to justice.

17.

On Holocaust Survivors and Children of Survivors

A. Writings by Survivors and General Accounts

Bauer, Yehuda. "The Initial Organization of the Holocaust Survivors in Bavaria." *YVS* 8 (1970): 127–158.

Bloch, Sam E. (ed.). *Holocaust and Rebirth: Bergen-Belsen, 1945–1965.* New York: Bergen-Belsen Memorial Press, 1965.

> A memorial book issued on the twentieth anniversary of the liberation by survivors of the camp; valuable information on camp life and on the fate of Holocaust survivors.

Brenner, Reeve Robert. *The Faith and Doubt of Holocaust Survivors.* New York: Free Press, 1980.

A pioneering study on the effects of the Holocaust on the survivors' religiosity which uses both subjective data (interviews) and objective sociological analysis.

Fishman, Joel S. "The Anneke Beekman Affair and the Dutch News Media." *JSS* 40, no. 1 (Winter 1978): 3–24.

The case of a Jewish orphan, a victim of Nazism, who was raised a Catholic, and the attempt by Jewish organizations to have her raised under Jewish auspices.

Goldberg, Michael. *Namesake.* New Haven, Conn.: Yale University Press, 1982.

A gripping memoir by an "assimilated" survivor of the Holocaust whose father was killed by the Nazis, and who tracked down, and confronted the question of killing, his father's murderer.

Heymont, Irving. *Among the Survivors of the Holocaust—1945: The Landsberg DP Camp Letters of Major Irving Heymont, United States Army.* Cincinnati and New York: American Jewish Archives/Ktav, 1983.

The letters cover the fall of 1945, and record the initially horrendous conditions the "displaced" persons faced, and Major Heymont's valiant attempts to improve them.

Kucher-Silberman, Lena. *One Hundred Children.* New York: Doubleday, 1961.

The author, upon returning to Poland after the war, found that her husband and children were dead. At a refugee center, she discovered a group of children who were frightened, starved, beaten, and scarred. The author worked with them and brought them to Israel.

Love, Shelly. *Jewish Holocaust Survivors' Attitudes Toward Contemporary Beliefs About Themselves.* Ann Arbor, Mich.: UMI Publications, 1984.

Based on 1,900 questionnaires distributed in the United States, Europe, and Israel, this study looks at survivors' responses to portrayals of the Holocaust, and of its victims and survivors, in the mass media and in literature.

Moskowitz, Sarah. *Love Despite Hate: Child Survivors of the Holocaust and Their Adult Lives.* New York: Schocken, 1982.

A thoughtful look at how twenty-four survivors who were children during the Holocaust reconstructed their lives in England.

Pinson, Koppel. "Jewish Life in Liberated Germany—A Study of the Jewish DP's." *JSS* 9, no. 2 (April 1947): 101–126.

Rabinowitz, Dorothy. *New Lives*. New York: Knopf, 1976, Avon, 1977.

Excellent, short biographical sketches of, and excerpts from interviews with, Holocaust survivors in America—their struggle to begin again in America, to remember, and to pass on the legacy to their children.

Rosensaft, Menachem Z. "The Mass Graves of Bergen-Belsen: Focus for Confrontation." *JSS* 41, no. 2 (Spring 1979): 155–179.

The history of Bergen-Belsen and the protection of its remains by its survivors.

Sachar, Abram L. *The Redemption of the Unwanted*. New York: St. Martin's/Marek, 1983.

Much of the first part of this book concerns the lives of the 400,000 Holocaust survivors in DP camps and the efforts of the Bricha organization to smuggle them to Palestine.

Vida, George. *From Doom to Dawn: A Jewish Chaplain's Story of Displaced Persons*. New York: Jonathan David, 1967.

The memoir of a chaplain who worked with DP's, helping them to recover hope and begin anew.

B. On Holocaust Survivors—Psychological and Related Studies; Legal Information

A comprehensive list of books and articles on this subject up to 1979 can be found in Eva Fogelman, *Survivors and Their Children: Psychosocial Impact of the Holocaust* (New York: National Jewish Resource Center/ZACHOR, 1979).

Bergman, Martin, and Jacoby, Milton E. *Generations of the Holocaust*. New York: Basic Books, 1982.

An anthology of studies by psychologists and psychiatrists on Holocaust survivors and children of survivors.

Bettelheim, Bruno. *Surviving and other Essays*. New York: Knopf, 1979; Vintage pb., 1980.

Essays on the Holocaust and its effects on those who survived.

Bloch, Herbert. "The Personality of Inmates of Concentration Camps." *American Journal of Sociology* 52 (1946–47): 335–341.

Bulka, Reuven P. **Holocaust Aftermath: The Continuing Impact of the Generations.* New York: Human Sciences Press, 1982.

A reproduction of the special issue of the *Journal of Psychology and Judaism* on survivors and children of survivors.

Danieli, Yael. "Differing Adaptational Styles in Families of Survivors of the Nazi Holocaust." *Children Today* 10, no. 5 (September–October 1981): 6–10.

———. "The Group Project for Holocaust Survivors and Their Children." *Children Today* 10, no. 5 (September–October 1981): 11 and 33.

Dimsdale, Joel. *Survivors, Victims and Perpetrators: Essays in the Nazi Holocaust.* Washington, D.C.: Hemisphere, 1981.

Psychological studies of concentration camps, anti-Semitism, and opposition to the Nazis.

Eitinger, Leo. *Concentration Camp Survivors in Norway and Israel.* London: Allen & Unwin, 1964.

One of the only comparative studies of concentration camp survivors analyzing the influence of environment.

Hogman, Flora. "Adaptive Mechanisms of Displaced Jewish Children During World War II and Their Later Adult Adjustment." *Shoah* 1, no. 3 (Winter 1979): 10–13.

Hoppe, Klaus P. "The Psychodynamics of Concentration Camp Victims." *Psychoanalytic Forum* 1 (1966): 76–85.

Jaffe, Ruth. "The Sense of Guilt Within Holocaust Survivors." *JSS* 32, no. 4 (October 1970): 307–314.

Krystal, Henry. *Massive Psychic Trauma.* New York: International Universities Press, 1968.

A major work on the effects of the Holocaust and other incidents of mass horror on the victims.

Luchterhand, Elmer. "Early and Late Effects of Imprisonment in Nazi Concentration Camps: Conflicting Interpretations in Survivor Research." *Social Psychiatry* 5, no. 2. (1970): 102–110.

Includes a valuable bibliography for references of works on survivor-related research.

————. "The Gondola-Car Transport." *International Journal of Social Psychiatry* 13 (1966–67): 316–325.

————. "Prisoner Behavior and Social System in the Nazi Concentration Camps." In *Mass Society in Crisis*, edited by Rosenberg, Gerber, and Hanton. 2d ed. New York: Macmillan, 1971.

Luel, Steven, and Marcus, Paul (eds.). *Psychoanalytic Reflections on the Holocaust: Selected Essays.* New York: Ktav, 1984.

Includes several essays by noted psychoanalytic authorities on the effects of the Holocaust on survivors and children of survivors.

Niederland, William, and Krystal, Henry (eds.). *Psychic Traumatization.* Boston: Little, Brown, 1971.

One of the basic anthologies on concentration camp survivors and their children—see especially the articles by Klein, Luchterhand, and Hoppe, as well as Hoppe's bibliography.

Porter, Jack Nusan. "On Therapy Research and Other Dangerous Phenomema." *Shoah* 1, no. 3 (Winter 1979): 14–17.

————. "Is There a Survivor's Syndrome? The Psychological and Sociopolitical Implications." *Journal of Psychology and Judaism* 6, no. 1 (Fall–Winter 1981): 33–52.

Quatymann, Wilfred (ed.). *Holocaust Survivors: Psychological and Social Sequalae.* New York: Human Sciences Press, 1980; pb., 1982.

An anthology, originally a special issue of the *Journal of Contemporary Psychotherapy*, dealing with the moral, psychological, and philosophical problems of Holocaust survivors.

Rappaport, Ernest A. "Survivor Guilt." *Midstream* 17 (August–September 1971): 41–47.

Discussed in relation to Jewish indemnity claims against Germany.

Schneider, Gertrude. "Survival and Guilt Feelings of Jewish Concentration Camp Victims." *JSS* 37, no. 1 (January 1975): 74–83.

Based on a study of twenty-five men and women, all in their forties, who spent three or more years in concentration camps.

Winnik, H. Z. "Contribution to Symposium on Psychic Traumatization Through Social Catastrophe." *International Journal of Psychoanalysis* 49 (1968): 298–301.

C. Writings by and about Children of Holocaust Survivors

Epstein, Helen. *Children of the Holocaust: Conversations with the Sons and Daughters of Survivors.* New York: Putnam's 1979, and Bantam, 1980.

> The author, a child of Auschwitz survivors, relates the sometimes tragic, sometimes triumphant story of the sons and daughters born to survivors of Hitler's concentration camps. She also tells of her own quest to come to terms with her parents' past, which, in spite of their efforts to protect her, she accepted as her own. In pursuit of this quest she met hundreds of children of Holocaust survivors, whose stories she has related for this book.

Fogelman, Eva. "Awareness Groups for Children of Survivors." *Shoah* 1, no. 1 (Spring 1978): 8.

Podietz, Lenore. "The Holocaust Revisited in the Next Generation." *Analysis* 54 (December 1975): 1–5.

Rosensaft, Menachem Z. "Reflections of a Child of Holocaust Survivors." *Midstream* 27, no. 9 (November 1981): 31–33.

Sigal, John. "Second Generation Effects of Massive Psychic Trauma." In *Psychic Traumatization*, edited by William Niederland and Henry Krystal, pp. 55–66. Boston: Little, Brown, 1971.

Steinitz, Lucy, and Szonyi, David (eds). *Living After the Holocaust: Reflections of the Post-War Generation in America.* New York: Bloch, 1976, 1979.

> The editors present childhood memories and scholarly research which relate to the survivors and their families, reveal their inner turmoil, and explore how people cope with the experience of the Holocaust a generation later.

18.

Theological, Philosophical, Historical, Psychological, and Communal Perspectives on the Holocaust

A. Jewish Theological, Philosophical, and Communal Responses

Agus, Jacob B. "God and the Catastrophe." *Judaism* 18 (Summer 1964): 13–21.

Berkovits, Eliezer. *Faith After the Holocaust.* New York: Ktav, 1973.

> On the possibility of believing in God and divine revelation after Auschwitz—an eloquent persuasive argument for the continuity of Jewish belief after the Holocaust.

Blumenthal, David R. "The Popular Jewish Response and the Holocaust: An Initial Reflection." *Shoah* 2, no. 1 (Spring–Summer 1980): 3–5.

Borowitz, Eugene B. "Auschwitz and the Death of God: A Sermon." In *How Can a Jew Speak of Faith Today?* Philadelphia: Westminster Press, 1969.

Buber, Martin. *The Eclipse of God.* New York: Harper & Row, 1952; Westport, Conn.: Greenwood, 1977.

> Studies in the relation between religion and philosophy on evil and suffering—Buber's only major written response to the Holocaust.

Cohen, Arthur A. (ed.). *Arguments and Doctrines.* New York: Harper & Row, 1970.

A collection of writings that represent the responses of major Jewish thinkers in the post-Holocaust era. Cohen's meditation on the Holocaust revolves around Rudolf Otto's idea of the "tremendum"—an awesome event which disrupts and reshapes our whole perspective on the world.

Fackenheim, Emil. *God's Presence in History.* New York: New York University Press, 1970; Harper & Row pb., 1972.

One of contemporary Judaism's most important philosophers discusses the Holocaust throughout this very influential work. He posits the "614th commandment" of "Thou shalt not give Hitler posthumous victories."

————. *The Jewish Return into History: Reflections in the Age of Auschwitz, and a New Jerusalem.* New York: Schocken, 1978; pb., 1980.

This selection of essays deals with the implications of the Holocaust on Jewish faith and life, the ethical challenge and touchstone that the event, along with the 1967 reunification of Jerusalem, represents for both Jews and non-Jews. Fackenheim shows the deep connection, in terms of both history and faith, between the Holocaust and the founding of Israel.

————. *To Mend the World: Foundations of Future Jewish Thought.* New York: Schocken, 1983.

Fackenheim's most in-depth of the relationship between the Holocaust and faith, between the Holocaust and covenant, and between the Holocaust and the rest of Jewish history.

————. *Quest for Past and Future.* Boston: Beacon, 1968; pb., 1970.

A wide-ranging philosophical and theological work, parts of which deal with the Jewish condition after Auschwitz.

————. Popkin, Richard; Steiner, George; and Wiesel, Elie. "Jewish Values in the Post-Holocaust Future." *Judaism* 16 (Summer 1967): 269–299.

A remarkable symposium with a number of different approaches to the implications of the Holocaust.

Friedlander, Saul. *Reflections on Nazism: An Essay on Kitsch and Death.* New York: Harper & Row, 1984.

A short (160-page) essay on the portrayal and distortion of the Holocaust in historical writing, memoirs, novels, and films.

Gordis, Robert. "A Cruel God or None—Is There No Other Choice?" *Judaism* 21 (1972): 277–285.

Greenberg, Irving. *Confronting the Holocaust and Israel.* New York: National Jewish Resource Center, n.d.

A thoughtful discussion of the "voluntary covenant," the Jewish return to power and history, and possible links between the Holocaust and the founding of the State of Israel.

———. *The Holocaust: The Need to Remember.* New York: National Jewish Resource Center, n.d.

———. "Judaism and Christianity After the Holocaust." *Journal of Ecumenical Studies* 12, no. 4 (Fall 1975): 521–553.

———. "The State of Israel and the Challenge of Power to Jewish and Christian Philosophy." *Shoah* 1, no. 2 (Fall 1978): 21–23.

Heschel, Abraham Joshua. "The Meaning of This Hour." In *Man's Quest for God.* New York: Scribner's, 1979.

Katz, Steven T. *Post-Holocaust Dialogues: Critical Studies in Modern Jewish Thought.* New York: New York University Press, 1983.

A major study of Jewish thought in the post-Holocaust period, with essays on Martin Buber, Eliezer Berkovits, Richard Rubenstein, Emil Fackenheim, and Ignaz Maybaum.

Neher, Andre. *The Exile of the Word: From the Silence of the Bible to the Silence of Auschwitz.* Translated by David Maisel. Philadelphia: Jewish Publication Society, 1980.

Neher delves into the silence of God and man at Auschwitz and elsewhere.

Neusner, Jacob. *Stranger at Home: "The Holocaust," Zionism and American Judaism.* Chicago: University of Chicago Press, 1981.

The distinguished and prolific historian decries the use of the word "Holocaust," and what he sees as the overemphasis on the Holocaust in American Jewish life, in three of these fifteen essays.

Roskies, David G. *Night Words: A Midrash on the Holocaust.* Washington, D.C.: B'nai B'rith Hillel Foundation, n.d.

An "interpretation" of the Holocaust using traditional and modern sources, and arranged for thirty-six parts.

Rubenstein, Richard L. *After Auschwitz.* New York: Bobbs-Merrill, 1966.

One of the most controversial of the theological reflections on the Holocaust—Rubenstein believes that the murder of six million Jews necessitates a radical reinterpretation of traditional Jewish and Christian theologies.

Schulweis, Harold. "The Holocaust Dybbuk." *Moment* 1 (February 1976): 36–41.

Siegel, Seymour. "Theological Reflections on the Destruction of European Jewry." *Conservative Judaism* 18 (Summer 1964): 2–9.

Wiesel, Elie. *Ani Ma'amin.* New York: Random House, 1974.

A remarkable poetic statement of post-Holocaust belief, doubt, and theological turbulence.

———. *A Jew Today.* New York: Random House, 1978; Vintage pb.

A collection of essays reflecting upon the place of today's Jew in a world which lives in the shadow of the Holocaust—includes an essay entitled "A Plea for the Survivor."

———. *One Generation After.* New York: Avon, 1971; Schocken pb., 1982.

Reflections on the meaning of the twenty-five years after the close of World War II by a survivor of Auschwitz.

Wyschogrod, Michael. "Faith and the Holocaust." *Judaism* 20 (Summer 1971): 280—294.

A review-essay of—and response to—Fackenheim's *God's Presence in History.*

B. Christian Theological and Personal Responses

Cargas, Harry James. *A Christian Response to the Holocaust.* New York: Stonehenge Books, 1982.

A leading "post-Auschwitz Christian" examines the legacy of Christian anti-Semitism, the future of Jewish-Christian relations, and some paths for post-Holocaust Christian theology.

——— (ed.). *When God and Man Failed.* New York: Macmillan, 1981.

Nineteen essays by such outstanding Protestant and Catholic thinkers as Eva Fleischner, Robert McAfee Brown, Edward H. Flannery, John F. Pawlikowski, Harry James Cargas, Alice and Roy Eckardt, and Thomas A. Indinopoulos.

Davies, Alan T. *Anti-Semitism and the Christian Mind: The Crisis of Conscience After Auschwitz.* New York: Herder, 1969.

A major work examining the multifaceted challenges to the traditional Christian perception of the Jew in light of the Holocaust.

Eckardt, A. Roy. *Your People, My People.* New York: Quadrangle, 1974.

Eckardt examines the Holocaust's implications in terms of both Christian thought and life and Jewish-Christian relations.

—— and Eckardt, Alice. *Long Night's Journey Into Day: Life and Faith After the Holocaust.* Detroit: Wayne State University Press, 1982.

Seven penetrating essays on the implications of the Holocaust for contemporary Christianity, by two of the most thoughtful contemporary Protestant thinkers.

Fleischner, Eva. *Judaism in German Christian Theology Since 1945.* Metuchen N.J.: Scarecrow Press, 1975.

A learned investigation of a highly important subject by a leading Christian theologian.

Hick, John. **Evil and the God of Love.* New York: Harper & Row, 1966, 1977.

Examination of Christian theologies and their relationship to theodicy after the Holocaust.

Littell, Franklin H. *The Crucifixion of the Jews.* New York: Harper & Row, 1974.

Littell reexamines Christian attitudes toward Jews in light of the Holocaust. He argues that Christians need to radically rethink these attitudes toward the Jews, who are now—in part because of large-scale Christian indifference during the Holocaust—a "crucified" people.

McGarry, Michael B. **Christology After Auschwitz.* New York: Paulist Press, 1977; pb., 1977.

A penetrating summary of various approaches to Christology since the Holocaust by a number of significant Jewish, Protestant, and Catholic thinkers.

Moltmann, Jurgen. *The Crucified God.* New York: Harper & Row, 1974.

An important, if highly controversial, work of post-Holocaust theology by a major German theologian.

————. "The Jewish People and the Holocaust." *Journal of the American Academy of Religion* 44 (December 1976): 675–691.

Pawlikowski, John T. "The Holocaust and Catholic Theology: Some Reflections." *Shoah* 2, no. 1 (Spring–Summer 1980): 6–9.

Peck, Abraham (ed.). *Jews and Christians After the Holocaust.* Philadelphia: Fortress Press, 1982.

Seven essays by leading Jewish and Christian theologians.

Rausch, David A. *The Legacy of Hatred: Christians Must Not Forget the Holocaust.* Chicago: Moody Press, 1984.

On the roots of the Holocaust, including Christian anti-Jewish teachings, and on the Holocaust as an object lesson in racial and religious hatred.

Sherman, Franklin. "Speaking of God After Auschwitz." *Worldview* 17, no. 9 (September 1974): 26–30.

A Christian articulation of a Heschelian position on the question of theodicy in light of the Holocaust.

Siirala, Aarne. *Voice of Illness.* Philadelphia: Fortress Press, 1964.

A Lutheran theologian's thoughtful reflections after a visit to a death camp.

Simon, Ulrich. *A Theology of Auschwitz.* Atlanta: John Knox Press, 1979.

An attempt to integrate the Holocaust into classical Christian categories.

Van Buren, Paul M. *Discerning the Way: A Theology of the Jewish-Christian Reality.* New York: Seabury Press, 1980.

A noted Christian theologian reflects on the implications of the Holocaust and the founding of the State of Israel for Jewish-Christian relations.

Willis, Robert. "Christian Theology After Auschwitz." *Journal of Ecumenical Studies* 12 (Fall 1975): 493–515.

C. German Responses

Bird, Keith. " 'Germany Awakes': The 'Holocaust'—Background and Aftermath." *Shoah* 1, no. 4 (Summer 1979): 5–9.

Eckardt, Alice, and Eckardt, Roy. "German Thinkers View the Holocaust." *Christian Century* 93, no. 9 (March 17, 1976): 249–252.

Herzfeld, Hans. "Germany: After the Catastrophe." *JCH* 2, no. 1 (January 1967): 79–93.

Jaspers, Karl. *The Question of German Guilt. New York: Dial, 1947: Capricorn pb., 1961; Westport, Conn.: Greenwood Press, 1978.

A fascinating treatment of this important topic by Germany's foremost philosophical minds—Jaspers acknowledges how popular the Nazis were with the German public.

———— and Augstein, Rudolf. "The Criminal State and German Responsibility." *Commentary* 40 (February 1966): 33–39.

A dialogue between Jaspers, one of the founders of modern existentialism, and Augstein, the publisher of Germany's largest weekly news magazine, on the issue of Nazi murderers, and the question of extending the statute of limitations on their prosecution.

Kalow, Gert. *The Shadow of Hitler: A Critique of Political Consciousness.* Translated from the German by Betsy Ross. London: Rapp & Whiting, 1968.

The author, a former Nazi, describes the German mind and ideology after Hitler.

Lang, Daniel. *A Backward Look: Germans Remember.* New York: McGraw-Hill, 1979.

Lang interviewed several dozen Germans who served in civilian units at the end of World War II, and captures their reflections on the Nazi period.

D. Philosophical and Moral Implications

Cargas, Harry James. "Letter to a Friend." *Shoah* 2, no. 1 (Spring–Summer 1980): 37–38.

On the issue of focusing on study of the Holocaust, to the "exclusion" of other instances of mass persecution.

Jonas, Hans. "Immorality and the Modern Temper." *Harvard Theological Review* 55 (1960): 1–20.

A philosophical-theological response to the Holocaust.

Langer, Lawrence. *Versions of Survival: The Holocaust and the Human Spirit.* Albany: State University of New York Press, 1982.

Four long, remarkable essays entitled "Language as Refuge," "Auschwitz: the Death of Choice," "Elie Wiesel—Divided Voice in a Divided Universe," and "Gertrud Kolmar and Nelly Sachs— Bright Visions and Songs of Lamentations."

Roth, John K. "The Holocaust and Freedom to Choose." *Shoah* 2, no. 1 (Spring–Summer 1980): 19–22.

Steiner, George. "A Kind of Survivor" (1965) and "Postscript" (1966). In *Language and Silence: Essays on Language, Literature and the Inhuman*, pp. 140–154 and 155–170. New York: Atheneum, 1967.

These essays comprise a section "Language Out of the Darkness," which connects the unreality of the human barbarism of the Holocaust with the European "civilization" of the time.

Wiesenthal, Simon. *The Sunflower*. New York: Schocken, 1976.

A symposium on views of the Nazi war crimes and the question of forgiving—it contains a short story followed by the comments of many individuals, religious and secular, dealing with the question of forgiveness.

E. Historical Perspectives

Bauer, Yehuda. *The Holocaust in Historical Perspective*. Seattle: University of Washington Press, 1978; pb., 1979.

Bauer includes an overview on the causes of the Holocaust and a long essay on the Joel Brand affair.

———. *The Jewish Emergence from Powerlessness*. Toronto: University of Toronto Press, 1979; pb., 1982.

Essays on the significance of the Holocaust in the context of modern Jewish history, particularly the relative powerlessness which Diaspora existence entailed.

———; Rotenstreich, Nathan; and Lowe, Malcolm (eds.). *The Holocaust as Historical Experience*. New York: Holmes & Meier, 1981.

An excellent anthology of articles by thirteen leading Israeli and American scholars on the "Background," "Witness and Case Studies," and "The Judenrat and the Jewish Response."

Dawidowicz, Lucy S. *The Holocaust and the Historians*. Cambridge, Mass.: Harvard University Press, 1981.

On the historiography of the Holocaust in England, Russia, Germany, Poland, and the United States.

Esh, Saul. "The Dignity of the Destroyed." *Judaism* 11 (Spring 1962): 99–111.

Fein, Helen. "A Formula for Genocide: Comparison of Turkish Genocide (1915) and German Holocaust (1939–1945)." *Comparative Studies in Sociology* 1 (1978): 271–293.

Feingold, Henry L. "Determining the Uniqueness of the Holocaust: The Factor of Historical Valence." *Shoah* 2, no. 1 (Spring 1981): 3–11.

Fleischner, Eva (ed.). *Auschwitz: Beginning of a New Era?* New York: Ktav, 1977.

A truly valuable volume of essays on the implications of the Holocaust by participants at an international symposium, including Elie Wiesel, Rosemary Radford Ruether, Irving Greenberg, Gregory Baum, and Emil Fackenheim.

Rubenstein, Richard L. *The Age of Triage: Fear and Hope in an Overcrowded World*. New York: Harper & Row, 1982.

———. *The Cunning of History*. New York: Harper & Row, 1975, pb., 1978.

In both these stimulating books, Rubenstein posits the hypothesis that the Holocaust represented but one—if the ultimate—attempt by a modern government to deal with the problem of "surplus population."

Starr, Joshua, and Shapiro, Leon. "Recent Population Data Regarding the Jews in Europe." *JSS* 8, no. 2 (April 1946): 75–86.

On the demographic catastrophe.

Tal, Uriel. "Excursus on the Term *Shoah*." *Shoah* 1, no. 4 (Summer 1979): 10–11.

F. Personal Reflections and Responses

Améry, Jean. *At the Mind's Limits*. Translated by Sidney and Stella P. Rosenfeld. Bloomington: Indiana University Press, 1980.

Five remarkable autobiographical essays by a survivor of Auschwitz which constitute profound contemplations on the death camp's mental, moral, and physical implications.

Berliner, Gert. "Living with the Knowledge of the Holocaust." *Midstream* 16 (June–July 1970): 33–40.

A photographic essay which includes photographs of concentration camp sites and seven poems related to the Holocaust.

Parker, Frank S. "A Visit to Majdanek." *Judaism* 25 (Spring 1976): 158–166.

Pisar, Samuel. *Of Blood and Hope*. Boston: Little, Brown, 1980.

> The memoir of a survivor of Auschwitz who is now an adviser on international trade relations. Pisar discusses the implications of the Holocaust for contemporary world affairs.

Wiesel, Elie. "Faces from the Holocaust." *Jewish Digest* 17 (August 1973): 43–46.

> An address given at the opening of an exhibition of captured Nazi photographs.

G. Psychological Responses

Frankl, Victor. *Man's Search for Meaning* (orig. title, *From Death Camp to Existentialism*). Boston: Beacon Press, 1963; New York: Washington Square Press, 1964; rev. ed., Touchstone/Simon & Schuster, 1984.

> The theory of logotherapy, by a professor of psychiatry and neurology at the University of Vienna who was imprisoned in concentration camps for over three years.

Kren, George M., and Rappoport, Leon. *The Holocaust and the Crisis of Human Behavior*. New York: Holmes & Meier, 1980.

> A controversial psychohistorical examination of the Holocaust which focuses equally on killers and victims.

Mitscherlich, Alexander, and Mitscherlich, Margarete. *The Inability to Mourn*. New York: Grove Press, 1975.

> Two German psychoanalysts explore the psychic defenses against guilt, remorse, and shame of their countrymen in the aftermath of the Nazi atrocities.

19.

Educating Others on the Holocaust: Learning About It; Scholarly and Methodological Issues

A. Teaching the Holocaust and Related Educational Issues

Anti-Defamation League of B'nai B'rith. *Holocaust and Genocide: A Search for Conscience*. New York: ADL, 1984.

> Two volumes designed for teaching a course or workshop on the Holocaust: *Curriculum Guide*, edited by Richard F. Flaim and Edwin W. Reynolds, includes an introductory overview, six teaching units, and audiovisual-resource guide; *Anthology for Students*, edited by Harry Furman, provides materials from diaries, novels, short stories, newspaper articles, and Nazi propaganda, as well as discussion topics and values-clarification exercises.

Baron, Lawrence. "Teaching the Holocaust to Non-Jews." *Shoah* 2, no. 2 (Spring 1981): 14–15.

Bayme, Steven, and Roberts, Julian. "Yeshiva University's Summer Institute on Teaching the Holocaust." *Shoah* 1, no. 3 (Winter 1979): 16–17.

Blumenkrantz, Bernhard. "How Holocaust History Is Not Taught— Shortcomings of French Textbooks." *Patterns of Prejudice* 9, no. 3 (May–June 1975): 8–12.

Carmon, Arye. "Teaching the Holocaust." *M&R* 6, no. 5 (May–June 1980): 12.

Davis, Perry. "The New York City Holocaust Curriculum." *Shoah* 2, no. 2 (Fall 1978): 4–7.

Des Pres, Terence. "The Dreaming Back." *Centerpoint* 4, no. 1 (Fall 1980): 13–18.

On the temptations and dangers in Holocaust studies.

Douglas, Donald M. "Teaching the Holocaust—The Kansas Experience." *Shoah* 1, no. 4 (Summer 1979): 17–18.

Fein, Helen. "The Treatment of Genocide in U.S. Sociology Textbooks." *Patterns of Prejudice* 13, nos. 2–3 (March–June 1979): 31–36.

Friedlander, Henry. *On the Holocaust.* New York: Anti-Defamation League, 1973.

A critique of the treatment of the Holocaust in history textbooks, accompanied by an annotated bibliography.

Goldman, Martin S. "Teaching the Holocaust: Some Suggestions for Comparative Analysis." *Journal of Intergroup Relations* 6 (December 1977): 23–30.

Hirt, Robert S., and Kessner, Thomas (eds.). *Issues in Teaching the Holocaust: A Guide.* New York: Yeshiva University Press, 1981.

The first major anthology which deals with the host of resources, approaches, and problematics in teaching the Holocaust, in eight brief essays.

"The Holocaust." *Social Education* 4, no. 4 (April 1978).

The entire issue is on teaching the Holocaust. Contributors discuss some of the key methodological issues and problems.

Kalfus, Richard. "Culture During the Nazi Era: An Interdisciplinary Course in the Community College." *Shoah* 2, no. 2 (Spring 1981): 16–18.

Kolinsky, Martin, and Kolinsky, Eva. "The Treatment of the Holocaust in West German Textbooks." *YVS* 10 (1974): 149–216.

Korman, Gerd. "Silence in American Textbooks." *YVS* 8 (1970): 183–202.

Lipstadt, Deborah E. "We Are Not Job's Children." *Shoah* 1, no. 4 (Summer 1979): 12–16.

A personal reflection on teaching the Holocaust at the college level.

Littell, Franklin. "Holocaust Studies in Philadelphia." *Shoah* 1, no. 1 (Spring 1978): 8.

Meisel, Esther. "The Use of Literature in the Teaching of the Holocaust." *Shoah* 2, no. 1 (Spring–Summer 1980): 26–30.

Muffs, Judith Herschlag. "U.S. Teaching on the Holocaust." *Patterns of Prejudice* 11, no. 3 (May–June 1977): 28–29.

Nick, Ann L. *Teacher's Guide to the Holocaust.* New York: Anti-Defamation League, 1977.

Pate, Glenn. "The Treatment of the Holocaust in United States History Textbooks." New York: Anti-Defamation League, 1980.

Raphael, Marc Lee. "Yom Ha-Shoah and Holocaust Education in an Israeli High School." *Shoah* 2, no. 2 (Spring 1981): 12–13.

Roskies, Diane K. *Teaching the Holocaust to Children.* New York: Ktav, 1975.

Roth, John K. "Difficulties Everywhere: Sober Reflections on Teaching About the Holocaust." *Shoah* 1, no. 2 (Fall 1978): 1–3.

Schallenberger, E. Horst, and Stein, Gerd. "Jewish History in German Textbooks." *Patterns of Prejudice.* (September–October 1976): 15–21.

Sherwin, Byron. "The Spertus College of Judaica Holocaust Studies Curriculum." *Shoah* 1, no. 1 (Spring 1978): 9–10.

Zornberg, Ira. *Classroom Strategies for Teaching About the Holocaust: Ten Lessons for Classroom Use.* New York: Anti-Defamation League, 1983.

> Provides a host of practical resources: recommended readings, discussion questions, classroom scenarios, and lesson plans.

B. Learning About the Holocaust in Memorials, Centers, Archives, and Through Travel

Crowe, David M., Sr. "The Holocaust: Documents in the National Archives of the United States." *AJH* 70, no. 3 (March 1981): 362–378.

Cummings, Susan. "The Montreal Holocaust Memorial." *Shoah* 1, no. 2 (Fall 1978): 20.

Dinur, Benzion. "Problems Confronting Yad Vashem in Its Work of Research." *YVS* 1 (1957): 7–30.

Etkind, Louise. "New Haven Dedicates a Memorial." *Shoah* 1, no. 1 (Spring 1978): 7.

Fine, Ellen S., and Knopp, Josephine A. "Witnesses—A Tour of Remembrance." *Shoah* 2, no. 1 (Spring–Summer 1980): 23–25, 30.

> On an educators' tour of Holocaust sites in Europe.

In Everlasting Remembrance. New York: American Jewish Congress,
1969.

> A 48-page pamphlet which is a guide to memorials and monu-
> ments throughout the world honoring the Jews murdered in the
> death camps.

Zuroff, Efraim. "Yad Vashem: More Than a Memorial, More Than a
'Name." *Shoah* 1, no. 3 (Winter 1979): 4–9.

C. Scholarly and Methodological Issues

Arendt, Hannah. "Social Science Techniques and the Study of the
Concentration Camps." *JSS* 12, no. 1 (January 1950): 49–64.

> An article which warns against, among other things, the dangers of
> using analogies when discussing the Holocaust.

Ball-Kaduri, K. Y. "Evidence of Witnesses, Its Value and Limitations."
YVS 3 (1959): 79–90.

Bar-On, Zvi, and Levin, Dov. "Problems Relating to a Questionnaire on
the Holocaust." *YVS* 3 (1959): 91–118.

Bauer, Yehuda. "Trends in Holocaust Research." *YVS* 12 (1977): 7–36.

Blumenthal, David R. "Scholarly Approaches to the Holocaust." *Shoah*
1, no. 3 (Winter 1979): 21–27.

Dawidowicz, Lucy S. "Lies About the Holocaust." *Commentary* 70, no.
6 (December 1980): 31–37.

> A survey of so-called revisionist historians, such as Arthur Butz,
> who distort history in an attempt to deny the Holocaust.

———. "Towards a History of the Holocaust." *Commentary* 47 (April
1969): 51–56.

Deml, Ferdinand. "Antisemitismus in German Encyclopedias." *WLB*
21, no. 9 (1967): 31–36.

Dorpaler, Andreas. "The Weimar Republic and Nazi Era in East German
Perspective." *CEH* 11, no. 3 (September 1978): 211–231.

Eliav, Binjamin. "The Holocaust in the *Encyclopaedia Judaica*." *YVS* 9
(1973): 247–254.

Fein, Helen. "Holocaust Chronicles." *Jewish Spectator* 34 (Fall 1974): 52–54.

Friedman, Philip. "Research and Literature on the Recent Jewish Tragedy." *JSS* 12, no. 1 (January 1950): 17–26.

———. "Preliminary and Methodological Problems of the Research on the Jewish Catastrophe in the Nazi Period." *YVS* 2 (1958): 95–132.

———. "Problems of Research on the Jewish Catastrophe." *YVS* 3 (1959): 25–40.

Gringanz, Samuel. "Some Methodological Problems in the Study of the Ghetto." *JSS* 12, no. 1 (January 1950): 65–72.

Huttenbach, Henry R. "The Holocaust as Seen by East Germany." *M&R* 7, no. 5 (May–June 1981): 16.

Katz, Jacob. "Was the Holocaust Predictable?" *Commentary* 59 (May 1975): 41–48.

Without definitely answering the question, Katz offers valuable insights into important areas of discussion and evaluation of historical portents.

Kermish, J. "Mutilated Versions of Ringelblum's Notes." *YIVO Annual* 8 (1953): 289–301.

Korman, Gerd. "The Holocaust in American Historical Writing." *Societas* 2, no. 3 (Summer 1972): 251–270.

———. "Silence in American Textbooks." *YVS* 8 (1970): 183–202.

Two valuable studies which attack American historians and American textbooks for ignoring Jewish victims in their study of the Holocaust.

———. "Warsaw Plus Thirty: Some Perceptions in the Sources and Written History of the Ghetto Uprising." *YIVO Annual* 15 (1974): 180–196.

Korzen, Meir. "Problems Arising out of Research into the History of Jewish Refugees in the USSR During the Second World War." *YVS* 3 (1959): 119–140.

Kwiet, Konrad. "Problems of Jewish Resistance Historiography." *LBI Yrbk* 24 (1979): 37–60.

Lamm, Hans. "Notes on the Number of Jewish Victims of National Socialism." *JSS* 21, no. 2 (April 1959): 132–134.

Luck, David. "Use and Abuse of Holocaust Documents: Reitlinger and 'How Many?' " *JSS* 41, no. 2 (Spring 1979): 95–122.

Mark, Bernard. "Problems Related to the Study of the Jewish Resistance Movement in the Second World War." *YVS* 3 (1959): 41–66.

Rothkirchen, Livia. "The Zionist Character of the 'Self-Government' of Terezin: A Study in Historiography." *YVS* 11 (1976): 56–90.

Tal, Uriel. "On the Study of Holocaust and Genocide." *YVS* 13 (1979): 7–52.

Yahil, Leni. "Historians of the Holocaust—A Plea for a New Approach." *WLB* 12, no. 10 (1967–68): 2–10.

———. "The Holocaust in Jewish Historiography." *YVS* 7 (1968): 57–74.

20.

The Art of the Holocaust: The Holocaust on Television, in Film, and in Photography

A. Art

Aptecker, George. *Beyond Despair*. Morristown, N.J.: Kahn & Kahn, 1981.

> Statements by Elie Wiesel and a number of major Jewish historians are juxtaposed with fifty-three black-and-white photographs in this photographic essay on the Holocaust.

Banasiewicz, Czeslaw Z. (ed.). *The Warsaw Ghetto: Drawings by Jozef Kaliszan*. New York: Thomas Yoseloff, 1968.

Blatter, Janet, and Milton, Sybil. **Art of the Holocaust*. New York: Rutledge Press, 1981.

Ten years in the making, this volume includes over 350 reproductions (32 in color) of art created in concentration and death camps by 150 artists, as well as separate essays on Holocaust art by Blatter and Milton, as well as an overview history of the Holocaust by Henry Friedlander.

Constanza, Mary S. *The Living Witness: Art in the Concentration Camps and the Ghettoes.* New York: Macmillan, 1982.

A volume combining more than 100 drawings and interviews with artist-survivors.

Dawidowicz, Lucy. *Spiritual Resistance: Art from Concentration Camps, 1940–1945.* Philadelphia: Jewish Publication Society, 1978, 1981.

Reproductions of about eighty works from concentration camps, with a valuable introduction by Dawidowicz.

Green, Gerald. *The Artists of Terezin.* New York: Hawthorn Books, 1969, and Schocken, 1978.

Focuses on art work of Otto Unger, Bedrich Fritter, Leo Haas, and Karel Fleischman.

Greenspan, Ida. "Drawings." *Centerpoint* 4, no. 1 (Fall 1980): 43–45.

Lasansky, Mauricio. *The Nazi Drawings.* Text by Edwin Honig, drawings by M. Lasansky. Philadelphia Museum of Art, 1967; Iowa City: University of Iowa Press, 1976.

These thirty sketches represent the Nazi horror. Lasansky wrote, "When mid-twentieth-century Germany did not let man live and die with this right [dignity], man became an animal." The sketches depict this animal.

Mendelson, Marcel L. "Selinger's Monument." *Centerpoint* 4, no. 1 (Fall 1980): 30–31.

Mendjinsky, Maurice. *To the Memory of the Martyr Fighters of the Warsaw Ghetto.* Translated by Mifa Martin. Scarsdale, N.Y.: Donald G. Reynolds, n.d.

Includes thirty-five drawings by Mendjinsky, a previously unpublished poem by Paul Eluard, and a text by Vercors.

Salomon, Charlotte. *A Diary in Pictures.* New York: Harcourt, Brace, 1963; Viking, 1981.

Drawings by a young Jewish girl made before her deportation to Auschwitz—a moving counterpart to Anne Frank's work. The 1981 edition is greatly expanded and includes all the drawings.

Toll, Nelly. *Without Surrender: Art of the Holocaust*. Philadelphia: Running Press, 1978.

While, unfortunately, none of the prints in this anthology are in color, it is still an excellent guide to Holocaust art and has a number of good accompanying essays.

Volakova, Hana (ed.). + *I Never Saw Another Butterfly*. New York: Schocken, 1983.

Children's drawings and poems from Theresienstadt—one of the most moving books on the Holocaust.

"Walter Spitzer: The Artist as Witness." *Centerpoint* 4, no. 1 (Fall 1980): 87–94.

Yaffe, Richard. *Nathan Rapoport: Monuments and Sculptures*. New York: Shengold, 1980.

A pictorial study of the visual art of the leading sculptor of Holocaust memorials and monuments.

B. Television

Allen, Charles R., Jr. "*Holocaust*: On Commercializing Genocide." *M&R* 4, no. 4 (May–June 1978): 8.

Blumenthal, David R. "*Holocaust* and the Holocaust." *M&R* 5, no. 1 (September–October 1978): 8.

Dawidowicz, Lucy. "Visualizing the Warsaw Ghetto." *Shoah* 1, no. 1 (Spring 1978): 5–6, 17–18.

A critique of the BBC film *The Warsaw Ghetto*.

Druks, Herbert. "Green vs. the Experts." *M&R* 4, no. 4 (May–June 1978): 10.

On Gerald Green's *Holocaust*.

Elliman, Wendy. "Israel and the Holocaust." *M&R* 5, no. 3 (January–February 1979): 4.

Israel and Green's *Holocaust*.

Feingold, Henry. "Four Days in April: A review of NBC's Dramatization of the Holocaust." *Shoah* 1, no. 1 (Spring 1978): 15–17.

Kuperstein, Isaiah. *"Playing for Time*: A Review." *Shoah* 2, no. 4 (Spring 1981): 19–20.

A review of the television dramatization of Fania Fenelon's memoir.

Wiesel, Elie. "Trivializing the Holocaust." *M&R* 4, no. 4 (May–June 1978): 9.

Response to Green's TV special, *Holocaust.*

C. Film

Doneson, Judith E. "The Jew as a Female Figure in Holocaust Film." *Shoah* 1, no. 1 (Spring 1978): 12–13.

Insdorf, Annette. **Indelible Shadows.* New York: Random House, 1983; Vintage pb., 1983.

A superb critical overview of major feature films on the Holocaust from many countries, this is certain to be the work on the subject for years to come.

Isaac, Dan. "Film and the Holocaust." *Centerpoint* 4, no. 1 (Fall 1980): 137–139.

Soudet, Pierre. "Misuses of the Holocaust by the Film Industry." *Centerpoint* 4, no. 1 (Fall 1980): 151–152.

D. Photography

Cargas, Harry James. "Holocaust Photography." *Centerpoint* 4, no. 1 (Fall 1980): 141–150.

21.

Non-Jewish Victims of the Holocaust

Note: To date there has been no good bibliography on non-Jewish victims of the Nazis, including gypsies, Poles, Russians, and other Slavs, political dissidents, and homosexuals. The list which follows—a few works culled from other bibliographies and my own research—represents only a very modest beginning.

A. Gypsies

Acton, Thomas. *Gypsy Politics and Social Change.* London and Boston: Routledge & Kegan Paul, 1974.

Cohn, Werner. *The Gypsies.* Reading, Mass: Addison-Wesley, 1973.

Friedman, Philip. "How the Gypsies Were Persecuted." *WLB* 3–4 (1950).

Kenrich, Donald, and Puxon, G. *The Destiny of Europe's Gypsies.* New York: Basic Books, 1972.

> The only book-length account in English of the gypsies' fate during the Holocaust

Puxon, Grattar. *Rom: Europe's Gypsies.* London: Minority Rights Group Report no. 14 (March 1973).

Schechtman, Joseph. "The Gypsy Problem." *Midstream,* November 1966, pp. 52–60.

Yates, Dora E. "Hitler and the Gypsies." *Commentary* 8, no. 5 (November 1949): 455–459.

Yoors, Jan. *Crossing.* New York: Simon & Schuster, 1971.

———. *The Gypsies.* New York: Simon & Schuster, 1967.

B. Homosexuals

Garde, Noel I. *Jonathan to Gide: The Homosexual in History.* New York: Vantage, 1964; New York: Nosbooks, 1969.

> Garde's work includes sections on Magnus Hirschfeld (pp. 674–677), Prince Evlenberg-Hertelfeld (pp. 679–683), and Ernst Röhm (pp. 722–727).

Heger, Heinz. *The Men with the Pink Triangle.* Translated by David Fernbach. Boston: Alyson Publications, 1980.

> A short account of the Nazi persecution of homosexuals.

Rector, Frank. *The Nazi Extermination of Homosexuals.* New York: Stein & Day, 1981.

> This is the first major book-length study in English of the Nazi persecution of homosexuals. It is clear and well written.

Young, Allen. "Magnus Hirschfeld: Gay Liberation's Zeyde (Grandfather)." In *Chutzpah: A Jewish Liberation Anthology.* San Francisco: New Glide Publications, 1977.

C. Slavic Victims

Hillel, Marc, and Henry, Clarissa. **Of Pure Blood.* New York: McGraw-Hill, 1977, and Pocket Books, 1978.

> The terrifying story of how Hitler's adjutants tried to organize a breeding plan to produce a Nordic race.

Thompson, Larry V. "Lebensborn and the Eugenics Policy of the Reichfuhrer-SS." *CEH* 4, No. 1 (March 1971): 54–78.

Wytwycky, Bohdan. **The Other Holocaust: Many Circles of Hell.* Washington, D.C.: Novak Report, 1981.

> A brief overview of the Nazi persecution and killing of gypsies, Poles, Ukrainians, and Belorussians.

22.

Bibliographies and Bibliographical Essays

A. General Bibliographies on the Holocaust

Cargas, Harry J. *The Holocaust: An Annotated Bibliography*. Haverford, Pa.: Catholic Library Association, 1977.

> A comprehensive bibliography of over 400 items arranged according to topics.

Joseph, Sharon. *The Holocaust: An Annotated Bibliography*. Montreal: National Holocaust Remembrance Committee of the Canadian Jewish Congress, 1980.

> A nicely designed, useful resource guide which also includes eleven nonbibliographical sections, including "photographic aids," "resource kits," and "teachers' guides and classroom libraries."

Friedlander, Henry. "The Holocaust: Anti-Semitism and the Jewish Tragedy." In *The Study of Judaism: Bibliographical Essays*, pp. 207–229. New York: Ktav and Anti-Defamation League, 1972.

Kehr, Helen (ed.). *Persecution and Resistance under the Nazis*. Part I: Reprint of Catalogue no. 1 (2d ed.); Part II: New Material and Amendments. London: Institute of Contemporary History, 1978.

> A catalogue of the extensive collection on the Nazi regime at the Institute for Contemporary History.

Muffs, Judith Herschlag. *The Holocaust in Books and Films: A Selected, Annotated List*. New York: Anti-Defamation League, 1981.

> A particularly useful, thoughtfully annotated guide targeted toward high school and college teachers.

Robinson, Jacob. *The Holocaust and After: Sources and Literature in English.* Jerusalem: Israel Universities Press; distributed by Transaction Books, New Brunswick, N.J., 1973.

A detailed resource work which is crucial for any student of the Holocaust.

————. *The Holocaust: The Nuremberg Evidence.* Jerusalem and New York: Yad Vashem and YIVO, 1966.

A cataloguing of the extensive evidence offered at the eleven-month trial, and additional books and articles on the subject.

———— and Bauer, Yehuda (eds.). *Guide to Unpublished Materials of the Holocaust Period.* 3 vols. Jerusalem: Ahva Cooperative Press, 1970–75.

This multivolume guide to unpublished memoirs and other works is an invaluable tool for the scholar.

———— and Friedman, Philip. *Guide to Jewish History under Nazi Impact.* New York and Jerusalem: YIVO and Yad Vashem, 1960; New York: Ktav, 1974.

This is by far the most comprehensive listing of works on Jewish life and scholarship during the Holocaust.

B. Specialized Bibliographies

Abramowitz, Molly. *Elie Wiesel: A Bibliography.* Metuchen, N.J.: Scarecrow Press, 1978.

Ball-Kaduri, K.Y. "Testimonies and Recollections about Activities Organized by German Jewry During the Years 1933–1945 (Catalogue of Manuscripts in the Yad Vashem Archives)." *YVS* 4 (1960): 317–339.

Ben-Yosef, Avraham. "Bibliography of Yiddish Publications in the U.S.S.R. During 1941–1948." *YVS* 4 (1960): 135–166.

Braham, Randolph. *The Hungarian Jewish Catastrophes: A Selected and Annotated Bibliography.* Jerusalem and New York: Yad Vashem and YIVO, 1962.

Hirshberg, Jeffrey. "The Holocaust in Literature, 1978–1979: A Bibliography." *Shoah* 2, no. 1 (Spring–Summer 1980): 31–36.

Singerman, Robert. *Anti-Semitic Propaganda: An Annotated Bibliography and Guide.* New York: Garland, 1982.

Contains 24,000 entries on anti-Semitic works in English.

Szmeruk, Ch. "Yiddish Publications in the U.S.S.R. (from the Late Thirties to 1948)." *YVS* 4 (1960): 99–134.

The Third Reich, 1933–1939: A Historical Bibliography. Santa Barbara, Calif.: ABC—Clio Research Guide no. 10, 1984.

An excellent resource of over 300 pages, which contains abstracts of 1,024 articles published throughout the world from 1973 to 1982.

Weimar Germany: A Historical Bibliography. Santa Barbara, Calif.: ABC—Clio Research Guide no. 9, 1983.

This 300-page volume contains 1,034 abstracts drawn from over 2,000 journals in forty-two languages.

C. Bibliographical Essays

Friedman, Philip. "American Jewish Research and Literature on the Jewish Catastrophe of 1939–1945." *JSS* 13, no. 3 (July 1951): 235–250.

——— and Pinson, Koppel S. "Some Books on the Jewish Catastrophe." *JSS* 12, no. 1 (January 1950): 83–94.

Lowenthal, E. G. "In the Shadow of Doom—Post-War Publications on Jewish Communal History in German." *LBI Yrbk* 11 (1966): 306–335.

Michaelis, Meir. "The Duce and the Jews: An Assessment of the Literature on Italian Jewry Under Fascism 1922–1945." *YVS* 11 (1976): 17–32.

Section I-B

Literature of the Holocaust: A Select Bibliography

by Jeffrey Hirshberg and David G. Roskies

Since 1940 there have been at least two literatures of the Holocaust: one written from within, the other written from outside the "concentrationary universe." Each body of writing has its own potential greatness, one that has been duly recognized in the work of the Nobel laureates—Agnon, Bellow, Milosz, Sachs, Singer—who have contributed to our understanding of the Holocaust from both literary perspectives. Each perspective, however, must also bear inherent limitations. For the survivor-as-writer these limitations are perhaps above all the strictures of language: no understandable syntax can be so contorted, and no vocabulary can be at once as objective and believable, as is necessary to describe the enormities of Auschwitz. For the outsider, whose first formidable task may often be to imagine the unimaginable, the limitations may be less linguistic than formal: the serious documentary literature of Hochhuth, Weiss, and Epstein on the one hand, and the melodrama of Uris and Green on the other—to say nothing of the sensationalism of *The Boys from Brazil* and its kin—are frequently too prone to stereotyped characterizations and attitudes to be effective as art.

Every art has its limitations, and the literature of the Holocaust is clearly no exception. Keeping both perspectives toward the Holocaust in mind, works have been included to suggest the wide range of subjects and time-periods with which writers have been concerned: events prior to Hitler's ascendancy; the ghettos; the concentration camps; liberation and camps for displaced persons; survivors and survival in Israel, the United States, and elsewhere; post-Holocaust revenge. Yet works for which the Holocaust is not essential have been excluded. Romances in DP camps which could have been set elsewhere, war stories focusing upon Jews in American battalions, and post-Holocaust pursuits of Nazis which differ only marginally from other novels of manhunts and revenge—works, in short, for which the Holocaust is reduced to a gratuitous series of events—will in general not be found here.

Nor will books and essays which are more properly considered memoirs and diaries, though the line between fiction and memoir is frequently blurred in Holocaust writings. There is no question here that many memoirs are among the most moving works of Holocaust literature, but the present bibliography remains limited to works of imaginative literature—fiction, poetry, and drama—and to literary criticism, all of which are available in English (though they have been translated from over a dozen tongues). The reader interested in pursuing Holocaust memoirs and eyewitness accounts would do well to start with the bibliographies by Cargas and Robinson cited in Section I-A of this Guide.

In the interests of space and maximum usability, books published by vanity presses or "off the beaten track" are not included here. Conversely, works known to have appeared in paperback as recently as 1983 are marked with an asterisk.

1. Anthologies

Eliach, Yaffa. *Hassidic Tales of the Holocaust. New York: Oxford University Press, 1982.

   Nearly ninety tales—some apparently true, some legends—which affirm the faith of both the protagonists and the talebearers.

Friedlander, Albert H. (ed.). *Out of the Whirlwind: A Reader of Holocaust Literature. New York: Union of American Hebrew Congregations, 1968; Schocken pb., 1976.

   Especially useful as an introduction to the literature.

Gordon-Mlotek, Eleanor, and Gottlieb, Malka (eds.). We Are Here: Songs of the Holocaust. Foreword by Elie Wiesel, singable translations by Roslyn Resnick-Perry, illustrations by Tsirl Waletzky. New York: Education Department of the Workmen's Circle, 1983.

   An important collection of ghetto and partisan songs—music was one of the Jews' most important means of communication during the Holocaust.

Kuncewicz, Maria (ed.). *The Modern Polish Mind: An Anthology of Stories and Essays by Writers Living in Poland Today.* New York: Universal Library pb., 1963.

Includes an impressive section of postwar writing on the Holocaust not available elsewhere.

Leftwich, Joseph (ed. and trans.). *The Golden Peacock: A Worldwide Treasury of Yiddish Poetry.* New York and London: Thomas Yoseloff, 1961.

Includes a section devoted to poems of the Holocaust.

Meltzer, Milton (ed.). *Never to Forget: The Jews of the Holocaust.* New York: Harper & Row, 1976; Dell pb., 1977.

Excerpts from poems, diaries, letters.

Robinson, Armin L. (ed.). *The Ten Commandments: Ten Short Novels of Hitler's War Against the Moral Code.* New York: Simon & Schuster, 1943.

Each of these ten brief novels, by such authors as Thomas Mann, Rebecca West, and André Maurois, deals with the Nazi desecration of one of the Ten Commandments.

2. Fiction

Adams, Nathan M. *The Fifth Horseman.* New York: Random House, 1967.

Israeli intelligence officer in pursuit of a Nazi war criminal.

Aichinger, Ilse. *Herod's Children.* Translated by Cornelia Schaeffer. New York: Atheneum, 1963.

Viennese children on a ship to nowhere; their youthful logic allows them to accept their situation.

Amichai, Yehuda. *Not of This Time, Not of This Place.* Translated by Shlomo Katz. New York: Harper & Row, 1968.

An Israeli returns to Germany to discover his identity through his past.

Andersch, Alfred. *Efraim's Book.* Garden City, N.Y.: Doubleday, 1970.

Inescapable torments of a survivor.

Apitz, Bruno. *Naked Among Wolves.* Translated by Edith Anderson. Berlin: Seven Seas Publishers, 1960.

Fictitious re-creation of Buchenwald concentration camp.

Appelfeld, Aharon. *Badenheim, 1939. Translated by Dalya Bilu. Boston: David Godine, 1980; Bantam pb., 1982.

Kafkaesque novel portraying the inattentiveness to their own doom of vacationers in a Jewish resort town on the eve of the Holocaust.

———. Tzili: The Story of a Life. Translated by Dalya Biln. New York: Dutton, 1983.

The story of a girl who survives in the forest, suffers terribly, and finds unexpected love.

Arieti, Silvano. The Parnas. New York: Basic Books, 1980.

Part-fiction, part-history—on the chief elder of the Sephardic congregation in Pisa, and his efforts to raise morale and save lives during the Holocaust.

Arnold, Elliott. *A Night of Watching. New York: Scribner's, 1967.

The smuggling of Danish Jews into Sweden in 1943.

Barcovitch, Reuben. Hasen. New York: Knopf, 1978.

Two youths pursued like animals by the Nazis.

Bartov, Hanoch. The Brigade. Translated by David Segal. Philadelphia: Jewish Publication Society, 1967.

A Palestinian Jew comes of age as he confronts the Holocaust.

Bassani, Giorgio. Five Stories of Ferrara. Translated by William Weaver. New York: Harcourt, Brace & Jovanovich, 1971.

Four of these stories deal with the 1943 deportation of half of Ferrara's Jewish population.

———. *The Garden of the Finzi-Continis. Translated by William Weaver. New York: Atheneum, 1965; Harcourt, Brace & Jovanovich pb., 1977.

A well-off, assimilated Italian-Jewish family's fate changes after the imposition of Mussolini's first anti-Semitic laws, and with the coming of the war.

———. The Heron. Translated by William Weaver. New York: Harcourt, Brace & World, 1970.

Novelistic reflections of an Italian Jew who survived the Holocaust by hiding in Switzerland.

Beauvais, Robert. *The Half Jew*. Translated by Harold J. Salemson. New York: Taplinger, 1980.

Satirical novel about Vichy France.

Becker, Jurek. **Jacob the Liar*. Translated by Michael Kornfield. New York: Harcourt, Brace & Jovanovich, 1975.

A comic novel about truth and falsehood in the Nazi ghetto; made into a fine East German film.

Bellow, Saul. **Mr. Sammler's Planet*. New York: Viking, 1970.

Survival in America of a Polish-Jewish intellectual, whose vision has been sharpened by his experiences escaping the Nazis.

Ben-Amotz, Dan. *To Remember, to Forget*. Translated by Eva Shapiro. Philadelphia: Jewish Publication Society, 1968.

A novel about a European-born Israeli who tries to confront post-war Germany.

Benchley, Nathaniel. *Bright Candles*. New York: Harper & Row, 1974.

A Danish youth's resistance conflicts with his parents' compliance with the Nazis.

Berger, Naomi. *Echoes of Yesterday*. New York: Playboy Books, 1981.

A novel about growing up in pre-Nazi Germany followed by a decade of horror and trauma.

Berger, Zdena. *Tell Me Another Morning*. New York: Harper, 1961.

Semiautobiographical account of the author's spiritual resistance in several concentration camps.

Berri, Claude. *The Two of Us*. Translated by Helen Weaver. New York: William Morrow, 1968.

The basis for the popular film which Berri also directed; a Jewish boy from Paris is sent to live with an elderly Christian farmer and his wife, and becomes attached to the old man.

Black, Campbell. *Death's Head*. Philadelphia: Lippincott, 1972.

A former Nazi doctor is recognized by a Jewish survivor.

Blunden, Godfrey. *The Time of the Assassins: A Novel*. Philadelphia: Lippincott, 1959.

On the Nazi occupation of Kharkov.

Boll, Heinrich. *Billiards at Half-Past Nine. Translated by Leila Venne-witz. New York: Signet, 1965; McGraw-Hill pb., 1973.

A novel that traces the scars left by the Nazi period on a German who loved people, art, and an orderly existence.

————. *"The Train Was on Time" and "Where Were You, Adam?"—Two Novels. Translated by Leila Vennewitz. New York: McGraw-Hill. 1970.

The Train was on Time is the recollection of five days in a German soldier's life from the time he boards a troop train in the Ruhr until his death on the Eastern front. Where Were You, Adam? recounts a series of strange, stupid, or arbitrary incidents, culminating in the protagonist's death.

Bor, Josef. *The Terezin Requiem. Translated by Edith Pargeter. London: Heineman, and New York: Knopf, 1963; Avon pb., 1978.

The heroic performance of Verdi's Requiem at Terezin (Theresien-stadt) in front of Adolf Eichmann.

Borowski, Tadeusz. *This Way to the Gas, Ladies and Gentlemen. Translated by Barbara Vedder with introduction by Jan Kott. New York: Viking, 1967; New York: Penguin Books, 1976.

Concentration camp stories remarkable for the seemingly dispassionate portrayal of the Nazi horrors. A unique work.

Boyarsky, Abraham. Schreiber. New York: Beaufort Books, 1981.

Survivor Menachem Schreiber is ensnared in intrigue involving a former Nazi.

Bryks, Rachmil. *A Cat in the Ghetto. Translated by S. Morris Engel; introduction by Solomon Liptzin; preface by Irving Howe. New York: Bloch, 1959.

Four short novels about the Lodz Ghetto and Auschwitz.

————. *Kiddush Hashem. Translated by S. Morris Engel. New York: Behrman House, 1977.

A novel about survival and faith in the ghetto.

Chanelcs, Sol. *Three Children of the Holocaust. New York: Avon, 1974.

The story of three children who, having survived Auschwitz, are adopted and raised by a well-to-do couple in New York.

Cohen, Arthur A. *In the Days of Simon Stern*. New York: Random House, 1973.

Wide-ranging novel about a Jewish millionaire's efforts to rescue survivors; explores the theological and historical implications of the Holocaust.

Comfort, Alex. *On This Side of Nothing*. New York: Viking, 1949.

A Jewish poet returns to his North African town as its ghetto is being closed by German occupation troops.

Condon, Richard. *An Infinity of Mirrors*. New York: Random House, 1964.

A French Jewess marries a German officer before the occupation of France.

Crawford, Oliver. *The Execution*. New York: St. Martin's Press, 1978; Popular Library, 1979.

Five women seek postwar revenge upon the doctor who tortured them in concentration camps.

Davis, Christopher. *The Shamir of Dachau*. New York: New American Library, 1966.

Two survivors of Dachau decide to remain in Germany after the war.

Dayan, Yael. *Death Had Two Sons*. New York: McGraw-Hill, 1968.

The conflict between two generations of Israelis, a major part of which stems from their differing relationships to, and interpretations of, the Holocaust.

Delbo, Charlotte. *None of Us Will Return*. Translated by John Githens. New York: Grove, 1968; Boston: Beacon pb., 1978.

Billed as a memoir but written as poetry and fiction, this is the only volume of a French trilogy which has been translated. Delbo was a member of the French resistance who was captured in 1942 and imprisoned in Auschwitz.

del Castillo, Michael. *Child of Our Time*. Translated by Peter Green. New York: Knopf, 1958.

Concentration camp experiences of a non-Jewish Spanish child.

Durrenmatt, Friedrich. *The Quarry*. Greenwich, Conn.: New York Graphic Society, 1962; New York: Warner Books, 1979.

Postwar pursuit of a Nazi doctor.

Elman, Richard M. *Lilo's Diary*. New York: Scribner's, 1968.

————. *The Reckoning*. New York: Scribner's, 1969.

————. *The Twenty-Eighth Day of Elul*. New York: Scribner's, 1967.

Variations upon the theme of the will to survive: this and the two preceding works form a trilogy, each recounting the same story of a Jewish family confronting the Nazi menace in Transylvania, but from the narrative perspective of a different member of the family.

Elon, Amos. *Timetable*. Garden City, N.Y.: Doubleday, 1980.

Documentary fiction: a novelistic account of the events surrounding Eichmann's 1944 offer to spare one million Jews in return for one hundred trucks and other supplies.

Epstein, Leslie. **King of the Jews*. New York: Coward, McCann & Geoghegan, 1979; Pocket Books, 1980.

An important if not always convincing attempt to understand the Jewish councils and their leaders; based on Mordecai Rumkowski of Lodz.

Ettinger, Elzbieta. *Kindergarten*. Boston: Houghton Mifflin, 1970.

Polish Jew Hermann Weil and his teen-aged granddaughter wander together from city to city as the Nazis overrun Poland.

Falstein, Louis. *Sole Survivor*. New York: Dell, 1954.

A survivor who has made his way to New York finds there the Nazi guard who murdered his brother in Buchenwald, and kills him.

Faust, Irvin. **Roar Lion Roar and Other Stories*. New York: Random House, 1965; Avon pb., 1973.

Several of these stories concern the Holocaust and survival.

Federman, Raymond. *The Twofold Vibration*. Bloomington: Indiana University Press, 1982.

An old man about to be deported to space colonies for the unwanted frees himself from the guilt of having survived the Holocaust.

————. *The Voice in the Closet*. Madison, Wis.: Coda Press, 1979.

A semiautobiographical story of a youth who spent the war period hiding in a closet to avoid Nazi persecutors.

Feuchtwanger, Lion. *The Devil in France: My Encounter with Him in the Summer of 1940.* Translated by Elisabeth Abbott. New York: Viking, 1941.

Early stories about concentration camp experiences.

Field, Hermann, and Mierzenski, Stanislaw. *Angry Harvest.* New York: Thomas Y. Crowell, 1958.

A young Jewish woman finds shelter with a farmer in her flight from the Germans in Poland, only to be turned out when the farmer fears for his own safety.

Fish, Robert L. **Pursuit.* Garden City, N.Y.: Doubleday, 1978; Berkley, 1979.

The past haunts a Nazi war criminal who attempts to pose as a Jew in Palestine.

Forsyth, Frederick. **The Odessa File.* New York: Viking, 1972.

Notable spy-thriller about a German journalist who learns that his war-hero father was murdered by the SS during the retreat from Riga. He tracks down the culprit and exacts revenge, in the process uncovering a clandestine neo-Nazi organization.

Freeden, Herbert H. *Grist to God's Mill.* London: Godfrey & Stephens, 1947.

A novel about *Kristallnacht* (Crystal Night).

Fuks, Ladislav. *Mr. Theodore Mundstock.* Translated by Iris Unwin. New York and London: Grossman Publishers (Orion Press) and Jonathan Cape, 1968.

A Jew in Prague continues to lead a normal life as he awaits deportation in 1942.

Gary, Romain. *The Dance of Genghis Cohn.* Translated by the author and Camilla Sykes. New York and Cleveland: World Publishing Co., 1968.

The ghost of a Jewish comedian haunts a Nazi officer.

Gascar, Pierre. **Beasts and Men.* Translated by Jean Stewart and Merloyd Lawrence. London: Methuen, 1956; New York: Meridian Books, 1960.

Allegorical and realistic horror stories written from the perspective of a French POW.

Gheorghiu, Constantin Virgil. *The Twenty-Fifth Hour*. Translated by Rita Eldon. Chicago: Regnery, 1950; Pocket Books, 1967.

A non-Jew suspected of being Jewish is thrown into a concentration camp.

Ginzburg, Natalia. *Family Sayings*. Translated by D. M. Low. New York: Dutton, 1967.

On the break-up of a Jewish family in fascist Italy.

——. *A Light for Fools*. Translated by Angus Davidson. New York: Dutton, 1967.

A German Jew is discovered hiding in Italy, and both he and his protector are executed.

Goes, Albrecht. *The Burnt Offering*. Translated by Michael Hamburger. New York: Pantheon, 1956.

A German woman tells of Jews being tormented by SS officers when they came to her butcher shop each Friday to gather scraps of meat. The horror proves too much for her, and she offers, as a burnt offering, herself.

Goldring-Goding, Henry. *Out of Hell*. Boston: Chapman & Grimes, 1955.

About a former Polish army officer and his wife, their suffering in the Warsaw Ghetto and concentration camps, and their miraculous escape.

Goldsmith, John. *Exodus 43*. New York: Coward, McCann & Geoghegan, 1982.

A novel of the Danish rescue looked at from both the German and the Jewish perspective.

Gorbatov, Boris. *Taras' Family*. Translated by Elizabeth Donnelly. London and New York: Hutchinson, 1944; New York: Cattell, 1946.

Ukrainian resistance to the Nazis.

Gouri, Haim. *The Chocolate Deal*. Translated by Seymour Simckes. New York: Holt, Rinehart & Winston, 1968.

Two survivors of Auschwitz in a German city after the war; one ultimately dies; the other deals in chocolate imported by the American army.

Grade, Chaim. *The Seven Little Lanes*. Translated by Curt Leviant. New York: Bergen-Belsen Memorial Press, 1972.

Grass, Günter. *The Tin Drum*. Translated by Ralph Manheim. New York: Random House, 1971.

> An upside-down *Bildungsroman* set in the German-Polish city of Danzig (Gdansk).

Green, Gerald. *Holocaust*. New York: Bantam Books, 1978.

> Novel based on the author's screenplay for the provocative, if somewhat melodramatic, television production tracing the interrelated lives and deaths in two families, one German and one Jewish, through the Holocaust.

———. *The Legion of Noble Christians*. New York: Trident Press, 1965.

> A Catholic accepts a job from a Jewish agency to search for Christians who risked their lives for Jews during the Holocaust.

Grossman, Ladislav. *The Shop on Main Street*. Translated by Iris Unwin. Garden City, N.Y.: Doubleday, 1970.

> The basis for the Oscar award winning film, in which an old Jewish woman is befriended by a simple man in a Slovak town in 1942.

Grynberg, Henryk. *Child of the Shadows*. Translated by Celina Wieniewoka. London: Vallentine, Mitchell, 1969.

> A survivor's semifictional account.

Haas, Ben. *The House of Christina*. New York: Dell pb., 1981.

> About a woman in Vienna during the Holocaust who is involved both with an Austrian sympathetic to the Nazi cause and with a Jew participating in an anti-Nazi plot.

Habe, Hans. *The Mission*. Translated by Michael Bullock. New York: Coward-McCann, 1966.

> A novel based on the Evian Conference on Refugees convened by Roosevelt in July 1938, at which the world community lost its opportunity to ransom Germany's Jewish population from Hitler.

Hersey, John. *The Wall*. New York: Knopf, 1950; Pocket Books, 1954; Modern Library, 1967; Bantam, 1967.

> The "classic" novel of the Warsaw Ghetto, based on the figure of Emmanuel Ringelblum.

Hilsenrath, Edgar. *The Nazi Who Lived as a Jew*. Translated by Andrew White. Garden City, N.Y.: Doubleday, 1971 (as *The Nazi and the Barber*); Manor Books, 1977.

On an SS sergeant and murderer who, after the war, assumes the identity of a former Jewish friend and is drawn to Zionism and Israel.

————. *Night*. Translated by Michael Roloff. Garden City, N.Y.: Doubleday, 1966; Manor Books, 1974.

Documentary novel about life and death in a Ukrainian ghetto in 1942.

Jabes, Edmond. *The Book of Questions*. Translated by Rosemarie Waldrop. Middletown, Conn.: Wesleyan University Press, 1976.

————. *The Book of Questions*, Vols. 2 and 3: *The Book of Yukel* and *The Return to the Book*. Translated by Rosemarie Waldrop. Middletown, Conn.: Wesleyan University Press, 1977.

Theological responses to the Holocaust written in the style of midrash.

Jacot, Michael. *The Last Butterfly*. Indianapolis: Bobbs-Merrill, 1974; Ballantine, 1975.

The compassion of a former clown who is imprisoned with Polish children in Terezin (Theresienstadt).

Julitte, Pierre. *Block 26: Sabotage at Buchenwald*. Translated by Francis Price. Garden City, N.Y.: Doubleday, 1971.

Documentary novel by a survivor of Buchenwald.

Kanfer, Stefan. *Fear Itself*. New York: Putnam, 1981.

Niccolo Levi, an Italian Jew who has escaped to America, plots to assassinate President Roosevelt when he realizes that the American government has acquiesced in the Nazi murder of his family and thousands of other European Jews.

————. *The Eighth Sin*. New York: Random House, 1978; Berkley, 1979.

Nazi persecution of the gypsies, and one gypsy's post-Holocaust revenge.

Kaniuk, Yoram. *Adam Resurrected*. Translated by Seymour Simckes. New York: Atheneum, 1971; Harper & Row, 1978.

Set in an Israeli hospital for those driven insane by their experiences under the Nazis, this novel presents the reflections of Adam Stein, whom the Nazis turned into a death camp clown to comfort other Jewish victims.

Karmel, Ilona. *An Estate of Memory*. Boston: Houghton Mifflin, 1969.

The survival, spiritual resistance, and friendship of four women prisoners in a Nazi concentration camp.

Karmel-Wolfe, Henia. *The Baders of Jacob Street*. Philadelphia and New York: Lippincott, 1970.

Autobiographical novel of Jewish life in Cracow under Nazi occupation.

————. *Marek and Lisa*. New York: Dodd, Mead, 1984.

A love story about suffering in the concentration camp, separation, and reunion.

Ka-Tzetnik 135633 [Yehiel Dinur]. *Atrocity*. London: Anthony Blond, 1961 (as *Piepel*); New York: Lyle Stuart, 1963.

An eleven-year-old boy is the sexual toy of block chiefs in Auschwitz.

————. **House of Dolls*. Translated by Moshe M. Kohn. New York: Simon & Schuster, 1955; Pyramid Books, 1958; Chicago: Academy Press pb., 1982.

The fictitious notebook of a fourteen-year-old girl who is forced to be a prostitute in a Nazi concentration camp.

Klainer, Albert, and Klainer, Jo-Ann. *The Judas Game*. New York: Ace Books, 1981.

A novel based on the Nazi "medical experiments" in concentration camps.

Klein, Edward. *The Parachutists*. New York: Doubleday, 1981.

A novel about seven parachutists who jump into Hungary in 1944 attempting to rescue 7,500 Jews condemned to die in Auschwitz.

Koestler, Arthur. *Scum of the Earth*. London: Jonathan Cape, 1941; reissued with a new preface by the author, New York: Macmillan, 1968.

Refugees in France.

Kolitz, Zvi. *The Tiger Beneath the Skin: Stories and Parables of the Years of Death*. New York: Creative Age, 1947.

Eleven stories, including "Yossel Rakover's Appeal to God," unified by common themes of death and faith during the Holocaust.

Kosinski, Jerzy. *The Painted Bird. Boston: Houghton Mifflin, 1965; New York: Bantam, 1972; 2d ed., with an introduction by the author, Boston: Houghton Mifflin, 1976.

An often surrealistic novel of a young boy, who may or may not be a Jew or a Pole, on the run through Hitler's Europe.

Kotowska, Monika. *The Bridge to the Other Side*. Garden City, N.Y.: Doubleday, 1970.

Children in Nazi-occupied Poland.

Kuznetsov, Anatoli. *Babi Yar. Translated by Jacob Guralsky. Censored ed., New York: Dial, 1966; Dell pb., 1967; rev. ed., New York: Farrar, Straus, & Giroux, 1970; Pocket Books, 1982.

The massacre at Babi Yar as personally witnessed by a Russian youth who later became a major writer and defected to the West.

Langfus, Anna. *The Lost Shore*. Translated by Peter Wiles. New York: Pantheon, 1963.

———. *The Whole Land Brimstone*. Translated by Peter Wiles. New York: Pantheon Books, 1962.

Semiautobiographical account of survival and escape from the Warsaw Ghetto.

Laqueur, Walter. *The Missing Years*. Boston: Little, Brown, 1980.

Laqueur's first novel, about a middle-class, German-Jewish survivor.

Lessner, Erwin Christian. *At the Devil's Booth*. Garden City, N.Y.: Doubleday, 1952.

The forced flight of an anti-Nazi Austrian nobleman.

Levi, Primo. *The Reawakening*. Translated by Stuart Woolf. London: Bodley Head, 1965 (as *The Truce*); Boston: Little, Brown, 1965.

Survivors of Auschwitz returning to their native Italy after their liberation.

Levin, Meyer. *Eva: A Novel of the Holocaust. New York: Simon & Schuster, 1959; Behrman House pb., 1979.

Based on fact, this novel tells of a Polish-Jewish girl who masquerades as an Aryan among the Nazis.

———. *The Harvest. New York: Simon & Schuster, 1978; Bantam pb., 1979.

Brings the Chaimovitch family, about whom Levin had written in *The Settlers* (1972), through the Holocaust and up to the Israeli War of Independence.

———. *My Father's House*. New York: Viking, 1947.

A boy is saved during a round-up in Cracow. After the war he searches in vain for his family, whose members were murdered by the Nazis.

———. **The Stronghold*. New York: Simon & Schuster, 1965; New York: Fawcett pb., 1966.

A novel about an Eichmann-like Nazi seeking absolution for his war crimes from the ex-leaders of a Nazi-occupied country in the last days of the war.

Lewis, Robert. *Michel, Michel*. New York: Simon & Schuster, 1967.

The Church becomes involved when, after the war, a Jewish woman reclaims her nephew, who was sheltered and baptized by a Catholic during the Holocaust.

Lewisohn, Ludwig. *Breathe Upon These*. Indianapolis: Bobbs-Merrill, 1944.

An American community is shocked to learn, from a survivor of the tragedy, of the mass drowning of refugees from a Romanian ghetto when the ship on which they were fleeing, the *Struma*, struck a mine in the Black Sea.

Lind, Jakov. *Ergo*. Translated by Ralph Manheim. London: Methuen, 1967.

A novella about the animosity between a minor Viennese customs official and a psychotic who tries to insulate himself in the official's house from the contamination of the world.

———. *Landscape in Concrete*. Translated by Ralph Manheim. New York: Grove, 1966.

Set in the closing days of World War II, this allegorical novel tells the story of a *Wehrmacht* sergeant who, having been discharged as mentally unfit, wanders through Europe in search of a unit in which he can fight and reestablish his manhood.

———. *Soul of Wood and Other Stories*. London: Jonathan Cape, 1964; New York: Grove, 1965; Fawcett pb., Crest, 1966.

A survivor evokes the madness of the Holocaust through black humor in these seven stories.

Lustig, Arnost. *Darkness Casts No Shadow.* Translated by Jeanne Nemcova. Washington, D.C.: Inscape, 1976; New York: Avon pb., 1978.

Two boys escape from a death train in 1945.

————. *Diamonds of the Night.* Translated by Jeanne Nemcova. Washington, D.C.: Inscape, 1976.

Semiautobiographical stories about the lives of Jewish adolescents in Theresienstadt.

————. *Dita Sax.* Translated by George Theiner. London: Hutchinson, 1966; New York: Harper & Row, 1980 (as *Dita Saxova*).

The story of a nineteen-year-old girl living in a hotel in Prague a few years after the Holocaust, and of the horrors and uncanny events she has witnessed.

————. *Night and Hope.* Translated by George Theiner. New York: Dutton, 1962; Washington, D.C.: Inscape, 1976; Avon, 1978.

This is the first volume of Lustig's *Children of the Holocaust* series, which was followed by *Darkness Casts No Shadow* and *Diamonds of the Night.* The seven stories in this volume portray children's visions of Terezin, which Lustig himself survived.

————. *A Prayer for Katerina Horovitzova.* Translated by Jeanne Nemcova. New York: Harper & Row, 1973; Avon pb., 1975.

A tale of failed Jewish mediation and German blackmail in the concentration camps.

Malaparte, Curzio. *Kaputt.* Translated by Cesare Foligno. New York: Dutton, 1946; Avon, 1966.

An extraordinary wartime reportage written by an Italian fascist, this work includes a unique portrait of Hans Frank.

Margolian, Abraham. *A Piece of Blue Heaven.* Fredericton, N.B.: New Elizabethan, 1956.

Based on diaries, this novel recounts the heroism of a surgeon who provided sanctuary for Dutch Jews in Amsterdam.

Mazzetti, Lorenza. *The Sky Falls.* Translated by Marguerite Waldman. New York: McKay, 1963.

A ten-year-old girl tells how she and her younger sister lived with their German-Jewish uncle in an Italian village near the front lines.

Morante, Elsa. *History: A Novel.* Translated by William Weaver. New York: Knopf, 1977; Avon pb., 1979.

A major novel that treats the Holocaust microscopically, through the life of an ordinary Italian-Jewish woman, her bastard son, and his dog.

Morgenstern, Soma. *The Third Pillar.* Translated by Ludwig Lewisohn. New York: Farrar, 1955.

The third pillar adumbrating the Redemption is the pillar of blood built by Hitler's slaughter of Jewish children.

Morgulas, Jerrold. *The Accused.* Garden City, N.Y.: Doubleday, 1967.

On Holocaust survivors in the Washington Heights section of Manhattan.

———. *The Twelfth Power of Evil.* New York: Seaview Press, Harper & Row, 1981.

A novel by a U.S. prosecutor at Nuremberg about two giant companies—one American, one German—pursuing "business as usual" in part with the assistance of slave labor.

Neumann, Robert. *By the Waters of Babylon.* New York: Simon & Schuster, 1940.

Early novel on the plight of Jewish refugees.

Obletz, Rose Meyerson. *The Long Road Home.* New York: Exposition, 1958.

Jewish refugees after the war.

Olivier, Stefan. *Rise Up in Anger.* New York: Putnam, 1963.

One German officer seeks postwar revenge on another, who sentenced him to Buchenwald for helping the Jews.

Orlev, Uri. *The Lead Soldiers.* Translated by Hillel Halkin. New York: Taplinger, 1980.

The Holocaust as seen through the eyes of two Polish-Jewish children whose parents renounced their Judaism.

Pawel, Ernst. *The Island in Time.* Garden City, N.Y.: Doubleday, 1951.

Love in a DP camp, between people waiting to emigrate to Palestine.

Persico, Joseph E. *The Spiderweb.* New York: Crown, 1979.

Thriller based on Nazi exploitation of Jewish printers to produce counterfeit American and British currency.

Pinkus, Oscar. *Friends and Lovers.* New York and Cleveland: World, 1963.

A physicist in Cambridge, Massachusetts, who witnessed his family's death in Warsaw, seeks a companion with whom to share his despair.

Presser, Jacob. *Breaking Point.* Translated by Barrows Mussey. New York and Cleveland: World, 1958.

Portrays the concentration camp in Westerbork, Holland, where Jews were forced to select those of their number who would be deported to Auschwitz.

Raphael, Frederic. *Lindmann: A Novel.* New York: Holt, Rinehart & Winston, 1964.

Fictitious account of Jacob Lindmann, one of two survivors of the S.S. *Broda,* which in 1942 sank off the Turkish coast with a cargo of Jewish refugees.

Rawicz, Piotr. *Blood from the Sky.* Translated by Peter Wiles. New York: Harcourt, Brace & World, 1964.

A major novel on survival and closeness. Based on the author's actual experiences.

Remarque, Erich Maria. *The Night in Lisbon.* Translated by Ralph Manheim. New York: Harcourt, Brace & World, 1964.

About refugees from Hitler, who forge a new life in Lisbon.

————. *Spark of Life.* Translated by James Stern. New York: Appleton-Century-Crofts, 1952.

Prisoner 509 tells the story of his comrades' determination to rekindle the spark of life after they were liberated.

Richter, Hans Werner. *They Fell from God's Hand.* Translated by Geoffrey Saintsbury. New York: Dutton, 1956.

Life in a DP camp near Nuremburg in 1950.

Rochman, Leyb. **The Pit and the Trap: A Chronicle of Survival.* Translated by Moshe Kohn and Sheila Friedling, with a foreword by Aharon Appelfeld. New York: Holocaust Library, 1983.

Five Jews in hiding among depraved Polish peasants. The realistic counterpart to Kosinski's *The Painted Bird.*

Romanowicz, Zofia. *Passage Through the Red Sea*. Translated by Virgilia Peterson. New York: Harcourt, 1962.

Reunion of two women who met in a slave labor camp.

Rosen, Norma. *Touching Evil*. New York: Harcourt, Brace & World, 1969; Curtis Books pb.

The implications of the Holocaust against a Manhattan backdrop.

Rostov, Mara. *Eroica*. New York: Putnam, 1977; B.J. Publishing Group pb., 1978.

A woman seeks to expose her father for the crimes he committed in Nazi death camps.

Rudnicki, Adolf. *Ascent to Heaven*. Translated by H. C. Stevens. New York, Toronto, and London: Roy McLeod, and Dennis Dobson, 1951.

Four stories of Warsaw, survival, and the fate of assimilated Jews by the foremost Polish-language writer on the Holocaust.

Rybakov, Anatoli. *Heavy Sand*. New York: Viking, 1981; Penguin pb., 1982.

An epic novel of a Russian-Jewish family from the turn of the century through the Russian Revolution to the Holocaust.

St. John, Robert. *The Man Who Played God*. Garden City, N.Y.: Doubleday, 1962.

Fictionalized account of the Kästner case: a Hungarian Jew who ransomed a few thousand Jews for several million dollars is tried in Israel after the war on charges of being a Nazi collaborator.

Salisbury-Davis, Dorothy, and Ross, Jerome. *God Speed the Night*. New York: Scribner's, 1968.

A nun assists French Jews fleeing from Hitler.

Samelson, William. *All Life in Wait*. Englewood Cliffs, N.J.: Prentice-Hall, 1969.

Semiautobiographical novel about survival.

Samuels, Gertrude. *Mottele*. New York: Harper & Row, 1976; New American pb., 1977.

Sayre, Joel. *The House Without a Roof*. New York: Farrar, Straus, 1948.

A Jewish family in Berlin as the Nazis rise to power; Sayre was a correspondent for the *New Yorker*, and first published this novelistic eyewitness account as a serial for that magazine.

Schaeffer, Susan Fromberg. *Anya. New York: Macmillan, 1974; Avon pb., 1976.

An ironic novel about a woman survivor of the Vilna Ghetto and concentration camps, this work received the Edward Lewis Wallant Award for the best work of Jewish fiction of 1974.

Schwarz-Bart, André. *The Last of the Just. Translated by Stephen Becker. New York: Atheneum, 1960; Bantam pb., 1969; Atheneum, 1977.

One of the most remarkable novels of the Holocaust, not only for its sustained sardonic vision, but for its effective blend of Jewish tradition and Nazi nightmare: Ernie Levy is a young boy who suffers for all mankind as he assumes the role of the last of the thirty-six righteous men.

Seiden, O. J. *The Survivors of Babi Yar*. Athens, Ohio: Stonehenge Books/Ohio University Press, 1980.

A novel about a young man who survives the massacre at Babi Yar, fights with Jewish partisans in the Ukraine, and attempts to enter Palestine after the war.

Semprun, Jorge. *The Long Voyage*. Translated by Richard Seaver. New York: Grove, 1964.

An award-winning novel about 120 prisoners on a five-day train ride bound for a concentration camp.

Serge, Victor. *The Long Dusk*. Translated by Ralph Manheim. New York: Dial Press, 1946.

Underground resistance to the German occupation of France.

Shaw, Robert. *The Man in the Glass Booth. New York: Harcourt, Brace, & World, 1967; Grove pb., 1969.

Novel based on the Eichmann trial.

Shilansky, Dov. *Musulman*. Tel Aviv: Menora Publishing House, 1962.

Resistance in Auschwitz.

Silberstang, Edwin. *Nightmare of the Dark*. New York: Knopf, 1967.

A twelve-year-old Jewish boy survives the concentration camp nightmare.

Singer, Isaac Bashevis. *Enemies: A Love Story.* New York: Farrar, Straus & Giroux, 1972; Fawcett, 1977.

The broodings and marital and erotic mishaps of a Holocaust survivor in New York.

Solomon, Michael. *The "Struma" Incident: A Novel of the Holocaust.* Translated by Carol Dunlop-Herbert. Toronto: McClelland & Stewart, 1979.

Documentary fiction about a doomed boat carrying refugees.

Sperber, Manes. *The Abyss.* Translated by Constantine Fitzgibbon. Garden City, N.Y.: Doubleday, 1952.

————. *Journey Without End.* Translated by Constantine Fitzgibbon. Garden City, N.Y.: Doubleday, 1954.

————. *. . . Than a Tear in the Seas.* Translated by Constantine Fitzgibbon with an introduction by André Malraux. New York and Tel-Aviv: Bergen-Belsen Memorial Press, 1967.

This and the preceding two novels form a trilogy on the Polish partisans, raising questions about the appropriate Jewish view of resistance.

Stebel, S. L. *The Collaborator.* New York: Random House, 1968.

A Jewish economist in Israel is accused of having collaborated with the Nazis.

Steiner, George. *The Portage to San Cristobal of A.H.* New York: Simon & Schuster, 1982.

A[dolph] H[itler] is hunted down in the Amazon jungle. In England, this work has also been adapted for the stage by Christopher Hampton.

Steiner, Jean-François. *Treblinka.* Translated by Helen Weaver. New York: Simon & Schuster, 1967; New American Library pb., 1968.

Powerful historical novel about psychological resistance and physical rebellion in the Treblinka concentration camp.

Stern, Daniel. *Who Shall Live, Who Shall Die?* New York: Crown, 1963.

Post-Holocaust revenge by one survivor against another person, also a survivor, responsible for his parents' deaths.

Stolzfuss, Ben. *The Eye of the Needle.* New York: Viking, 1967.

The story of an adolescent boy living through the Nazi occupation, as told in his diary and by his psychiatrist.

Styron, William. *Sophie's Choice. New York: Random House, 1979; Bantam pb., 1980.

An important book about the ability—or inability—of Americans to come to grips with the Holocaust.

Suhl, Yuri. *On the Other Side of the Gate. New York: Avon pb., 1976.

Novel about smuggling an infant out of the ghetto.

———. *Uncle Misha's Partisans. New York: Four Winds Press, 1973.

About perhaps the most important partisan band.

Talmy, Shel. *The Web. New York: Dell Books, 1981.

Four years old when his mother is raped and both his parents are killed by the Gestapo, successful businessman Mark Sebastion, now forty-four, searches for the killers through three continents.

Taube, Herman, and Taube, Suzanne. *Remember.* Translated by Helena Frank. Baltimore: Nicholas A. Grossman, 1951.

Eight stories of concentration camp horrors.

Tennenbaum, Silvia. *Yesterday's Streets.* New York: Random House, 1981.

A novel about the Westheims of Frankfurt, a nonreligious, fairly assimilated family, between 1903 and 1945.

Thomas, D. M. *The White Hotel. New York: Viking Press, 1981; Pocket Books, 1982.

A woman's odyssey from psychoanalysis to *Babi Yar* and beyond—a remarkable novel.

Tomkiewicz, Mina. *Of Bombs and Mice.* Translated by Stefan Grazel. New York: Thomas Yoseloff, 1970.

Life in the Warsaw Ghetto seen through the eyes of a girl from a prosperous family.

Tournier, Michel. *The Ogre. Translated by Barbara Bray. New York: Doubleday, 1972, Dell pb., 1973.

The Holocaust told through myth; the Christian counterpart to *The Last of the Just.* Tournier is considered by some the foremost contemporary French novelist.

Traub, Barbara Fishman. *The Matrushka Doll.* New York: Richard Marek, 1979.

About a Hungarian survivor after the war.

Uhlman, Fred. *Reunion. New York: Farrar, Straus & Giroux, 1977; Penguin pb., 1978.

Reunion after thirty years of two boyhood friends, one a Jew and the other a German aristocrat, who were separated during the Hitler era.

Uris, Leon. *Exodus. Garden City, N.Y.: Doubleday, 1958; Bantam pb., 1962.

The plight of refugees aboard the Exodus and their subsequent struggle in the Israeli War of Independence.

———. *Mila 18. Garden City, N.Y.: Doubleday, 1961; Bantam pb., 1962.

The uprising in the Warsaw Ghetto.

———. *QB VII. Garden City, N.Y.: Doubleday, 1970; Bantam pb., 1972.

A former concentration camp inmate sues an American novelist for writing that the survivor performed sterilization surgery on fellow inmates.

Van Rjndt, Phillipe. *The Trial of Adolf Hitler. New York: Simon & Schuster, 1978; Bantam pb., 1980.

Hitler reveals himself twenty-five years after World War II and is tried at the United Nations.

Von Rezzori, Gregor. *Memoirs of an Anti-Semite: A Novel in Five Stories. New York: Penguin, 1982.

An intriguing story which portrays a "cultured" anti-Semite from 1919 to the present.

Wallant, Edward Lewis. *The Pawnbroker. New York: Harcourt, Brace & World, 1961; Macfadden Books pb., 1964; Harcourt, Brace & World, 1978.

A survivor who is now a pawnbroker in Harlem is haunted by memories of concentration camp horrors.

Weil, Grete. *My Sister, My Antigone. New York: Avon Books, 1984.

A taut, moving novel about a Holocaust victim who confronts the guilt of surviving through her obsession with the mythic Greek heroine who died for her beliefs.

Weinberg, Marcel. Spots of the Time. New York: Macmillan, 1972.

About an orphan's struggles and survival through the Holocaust.

Weiss, David. *The Guilt Makers*. New York: Rinehart, 1953.

> A young survivor's experiences of cruelty in America, despite his friendship with a social worker, lead him to an act of violence for which he receives a severe prison sentence.

Wertheim, Moritz. *The Last of the Levanos*. New York: Thomas Yoseloff, 1967.

> A Dutch novel about a sixty-five-year-old Jew who cannot forget the Nazi murder of his wife and children.

Wertmuller, Lina. *Head of Alvise*. New York: William Morrow, 1982.

> A promising first novel by the Italian film director about two very different boys and their journey to a concentration camp, flight across Europe and to America.

White, Patrick. *Riders in the Chariot*. New York: Viking, 1961; Avon pb., 1975.

> Post-Holocaust suffering of a survivor who fled to Australia.

Wiechert, Ernst. *The Forest of the Dead*. Translated by Ursula Stechow. New York: Greenberg Publishers, 1947.

> Thinly veiled autobiographical account of concentration camp experiences.

Wiesel, Elie. *The Accident*. Translated by Anne Borchardt. New York: Hill & Wang, 1962; Bantam pb., 1982.

> About one man's conflict over the will to live after the Holocaust.

———. *Dawn*. Translated by Anne Borchardt. New York: Hill & Wang, 1961; Avon pb., 1970; Bantam pb., 1982.

> Does the Holocaust justify a political murder on the part of young Zionists fighting the British? Wiesel's short novel deals with this complex question.

———. *The Gates of the Forest*. Translated by Frances Frenaye. New York: Holt, Rinehart & Winston, 1966; Schocken pb., 1982; Bantam pb., 1982.

> Jewish tradition is fused with Holocaust nightmare as Wiesel tells the tale of a Hungarian youth who survived in caves, in forests, and among the partisans.

———. *Legends of Our Time*. New York: Holt, Rinehart & Winston, 1968; Avon pb., 1972.

Includes some previously published short stories as well as essays and autobiographical sketches.

———. *Night*. Translated by Stella Rodway. New York: Hill & Wang, 1960; Hill & Wang pb., 1960; Avon, 1972; Bantam, 1982.

Semiautobiographical account of the Nazis' destruction of the author's native Sighet, Hungary, and of his concentration camp experience while still a young boy.

———. *One Generation After*. New York: Random House, 1970; Avon pb., 1971; Pocket pb., 1981.

Essays and stories about survivors and survival.

———. *The Town Beyond the Wall*. Translated by Stephen Becker. New York: Atheneum, 1964; rev. ed., New York and Tel Aviv: Bergen-Belsen Memorial Press, 1967, Schocken, 1982.

A Jew is captured and tortured by the Russians when he returns to his native Hungary after the war.

Wiesenthal, Simon. *Max and Helen*. New York: William Morrow, 1982.

A "remarkable true love story" about lovers who were witnesses to concentration camp atrocities and yet, for the sake of a greater mercy, did not reveal most of what they had seen.

———. *The Sunflower*. Translated by H. A. Piehler, with a symposium translated by Carol Pimentol Pinto. London: W. H. Allen, 1970; New York: Schocken, 1976.

A provocative short story asking whether a Jew should forgive a former Nazi; the "symposium" consists of commentary on the story by distinguished theologians and philosophers.

Wiseman, Thomas. *Journey of a Man*. Garden City, N.Y.: Doubleday, 1967.

A survivor's guilt about both the general lack of resistance and his own survival.

———. *The Quick and the Dead*. New York: Viking, 1968.

A first-person narrative about a half-Jew who escapes death in Vienna during the Holocaust with the help of Nazi patronage.

Wood, Bari. *The Tribe*. New York: New American Library, 1981.

A novel about five people who survived Bergen-Belsen in mysterious circumstances, and their fate in America.

Wouk, Herman. *The Winds of War. Boston: Little, Brown, 1971; Pocket Books, 1977.

———. *War and Remembrance. Boston: Little, Brown, 1978; Pocket Books, 1980.

The sequel to Winds of War, which brings the Jastrow family through the Holocaust era in Germany and to the United States.

Wurio, Eva-lis. To Fight in Silence. New York: Holt, Rinehart & Winston, 1973.

Novel of Scandinavian resistance.

Yaffe, James. The Voyage of the "Franz Joseph." New York: Putnam, 1970.

The story of a ship which carried one thousand Jewish refugees across the Atlantic in 1939.

Zieman, Joseph. *The Cigarette Sellers of Three Crosses Square. London: Vallentine & Mitchell, 1970; Minneapolis: Lerner, 1975; New York: Avon, 1977.

The true story of Jewish children on the Aryan side of Warsaw.

Zweig, Arnold. The Axe of Wandbek. New York: Viking, 1947.

A German butcher commits suicide rather than execute Jews for the Nazis.

3. Drama

Anthology

Skloot, Robert. *The Theatre of the Holocaust. Madison: University of Wisconsin Press, 1983.

Four plays: Shimon Wincelbergs's Resort 76 (based on Bryks's A Cat in the Ghetto, and also published as The Windows of Heaven), Harold and Edith Lieberman's Throne of Straw (dramatizing the experience of Mordechai Chaim Rumkowski, the leader of the Lodz Jewish Council), George Tabori's The Cannibals (on the moral question facing starving concentration camp inmates who must choose between cannibalism and death), and Charlotte Delbo's Who Will Carry the Word (a poetic dramatization of life in the concentration camps), along with a fine introductory essay by Skloot.

Other Plays

Amichai, Yehuda. "Bells and Trains." *Midstream* 12 (October 1966): 55–66.

A radio play portraying a visit to an old age home for survivors.

Amir, Anda. *This Kind, Too.* Translated by Shoshana Perla. New York: World Zionist Organization, 1972.

Borchert, Wolfgang. *The Outsider.* In **Postwar German Theatre: An Anthology of Plays,* edited and translated by Michael Benedikt and George E. Wellwarth, pp. 52–113. New York: Dutton, 1967.

Dagan, Gabriel. "The Reunion." *Midstream* 19 (April 1973): 3–32.

An Israeli dramatically questions the failure of the Jews to resist the Nazi onslaught.

Eliach, Yaffa, and Eliach, Uri. *The Last Jew.* Translated by Yaffa Eliach. Israel: Alef-Alef Theatre Publications, 1977.

Frisch, Max. *Andorra.* Translated by Michael Bullock. New York: Hill & Wang, 1964.

Allegorical play on the problem of complicity with evil.

Goldberg, Leah. *The Lady of the Castle.* Translated by T. Carmi. Tel Aviv: Institute for the Translation of Hebrew Literature, 1974.

Goodrich, Frances, and Hackett, Albert. *The Diary of Anne Frank.* New York: Random House, 1956.

Hochhuth, Rolf. **The Deputy.* Translated by Richard and Clara Winston. New York: Grove Press, 1964.

A German Protestant's dramatic indictment of the silence of Pius XIII—a powerful statement on the use and abuse of language, and doubtless one of the century's most controversial plays. Hochhuth's drama is perhaps better read and studied than performed or witnessed.

Lampell, Millard. *The Wall: A Play in Two Acts Based on the Novel by John Hersey.* New York: Knopf, 1961.

Lind, Jakov. *Ergo: A Comedy.* New York: Hill & Wang, 1968.

Dramatization of the author's novel of the same title.

Megged, Aharon. *The Burning Bush.* Translated by Shoshana Perla, New York: World Zionist Organization, 1972.

Miller, Arthur, *Incident at Vichy. New York: Viking, 1965; Bantam pb., 1967.

> Nine men and a boy, all suspected of being Jews, have been rounded up and now wait their common fate.

Pilchik, Ely E. Strength: A Play in Three Acts. New York: Bloch, 1964.

Sachs, Nelly. Eli: A Mystery Play of the Sufferings of Israel. Translated by Christopher Holme. In *O The Chimneys! New York: Farrar, Straus, & Giroux, 1967.

Sartre, Jean-Paul. *The Condemned of Altona. Translated by Sylvia and George Leeson. New York: Knopf, 1961; Norton pb., 1978.

Sherman, Martin. *Bent. New York: Avon, 1980.

> On the Nazi persecution of homosexuals.

Sylvanus, Erwin. Dr. Korczak and the Children. In *Postwar German Theatre: An Anthology of Plays, edited and translated by Michael Benedikt and George E. Wellwarth, pp. 115–157. New York: Dutton, 1967.

Tomer, Ben-Zion. Children of the Shadows. Translated by Hillel Halkin. New York: World Zionist Organization, n.d..

Walser, Martin. The Rabbit Race. Adapted by Ronald Duncan, translated by Richard Gruneberger. London: J. Calder, 1963.

Werfel, Franz V., and Behrman, S. N. Jacobowsky and the Colonel. New York: Random House, 1944.

> Play based on the novel by Werfel: a Polish-Jewish refugee and a reactionary Polish colonel discover their need for each other in their common flight from the Nazis.

Wiesel, Elie. The Trial of God. Translated by Marion Wiesel. New York: Random House, 1979.

———. Zalman; or, The Madness of God. Translated by Nathan Edelman and adapted for the stage by Marion Wiesel. New York: Random House, 1974.

Wincelberg, Shimon. "The Windows of Heaven (A Condensation of a Full-Length Play)." Midstream 8 (December 1962): 44–64.

> Play based on Rachmil Bryks's A Cat in the Ghetto.

Zuckmayer, Carl. The Devil's General. In Masters of Modern Drama, edited by Haskell M. Bloch and Robert G. Shedd. New York: Random House, 1962.

4. Poetry

Celan, Paul. *Selected Poems*. Translated by Michael Hamburger and Christopher Middleton. Middlesex: Penguin Books, 1972.

————. *Speech-Grille and Selected Poems*. Translated by Joachim Neugroschel. New York: Dutton, 1971.

Fast, Howard. *Never to Forget*. New York: Jewish People's Fraternal Book League, 1946.

Narrative poem of the Warsaw Ghetto uprising.

Feldman, Irving. *The Pripet Marshes and Other Poems*. New York: Viking, 1965.

Includes several poems on the Holocaust.

Gershon, Karen. *Selected Poems*. New York: Harcourt, Brace & World, 1966.

Gillon, Adam. "Here as in Jerusalem: Selected Poems of the Ghetto." *Polish Review* 10, no. 3 (1965): 22–45.

English translation of Polish poetry in and on the Holocaust.

Glatstein, Jacob. *Poems*. Translated by Etta Blum. Tel Aviv: I. L. Peretz, 1970.

————. **The Selected Poems of Jacob Glatstein*. Translated by Ruth Whitman. New York: October House, 1972.

Both volumes contain some of Glatstein's better-known poems on the Holocaust, written from 1938 on.

Greenberg, Uri Zvi. From *Streets of the River*. Translated by Robert Friend and others. In *Anthology of Modern Hebrew Poetry*, edited by S. Y. Penneli and A. Ukhmani, vol. 2, pp. 259–280. Jerusalem: Israel Universities Press, 1966.

A small but significant selection from this central response to the Holocaust in modern Hebrew poetry.

Hecht, Anthony. **The Hard Hours*. New York: Atheneum, 1967.

See especially "More Light! More Light!" This collection received a Pulitzer Prize in 1968.

————. *Millions of Strange Shadows*. New York: Atheneum, 1978.

Heyen, William. *The Swastika Poems*. New York: Vanguard, 1977.

Hill, Geoffrey. **Somewhere Is Such a Kingdom: Poems 1952–1971*. Boston: Houghton Mifflin, 1975.

Jackson, Ada. *Behold the Jew*. New York: Macmillan, 1944.

Jarrell, Randall. "A Camp in the Prussian Forests." In *Losses*. New York, Harcourt, Brace, 1948.

Katzenelson, Yitzhak. *The Song of the Murdered Jewish People*. Translated by N. H. Rosenbloom, revised by Y. Tobin. Israel: Ghetto Fighters' House, 1980; bilingual facsimile ed.

The major lament written in the Holocaust, still not adequately translated.

Klein, A. M. *Collected Poems*. Toronto: McGraw-Hill, Ryerson, 1974.

A neoclassical response from the most Hebraic of Anglo-Jewish poets.

Kolmar, Gertrud. *Dark Soliloquy: The Selected Poems of Gertrud Kolmar*. Translated by Henry A. Smith. Bilingual ed. New York: Seabury Press, 1975.

Kovner, Abba, and Sachs, Nelly. *Selected Poems of Abba Kovner and Nelly Sachs*. Translated by Shirley Kaufman and Nurit Orchan. Middlesex: Penguin Books pb., 1971.

Lask, Israel Meir. *Songs of the Ghettoes*. Tel Aviv: Eked, 1976.

Leftwich, Joseph (ed. and trans.). "Songs of the Death Camps—A Selection with Commentary." *Commentary* 12 (1951): 269–274.

Levertov, Denise. "During the Eichmann Trial." In *Jacob's Ladder*. New York: New Directions, 1958; pb., 1961.

Levi, Primo. *Shema: Collected Poems of Primo Levi*. Translated by Ruth Feldman and Brian Swann. London: Menard Press, 1976.

Meyers, Bert. *The Dark Birds*. Garden City, N.Y.: Doubleday, 1969.

Mezey, Robert. "Theresienstadt Poems." In *Naked Poetry: Recent American Poetry in Open Forms*, edited by Stephen Berg and Robert Mezey. Indianapolis: Bobbs-Merrill, 1969.

Milosz, Czeslaw. *Selected Poems*. New York: Seabury Press, 1973; rev. ed., Ecco Press, 1980 pb.

Pagis, Dan. *Points of Departure*. Translated by Stephen Mitchell, introduction by Robert Alter. Bilingual ed. Philadelphia: Jewish Publication Society, 1981.

An award-winning translation of the major contemporary Hebrew poet on the Holocaust.

Pilinszky, Janos. *Selected Poems. Translated by Ted Hughes and Janos Csokits. New York: Persea Books, 1976.

Plath, Sylvia. *Ariel. New York: Harper & Row, 1965.

   Various aspects of the Holocaust become metaphors for personal suffering in some of the poems in this collection.

Radnoti, Miklos. Clouded Sky. Translated by Steven Polgar, Stephen Berg, and S. J. Marks. New York: Harper & Row, 1972.

Reznikoff, Charles. *Holocaust. Los Angeles: Black Sparrow Press, 1975.

Rosensaft, Menachem Z. Fragments: Past and Future. New York: Shengold, 1968.

Rozewicz, Tadeusz. *"The Survivor" and Other Poems. Translated by Magnus J. Krynski and Robert McGuire. Princeton: Princeton University Press, 1976.

Sachs, Nelly. *O the Chimneys! Translated by Michael Hamburger, Ruth and Matthew Mead, and Michael Roloff. Bilingual ed. New York: Farrar, Straus & Giroux, 1967.

———. The Seeker and Other Poems. Translated by Ruth and Matthew Mead and Michael Hamburger. New York: Farrar, Straus & Giroux, 1970.

Schmuller, Aaron. Treblinka Grass. New York: Shulsinger Brothers, 1957.

———. While Man Exists: Poems and Translations. Brooklyn, N.Y.: Pantheon, 1970.

Siegel, Danny. Nine Entered Paradise Alive. New York: Town House Press, 1980.

Sklarew, Myra. *From the Backyard of the Diaspora. Washington, D.C.: Dryad Press, 1976.

Snodgrass, W. D. The Führer Bunker. Brockport, N.Y.: BOA Editions, 1977.

Sutzkever, Abraham. *Burnt Pearls: Ghetto Poems of Abraham Sutzkever. Translated by Seymour Mayne, introduction by Ruth R. Wisse. Mosaic Press/Valley Editions, 1981. Available only from the publisher, P.O. Box 1032, Oakville, Ont., Canada L6J 5E9.

   The first English collection of this major Yiddish poet of the Holocaust.

————. "Green Aquarium." Translated by Ruth R. Wisse. *Prooftexts: A Journal of Jewish Literary History* 2, no. 1 (January 1982): 95–121.

Fifteen prose poems on the author's experiences in the Vilna Ghetto and forests.

Taube, Herman. *A Chain of Images.* New York: Shulsinger Brothers, 1979.

Volakova, Hana (ed.). *I Never Saw Another Butterfly.* Translated by Jeanne Nemcova. New York: McGraw-Hill, 1964.

Remarkable collection of poetry and drawings by children in Terezin concentration camp.

Wiesel, Elie. *Ani Maamin: A Song Lost and Found Again.* Translated by Marion Wiesel. New York: Random House, 1973.

Wolfskehl, Karl. *1933—A Poem Sequence.* Translated by Carol North Valhope and Ernst Morwitz. New York: Schocken, 1947.

A German Jew's poetic attempts to understand the events surrounding Hitler's ascendancy in 1933.

Yevtushenko, Yevgeny. "Babi Yar." In *Selected Poems,* translated by Robin Milner-Gulland and Peter Levi. Baltimore: Penguin, 1974.

Other translations of "Babi Yar" may be found in *Hadassah Magazine,* March 1962, p. 15; *Jewish Currents,* December 1961, pp. 7–10; and the *Reconstructionist,* April 6, 1962, pp. 15–17.

5. Literary Criticism

Alexander, Edward. *The Resonance of Dust: Essays on Holocaust Literature and Jewish Fate.* Columbus: Ohio State University Press, 1979.

Literature of the Holocaust as a reflection of the Jewish role in and response to history, and of the failure of Jews to recognize the enormity of the events surrounding them.

Alter, Robert. *After the Tradition: Essays on Modern Jewish Writing.* New York: Dutton, 1969.

Includes provocative discussions of Wiesel, Guri, Amichai, and Bartov.

————. *Defenses of the Imagination: Jewish Writers and Modern Historical Crisis.* Philadelphia: Jewish Publication Society of America, 1977.

See his essays on Uri Zvi Greenberg, Charles Reznikoff, and Jewish humor.

Alvarez, A. "The Literature of the Holocaust." *Commentary* 38 (November 1964): 65–69. Reprinted in *Beyond All This Fiddle*, pp. 22–33. New York: Random House, 1969.

A good discussion of Rawicz's *Blood from the Sky.*

Bentley, Eric (ed.). *The Storm Over "The Deputy."* New York: Grove, 1965.

Valuable anthology of responses to Hochhuth's play as both text and drama, including literary, philosophical, and historical criticism, and a full bibliography of reviews by David Beams.

Bilik, Dorothy Seidman. *Immigrant Survivors: Post Holocaust Consciousness in Recent Jewish American Literature.* Middletown, Conn: Wesleyan University Press, 1981.

On Holocaust-related themes in the writings of Bellow, Singer, Malamud, and others

Bosmejiar, Hamida. *Metaphors of Evil: Contemporary German Literature and the Shadow of Nazism.* Iowa City: University of Iowa Press, 1979.

A sober evaluation from a non-Jewish perspective.

Brown, Robert McAfee. *Elie Wiesel: Messenger to All Humanity.* Notre Dame, Ind.: Notre Dame University Press, 1983.

Incorporating excerpts from Weisel's books, articles, talks, and conversations with the author, this is a fine introduction to his life and work.

Ezrahi, Sidra DeKoven. *By Words Alone: The Holocaust in Literature.* Chicago and London: University of Chicago Press, 1980; pb. 1982.

Includes brief but penetrating discussions of numerous works, while concentrating upon ways the same facts have been transformed into literature by different writers.

Fine, Ellen S. *Legacy of Night: The Literary Universe of Elie Wiesel.* New York: State University of New York Press, 1982.

Knopp, Josephine Zadovsky. *The Trial of Judaism in Contemporary Jewish Writing.* Urbana: University of Illinois Press, 1975.

Discusses Wiesel, Sachs, Singer, and Schwarz-Bart, as well as other authors less immediately concerned with the Holocaust.

Langer, Lawrence L. *The Age of Atrocity: Death in Modern Literature*. Boston: Beacon, 1978.

"Imaginative strategies" for dealing with "inappropriate death" in the writings of Thomas Mann, Camus, Solzhenitsyn, and Charlotte Delbo.

——. *The Holocaust and the Literary Imagination*. New Haven: Yale University Press. 1975.

The first major full-length study of the aesthetics of Holocaust writing, including penetrating discussions of the works of Schwarz-Bart, Wiesel, Celan, Sachs, and Hecht, among others, as well as some provocative distinctions between successes and failures in Holocaust literature.

——. *Versions of Survival: The Holocaust and the Human Spirit*. Albany: State University of New York Press, 1982.

Four long, remarkable essays entitled "Language as Refuge," "Auschwitz: The Death of Choice," "Elie Wiesel—Divided Voice in a Divided Universe," and "Gertrud Kolmer and Nelly Sachs—Bright Visions and Songs of Lamentations."

Milosz, Czeslaw. *The Witness of Poetry*. Cambridge, Mass.: Harvard University Press, 1983.

See especially "Ruins and Poetry."

Mintz, Alan. *Hurban: Responses to Catastrophe in Hebrew Literature*. New York: Columbia University Press, 1984.

A fine series of essays on literary responses to three great catastrophes: the destruction of the Second Temple, the Russian pogroms of the early twentieth century, and the Holocaust.

Rosenfeld, Alvin H. *A Double Dying: Reflections on Holocaust Literature*. Bloomington and London: Indiana University Press, 1980.

A thoroughgoing, generic survey of diaries, memoirs, fiction, poetry, and drama of the Holocaust, which raises essential questions about the criteria by which this literature is to be evaluated; includes an excellent bibliography.

—— and Greenberg, Irving (eds.). *Confronting the Holocaust: The Impact of Elie Wiesel*. Bloomington and London: Indiana University Press, 1979.

A dozen essays examining Wiesel's work from literary, historical, psychological, and theological perspectives.

Roskies, David G. *Against the Apocalypse: Responses to Catastrophe in Modern Jewish Culture.* Cambridge, Mass.: Harvard University Press, 1984.

Treats the literature of the Holocaust within the context of East European Jewish culture in the nineteenth and twentieth centuries.

Steiner, George. **Language and Silence: Essays on Language, Literature, and the Inhuman.* New York: Atheneum, 1967, pb. 1970.

The title adequately captures Steiner's principal concerns, but not the genius with which he provocatively treats them. Many of these essays, including "The Hollow Miracle," seek to develop a "philosophy of language" at the heart of which lies the artist's special responsibility to his reader and to his subject.

Section I-C

Bibliographies on the Holocaust for Young People

by Bea Stadtler

1. Nonfiction, Fictionalized Biography, and Fictionalized Autobiography

Abells, Chana Byers. *The Children We Remember*. Rockville, Md.: Kar-Ben Copies, 1983.

> A book of photographs from Yad Vashem of the Jewish children under Nazi domination, some who perished and some who survived; its forty-one photos and several hundred words are appropriate for the third and fourth grades, with a teacher's guide. Ages 7–10.

Altshuler, David. *Hitler's War Against the Jews*. New York: Behrman House, 1978.

> This adaptation of Lucy Dawidowicz's *The War Against the Jews* is divided into two parts: Part I, The Final Solution; Part II, The Holocaust. Maps and photos are included, and at the end, "Some Dates to Remember." Each chapter ends with a small section entitled "Issues and Values." Although the book is divided thematically and clearly printed, the language is suitable only for ages 14 and up.

Anti-Defamation League of B'nai B'rith and National Council for the Social Sciences (NCSS). *The Record: The Holocaust in History*. New York: ADL and NCSS, 1978.

A good introduction to the Holocaust in the form of a historical tabloid with key names, dates, and events, along with maps and other graphics. Age 14 and up.

Appel, Benjamin. *Hitler: From Power to Ruin*. New York: Grosset & Dunlap, 1964.

From the years Hitler was a nobody to his rise and ultimate defeat and suicide, this book tells his history. It is printed in bold, large letters and includes black-and-white photos. Ages 11–13.

Baer, Edith. *A Frost in the Night*. New York: Pantheon Books, 1980.

Eve Bentheim lived a happy, peaceful life in Thalstadt, Germany. She was an only child, doted on by her parents, grandfather, and assorted relatives. Soon, she heard remarks being made about Jews, which became more frequent and vicious. The book ends with Hitler's appointment as Chancellor of Germany. The plot never really gets off the ground, in part because there is too much descriptive material on Eve's town, house, and relatives. Ages 11–13.

Baldwin, Margaret. *The Boys Who Saved the Children*. New York: Julian Messner, 1981.

Ben Edelbaum's experiences in the Lodz ghetto are told in a very simple and moving way. Ben and other boys working in the fur factory in Lodz save the ghetto's children for a time by making a fur coat for the wife of the German officer in charge of the ghetto. Ages 11–13.

Bar Oni, Bryna. *The Vapor*. Chicago: Visual Impact, 1976.

Bryna's story began in 1937, when she was twelve years old. Two weeks later the Nazis conquered Poland, bringing terror and blood-shed in their wake. This is the author's story of her resistance, her fears, and her experiences. Age 14 and up.

Bergman, David. *Never Forget and Never Forgive*. Chicago: Remembrance Educational Media, 1979 (with taped narration).

The format of this book is a looseleaf notebook, with photographs and sketches. Short, succinct passages tell about Bergman's experiences during the Holocaust years. Ages 11–13.

Cowan, Lori. *Children of the Resistance*. New York: Archwa, 1969.

Eight stories about teenagers who were active in the resistance. Age 14 and up.

Dribben, Judith. *And Some Shall Live*. Jerusalem: Keter Books, 1969.

Judith Strick was in Poland at the beginning of World War II. She was able to join the partisans in the forest and managed to fight against the Germans in many ways, including spying, bombing trains, killing German soldiers, and other activities. Age 14 and up.

Edelstein, Dov. *Worlds Torn Asunder*. New York: Ktav, 1984.

The author, a pious Hasidic youth from the town of Szatmár in Hungary, was sent to Auschwitz at the age of seventeen. A moving, religiously sensitive, and exceptionally well written account of life in the camp. Age 14 and up.

Eliav, Arie. *The Voyage of the "Ulua."* Translated from Hebrew by Israel Taslitt. New York: Sabra Books, 1969.

The *Ulua* was a ship carrying "illegal" immigrants (a group of 800 survivors) to Israel, while the British blockaded the seaports. The author, who captained the ship, tells how the *Ulua* beat the British blockade and entered Israel illegally, in this fine, exciting work. Age 14 and up.

Ferderber-Salz, Bertha. *And the Sun Kept Shining*. New York: Holocaust Library, 1980.

A survivor and the mother of two daughters relates with simplicity and realism the heroism and humanism of most of the other Jews in a ghetto and camp, as well as how she was eventually reunited with her daughters. *And the Sun Kept Shining* is much more realistic and sensitive than most other Holocaust books. Age 14 and up.

Flinker, Moshe. *Young Moshe's Diary*. Introduction by Saul Esh and Geoffrey Wigoder. Jerusalem: Yad Vashem, 1965.

The diary of a sixteen-year-old Orthodox Jewish boy who died in Auschwitz; his thoughts are mature and philosophical. This is a real classic. Age 14 and up.

Foreman, James. *Ceremony of Innocence*. New York: Hawthorn Books, 1970.

A German brother and sister engage in brave resistance to the Nazis. This is a story about two individuals involved in a resistance group that really existed. Age 14 and up.

———. *Nazism*. New York: Franklin Watts, 1978; Dell Laurel Leaf, 1980.

A good short introduction; focusing on Hitler and on Nazi ideology. Age 14 and up.

————. *The White Crow*. New York: Farrar, Straus & Giroux, 1976.

This is a fictionalized retelling of Hitler's youth, from 1907, when he was eighteen, until the unsuccessful attempt to gain power in Munich in 1923; a portrait of a fanatic, showing the roots of the anger and hatred that later engulfed the world. Age 14 and up.

Frank, Anne. *The Diary of a Young Girl*. New York: Globe, 1958.

Anne Frank's diary is adapted for the younger child in an edition that includes photos, an excellent short epilogue, and questions for students. Age 14 and up.

————. *The Diary of a Young Girl*. Introduction by Eleanor Roosevelt; translated from the Dutch by B. M. Mooyaart. New York: Doubleday, 1967; Pocket Books, 1967.

Anne Frank's diary encompasses the period from June 1942 to July 1944, during which time the Frank family was hidden by Dutch friends in a warehouse. The first few entries deal with life in Holland before their hiding. There is an "Afterword" in this book, which gives a short historical synopsis of German history from the beginning of the twentieth century. Age 14 and up.

Friedlander, Albert H. *Out of the Whirlwind: A Reader of Holocaust Literature*. New York: Union of American Hebrew Congregations, 1968; Schocken pb., 1976.

This volume constitutes a major contribution to Holocaust studies and can be read by individuals or used as a classroom text. It incorporates literary selections from such diverse sources as *The Last of the Just, The Town Beyond the Wall*, and *The Diary of a Young Girl: Anne Frank*. In addition, it includes scholarly selections from Salo W. Baron, Bruno Bettelheim, Alexander Donat, and many others. The last section of this excellent overview is concerned with "Questions After the Storm." Age 14 and up.

Gilbert, Martin. *The Holocaust: Maps and Photographs*. New York: Hill & Wang, 1978.

Gilbert includes invaluable maps and photos with short notes. Ages 11–13.

Goldston, Robert. *Sinister Touches: The Secret War Against Hitler*. New York: Dial Press. 1982.

On the anti-Nazi resistance movement in Europe; a short, readable account for younger readers. Age 14 and up.

Gurdis, Luba Krugman. *The Death Train*. New York: Holocaust Library, 1978.

A survivor recounts her memories of suffering during World War II and includes sketches she made of her experiences. At one hideout, she and her family were near the tracks on which ran the trains taking Jews to Belzec, a death camp. She was also a survivor of Majdanek concentration camp. Age 14 and up.

Hannan, Charles. *A Boy in That Situation: An Autobiography*. New York: Harper & Row, 1978.

In this self-portrait, a Jew in Hitler's Germany recalls how he had too much *chutzpa* (daring or gall) for a boy in his situation. Ages 11–13.

Heyman, Eva. *The Diary of Eva Heyman*. Translated from Hebrew by Moshe Kohn. Jerusalem: Yad Vashem, Alpha Press, 1974.

Thirteen-year-old Eva Heyman left a diary that she kept from February 13 to May 30, 1944, in which she describes her life in a small Hungarian town under Nazi occupation. After her mother and stepfather fled, Eva lived with her grandparents before she and they were taken to Auschwitz and murdered. Ages 11–13.

Hoffman, Judy. *Joseph and Me in the Days of the Holocaust*. New York: Ktav, 1979.

The first chapter of this illustrated booklet gives the background of the Jews in Europe and the rise of Hitler and Nazi Germany. The author proceeds to tell the story of her survival during the Holocaust and arrival in Israel. A useful glossary explains many words in the book. Ages 11–13.

Hyams, Joseph. *A Field of Buttercups*. Englewood Cliffs, N.J.: Prentice-Hall, 1968.

Janusz Korczak was a famous Polish-Jewish doctor and educator. He felt children should largely govern themselves, and practiced these theories in the orphanage he established in Warsaw. This book tells of his experiences from the time the orphanage was transferred to the ghetto, during the Nazi occupation of Poland, until the children were sent to the Treblinka death camp. When they disposed of their yellow stars at the *Umschlagplatz* (transfer point for deportation), it looked like "a field of buttercups." The good doctor would not abandon his small charges and, although he was offered his freedom, went with them to his death. Age 14 and up.

Joffo, Joseph. *A Bag of Marbles*. Translated from French by Martin Sokolensky. Boston: Houghton Mifflin, 1974.

A true story by the author, who was ten years old in 1941 and who, with his twelve-year-old brother, Maurice, was sent away by their barber father to escape from the Nazis. The story begins when Jo trades his yellow star for a bag of marbles. Age 14 and up.

Kerr, Judith. *When Hitler Stole the Pink Rabbit*. New York: Coward, McCann & Geoghegan, 1972.

Based on her own experiences, Kerr has written of her escape as a child to Switzerland, and finally to England, together with her family. The pink rabbit was a stuffed animal that was left behind in the rush to leave Germany. Ages 11–13..

Kluger, Ruth, and Mann, Peggy. *The Secret Ship*. New York: Doubleday, 1978.

A young person's version of *The Last Escape*, which personally recounts Ruth Kluger's work with illegal *aliya* (immigration) into Palestine in 1939. Ages 11–13.

Koehn, Ilse. *Mischling, Second Degree*. New York: Greenwillow Books, 1977; Bantam pb.

The author is a child of a Jewish father and a non-Jewish mother, with one Jewish grandparent, which made her a *Mischling*, second degree, according to the Nazis. Her experience in Hitler Youth camps is recounted in a very straightforward way. Ages 11–13.

Kohn, Nahum, and Roiter, Howard. *A Voice from the Forest*. New York: Holocaust Library, 1980.

Of the many books written about the Holocaust, few have been about the partisans in the forest. This exciting book is particularly welcome because of its dispassionate, factual approach. Age 14 and up.

Kuper, Jack. *Child of the Holocaust*. New York: Doubleday, 1968.

Nine-year-old Jankel returns to his hometown in Poland to find that his family has been captured by the Nazis. He pretends he is not a Jew and, during the next four years, passes as a Gentile, almost coming to believe he is one. Age 14 and up.

Kulski, Julian Eugeniusz. *Dying, We Live*. New York: Holt, Rinehart & Winston, 1979.

The author of this book was the son of the mayor of Warsaw during the Nazi occupation and was ten years old when the war began. He became involved with the Polish resistance movement and speaks with admiration about the courage of the Jews in the ghetto. He presents his story in a kind of diary, which he reconstructed long after the war. His family was exceptional and was not, unfortunately, typical of Polish attitudes towards the Jews. His book is well written and interesting. Age 13 and up.

Lyttle, Richard B. *Nazi Hunting*. New York: Franklin Watts, 1982.

A study for younger readers of the search for six Nazis, including Adolf Eichmann, Josef Mengele, and Martin Bormann. Ages 11–13.

Meltzer, Milton. *Never to Forget*. New York: Harper & Row, 1976.

"Why remember?", an introductory two pages at the beginning of the book, is filled with things to think about. The rest of the volume is divided into parts entitled: "History of Hatred," "Destruction of the Jews," and "The Spirit of Resistance." *Never to Forget* includes a chronology, maps, and a bibliography that is largely composed of adult books not really suitable to young readers. Age 14 and up.

Nazi Germany. New York: Longman Schools Division, 1982.

A resource package of nine units, each with a narrative, primary source material, and illustrations. Ages 11–13.

Noble, Iris. *Nazi Hunter: Simon Wiesenthal*. New York: Julian Messner, 1979.

This book is a biography of Simon Wiesenthal, a hunter of Nazis who, through a streak of coincidences and bulldog tenacity, discovered the whereabouts of Adolf Eichmann. It also tells of his successes and failures in hunting other Nazis in America and elsewhere. Age 14 and up.

Orlev, Uri. *The Lead Soldiers*. Translated from Hebrew by Hillel Halkin. New York: Taplinger, 1980.

The Nazi occupation of Poland is seen through the eyes of Yurik, a young boy, and his younger brother, Kazik. From Warsaw the youngsters are sent to Bergen-Belsen and, after their liberation, proceed to Israel. Age 14 and up.

Patterson, Charles. *Anti-Semitism: The Road to the Holocaust and Beyond*. New York: Walker, 1982.

Patterson explains how the Holocaust was not an isolated chapter in history, but rather a culmination of centuries of persecution of the Jewish people. From the roots of anti-Semitism in ancient history to an examination of present-day anti-Semitism, the author takes the reader along the long history of anti-Semitic discrimination, violence, terror, and murder. Age 14 and up.

Pilch, Judah (ed.). *The Jewish Catastrophe in Europe*. New York: American Association for Jewish Education, 1968.

With chapters on the roots of the Holocaust, and overview of its unfolding, the apathy of "spectators," resistance, and the literature of the Holocaust, this handbook is an interesting, readable introduction. Age 14 and up.

Prager, Moshe. *Sparks of Glory*. Translated from Hebrew by Mordecai Schreiber. New York: Shengold, 1974.

Here are stories about spiritual resistance during the Holocaust, about those with ultimate faith in God. The author interviewed survivors after the war and retells their experiences. Age 14 and up.

Rabinowitz, Dorothy. *About the Holocaust*. New York: American Jewish Committee, 1979.

This pamplet contains invaluable information that refutes the arguments of those who doubt the reality of the Holocaust. Age 14 and up.

Rabinsky, Beatrice, and Mann, Gertrude. *Journey of Conscience*. New York: Collins-World, 1979.

High school students tell of their trip to sites of the Holocaust. The booklet indicates how some high school teachers make learning about the Holocaust a meaningful, thoughtful experience for their students. Ages 11–13.

Reisman, Arnold, and Reisman, Ellen. *Welcome Tomorrow*. Cleveland: North Coast Publishing, 1983.

These memoirs relate the author's early boyhood in Lodz, his native city, and then his many incredible adventures. Reisman tells how his family escaped to Russia and the experiences they had fleeing from one area in Russia to another as the Nazis conquered more and more territory. Experiencing a different kind of persecution, terror, flight, and incarceration than other Jews did under the Nazis, the resilient little boy managed to survive and even helped his mother to endure. Although Lionia, as Arnold

Reisman was called, originally wanted to settle in Israel, his parents persuaded him to emigrate to America, where he is now a professor of management and systems analysis. Age 14 and up.

Reiss, Johanna. *The Upstairs Room. New York: Crowell, 1972; Bantam pb., 1973.

The author describes her experiences as a Jewish child in Holland after Hitler's invasion. Ages 11–13.

———. *The Journey Back.* New York: Crowell, 1982.

When peace is declared, the author and her sister journey back home to begin life once more as a family. They must adjust to many things, including a stepmother who has replaced the mother murdered in the Holocaust, and a sister who has converted to Christianity. This is a moving sequel to *The Upstairs Room.* Ages 11–13.

Rossel, Seymour. *The Holocaust.* New York: Franklin Watts, 1981.

The book tells how the Nazis planned, and carried out, their program of extermination against the Jews and how the Holocaust affects us today. Age 14 and up.

Rubin, Arnold P. *Hitler and the Nazis: The Evil That Men Do. New York: Julian Messner, 1977; Bantam, 1979 (as *The Evil That Men Do: The Story of the Nazis*).

Many aspects of the Holocaust are included in this book: relations between Jews and Christians, anti-Semitism, and the silence and passivity of the world. Age 14 and up.

Salomon, Charlotte. *Charlotte.* New York: Harcourt, Brace & World, 1963; Viking, 1982.

Charlotte was born in Berlin in April 1917. In 1933, at age sixteen, she left school, where she had been humiliated because she was Jewish. She then went to art school. In 1939, her father sent her to her grandparents in southern France, thinking she would be safe there. Lonely and unhappy, she told her story in words and in hundreds of pictures. In 1943, she was captured and murdered in Auschwitz. (The 1982 edition alone includes the complete drawings.) Age 14 and up.

Schweifert, Peter. *The Bird Has Wings: Letters of Peter Schweifert.* Edited by Claude Lanzman; translated from French by Barbara Lucas. New York: St. Martin's Press, 1976.

Peter Schweifert left Germany when he was twenty-one and was killed when he was twenty-seven. These letters are to his mother, who tries to deny she is Jewish. In the letters, he urges her to declare herself a Jew and to be proud of her identity. Age 14 and up.

Siegel, Aranka. *Upon the Head of a Goat. New York: Farrar, Straus & Giroux, 1981.

Nine-year-old Piri, visiting her grandmother in the Ukraine, is at first not able to return home to Hungary when the war breaks out. Finally, she does return to yellow badges, rations, avoidance by old friends, and a forced move into a ghetto. Through her mother's determination, her family is held together for a long time before being deported to Auschwitz, where they are separated and meet different fates. Ages 11–13.

Stadtler, Bea. *The Holocaust: A History of Courage and Resistance. New York: Behrman House, 1975.

These twenty-two short chapters include the time from World War I to the Nuremberg trials; they cover spiritual and physical resistance and highlight the dilemmas Jews and Jewish leaders encountered. Excerpts from documents and the questions at the end of each chapter make this a particularly thoughtful book. Ages 11–13.

Stanke, Alain. So Much to Forget. Translated from French by Susan Altschul. Agincourt, Ont.: Gage, 1977.

Through the eyes of a six-year-old boy, the author tells his story of the Russian, and then Nazi, occupation of Lithuania. Stanke, who is not Jewish, relates his story simply and well. Age 14 and up.

Steenmeijer, Anneke (in collaboration with Otto Frank). A Tribute to Anne Frank. New York: Doubleday, 1971.

This is a collection of letters and tributes received by Otto Frank after the publication of The Diary of a Young Girl. The volume has beautiful photographs and many moving entries. Age 14 and up.

Stern, Ellen Norman. Elie Weisel: Witness For Life. New York: Ktav, 1982.

This biography of the most famous writer of the Holocaust traces the reasons for his mystical leanings. The book takes the reader from Wiesel's childhood in Sighet through the Holocaust and after. Age 14 and up.

Suhl, Yuri. Uncle Misha's Partisans. New York: Four Winds Press, 1973.

This is a true, exciting, and suspenseful story of resistance against the Nazis by a small band of Jewish fighters in the forest under the leadership of Diadia Misha, better known as Uncle Misha. Ages 11–13.

Volakova, Hana (ed.). *I Never Saw Another Butterfly*. New York: Schocken, 1983.

This famous anthology includes poems and drawings by children in the concentration camp at Theresienstadt, Czechoslovakia, along with a note on each poem and its author. The children were subsequently sent to their deaths. Age 10 and up.

Weissman-Klein, Gerda. *Promise of a New Spring*. Chappaqua, N.Y.: Rossell Books, 1982.

Using different kinds of illustrations, this book is a simple, appropriately restrained introduction to what was lost in the Holocaust, and how the Jewish people began to recover—appropriate for very young readers. Ages 7–10.

Werstein, Irving. *That Denmark Might Live*. Philadelphia: Marcus Smith, 1967.

This book deals with the Danish resistance against the Nazis and the protection of the country's Jews. "Although Denmark did not actually fight on the Allied side, she contributed much to the defeat of Germany," according to Field Marshal Montgomery, who added, "The Danish resistance was worth ten divisions." Ages 11–13.

———. *The Uprising of the Warsaw Ghetto*. New York: Norton, 1968.

The author uses interviews, trial records, and survivor journals to tell the story of the Warsaw Ghetto Uprising, which lasted longer than the battle of the whole Polish army against the invasion of Germany. Here is an authentic, historical account. Age 14 and up.

Wiesel, Elie. *Night*. New York: Hill & Wang, 1960; Avon pb., 1969; Bantam pb.

Wiesel's memoir was one of the first books by a survivor about his experiences during the Holocaust years. It is a slim volume but undoubtedly one of the best ever written. Elie Wiesel struggles to maintain his belief in a good and merciful God, in the face of the Jewish experience during the Hitler years. Age 14 and up.

Wolfe, Burton. *Hitler and the Nazis*. New York: Putnam, 1970.

From Adolf Hitler's beginnings to his miserable end, this book relates, in simple language, the story of the rise of the Nazi party and Hitler. Ages 11–13.

Zei, Alki. *Petros' War*. New York: Dutton, 1972.

Alki Zei has written an exciting book, based on some of his own experiences in German-occupied Greece. Petros and his sister, Antigone, are part of a resistance movement in which Rita, a Jewish girl, participates until they have to hide her. Ages 11–13.

Zieman, Joseph. *The Cigarette Sellers of the Three Crosses Square*. Translated from Polish by Janina David. Minneapolis: Lerner Publications, 1975.

A band of children and teenagers help each other survive in Nazi-occupied Poland. These Jewish children manage to escape from the ghetto to the Aryan section of Warsaw. The author meets them and records their conversations and experiences. Age 14 and up.

2. Fiction

Ambrose, Kenneth. *The Story of Peter Cronheim*. New York: Duell, Sloan & Pearce, 1962.

Peter lives in a town in north Germany, and in 1932 celebrates his *Bar Mitzvah*. But after that things begin to change for the Jews, first slowly and then more and more rapidly. Soon he sees hate and brutality out in the open. He arrives in England at the end of the story. Ages 11–13.

Arnold, Elliot. *A Kind of Secret Weapon*. New York: Scribner's, 1969.

Denmark is occupied by the Nazis in 1940. Peter Andersen's parents are involved in printing an underground newspaper calling for resistance against the Germans. Peter soon becomes involved in this activity and has many adventures in his clandestine work. Ages 11–13.

———. *A Night of Watching*. New York: Scribner's, 1967.

Here is one of the few novels about the Danish uprising on behalf of the Jews in 1943. Age 14 and up.

Arrick, Fran. *Chernowitz*. Scarsdale, N.Y.: Bradbury Press, 1981.

Bobby Cherno, a Jewish boy in the ninth grade in an American high school, is tormented by an anti-Semitic peer. The bully gathers a group around him, and the Jew-baiting extends to Bobby's family. The ultimate outcome is an assembly at school where films are shown of concentration camps and their victims, causing many of the students to become ill. Still, this does not change the anti-Semitic bully's attitude. Age 14 and up.

Benchley, Nathaniel. *Bright Candles: A Novel of the Danish Resistance.* New York: Harper & Row, 1974

When actions were taken by the Nazis against Danish Jews, cooperation with the Germans was no longer possible for people of conscience. This is the story of the Danish resistance against German oppression. Ages 11–13.

Bezedekova, Zdenka. *They Called Me Leni.* Translated from Czech by Stuart R. Amor. New York: Bobbs Merrill, 1973.

A young Czech girl, abducted from her home, is placed with a Nazi family to be "reeducated." The book is concerned with her search for her true identity. Ages 8–10.

Bishop, Claire Huchet. *Twenty and Ten.* New York: Viking Press, 1952.

Twenty children in a Catholic children's home take in ten Jewish children. Sister Gabriel, the orphanage's director, is captured by the Nazis, who come to the orphanage to try to force the children to reveal the hiding place of the Jewish children. But the orphans manage to conceal their secret very well. Ages 8–10.

Block, Marie. *Displaced Person.* New York: Lothrop, Lee & Shepard, 1978.

Stefan has come to a displaced persons' camp in Germany from Russia. Life in the camp is hard. The book deals with his struggle with the concepts of freedom and survival. Age 14 and up.

Bunting, Eve. *Terrible Things.* Illustrated by Stephen Gansmell. New York: Harper & Row, 1980.

A marvelous picture-book story showing how, group by group, the animals in the forest are taken away by the Terrible Things, until White Rabbit finds reasons for each of these "round-ups." Martin Niemoeller's famous statement translated into a language children can understand. Ages 7–10.

Dank, Milton. *The Dangerous Game.* New York: Lippincott, 1977.

Charles Marceau, son of a French father and an American mother, joins a resistance group in Paris and has many close calls with the Nazis. Ages 11–13.

Demetz, Hanna. *The House on Prague Street.* New York: St. Martin's Press, 1980; Avon pb., 1983.

This is the story of Helene Richter and the house in which she lived in Czechoslovakia with her grandfather, who was more Czech than Jewish. The gradual deterioration of the family is shown as things in Czechoslovakia become more desperate for the Jews. Hanna Demetz has written a tender, sensitive book. Age 14 and up.

Eisenberg, Azriel, and Globe, Leah Ain (eds.). *The Secret Weapon and Other Tales of Faith and Valor*. New York: Soncino Press, 1966.

This is a collection of stories, several of which deal with World War II. One story, by Baruch Hermanowitz, is about how a pair of *tefillin* (phylacteries) become a secret weapon against the Nazis. Ages 11–13.

Firer, Ben Zion. *Twins*. New York: Phillip Feldheim, 1981.

About twins (a boy and a girl) who are separated during the Holocaust—he to Israel, she to a Polish convent—and about their eventual reunion. Age 14 and up.

Kay, Mara. *In the Face of Danger*. New York: Crown, 1977.

Ann Lindsay is caught in Nazi Germany when her uncle is injured in an auto accident. Her discovery of two Jewish girls hidden in her house and her attempts to save them are part of an exciting story. Ages 11–13.

Kerr, M. E. *Gentlehands*. New York: Harper & Row, 1978.

Buddy Boyle, a poor boy, falls in love with Skye Pennington, a very rich girl. In the course of their relationship, Buddy and Skye discover that Buddy's grandfather is a former Nazi who beat and tortured the Jewish women prisoners at a concentration camp. This has a devastating effect on Buddy and his relationship with Skye. Age 14 and up.

Kranzler, Gershon. *Seder in Berlin and Other Stories*. New York: Merkos L'inyonei Chinuch, 1975.

These are stories based on religious *mitzvot* (commandments). A few of these stories are about the Holocaust, including "The Little Red Shoe," "The Miracle of Manheim," and "Seder in Berlin." The coincidences in these stories make sense when we consider what really happened to survivors. Ages 11–13.

Levin, Jane. *Star of Danger*. New York: Harcourt, Brace & World, 1966.

By concentrating on two good friends, Karl and Peter, *Star of Danger* tells the story of the Danish resistance. Age 14 and up.

Levitan, Sonia. *Journey to America*. New York: Atheneum, 1970.

Lisa's papa goes to America to set up his business and living quarters for his family, which remains behind in Germany. The book deals with the heartbreak of leaving friends and belongings behind when the family finally departs. It also deals with the poverty that they experience and the trauma of beginning again. Ages 11–13.

Levoy, Myron. *Alan and Naomi*. New York: Harper & Row, 1977.

Alan lives in New York City and likes to play stickball more than anything else. But it is 1944, and Naomi Kirshenbaum lives upstairs. She was in France during the Nazi occupation and suffered a great deal. She is very withdrawn and does not participate in anything. Alan tries to help her become adjusted to living again. In the end, he is successful. Ages 11–13.

Mace, Elizabeth. *Brother Enemy*. New York: Beaufort Books, 1981.

At age nine, Andreas, a *Mischling*, was sent from Hamburg to London. He returns ten years later to find that his mother is dead, his half-brother vastly changed. Age 14 and up.

Moskin, Marietta. *I Am Rosemarie*. New York: John Day, 1972.

This book is about a Jewish girl in Amsterdam caught in Hitler's net in 1940. She goes from the transit camp at Westerbork to Bergen-Belsen and from there to Biberach, another concentration camp. Ages 11–13.

Murray, Michele. *The Crystal Night*. New York: Laurel Leaf (Dell), 1975.

The pre-1940 anti-Semitism of Germany reaches into the life of a farm family in Connecticut. Age 14 and up.

Neshamit, Sara. *Children of Mapu Street*. Philadelphia: Jewish Publication Society, 1970.

In 1941, Kovno, Lithuania, was invaded by the Nazis. This is the story of the Jewish children who lived in a courtyard on Mapu Street during the German invasion, along with the hatred of some of their non-Jewish neighbors, and the courage of others. Shmuelik, the protagonist, who is captured and who escapes from a train taking him to a concentration camp, stands out in this tender and exciting novel. Age 14 and up.

Orgel, Doris. *A Certain Magic*. New York: Dial Press, 1976.

Two lives, thirty-six years apart, seem to come together when eleven-year-old Jenny finds her aunt's diary. The diary tells about the aunt's experiences as a Jewish refugee living in England. The story blends fantasy and realism and seems to merge past and present. Ages 11–13.

———. *The Devil in Vienna*. New York: Dial Press, 1978.

The plot focuses on the friendship between a Jewish girl and a Catholic girl whose father is a Nazi during the Hitler years. Their separation, correspondence, and reunion are touching and enlightening. The Jewish family is saved by the Catholic girl's uncle, who is a priest. Ages 11–13.

Richter, Hans Peter. **Friedrich*. Translated from German by Edith Kroll. New York: Laurel Leaf (Dell), 1973.

The story is told by Friedrich's friend, who is non-Jewish. The gradual deterioration of his friendship with Friedrich is realistically described. Ages 11–13.

Rose, Anne. *Refugee*. New York: Dial, 1977.

Refugee is about the author's experiences fleeing Nazi Europe and her apprehension as she waits for her parents to join her in America. Ages 11–13.

Sachs, Marilyn. *A Pocketful of Seeds*. New York: Doubleday, 1973.

Nicole Neiman is separated from her parents during the Nazi invasion of France. During the war, she changes from a sheltered and immature eight-year-old to a courageous thirteen-year old. Marilyn Sachs's novel is based on the true experiences of one of her friends. Despite some factual errors in the Seder scene, this is an absorbing story. Ages 11–13.

Samuels, Gertrude. *Mottele: A Partisan Odyssey*. New York: Harper, 1976.

Mottele returns from his music lesson to find the Germans have destroyed his home and murdered his family. The twelve-year-old flees to the forest and then takes revenge on the Germans in their officers' club. This fictionalized account of Jewish partisan experiences is based on true episodes. Ages 11–13.

Shemin, Margaretha. *The Empty Moat*. New York: Coward-McCann, 1969.

In this lovely story, Elizabeth van Swaenenburgh lives in a beautiful castle in Holland, now shared by German soldiers. The moat around the castle has swans, and as long as they are there, legend has it that no harm will befall the castle. In the dungeon, Elizabeth hides first a British soldier and then a Jewish girl. Courageous, though fearful, she sees the Jewish transports to the concentration camp, and cannot forget them. Ages 11–13.

Suhl, Yuri. *On the Other Side of the Gate.* New York: Avon Books, 1975.

Here is the story of a young boy who was handed over the wall of the Warsaw Ghetto to a non-Jewish family to be taken care of during the war. The book focuses on the feelings of the child's family as they make the difficult decision to hide him among sympathetic Poles. An "afterword" tells about what really happened to the Jewish children who went to the "other side of the wall." Although this is a novel, the story could be, and probably is, true. Age 14 and up.

Van Stockum, Hilda. *The Borrowed House.* New York: Farrar, Straus & Giroux, 1975.

Twelve-year-old Janna, a German girl, moves into a "borrowed" house in Amsterdam with her actor parents. In exploring the house, she finds artifacts of the previous Jewish owners, as well as a closet full of clothes for a girl her own age. In questioning servants and neighbors, she learns a great deal about the Jewish family that previously owned the house. This gives her a disturbing picture of the Hitler Youth organization to which she once belonged. Ages 11–13.

Vivier, Collette. *House of the Four Winds.* Translated from French by Miriam Morton. New York: Doubleday, 1969.

A young Parisian boy becomes involved with an underground resistance group during the German occupation of France. Ages 11–13.

Wuorio, Eva-Lis. *Code: Polonaise.* New York: Holt, Rinehart & Winston, 1971.

A small band of young Polish patriots secretly work for their country's freedom. Although this book does deal with the Nazis and the Polish resistance, nothing is said about Jews, Jewish persecution, or Jewish resistance. Ages 11–13.

3. Short Story Anthologies

Belth, Norton (ed.). *The First "World Over" Story Book*. New York: Jewish Education Committee of New York, 1952.

> This anthology includes three stories on the Holocaust: Stephen Fein's "Hanukkah Light in Warsaw," Elchanan Indelman's "Underground Brigade," and Azriel Eisenberg and Abraham Segal's "Stowaway."

————. *The Second "World Over" Story Book*. New York: Jewish Education Committee of New York, 1952.

> Included here are two stories of Jewish heroism during the Holocaust: Reuben Davis's "Hannah Szenes, She Fought for Freedom," and Curtis Lubinski's "The Heroes of Warsaw."

Section II

Audio-Visual Materials on the Holocaust

by Eric A. Goldman and Nama Frenkel

The following is a list of recommended films on the Holocaust. We have endeavored to choose films and videotapes that are in readily usable formats (16-mm film, ½-inch Beta/UHS and ¾-inch U-Matic video-tape) and are *presently available for rental*. (All audio-visual materials are 16mm unless otherwise indicated. Rental fees are indicated as of the fall of 1983, and are subject to change.) The film's distributor and current rental or purchase price, when known, are indicated at the end of each entry. A list of distributors, including addresses, is provided at the end of the chapter.

This filmography cannot possibly be complete and comprehensive, but we feel that the materials listed should provide an adequate base for programming related to the subject.

1. Short Films

Ambulance, a film by Janusz Morganstern (1962, age 16 up, 9 min., b&w), is a trigger film that gives perceptive viewers a microcosm of the Holocaust. Beginning with the menacing sound of German marching music that keeps time to the rantings of Hitler, the first minutes are interspersed with coughs of exhaust from an ambu-lance. Children, under guard, play nearby. Birds overhead fly free. A dog runs back and forth. Only the children and their adult companion have no escape. By the end, a Yiddish folk song has turned into Kaddish. The children and their teacher are gone. The message of this little piece, however, haunts the viewer long after the more graphic and horrifying films have been rejected by the mind's eye, which can only take in so much.

Jewish Media Service/JWB, rental fee $20.

The Arrival of Hitler, directed by Leni Riefenstahl (1974, age 14 up, 12 min., b&w), is the opening sequence from *Triumph of the Will*. After an overture, Hitler's plane appears, casting a shadow over the town. As his motorcade progresses through Nuremberg, there is a sense of drama: crowds cheering, saluting, and waving. This film extract can be an important teaching tool documenting Hitler's charismatic appeal to the German masses. The teacher or group leader might raise questions such as: Why was this film made? How does this film reflect Hitler's illusions of grandeur? How does this film illustrate the potential of the media as a propaganda tool?

Films, Inc., rental fee $40.

The Avenue of the Just, produced by the ADL, directed by Samuel Elfert, written by Arnold Foster (1978, age 12 up, 55 min., color), refers to the tree-lined walk at Yad Vashem, Israel's Holocaust memorial, that pays tribute to Christians who saved Jewish lives. This film celebrates ten of those valiant people. Recognizing that these people risked personal safety and even brought their families into jeopardy, it is a celebration of heroism at a time when most of humanity turned away. There are interviews with men and women who sacrificed for others and with some of the people they saved. It includes interviews with Anne Frank's father, the people who hid the Frank family in Amsterdam, and sequences showing that famous house today.

Anti-Defamation League of B'nai B'rith, rental fee $40.

Cages (1967, age 14 up, 9 min., b&w) is an animated film about a man in a cage. As freedom is given to the prisoner by the jailer, the prisoner takes more than the jailer intended. As the camera moves back, we see that not only is the prisoner in a cage, but the jailer is in a cage, and so on. It would serve as a good trigger film on freedom, authority, and imprisonment themes.

Michigan Media Rental, $10.25.

The Camera of My Family, a film by Catherine Noren (1979, age 12 up, filmstrip with accompanying audiocassette, 18 min., color), brings four generations of a German family to life. They lived from 1845 to 1945. The world as they knew it came to an end with Hitler. Catherine Noren, a professional photographer, grew up in a family that wanted to suppress all memories of that old life. With her curiosity aroused by an old photo album, she began a search for the story of her family that unlocked the past. She learned that twenty-six members of the family were sent to concentration camps. Nineteen died—by gas, bullets, starvation, or suicide. This filmstrip is a striking change from most Holocaust confrontations. The photographs are, for the most part, real family portraits. The artist integrates facts with family history and makes her statement most poignantly.

Anti-Defamation League of B'nai B'rith, purchase only, $35. Videocassette purchase, $110. Rental, $20.

Camps of the Dead, produced by France Libre Actualities and Allied cameramen (1945, for sophisticated audiences only, 19 min., b&w), is a documentary view of the death camps as they were liberated in 1945. The footage, made up entirely of material provided by Allied army cameramen, shows the camps as they were: with living skeletons, bodies strewn everywhere, the crematoria and the mass graves. This film is excruciating to watch, and extreme care should be taken in its use. It would not be responsible for a group leader to use it in programming for general audiences. Rather, it lends itself to serious use in teacher-sensitization sessions and in academic settings.

Radim Films, rental fee $25.

Cemetery at Remu (15 min., age 14 and up, b&w) is a montage of sequences in an abandoned Polish synagogue. The film shows loneliness and emptiness, with snow falling on the Jewish cemetery. It carries a disquieting message.

Alden Films, Inc., rental fee $12.

Denmark '43, directed by Arthur Ornitz (1972, age 13 up, 22 min., color). Active resistance to evil is illustrated in this film, "an experiment in historical imagination," in which a present-day Danish high school teacher guides his students through a reenactment—on location—of the courageous rescue of Jews by a Danish fishing village during the Nazi occupation. Though in seeing this film we are twice-removed from the original events, and though the simulation is a transparent one, the superlative photography and music combine with the unaffected modesty of the "players" to create a stirring effect.

Jewish Media Service/JWB, rental fee $20.

Genocide, directed by Arnold Schwartzman (1975, age 16 up, 52 min., b&w and color), is an explicit and complete documentary of the methodical extermination of six million Jews under Hitler. The film chronologically moves from the exposition of the master-race theory in the early 1930s through the persecution, ghettoization, deportation, and mass murder of European Jewry. It was produced by Thames-TV as part of the *World at War* television series, with the detached and straightforward tone of a television documentary.

Anti-Defamation League of B'nai B'rith, rental fee $50.

The Hangman, directed by Melrose Productions (1964, age 14 up, 12 min., color animation). In this animated parable based on the poem by Maurice Ogden, the people of a town are condemned to be hanged, one by one, by a mysterious stranger who erects a gallows in the town square. For each hanging, the remaining townspeople, in their fear, indifference, or prejudice, find a rationale. But the hangman's rope is really intended for "he who serves me best": the last survivor, he who has failed all along to raise his voice in protest and now shudders to find there is no one left to protest on his behalf.

Jewish Media Service, rental fee $25.

Hitler: Anatomy of a Dictatorship, produced by Learning Corporation of America (1969, age 14 up, 22 min., b&w), is an overview of the story of Hitler's rise to power. Using historical footage, the film adequately covers the early history of the German economic and political climate between the wars. However, its attempt at political analysis is cursory and without depth. Although the film is limited in scope, leaving out such major areas of concern as Hitler's racist theories and the destruction of the Jews, it can provide a worthwhile capsule history of the events leading up to the Holocaust.

Learning Corporation of America, rental fee $25.

The Holocaust, produced by Audio-Visual Narrative Arts, Inc. (1977, age 14 up, 2 filmstrips with accompanying cassettes and teacher's guide, 16 min. each, b&w), is a two-part overview of the Holocaust and the period in which it occurred. Part I, *Without Pity*, is a sensitive, emotional presentation about the brutality of the Holocaust. Part II, *Dream into Reality*, is an attempt to analyze the historical and cultural context of the Holocaust—including a short history of anti-Semitism in Germany through the centuries—in order to better understand how and why it happened.

Audio-Visual Narrative Arts, Inc., purchase price $74.50.

The Holocaust: 1933–1945, produced by Theodore Z. Weiss and the Board of Jewish Education of Chicago (1975, age 14 up, 24 min., b&w), is a concise, documentary overview using Nazi footage and stills, which places the events of the Holocaust into historical perspective. Produced by Yad Vashem and the Israel Film Service, the film tells of the road to death: early laws against the Jews, ghettoization, deportation, and death camps. The film deals with the early years under Hitler within the context of the larger world situation and the Jewish struggle for the right to live. Although short, thereby of necessity presenting history in a capsuled, dispassionate style, the film provides a factual overview of the Holocaust in historical context.

Alden Films, rental fee $35.

The Holocaust in Stamps, produced by Samuel Grand (1979, age 10 up, sound filmstrip, 20 min.). One of the ways we can view a worldwide tragedy is in the cultural artifacts people chose to create to embody it. From this oblique angle, a sense of poignancy is created through understatement that is somehow more lasting than horror images. This program gives a complete historical and factual overview and, therefore, can be used with a group unfamiliar with the material. For those with greater background, their awareness can be renewed by the unique vehicle of those tiny art works—postage stamps.

World Zionist Organization, Department of Education and Culture, purchase price $18.

I Never Saw Another Butterfly (1975, age 12 up, 15 min., color). This is an adaptation of the well-known book of children's drawings and poems from the Theresienstadt concentration camp. With sensitive choral music by Charles Davidson, well performed by a children's choir; it is a very nice mood piece for Holocaust observances and classes.

Board of Jewish Education, New York, rental fee $10 (available only in New York City area for precollegiate-age programming).

I Never Saw Another Butterfly, produced by Martin Hoade and Doris Ann; script by Virginia Mazer (1965, age 12 up, 30 min., b&w), is a fictionalized account of one of the children who passed through Theresienstadt, the Nazi show camp. It includes documentary footage of Prague and Theresienstadt.

Eternal Light Film Library/United Synagogue of America, rental fee $19 (must be ordered at least five weeks in advance).

In Dark Places: Remembering the Holocaust, directed by Gina Blumenfeld (1979, age 14 up, 58 min., color). This is a profound, thought-provoking film, focusing on children of Holocaust survivors as they try to come to grips with the experience that changed their entire generation. It includes personal stories of survivors, a portion of a play depicting the experience of the transports, and a discussion of media exploitation of the Holocaust.

Phoenix Films, rental fee $65.

Joseph Schultz, directed by Predrag Golobovic (1973, age 12 up, 13 min., color). In this film, a German soldier who has taken part in the destruction of a small Yugoslav village refuses to join the firing-squad execution of its male inhabitants, preferring, with quiet dignity, to share their fate. Based on a true incident, this subtle, realistic film depicts neither active resistance nor complicity, but rather the martyr's passive refusal to lend a hand to evil.

Jewish Media Service/JWB, rental fee $17.

A Journey of Conscience, produced by Leatrice Rabinsky (1976, age 12 up, filmstrip with accompanying audiocassette, 30 min., color), is subtitled "A New Generation Responds to the Holocaust." Using slides taken on a journey of conscience by students of Cleveland Heights High School, this filmstrip documents their confrontation with sites of the Holocaust period. It also follows the group, their teachers, and a survivor of Birkenau, Bertha Lautman, to Israel and Holland. Each narrator speaks movingly, expressing sincere questions about "Why?" and "How?" There is deep emotion and a real sense of mission throughout that should successfully reach viewers of a similar age who are facing some of life's harshest realities straight-on. Adults might find the students' lofty goals a bit too grand and naive.

Cleveland Board of Jewish Education/Bookstore, purchase only, $25.

The Legacy: Children of Holocaust Survivors, produced by Miriam Strilky Rosenbush (1980, age 16 up, 23 min., color), concentrates on five articulate, thoughtful people who are the children of Holocaust survivors. They speak of the "conspiracy of silence," or the overprotection by parents who had already lost their families. The interviews are carefully staged in attractive settings whenever the camera is not turning back into the past through photographs of prewar days in Vienna or of families wiped out in all but the memories of the lone survivors.

Films, Inc., rental fee $50.

The Legacy of Anne Frank, produced by Martin Hoade and Doris Ann; script by Virginia Mazer (1967, age 12 up, 28 min., b&w), is a television documentary (part of the *Eternal Light* series), shot on location, of the story of Anne and her family. Including some historical footage, the film tells the story of Dutch Jews who found themselves victims of the Nazis. It is also a tribute to those non-Jews who jeopardized their lives to save Jews during this period and includes a segment on the famous dockworkers' strike. Including photographs and interviews, the film is mainly the story of a young girl—her school days, her growing up, her family, and her fears. Although the film is well written and narrated in a clear, straightforward style, it lacks the emotion and sensitivity that the subject demands.

Eternal Light Film Library/United Synagogue of America, rental fee $25.

Let My People Go, produced by Marshall Flaou (1972, age 14 up, 54 min., b&w), is a chronological documentary story of modern Zionist history, using authentic film footage. Originally produced as a television special, the film tells the story of early pioneering in Israel, the riots of the 1930s, and emphasizes the Holocaust (including explicit footage of the death camps). The second half tells of the rebirth: the illegal immigration, the War of Independence, and the Ingathering of the Exiles. The film is a memorable one, placing major events in the context of modern Jewish history, with a superbly written and paced narration and a sensitive use of music. It is an effective and moving film stirring strong emotional feelings in many viewers—an excellent overview of the broad outlines of the Holocaust and the rise of modern Zionism, especially for audiences with limited backgrounds.

Films, Inc., rental fee $65.

The Life That Disappeared (1971, age 14 up, 80 slides with accompanying cassette and teacher's guide, 16 min., b&w) provides an intimate glimpse of everyday Jewish life in Poland's cities and villages in the years immediately preceding the Holocaust. Photographed and narrated (in heavily accented English) by Roman Vishniac, the slide-tape program depicts the hardships of life in Poland—the discrimination, the fear of anti-Semitism, the difficulties of daily life, and the valiant efforts made at keeping alive a unique culture and religion. The effectiveness of the program lies in its authenticity—Vishniac's photographs taken at a time when Polish Jewry was already in the Nazi shadow, and his quiet, wistful description of a life which has literally disappeared.

Jewish Media Service/JWB, rental fee $20.

Memorandum, produced by John Spotton and Donald Brittain (1966, age 14 up, 58 min., b&w), is an interpretative documentary, interweaving events which took place after the war with scenes from the Holocaust itself. It is the story of a survivor, Bernard Laufer, now a glasscutter in Toronto, who returns to Bergen-Belsen, which was liberated by the British twenty years before the film was made. Produced by the National Film Board of Canada, this moving portrait raises questions and provides a context in dealing with issues which we, living in the aftermath of the Holocaust, must confront: What does our responsibility to remember imply? How can we achieve a personal perspective vis-à-vis the Holocaust? Although the film is somewhat dated stylistically, it is an effective portrayal of a survivor, his memories and his inner struggles.

Anti-Defamation League of B'nai B'rith, rental fee $30.

Music of Auschwitz (1978, age 12 up, 16 min., color). CBS TV's *60 Minutes* interviewer Morley Safer introduces us to a tiny sixty-year-old singer named Fania Fenelon, who is the author of *Playing for Time*. We meet her at a reunion of Holocaust survivors in France. She agrees to return with him to Auschwitz, where she survived because she could sing "Madame Butterfly." Fenelon was a member of the all-female prisoners orchestra that made music to sedate the new arrivals into a sense of calm and to give relief to Nazis after long days and nights of killing. She plays the music of Puccini as background to photographs of piles of human hair and eyeglasses and actual film clips. The sharp contrast between the beauty of what the ear hears and the horror of what the eye sees is as shocking now as when the prisoners gave concerts outside the crematoria.

Anti-Defamation League of B'nai B'rith, rental fee $30.
Carousel Films, purchase price $325.

Night and Fog, directed by Alain Resnais (1955, French with English subtitles, age 16 up, 31 min., b&w and color), is a brutally graphic, artistic depiction of life and death in a Nazi extermination camp. It combines ghostly scenes of the abandoned camp today with Nazi and Allied film footage and stills. This juxtaposition between past and present is seen in the stark contrast between the contemporary sequences shot in color and the black-and-white of the historical footage. Excellently produced and directed by Alain Resnais, the film is a personal statement about the banality of evil in our time. Although the film is an old one, it remains one of the best documents of its kind due to its content and its length, both of which permit a wide range of programming uses. There is no special emphasis on Jews.

Films, Inc., rental fee $55.

Nightmare: The Immigration of Joachim and Rachael, a film by Tom Robertson (1976, age 10 up, 21 min., b&w and color), is based on the accounts of several survivors of the Warsaw Ghetto. In a highly effective way, he integrates many real stories into one moving experience of two small children. Major stages of the Holocaust, including ghettoization, deportation, and the Final Solution, are vivid parts of this dramatization, which moves determinedly from point to point. Information that cannot be reduced to a story easily "spoon-fed" to youngsters is handled in a responsible and respectful manner that still makes it highly accessible to the viewer. It is easy to become involved with these children, a brother and sister, so we are able to suspend judgment and avoid questioning the coincidence factor that allows them to be present at all the critical times.

Jewish Media Service/JWB, rental fee $35.

Obedience (1962, age 14 up, 45 min., b&w) is a clinical, "candid-camera" documentary of the famous Milgram experiments at Yale. The experiments tested subjects' willingness to obey orders requiring them to inflict pain, in the form of a graduated series of electric shocks, on others. The "shock" device was a dummy, and the "victims" actors. But not knowing this, more than half the subjects were willing to continue the "shocks" to the end of the test sequence, despite evidence that real harm had been done. The conclusion of the film (and the experiment) is the disturbing possibility that people very much like ourselves are capable of carrying out even the most immoral of orders, provided they come from a sufficiently "respectable" authority, not unlike the situation in Nazi Germany.

Michigan Media, $15.95. For use by educators only.

Resistance: Jewish Ghetto Fighters and Partisans (1976, age 12 up, filmstrip with cassette and discussion guide, 18 min., color) is a factual overview of the incidents of resistance by the Jewish ghetto fighters and partisans during the Holocaust. Using maps and photographs, the filmstrip deals with armed resistance—there were about fifty such incidents. Although it does not deal with the topic in sufficient depth, nor with the larger issue of general acquiescence on the part of most victims, the filmstrip factually describes incidents of armed resistance against the Nazis. In addition, it is successful in not falling prey to the temptation of exaggerating the impact of the incidents to which it refers.

Board of Jewish Education, New York, purchase price $18.

Sosua (1981, age 14 up, 30 min., color). A film by Harriet Taub and Harry Kafka, *Sosua* is the story of a unique community in the Dominican Republic founded forty years ago as a haven for Jews fleeing the Nazi terror. The film, which is well edited and a pleasure to watch, illuminates inherent conflicts, as young and old express a wide range of opinions about what it means to be a Jew and what the future holds for Sosua as a Jewish community. The film contains rich archival footage of the Evian Conference, of Trujillo, and of Sosua's earliest days.

Sosua-Sol Productions, Inc., rental fee $50.

Springman and the SS, directed by Jiri Trnka (1960, age 8 up, 15 min., b&w animation). A "Mighty Mouse" figure resists and defeats the real "bad guys," Nazi SS men, by outbouncing them on springs. The characterization of Nazis is excellent and can be elaborated upon in discussion. Their arrogance, their fear of any type of difference, their arbitrary and stupid brutality are communicated with a light touch, but uncompromisingly. One always wonders whether dramatizing and simplifying this experience for children results in loss of impact, but this Czechoslovakian animator was deadly serious.

Phoenix Films, rental fee $20.

Thirty-Four Years After Hitler, produced by William K. McClure (1978, age 12 up, 19 min., color). This is an astonishing documentary about the neo-Nazi movement in West Germany and its similarities to Hitler's party. It is particularly interesting that much of the movement is financed by its American membership.

Anti-Defamation League, purchase price $350; rental fee $35.

A Time to Remember, a film by C. J. Pressma (1980, age 16 up, also available on videocassette, color). To give the numbers meaning and the historical memory substance, this film focuses on the stories of four individuals. Each person recalls the past as photographs of Holocaust atrocities flash on the screen. The effect is chilling, and the message is direct. Those who have lost everyone say that we are our brother's keeper.

Jewish Media Service/JWB, rental fee $50 (video or 16mm); purchase price $300 (video), $350 (16mm).

Tomorrow Came Much Later: A Journey of Conscience, produced by the Cleveland Heights–University Heights School District and WVIZ-TV (1980, age 14 up, 58 min., color). This film documents the pilgrimage to the past via Europe and Israel by Bertha Lautman, her nineteen-year-old son, and a group of students completing a Literature of the Holocaust course. Mrs. Lautman, inmate no. 1048 at Birkenau, retraces her steps with grim and forceful memory that impacts movingly on her fellow travelers and the viewer. Modern-day Europe comes into sharp contrast with the old world that is no more. Ultimately, however, the intensity and purpose get lost. Perhaps this is because the camera no longer focuses through Bertha Lautman, whose personal perspective gives the beginning of the film the unique vision that only someone who has survived can impart.

University of Illinois Film Center, rental fee $34.50.
Centron Films, purchase price, $1,195 (film); $299 (video).

Trial at Nuremberg, produced by Burton Benjamin (1958, age 12 up, 24 min., b&w), is a CBS News documentary (narrated by Walter Cronkite) of the Nuremberg court drama as it unfolded immediately after the war. It is the story of the confrontation of Hitler's top-ranking henchmen with the evidence of their crimes; their facial expressions, alternating between arrogance and shame; their consistent denials and claims of ignorance. The film is just the record of a trial, offering little explication of the crimes, of the role and fate of the masses of these men's underlings, or of the legal and moral implications of the trial itself.

CRM/McGraw-Hill Films, rental fee $115.

Verdict for Tomorrow (1969, cleared for television, 28 min., b&w). This well-documented analysis of the Eichmann trial uses excerpts from the trial itself (with voice-over translation) accompanied by commentary and narration by Lowell Thomas. Although melodramatic and dated in style, the film clearly presents the major issues of both the defense and the prosecution.

Anti-Defamation League of B'nai B'rith, rental fee $20; purchase, $200 (16mm); $125 (video).

The Warsaw Ghetto (1966, age 16 up, also available for purchase on videotape, 51 min., b&w) is a powerful yet low-keyed documentation of one chapter in the story of German barbarism against the Jews. Produced by BBC-TV, the film, compiled from Nazi photographic records, including propaganda films, tells the story of the ghetto from its creation in 1940 to its destruction in 1943. This sensitive film documents, in tightly edited detail, atrocity and barbarity on the one hand and an attempt at maintaining human dignity on the other.

Anti-Defamation League of B'nai B'rith, rental fee $30.

Warsaw Ghetto: Holocaust and Resistance (1974, age 12 up, filmstrip with cassette, 19 min., b&w) is a moving, authentic story of Jewish struggle, dignity, and resistance. Narrated by Theodore Bikel with the voice and testimony of Vladka Meed, a survivor of the Jewish underground, the filmstrip sensitively documents the story of the Warsaw Ghetto: the Nazi occupation of Poland, the formation of the ghetto in 1940, the starvation, the mass burials, the deportations, and the total destruction.

Jewish Labor Committee, purchase price $13.

We Must Never Forget (1979, age 14 up, ³/₄-in. U-Matic videotape, 30 min., color) was produced by the Roman Catholic diocese of Rockville Centre, N.Y., on the assumption that only first-hand accounts can make the Holocaust real to succeeding generations. Lillian Dubsky, a committed, intelligent woman, recalls her life as a Jewish girl in Vienna as Hitler came to power. The second speaker is a nameless girl, who obviously represents many who were in Auschwitz. In the third segment, Father Thomas Hart, an earnest young priest, asks questions that can never be satisfactorily answered: Why? How? Who was responsible?

Diocesan TV Center, purchase only, $150.

We Were German Jews, directed by Michael Blackwood (1981, age 16 up, 58 min., b&w and color), is the story of two young Jews who escaped from the Gestapo in October 1942. Although the film begins slowly, the story of Herbert Strauss, today a professor of history at the City University of New York, and his wife Lotte, is a moving and revealing documentation of the period in Germany. Strauss returns to his home, Wurzberg, to Berlin, and to the Swiss border, where he had fled forty years earlier.

Blackwood Productions, rental fee $90.

2. Feature Films

Note: All films in this section are distributed by the Jewish Media Services/JWB unless otherwise indicated.

Affaire Blum (West Germany, 1948, directed by Erich Engel, German with English subtitles, 103 min., b&w). *Affaire Blum* is a true story about Germany in the 1920s. Based on a celebrated 1926 murder trial which had Dreyfus-like overtones, a rightist judge and police commissioner try to frame a Jewish industrialist for a murder by a Nazi petty criminal. A socialist politician whom the Jew had supported helps him clear himself, but he retains a sense of foreboding about the future. The case concerns Dr. Blum, a Jewish manufacturer, falsely accused of killing his bookkeeper. Even when the identity of the real killer becomes evident, the state prosecutor refuses to accept Blum's innocence. Made in postwar Germany, it is wordy, complex, and sometimes dull, but provides some interesting insights.

Films, Inc., inquire about rental fee.

As If It Were Yesterday (Belgium, 1980, directed by Myriam Abramowicz and Esther Hoffenberg, French with English subtitles, 86 min., b&w). Here is the story of how 4,000 Jewish children were saved in Belgium during the Nazi occupation. Using interviews with some of those who helped in this effort, often risking their lives, the film provides insights and a deeper understanding of resistance and complicity.

Rental scaled according to use.

Black Thursday (France, 1974, directed by Michel Mitrani, French with English subtitles, 96 min., color). *Black Thursday* is the story of July 16, 1942, the day that the French police began a massive round-up of 13,000 Jews in occupied Paris. The film follows a twenty-year-old Gentile student whose desperate and futile attempt to save as many lives as possible results in a tragic personal loss. Examining "romantic fascism" as it does, it stands as a fine example of a recent French cinema movement that deals with the amorality of the French during the Nazi occupation.

Rental fee $175.

The Boat Is Full (Switzerland, 1980, directed by Markus Imhoof, German with English subtitles, 100 minutes, color). This award-winning film is about five Jews and a Nazi deserter who decide to pass as a family and flee Germany to escape death. This is a revealing study of Swiss complicity in Nazi genocide.

Rental fee $225.

Border Street (Poland, 1948, directed by Aleksander Ford, Polish with English subtitles, 110 min., b&w). *Border Street*, which offers an authentic re-creation of the doomed Warsaw Ghetto Uprising, is the story of the Jews who chose to take up arms and die fighting. This is an important film, the first to be made by a Jew in Poland after the Holocaust, and about the Holocaust.

For rental information, contact Jewish Media Service.

Cabaret (United States, 1972, directed by Bob Fosse, 123 min., color). This is the story of the life of an American cabaret singer, set against the backdrop of early 1930s Nazi Germany. While being a most entertaining musical film, it also provides a fine insight into early Nazism and the general terror of the country. It stars Liza Minnelli and Joel Gray.

Hurlock Cine World, rental fee $375.

California Reich (United States, 1975, directed by Walter Parkas and Keith Critchlow, age 16 up, 60 min., color) is a tightly edited documentary (no voice-over narrator), depicting the activities, the members, and the views of the National Socialist White People's party. A purportedly objective film, the camera reveals the sick minds of active American Nazis: the footage includes blatantly racist speeches, interviews with Nazi members and their families, vignettes of social gatherings. It provides an insight into the minds and lives of the dissatisfied working-class Americans who are attracted to neo-Nazism. For those already acquainted with the theories and policies of the Third Reich, the film is a shockingly real introduction to an American reality—for all complacent souls who say it could never happen again.

Film, Inc., rental fee $185.

Conspiracy of Hearts (England, 1960, directed by Ralph Thomas, 113 min., b&w). *Conspiracy of Hearts* is about the efforts of a group of nuns, situated in a convent to the south of Florence, to help Jewish children escape from a local prison camp. Aware that such activity puts them in mortal danger, they persist in their efforts. Nicely acted, this is a moving story of one of many such rescue movements.

Rental fee $80.

Diary of Anne Frank (United States, 1959, directed by George Stevens, 180 min., b&w). This is one of the most affecting human documents of our time, based on the diary of a young Jewish girl before she was killed in a Nazi concentration camp. Written during the two years of hiding in an Amsterdam attic, her diary faithfully records the daily routine, alarms, quarrels, reconciliations, and mutual comfort of eight frightened people. A moving portrait with a good cast.

Rental fee $100.

Distant Journey (Czechoslovakia, 1950, directed by Alfred Radok, Czech with English subtitles, 95 min., b&w). Focusing on one

Prague family and the separate paths taken by each of the members, *Distant Journey* is a moving dramatization of the Nazi persecution and imprisonment of Czech Jews. Using newsreels juxtaposed with dramatization, the film manifests sensitivity for the period.

For rental information, contact Jewish Media Service.

The Eighty-First Blow, produced by David Bergman, Jacques Ehrlich, and Haim Gouri (Israel, 1975, in Hebrew with English subtitles, age 16 up, 150 min., b&w), is a chronological documentary of the Holocaust. The film is an historical document made up of footage and stills shot by the Nazis themselves, using an authentic compilation of quotes and stories from the Eichmann trial as narrative. Produced by Holocaust survivors in Israel, the film is an attempt at preventing the "final blow" of meeting people after the Holocaust who refuse to hear the tale or believe that it happened. A meticulous documentation, the film is slow and deliberate. The footage of the atrocities committed against the Jews is painfully explicit, all of which makes such an authentic document difficult to view in its entirety.

Alden Films, rental fee $100.

The Fifth Horseman Is Fear (Czechoslovakia, 1966, directed by Zbynek Brynych, Czech with English subtitles, cinemascope, 100 min., b&w). *The Fifth Horseman Is Fear* presents the story of a Jewish physician who is reduced by the Nazis to a position as inventory taker in a warehouse of confiscated Jewish property. As he goes through the fear-ridden city, all objects and people seem dangerous, foreboding, and nightmarish. The film concerns man's responsibility to his fellow man during the Nazi occupation.

Rental fee $145.

Forever Yesterday (United States, 1980, directed by Zbynek Brynych, 60 min., color). This documentary presents interviews with survivors, who talk about various parts of their past: pre-Nazi life in Europe, the round-up of Jews, the transports, life in the camps, and liberation. The one disturbing aspect is constant questioning by an interviewer who often probes to elicit details that could have been left out. Either she assumed that the audience could be expected to know absolutely nothing about the Holocaust—which might be true in many instances—or she felt that those being interviewed were not making their points dramatically enough.

Anti-Defamation League (3/4 in. video only), $30.

The Garden of the Finzi-Continis (Italy, 1971, directed by Vittorio De Sica, Italian with English subtitles, 96 min., color). This film is set in 1938 Italy, when Mussolini's anti-Semitic edicts began to isolate Jews from their fellow Italians. This is the story of an aristocratic Jewish family forced, for the first time, to acknowledge its Jewishness and the world around it.

Libra Cinema 5 Films, rental scaled according to use.

The Great Dictator (United States, 1940, directed by Charlie Chaplin, 128 min., b&w). This is Charlie Chaplin's monumental work of a barber and his Jewish girlfriend who are persecuted in the mythical country of Tomania. Using satire to tell the world of Nazi conditions, Chaplin plays both barber and Hitler-like tyrant, lookalikes who are mistaken for each other. Although the ending might seem out of date, the film is both powerful and moving.

Rental fee $100.

Image Before My Eyes (United States, 1981, directed by Josh Waletzky, 90 min., b&w and color) is a moving, insightful look at the vibrant political, cultural, and religious life of Polish Jewry between the wars. Director Josh Waletzky uses a series of interviews, photographs, and rare film footage shot during the 1920s and 1930s to recreate the unique civilization destroyed by the Nazis.

Libra Cinema 5 Films, rental scaled according to use.

Jakob the Liar (East Germany, 1976, directed by Frank Beyer, German with English subtitles, 95 min., color). The film raises timeless items of human survival in the context of the Holocaust. It proves that the last word has not been said about the Holocaust so long as human hearts and minds try to explore its meaning for each age. Sealed in the ghettos of Poland, thousands of Jews await death by starvation or deportation to the extermination centers of the East. Among them is Jakob, a fellow sufferer who differs from the rest in that his imagination and "lies" refuse to acknowledge any walls or boundaries. Jakob's "lies" do not prevent the Jews from being loaded into freight cars and transported to Auschwitz and Treblinka. But they do constitute a higher morality, one which recognizes that the basic right to live necessarily presumes the right to hope against hope.

Rental fee $175.

Judgment at Nuremberg (United States, 1961, directed by Stanley Kramer, 186 min., b&w). A full evening program, *Judgment at Nuremberg* is a dramatization of the confrontation between a conscientious, decent-hearted, somewhat provincial American judge (Spencer Tracy) and the former Nazi magistrates he is asked by the occupation authorities to try. His task turns out to be more difficult then he expected, for not all the defendants are "evil" in conventional, unambiguous ways. Would he have acted any differently himself? The film is an all-star, "Hollywood-style" production, absorbing and thought-provoking nonetheless.

Rental fee $175.

The Juggler (United States, 1953, directed by Edward Dmytryk, especially for young teenagers, 88 min., b&w). Kirk Douglas gives a convincing performance as an emotionally scarred concentration camp survivor, brought to Israel in 1949, whose obsessive fear of men in uniform leads him to assault a well-meaning policeman. In flight from the law, he finds his way to a border kibbutz, where the warm concern of the members and the love of one of them set him on the road to recovery. Despite its somewhat dated Hollywood style, this is a stirring, fast-moving, suspenseful film that is congruent with history.

Rental fee $95.

Julia (United States, 1977, directed by Fred Zinnemann, 117 min., color). Lillian Hellman's story of her attempts to smuggle money into Nazi Germany to help secure freedom for Jews and political prisoners, and her closeness to her friend Julia. The film stars Jane Fonda, Vanessa Redgrave, and Jason Robards.

Rental fee $175.

Kapo (Italy, 1959, directed by Gillo Pontecorvo, Italian with English subtitles, 116 min., b&w). A moving study of hope and humiliation in Nazi concentration camps. A Jewish family, living in Paris during World War II, is arrested by the Nazis and shipped to a concentration camp. There, a sympathetic doctor convinces Edith, the fourteen-year-old daughter, to assume the identity of a French thief, saving her from execution. Here is the story of how concentration camp life destroyed not only the body but the spirit, with a poignant portrayal by Susan Strasberg.

Rental fee $95.

Kitty: A Return to Auschwitz (United States, 1980, directed by Alfred Radok, also available in 3/4 in. videocassette, 90 min., color). Kitty Felix Hart talks about her past as a teenager in Auschwitz, inmate no. 39934. She survived; over thirty members of her family and many of her school friends did not. The background for her trip into the past is her present home in Birmingham, England, and the grounds of the concentration camp, where she walks with her grown son thirty-four years after her liberation. They find one tiny human bone to testify to the millions who died. Their discovery is as chilling and penetrating as any of the photographs of piles of skeletons or humans bones that are usually included in Holocaust documents.

Films Inc., rental $125.

Lacombe, Lucien (France, 1973, directed by Louis Malle, French with English subtitles, mature teenagers and adults, 140 min., color). A weak-minded French teenager with a penchant for power is drawn into complicity with the Nazi occupation authorities and becomes a willing tool of their barbarism. But his attraction to a Jewish girl, whose helpless family he is assigned to "watch," brings him a new, and ultimately fated, sense of moral responsibility. The film is a masterpiece of subtle characterization and a powerful illustration of the ambiguities of complicity and resistance.

Rental fee $275.

The Last Chapter (United States, 1965, directed by Benjamin and Lawrence Rothman, 90 min., b&w) is a thorough and artistic documentary of 1,000 years of Jewish life in Poland. Its lyrical music and narrative (read by Theodore Bikel) combine with fascinating, rare footage of Jewish life in twentieth-century Poland and the relics of its earlier history to give us a deeply moving portrait of a world that is no more. The film concerns itself not only with folk culture but also with the great achievements of Jewish scholars, artists, and leaders; not only with the beauty of Polish-Jewish life but also with harsh economic and political circumstances. Its documentation of the destruction of Polish Jewry (the final portion of the film) is one of the most sensitive and dramatic compilations of Holocaust footage available.

Rental fee $100.

Man in the Glass Booth (United States, 1974, directed by Arthur Hiller, 117 min., color). This is the filmed theater story of a man (modeled after Adolf Eichmann) tried by Israel for war crimes. This stunning "intellectual mystery tale" stars Maximilian Schell in a piercing performance.

Rental fee $200.

The Martyr (Germany/Israel, 1976, directed by Aleksander Ford, available in English, 90 min., color). *The Martyr* is the story of Dr.

Janusz Korczak, a physician, social worker, and writer of children's books, who ran an orphanage in the Warsaw Ghetto. The film tells of his struggle to keep his 200 orphans fed in the face of Nazi occupation and persecution. Although marred by a slow plot development, the film still serves as a moving testament to one man's humanitarianism and heroism in the face of tyranny.

Rental fee $150.

Me and the Colonel (England, 1958, directed by Peter Glenville, 109 min., b&w). Danny Kaye is Jacobowsky, a Jewish tradesman who is forced to share an ancient Rolls-Royce with a blustering, bigoted Polish colonel. Both refugees are fleeing the German army in an escape route across occupied France. Here is a satiric story of kindly, even gallant behavior in the face of absurdity and adversity.

Rental fee $65.

Mr. Klein (France, 1976, directed by Joseph Losey, French with English subtitles, 124 min., color) is a moving film about a self-centered, amoral man in Nazi-occupied France whose life is altered when he is mistaken for another Mr. Klein who is Jewish. The film stars Alain Delon and Jeanne Moreau.

Rental fee $200.

My Father's House (Israel, 1946, directed by Herbert Kline, available in English, 65 min., b&w). Written by Meyer Levin, this is the touching story of a ten-year-old Bergen-Belsen survivor who, brought legally into Palestine after the war, searches unsuccessfully for his family. Learning that they have perished, he accepts as a surrogate family the Palestinian Jews and fellow survivors who take him in. *My Father's House* is an excellent vehicle for educating children about the Holocaust.

Rental fee $95.

The Odessa File (United States, 1974, directed by Ronald Leame, 128 min., color). *The Odessa File* is about a German newspaper reporter's search for the Nazi murderer of his war-hero father. As he hunts the man, the reporter learns that this former SS officer is only one of many who are planning to resurrect the Nazi cause.

Rental fee $125.

The Only Way (Denmark, 1967, directed by Bent Christiansen, available in English, age 14 up, 63 min., color) is a feature-length film based on the Danish rescue of more than 7,000 Jews. The film concentrates on the compelling and spontaneous manner in which the Danes risked their lives and their possessions to rescue thousands of potential victims of Nazi tyranny. It stars Martin Potter and Jane Seymour. Many of the citizens of Copenhagen, both Christian and Jew, who were involved in the real events, appear.

Rental fee $75.

The Passenger (Poland, 1961, directed by Andrzej Munk, Polish with English subtitles, cinemascope only, 60 min., b&w). A German woman sees a passenger aboard a luxury liner whom she recognizes from the concentration camp where she was a guard. Her memory is stirred, and we return with her to the stark reality of the camp. The film is important in that it recounts the story from the perspective of the executioner.

Rental fee $115.

The Pawnbroker (United States, 1965, directed by Sidney Lumet, 114 min., color). The Pawnbroker is a memorable portrait of a man who survived the concentration camps only to encounter further horrors in Harlem. In the shabbiness of his daily surroundings the old man continually relives his past. Present scenes are intercut with subliminal flashbacks. In one incredible moment of self-awareness, the old man realizes his responsibility to humanity.

Rental fee $140.

Samson (Poland, 1961, directed by Andrzej Wajda, Polish with English subtitles, cinemascope only, 119 min., b&w). Samson is about a Jewish ruffian, released from prison with the outbreak of World War II, who suddenly finds himself ostracized in a world of non-Jews. Set in Warsaw at the time of the revolt, this film provides a most moving and realistic insight into mass fear contrasted with the courage of one individual.

Rental fee $85.

The Search (United States, 1948, directed by Fred Zinnemann, 103 min., b&w). A Czech woman roams through bomb-shattered Germany looking for the small son the Nazis took from her. The boy, hiding like a wild animal, is befriended by two American soldiers. In part a documentary, the film concerns the plight of thousands of refugee children in postwar Europe, as well as the role of UNRRA, the organization formed to rehabilitate these displaced children.

Rental fee $60.

The Shop on Main Street (Czechoslovakia, 1965, directed by Jan Kadar and Elmar Klos, Czech with English subtitles, 128 min., b&w). The

Shop on Main Street won an Academy Award for best foreign film. It is a haunting tragicomedy set in a small Czech town during the early days of the Nazi occupation. Ida Kaminska stars as a stubborn but lovable old Jewish widow who, in her innocence and deafness, is unable to comprehend the meaning of the grim events taking place around her.

Rental fee $160.

The Song and the Silence (United States, 1969, directed by Nathan Cohen, age 16 up, 80 min., b&w). The film takes place in a small Jewish community in Poland at the time of the Nazi occupation in 1939. Through Rabbi Shlomo and his family, we come to know the spirit of the common people, their joys and sorrows, their rich religious and communal life. We see too how the dream of Palestine and freedom gives hope and courage to the community as it fights for its survival.

Rental fee $100.

The Sorrow and the Pity (France, 1972, directed by Marcel Ophuls, French and German with English subtitles, 260 min., b&w). This is a moving epic about collaboration and resistance. People who lived through the German occupation share with us their activities during the period. We see and hear evidence that often corroborates their statements but sometimes flatly contradicts them. An extremely lengthy film but a most informative one.

Libra Cinema 5 Films, rental scaled according to use.

Stars (Bulgaria, 1958, directed by Konrad Wolf, Bulgarian with English subtitles, 94 min., b&w). *Stars* is a simple story of the love between a Nazi sergeant and a doomed Jewish girl. The sergeant, embittered by the war, has become cynical. But when he meets the girl, he begins to realize that he can accept something other than evil. Although powerless to save her, he acquires some of her courage and belief in humanity.

Rental fee $75.

Sweet Light in a Dark Room (Czechoslovakia, 1960, directed by Jiri Weiss, Czech with English subtitles, 93 min., b&w). *Sweet Light in a Dark Room* provides a meaningful exploration of human kindness, love, suspicion, and tragedy in the face of war and destruction. It is the story of Pavel, a young Aryan student, who risks his life by hiding Hana, a young Jewish girl, and providing her with food.

Rental fee $80.

Triumph of the Will (Germany, 1935, directed by Leni Riefenstahl, English narrator, 120 min.; shorter version: 50 min., b&w) is the now-famous propaganda film of the 1934 Nazi party rally held in Nuremberg. The film, commissioned by Hitler to generate enthusiasm for the party among the German people and to demonstrate his strength to the world, includes spectacular torchlight parades and mesmerizing goose-stepping demonstrations. It is an effective document for learning about Hitler's image of himself, his manipulation of crowds, and his use of film as a propaganda tool. The original version, in German with no subtitles, is extremely long and repetitious. However, the shorter version, which includes English subtitles over the speeches, provides a chilling experience recommended for sophisticated audiences.

Films Inc., rental fee $50 (longer version). $40 (shorter version).

The Two of Us (France, 1967, directed by Claude Berri, French with English subtitles, 86 min., b&w). This is the story of the love and generosity shown by an old man, a good-humored farmer, to a young Jewish boy during the Vichy regime. The boy is hidden in the countryside with the old farmer, who finds the child's company a way of rediscovering youth. Filled with pathos, this is a moving and most sensitive portrait. Michel Simon is superb as the old man.

For rental information, contact Jewish Media Service.

Les Violons du Bal (France, 1974, directed by Michel Drach, 110 min., b&w and color) is a film within a film. The larger story is about Drach's efforts to recreate his experiences as a Jewish boy during the German occupation of France. Compelled to remain faithful to his chosen medium, the filmmaker perseveres, and the process of creating becomes a major component of the movie itself. Drach blends the past and the present in an exciting, highly effective way. The result is an absorbing record of one man's personal history recreated through his art.

Rental fee $175.

Voyage of the Damned (United States, 1976, directed by Stuart Rosenberg, 158 min., color). This is a documentary/drama about the German ship *St. Louis*, which set sail in 1939 from Hamburg with 937 Jewish passengers aboard for Cuba. Denied entry in Cuba, the United States, and Canada, they were finally permitted to dock at Antwerp. The film is a bit overdramatized, but it does provide an understanding of the plight of the refugee.

Rental fee $125.

Who Shall Live and Who Shall Die (United States, 1981, directed by Lawrence Jarvik, 90 min., color). A study of the role the United States government and the American Jewish community took in working toward preventing the extermination of Jews during the Second World War. The film takes us through the history of the war and points out a controversial, often lopsided, picture of American Jewish apathy. Though the viewpoints of the film may be steadfastly rejected, it still successfully raises a variety of issues which make for worthwhile discussion and evoke deeply felt responses.

Kino International, rental scaled according to use.

The Witnesses (France, 1962, available in French, 82 min., b&w). Frederic Rossif *(To Die in Madrid, The Animals)* compiled this startling film from footage taken by the Germans in the Warsaw Ghetto between 1940 and 1943. It depicts the unmitigated torment suffered by 600,000 Jews, all but 500 of whom died at the hands of the Nazis. Survivors tell of their shocking experiences, and Madeleine Chapsal's poetic screenplay heightens the impact of their words.

Rental fee $80.

Distributors

Alden Films
7820 20th Avenue
Brooklyn, N.Y. 11214

Anti-Defamation League of
   B'nai B'rith
823 United Nations Plaza
New York, N.Y. 10017

Audio-Visual Narrative Arts, Inc.
Box 9
Pleasantville, N.Y. 10570

Blackwood Productions
251 West 57th Street
New York, N.Y. 10019

Board of Jewish Education,
   New York
426 West 58th Street
New York, N.Y. 10019

Carousel Films
241 East 34th Street
Room 304
New York, N.Y. 10016

Centron Films
65 East South Water Street
Chicago, Ill. 60601

Cleveland Board of Jewish
   Education Bookstore
2030 South Taylor Road
Cleveland, Ohio 44118

CRM/McGraw-Hill Films
Del Mar, Calif. 92014

Diocesan TV Center
1345 Admiral Lane
Uniondale, N.Y. 11553

Eternal Light Film Library
United Synagogue of America
155 Fifth Avenue
New York, N.Y. 10010

Films, Inc.
733 Green Bay Road
Wilmette, Ill. 60091

Hurlock Cine World
13 Arcadia Road
Old Greenwich, Conn. 06870

The Images Film Archive
300 Phillips Park Road
Mamaroneck, N.Y. 10543

Jewish Education Press
426 West 58th Street
New York, N.Y. 10019

Jewish Labor Committee
25 East 78th Street
New York, N.Y. 10021

Jewish Media Service
Jewish Welfare Board
15 East 26th Street
New York, N.Y. 10010

Kino International
250 West 57th Street
New York, N.Y. 10019

Learning Corporation of America
1350 Avenue of the Americas
New York, N.Y. 10019

Libra Cinema 5 Films
1585 Broadway, Third Floor
New York, N.Y. 10019

Michigan Media
400 Fourth Street
Ann Arbor, Mich. 48109

Phoenix Films
468 Park Avenue South
New York, N.Y. 10016

Radim Films
1034 Lake Street
Oak Park, Ill. 60301

Sosua-Sol Productions
Box 315
Franklin Lakes, N.J. 07417

University of Illinois Film Center
1325 South Oak
Champaign, Ill. 61820

World Zionist Organization
Department of Education and
   Culture
515 Park Avenue
New York, N.Y. 10022

Section III

Jewish Music Resources for Holocaust Programming

by Irene Heskes

This resource listing is a guide to a wide variety of music suitable for performance in commemoration of the Holocaust. Included are materials by the victims or the survivors themselves and, significantly, selections by creative artists who have been inspired over the past decades to compose new music both as memorials to the martyrs and as messages of concern to the present and future generations. Notably, much of this recent creativity has been encouraged by patronage and commissions. The variety, quality, and vitality of all of this music—of legacy and of inspiration—points up the critical role of the arts in society as not apart from social and political history, but rather as intrinsic to total human experience.

Throughout their rule, the Nazis purposefully did not document any positive qualities of Jewish life. They blacked out education and culture, and musical expression in particular. In view of their attitudes toward their own musical expressions, this was a deliberately vicious policy. Nazi political dogma cited music as a prime mover of human emotions and therefore a mechanism for the control and manipulation of people. To carry forward their objectives, the Nazis adapted in the 1920s the "Horst Wessel Lied" from an old popular folk ballad. Their propagandists utilized music to shape public behavior, forming a special music section in the Nazi party for work at party rallies and public events. Up to the very last days of the war, prescribed music broadcasts deluged factories, offices, and all public places. The Reich Chamber of Music exercised full control over all music activities. In 1938, Goebbels created "eight commandments" for German music and musicians. For a few years, musicians were exempted from active military service. Those "Aryan" musicians who remained active in Nazi Europe were "seduced" into assertions that good music could negate any evil, including concentration camps!

Thus, music was used to create an atmosphere in which murder could be justified as patriotic duty and the victims as nonhuman. A good tune, pleasingly arranged with a strong political message, indoctrinated the public—most of whom seemed all too ready and willing. Nazi political, social, economic, and military songs were created in abundance. Even the concentration camps had to have music, but of a particular sort. All arrivals at the camps were questioned about their musical abilities. At Auschwitz, an all-female orchestra was organized, saving some of the players from death in the gas chambers. As early as 1938, a *Lagers Musikkapelle* (prisoners' band) was established at Buchenwald. In the concentration camps, the musicians played and sang constantly—not Jewish music or music by "Jewish" composers, except for parodies demanded for particular occasions. Sometimes they were relieved from work details for performances. In the early years of the camps, funds were allocated for music scores and instruments. The ensembles played concerts, for exercises and drills of the guards and for SS "relaxations." Some were given different clothes to wear as uniforms. Often, their music accompanied the marching of victims to the gas chambers. Radio broadcasts of music were frequently heard in the camps, and survivors have recalled hearing the Berlin Philharmonic Orchestra as people were being tortured, gassed, and burned.

Since the Nazis actively endeavored to destroy Jewish culture, denigrating and deliberately distorting such expressions, precious little music of the Holocaust remains for us. The music that has survived had to be written down in notation, secretly saved, or else preserved by word of mouth and orally transmitted by those who did not perish. The late Shmerke Kacerginsky provided a priceless form of remembrance in collecting many of the songs which the Jews wrote and sang during that era. Others have gathered the remnants of instrumental and art-song selections. Undoubtedly, very much more is lost to us. At the Yad Vashem Museum in Jerusalem, there are some photographs of music groups—an orchestra in the Kovno Ghetto and childrens' concerts in the Lodz and Warsaw Ghettos. Of course, the musical activity at Terezin camp constitutes an extraordinary account in itself.

Many musicians perished, and often their names are now known only by their very last musical work. Some martyrs particularize this enormous loss. David Eisenstadt was an outstanding scholar and musician who organized a symphonic ensemble as well as a chorus in the Warsaw Ghetto. His daughter, Maryasha Eisenstadt, was called "the nightingale of the ghetto." Both were shot by the SS troops in 1942.

Israel Faiveshes organized a contest of children's choirs of the ghettos of Lodz, Warsaw, and Vilna. Shipped to Piantova camp, he continued, until his death, to gather the children and teach them music. Israel Glatschtein wrote theatrical songs and performed them to the end at Treblinka; Abraham Slep, who had established a Jewish music institute in Vilna and taught the ghetto songs wherever he went, perished in Estonia. Mordecai Gebirtig, great poet and folksong creator, was specifically sought out and murdered. Hirsch Glick, martyr of martyrs, lives forever in his partisan hymn "Zog Nit Keinmol." While Yiddish was the predominant language in the camps and ghettos, mingled with their fellow Jews were many Sephardim from various countries, who sang their Ladino songs before they lost their lives.

The Jews' cultural loss from the Holocaust has been staggering. Truly, there has been a diminution of twentieth-century Jewish artistic creativity. The remnants of Jewish music from the Holocaust era can never be judged by the usual rules of esthetic evaluation. The poems and the songs are like old, faded, and torn photographs, precious because they are all that is left. They must respectfully be presented in the context of their origins. Any musical works now left symbolize unfinished lives and broken continuity. Now, we must nurture all types of new musical inspirations arising out of the desolation of the Holocaust and out of the determination by the artists never to disappear culturally into the oblivion which the Nazis had designed for them. Specifically, more music, ever much more music!

This listing is dedicated, therefore, to compositions not yet written, and to those who will encourage, guide, and assist the composers and the performers.

1. Collections of Holocaust Songs

Di Golden Pave—The Golden Peacock
    Collections of Yiddish songs from survivors in Israel.
    Editors: Gorali—Almagor—Bick.
    Voice lines and texts.
    70 songs; 142 pp.
    Haifa Music Museum and AMLI Library in Israel, 1970.

Geto Lider Aus Littland und Littauer
    Compiled by Johanna Spector (Vienna).
    Voice and texts.
    59 pp.
    American Joint Distribution Committee, 1947.

Kedoshim—Martyrs
Music and poetry of the martyrs, with art works.
Musical settings by Henoch Kon.
Voice lines and texts; ten songs.
Artist-illustrator: Isaac Lichtenstein.
Unpaginated.
CYCO—Congress for Jewish Culture, 1947.

*Lider fun di Getos un Lagern—Songs of the Ghettos and
Concentration Camps*
Collected and annotated by Shmerke Kacerginsky.
Edited by H. Leivick; music arranged by M. Gelbart.
(Expansion of *Dos Gezang fun Vilner Geto,* published in Paris in
1947.)
435 pp.
CYCO—Congress for Jewish Culture, 1948.

*Min Hametsar—Mi-Shirei Ha-Getos—
Out of the Depths—From the Songs of the Ghettos.*
Prepared by Ernest Horvitz.
Voice lines with some piano accompaniment.
31 songs.
70 pp., Hebrew translations of texts.
Ha-merkaz Letarbuth in Israel, 1949.

Mordecai Gebirtig: Troubadour of Our People
Music and texts by Gebirtig.
With narration, as compiled by Joseph Mlotek.
20 pp.
Workmen's Circle, 1970.

Never Forget—Songs and Poems
By Rana Rosenzweig (survivor).
Voice and piano accompaniment.
14 songs; 48 pp.
Moonlight Publishers, 1973.

Songs of the Concentration Camps
Collected by Emma Schaver.
Voice and piano accompaniment.
4 songs; arranged by Lazar Weiner.
10 pp.
Transcontinental/UAHC, 1948.

Songs of the Ghetto
　　Collected by Henoch Kon.
　　Voice and piano accompaniment.
　　Volume One: 30 songs; 64 pp.
　　Volume Two: 20 songs; 32 pp.
　　CYCO—Congress for Jewish Culture 1960 (Vol. 1) and 1972
　　　(Vol. 2).

Songs of the Martyrs
　　20 Hassidic melodies of the Jews of Maramures in the Carpathian
　　　region.
　　Arranged by Max Eisikovitz.
　　Voice and piano accompaniment.
　　62 pp.
　　Sepher Hermon Press, 1980.

Twenty-Five Ghetto Songs
　　Compiled and arranged by Malka Gottlieb and Chana Mlotek.
　　Voice lines and texts.
　　54 pp.
　　Workmen's Circle, 1968.

A Warsaw Ghetto Program
　　Seven songs with text materials.
　　Prepared by Ruth Rubin.
　　21 pp.
　　Workmen's Circle, 1967.

2. Song Collections Which Include Holocaust Selections

Broder—Zyngier
　　(*Los Cantores de Brody* volume in the collection *El Judaismo
　　　Polaco,* funded by the Conference on Jewish Material Claims
　　　Against Germany.)
　　Collected and edited by Shlomo Pryzament.
　　In Yiddish only.
　　Text materials, poetry and music.
　　240 pp.
　　Unión Central Israelita Polaca en la Argentina, 1960.

Doros Zinger—Songs of Our People
　　Collected by Samuel Bugatch.
　　Voice lines and texts.
　　200 songs, 298 pp.
　　Farband Labor Zionists, 1959.

Heritage of Music—The Music of the Jewish People
   (Lecture texts with musical illustrations.)
   Compiled and written by Judith Kaplan Eisenstein.
   28 topics, including aspects of Holocaust era.
   340 pp.
   Union of American Hebrew Congregations, 1972.

The Jewish Center Songster
   Edited by Bernard Carp.
   Voice lines and texts.
   96 songs; 96 pp.
   Jewish Welfare Board, 1949.

Mir Trogn a Gezang
   Collected by Eleanor Gordon Mlotek.
   Voice lines, with guitar chords.
   106 songs; 240 pp.
   Workmen's Circle, 1977.

A Treasury of Jewish Folksong
   Collected by Ruth Rubin.
   Voice with piano accompaniment.
   110 songs; 225 pp.
   Schocken Books, 1950.

Voices of a People
   Collected by Ruth Rubin.
   Texts with some music.
   558 pp.
   McGraw-Hill or Tara Publishers, 1973.

Yiddishe Dichter in Gesang—Yiddish Poets in Song
   Edited by Mordecai Yardeini.
   Solo and choral voices, with piano accompaniment.
   70 songs; 346 pp.
   Jewish Music Alliance, 1966.

Yidische Folkslider mit Melodien—Yiddish Folksongs with Melodies
   Collected by Yehuda Leib Cahan.
   Edited by Max Weinreich.
   (Compiled up to 1939 as ethnomusicological study of Eastern
      European communities by YIVO and sent to New York in time to
      escape Nazi destruction.)
   560 songs and texts; voice lines.
   562 pp.
   YIVO Institute for Jewish Research, 1957.

3. Recordings

Ballads of Matthausen
Composed by Mikia Theodorakis.
Text by Yekbus Karambanlis.
Hebrew translation by Michael Snunit.
Performed by Maria Farmandori.
Department of Culture—World Zionist Organization, Jerusalem.

Babi Yar, Symphony No. 13
Composed by Dmitri Shostakovich.
Orchestra
Angel SR-40212, or Everest 3181E.

De Profundis: A Psalm
Composed by Arnold Schoenberg.
Voice and orchestra.
Columbia M2S-780.

Dies Irae: Auschwitz Oratorio
Composed by Krzysztof Penderecki.
Solos, chorus, and orchestra.
Philodor 839-701.

The Final Ingredient
(Passover Seder preparations in a concentration camp—
TV opera.)
Composed by David Amram.
Libretto by Reginald Rose.
Solos, chorus, and instruments.
ABC-TV Department of Religious Programs.

From the Heart of a People
"Songs of the Shtetl and Lager."
Performed by Emma Schaver.
Mercury M6-20052.

Ghetto Songs
Performed by Louis Danto.
DaVinci DM-201.

I Never Saw Another Butterfly
Composed by Charles Davidson.
Poetry of Terezin Children.
Solos, chorus, and instruments.
Ashbourne Recording.

Jewish Folk Songs
    Performed by Martha Schlamme.
    Vanguard 9011 and 73004.

Kaddish
    Composed by Arthur Cohen.
    Orchestra.
    CRI S259.

Kaddish—Requiem
    Composed by Richard Wernick.
    Solos and instruments.
    Nonesuch 71303.

Lament for the Victims of the Warsaw Ghetto
    Composed by Arthur Gelbrun.
    Solos and orchestra.
    Everest 3273D.

How Long, O Lord (cantata)
    Composed by Jacob Avashalomov.
    Soloist, chorus, and orchestra.
    CRI S210.

O, The Chimneys
    Composed by Shulamith Ran.
    (Setting poetry by Nelly Sachs.)
    Narrator, solo, and instruments.
    Turnabout VOX TVS O 34435.

Out of the Ghetto
    Performed by Leon Lishner.
    Vanguard M-9068.

Songs of Ghetto and Shtetl
    (Recorded in Poland.)
    Performed by Abraham Rettig.
    MUZA XL-0163.

Songs of the Ghetto
    Performed by Abraham Brun.
    Folkways-FW 8739.

Songs of the Ghetto
    (Recorded in Czechoslovakia.)
    Solos and group.
    ARTA Supraphon SUC-ST-52140.

Songs of the Ghettos
>   Solos, group, and instrumentals.
>   Beit Lohamei Haghettaot—Ghetto Fighters House in Israel.
>   Hed Arzi—PRT 14586.

Songs of the Vilna Ghetto
>   Solos and group.
>   CBS-63345 or Hed Arzi BAN-14080.

A Survivor from Warsaw
>   Composed by Arnold Schoenberg.
>   Narrator, chorus, and orchestra.
>   (Text by Arnold Schoenberg.)
>   In Albums: 2RCA-LSC 7055; 2 Columbia-M2S 679.
>   Columbia ML-4664.

Symphonic Suite, From "Holocaust"
>   Music sound-track to the TV series.
>   Composed by Morton Gould.
>   Orchestra.
>   Disc: RCA ARLI 2785.
>   Cassette: RCA ARKI 2785.
>   8-track: RCA ARSI 2785 .

Terezin
>   Composed by Robert Stern.
>   Solos and instruments.
>   CRI S264.

Yiskor: In Memoriam
>   Composed by Oedoen Partos.
>   Viola and piano.
>   Mace 5-10033.
>   Version for violin and piano.
>   Music Heritage Series 1653.

Sources (Sections 1, 2 and 3)

Local recording stores will order all stock records by specified label and number. Basic general listing is:

>   Schwann Record Catalog
>   (monthly edition and semiannual supplement)
>   137 Newberry Street
>   Boston, Mass. 02116

American Joint Distribution
  Committee
60 East 42nd Street
New York, N.Y. 10017

Beit Lohamei Haghettaot
Ghetto Fighters House
Asherat, Israel

CBS-Israel Ltd. (Israel Records)
P.O. Box 681
Tel Aviv, Israel

CRI Recordings
170 W. 74th Street
New York, N.Y. 10023

Congress for Jewish Culture
25 East 78th Street
New York, N.Y. 10021

Farband Labor Zionists
Labor Zionist Alliance
575 Sixth Avenue
New York, N.Y. 10011

Haifa Music Museum and AMLI
  Library
Herman Struck House
P.O. Box 5111
Haifa, Israel

Jewish Music Alliance
One Union Square West
New York, N.Y. 10003

Jewish Welfare Board
15 East 26th Street
New York, N.Y. 10010

Ha-Merkaz Le-Tarbuth in Israel
World Zionist Organization—
  American Section
515 Park Avenue
New York, N.Y. 10022

McGraw-Hill Publishers
1221 Avenue of the Americas
New York, N.Y. 10021

Moonlight Publishers
947 East 83rd Street
Brooklyn, N.Y. 11236

Schocken Books
200 Madison Avenue
New York, N.Y. 10016

Sepher Hermon Press
175 Fifth Avenue
New York, N.Y. 10010

Tara Publications
29 Derby Avenue
Cedarhurst, N.Y. 11516

Transcontinental Music/UAHC
838 Fifth Avenue
New York, N.Y. 10021

Unión Central Israelita Polaca en
  la Argentina
% World Jewish Congress
One Park Avenue
New York, N.Y. 10016

Union of American Hebrew
  Congregations
838 Fifth Avenue
New York, N.Y. 10021

Workmen's Circle
45 East 33rd Street
New York, N.Y. 10016

Worldtone (International)
56-40 187th Street
Flushing, N.Y. 11365

YIVO Institute for Jewish
  Research
1048 Fifth Avenue
New York, N.Y. 10028

4. Performance Scores

A. Operas, Musico-Dramas, and Cantatas

Note: Chorus SATB (Soprano, Alto, Tenor, Bass) unless otherwise indicated.

Anna Frank (cantata)
> Composed by Joseph Shrogin, with adapted folk melodies.
> Text (English and Yiddish versions) by Moshe Taif, based upon the *Diary.*
> Narrator, soloists, chorus, and piano.
> Jewish Music Alliance.

The Binding: Modern Akeda (musico-drama)
> Composed by Samuel Adler.
> Libretto by Albert Friedlander.
> Child narrator, soloists, chorus, and orchestra.
> Available from Samuel Adler.

Brundibar—Children's Opera of Terezin
> Composed by Hans Krasa.
> (Composer was martyred Czech leader of Prague Jewish orphans.)
> Libretto based upon folktale.
> Soloists, chorus, and orchestra.
> Arranged by Joza Karas.
> Available from Joza Karas or Judith Berman.

Cantata Judaica (Finale)
> Composed by Zigmund Schul.
> Text by composer (martyred at Terezin).
> Male solo and male TB, chorus and piano.
> Available from Joza Karas.

Childhood Memories (musico-drama)
> With Holocaust melodies and original music.
> Composed and arranged by Stephen Freedman.
> Libretto adapted from Holocaust literature.
> Narrator, soloists, children's choir, and guitar or piano.
> Available from Stephen Freedman.

Diary of Anne Frank (one-act opera)
> Composed by Grigori Frid (Russian Jew in USSR).
> Libretto adapted by composer from the *Diary.*
> English translation by Donald Miller.
> Soloists and chamber orchestra.
> Available from Rafael Sobolevsky.

Diary of Anne Frank (cantata)
    Composed by Oscar Morawetz.
    Text adapted by the composer from the *Diary*.
    Narrator, soloists, chorus, and orchestra.
    Toronto Jewish Congress.

Di Naye Hagoda (cantata)
    "The Last Day of the Warsaw Ghetto."
    Composed by Max Helfman (with folksong adaptations).
    Text (English and Yiddish versions) by Itzik Pfeffer.
    Narrators, soloists, chorus, and piano.
    Jewish Music Alliance.

Echoes of Children (cantata)
    Composed by Ben Steinberg.
    Text adapted by the composer from poetry, diaries, and "testimo-
        nies" of martyred children and adults—materials from Yad
        Vashem Archives in Israel.
    Narrators, soloists, chorus, and orchestra.
    Toronto Jewish Congress.

The Emperor of Atlantis; or, Death Abdicates (chamber opera)
    Composed by Victor Ullman.
    Libretto by Peter Klein.
    (Both perished at Auschwitz—score as written and performed at
        Terezin.)
    Translated from original German into English by Kerry Woodward,
        who survived and edited the opera.
    Soloists, chorus, and instrumentation as originally done in the
        camp: saxophone, banjo, harpsichord, and harmonium.
    Available from Kerry Woodward.

Es Brennt (cantata)
    Based upon music and poetry by Mordecai Gebirtig.
    Music arranged by Julius Drossin.
    Text written by the arranger.
    Soloists, chorus, and piano.
    Cleveland Jewish Singing Society.

The Fence (cantata)
    Composed by Yehuda Wohl.
    Text adapted by the composer from Holocaust literature.
    Soloists, chorus, and orchestra.
    SESAC/IPA Publishers.

The Final Ingredient (one-act opera)
    "A Concentration Camp Seder."
    Composed by David Amram.
    Libretto by Reginald Rose.
    Soloists (Male, TB), choir and chamber orchestra.
    C. F. Peters/Alexander Broude.

Memoirs from the Holocaust (one-act opera)
    Composed by Michael Braz.
    Libretto adapted by composer from accounts of survivors.
    Soloists, chorus, and orchestra.
    Central Agency for Jewish Education in Miami.

Memorial Cantata
    Composed by Herbert Fromm.
    Text biblical selections by the composer in Hebrew and English.
    Male solo, mixed chorus, and orchestra or organ.
    Transcontinental/UAHC.

Nine Rivers from Jordan (opera)
    Composed by Hugo Weisgall.
    Libretto by Denis Johnston.
    Soloists, chorus, and orchestra.
    Theodore Presser Publishers.

The Ravine (musico-drama)
    Composed by Arthur Bergida Binder.
    Libretto adapted from the poetry of Nelly Sachs and translated into
       English by Irene LeHerissier.
    Narrator, soloists, and piano.
    Available from Arthur Bergida Binder.

Reign of Terror (opera)
    Composed by Solomon Pimsleur.
    Libretto: adapted by composer from play *Till the Day I Die* by
       Clifford Odets.
    Soloists, chorus, and orchestra.

Song of Terezin (cantata)
    Composed by Franz Waxman.
    Text adapted by the composer from Holocaust literature (including
       children's poems).
    Female solo, children's chorus, adult chorus, and orchestra.
    Theodore Presser Publishers.

A Survivor from Warsaw (musico-drama)
    Composed by Arnold Schoenberg.
    Libretto by the composer.
    Narrator, men's chorus, and orchestra.
    Belmont Publishers.

A Warsaw Opera (musico-drama)
    Composed by Nancy Heikin.
    Libretto by composer.
    Narrators, soloists, and piano.
    CUNY Graduate School.

We Remember (cantata)
    Composed by Alex Zimmer.
    Text adapted from liturgy by composer.
    Narrator, soloists, mixed choir, violin, and piano.
    Transcontinental/UAHC.

Sources

Samuel Adler
Eastman School of Music
26 Gibbs Street
Rochester, N.Y. 13604

Alexander Broude Company
225 West 57th Street
New York, N.Y. 10019

Belmont Publishers
P.O. Box 49961
Los Angeles, Calif. 90049
            or
% Arnold Schoenberg Institute
University of Southern California
Los Angeles, Calif. 90007

Judith Berman
5358 Ostrom Avenue
Encino, Calif. 91316

Arthur Bergida Binder
204 Washington Park
Brooklyn, N.Y. 11205

Central Agency for Jewish
    Education in Miami
4200 Biscayne Boulevard
Miami, Fla. 33137

Cleveland Jewish Singing Society
Jewish Community Center of
    Cleveland
3505 Mayfield Road
Cleveland Heights, Ohio 44118

Stephen Freedman
% Temple Isaiah
55 Lincoln Street
Lexington, Mass. 02173

Graduate Music Department
CUNY Graduate School
33 West 42nd Street
New York, N.Y. 10036

Jewish Music Alliance
One Union Square West
New York, N.Y. 10003

Joza Karas
212 Duncaster Road
Bloomfield, Conn. 06002

C. F. Peters Publishers
373 Park Avenue South
New York, N.Y. 10016

Theodore Presser Publishers
Presser Place
Bryn Mawr, Pa. 19010

SESAC/IPA Publishers
10 Columbus Circle
New York, N.Y. 10023

Rafael Sobolevsky
Department of Music—Crouse
   College
Syracuse University
Syracuse, N.Y. 13210

Toronto Jewish Contress
(Canadian Jewish
   Congress—Central Region)
150 Beverly Street
Toronto, Ont. MST 1T6
Canada

Transcontinental Music/UAHC
838 Fifth Avenue
New York, N.Y. 10021

Kerry Woodward (London
   Philharmonic)
% Yohanan Boehm
Jerusalem Post Editorial Bureau
405 East 42nd Street
New York, N.Y. 10017

B. Vocal Solo and Choral Works

Note: Chorus is SATB unless otherwise indicated.

Annotations of Auschwitz
   Composed by David Lumsdaine.
   Text by Peter Porter.
   Solo voice (female S), instrumental ensemble, and piano.
   Universal/Joseph Boonin Publishers.

Babi Yar
   Composed by Victor Semjonov (Soviet Jew).
   Text by Shimke Driz (Soviet Jew).
   Solo voice (med.) and piano.
   Available from Joachim Braun.

De Profundis
   Composed by Arnold Schoenberg.
   Text: Psalm 130.
   SSATBB chorus, a capella.
   Belmont Music Publishers.

Ein Jüdisches Kind (lullaby)
   Composed by Carlo S. Taube (martyred at Terezin).

The Fire and the Mountains
"Holocaust to Rebirth."
Composed by Moshe Cotel.
Text by Israel Kliras.
Soloists (female S and male TB), children's choir, adult chorus, and percussion.
Transcontinental Music/UAHC.

I Cried Unto the Lord
Composed by Julius Chajes.
Text adapted from Psalms by composer.
Chorus and organ.
Transcontinental Music/UAHC.

I Never Saw Another Butterfly
Composed by Charles Davidson.
Text adapted by the composer from the poetry of the children of Terezin.
Soloists/boy choir (SA), and organ or piano.
Ashbourne Publishers.

I Never Saw Another Butterfly
"A Song Cycle."
Composed by Srul Irving Glick.
Text adapted by the composer from the poetry of the children of Terezin.
Solo voice (med.) and piano.
Available from Srul Irving Glick.

Kaddish in Memory of the Six Million
Composed by Lazar Weiner.
Text adapted from liturgy by the composer.
Solo voice (med.), chorus, and piano.
Cantors Assembly of America.

Kaddish—Requiem
Composed by Richard Wernick.
Text adapted by the composer.
Soloist (female A), chamber instrumental ensemble, and electronic tape.
Theodore Presser Publishers.

The Last of the Judgment
Composed by Elia Tannenbaum.
Text adapted by the composer from *The Last of the Just* by André Schwarz-Bart.
Chorus and orchestra.
American Composers Alliance.

Lest We Forget
   "Memoriam to the Six Million."
   Composed by Heinrich Schalit.
   Liturgical text adapted by the composer.
   Chorus and orchestra or organ.
   Transcontinental Music/UAHC.

Lord, Hear My Prayer
   Composed by Yehudi Wyner.
   Text: Psalm 143.
   Chorus, a capella.
   Associated Music Publishers.

Metai
   "My Dead Ones"
   Composed by Tzipora Jochsberger.
   Chorus, a capella.
   Hebrew Arts School.

My People—Ami (5 songs)
   Composed by Erich W. Sternberg.
   Poetic texts by Else Lasker-Schueler.
   German, English, and Hebrew versions.
   Solo voice (high) and piano.
   Israel Music Institute

Nachamu Ami
   "Comfort Ye, My People."
   Composed by Emanuel Amiran.
   Text from the Bible.
   Chorus and orchestra.
   Israel Music Institute.

Night—In Memory of the Six Million
   Composed by Geraldine Schwartz.
   Text adapted by the composer from Holocaust literature.
   Solo voice (female S), chorus, percussion, and piano
   Temple Beth El (Birmingham, Mich).

O, The Chimneys
   Composed by Shulamith Ran.
   Text adapted by the composer from the poetry of Nelly Sachs.
   Solo (female A), instrumental ensemble, and electronic tape.
   Available from Shulamith Ran.

Rabat Tsararuni
"Oft Have They Afflicted Me."
Composed by Oedoen Partos.
Biblical text adapted by the composer
Chorus, a capella.
Israel Music Institute.

Requiem—Kaddish (for the Six Million)
Composed by Wilfred Josephs.
Solo (male B), chorus, string quartet, and orchestra.
G. Schirmer Publisher.

Requiem—Yizkor
Composed by Abraham W. Binder.
Liturgical text adapted by the composer.
Solo voice (male B), chorus, and organ.
Transcontinental Music/UAHC.

Saerspruch, a song
Composed by Victor Ullmann (martyred at Terezin).
Text by composer.
Solo voice (low) and piano.
Available from Joza Karas.

A Song Cycle (seven selections)
Composed by Ilse Weber (martyred at Terezin).
Hebrew poetry texts.
Solo Voice (high) and piano.
Available from Joza Karas.

Song of Anguish
Composed by Lukas Foss.
Text by the composer.
Vocal solo and orchestra.
Carl Fischer Publishers.

A Survivor from Warsaw
Composed by Arnold Schoenberg.
Text by the composer.
Narrator, TTBB chorus, and orchestra.
Belmont Music Publishers.

Three Pieces from Terezin
Composed by Max Stern.
Text adapted from Holocaust literature by the composer.
Solo voice (med.) and piano.
Theodore Presser Publishers.

Two Songs: Vilna—Summer, 1944; Anna Frank
    Composed by Aleksandr Vustin (Soviet Jew).
    Text by Moshe Taif (Soviet Jew).
    Solo voice (med.) and piano.
    Available from Joachim Braun.

Yad Vashem
    Composed by Saul Chapman.
    Text by Primo Levi (survivor).
    Soloists (SATB), chorus, instrumental ensemble, and electronic
      tape.
    Holy Blossom Temple, Toronto.

Yizkor: In Memory of the Six Million
    Composed by Shalom Secunda.
    Text by Samuel Rosenbaum.
    Solo Voice (med.), chorus, and orchestra.
    Belmont Music Publishers.

Sources

American Composers Alliance
170 West 74th Street
New York, N.Y. 10023

Ashbourne Publishers
425 Ashbourne Road
Elkins Park, Pa. 19117

Associated Music Publishers
866 Third Avenue
New York, N.Y. 10022

Belmont Music Publishers
% Arnold Schoenberg Institute
University of Southern California
Los Angeles, Calif. 90007

Joachim Braun
Music Department
Bar-Ilan University
Ramat Gan, Israel

Cantors Assembly of America
150 Fifth Avenue
New York, N.Y. 10011

Carl Fischer Publishers
56 Cooper Square
New York, N.Y. 10003

Srul Irving Glick
P. O. Box 500, Station A
Toronto, Ont. M5W 1E6
Canada

Hebrew Arts School
129 West 67th Street
New York, N.Y. 10023

Holy Blossom Temple
% Toronto Jewish Congress
150 Beverly Street
Toronto, Ont. M5T 1Y6
Canada

Israel Music Institute
P. O. Box 11253
Tel Aviv, Israel

Joza Karas
212 Duncaster Road
Bloomfield, Conn. 06002

Theodore Presser Publishers
Presser Place
Bryn Mawr, Pa. 19010

Shulamith Ran
% American Composers Alliance
170 West 74th Street
New York, N.Y. 10023

G. Schirmer
866 Third Avenue
New York, N.Y. 10022

Temple Beth-El of Birmingham
7400 Telegraph at 14 Mile Road
Birmingham, Mich. 48010

Transcontinental Music/UAHC
838 Fifth Avenue
New York, N.Y. 10021

Universal/Boonin Publishers
P. O. Box 2124
South Hackensack, N.J. 07606

C. Orchestra, Ensemble, and Solo Instruments

1. Full Orchestra

Ani Ma-Amin (arrangement) and *Zog Nit Keinmol* (arrangement)
    Arranged by Warner Bass.
    Transcontinental Music/UAHC.

Hazkarah
    Composed by Robert Stern.
    Includes cello solo.
    Institute of American Music.

Kaddish
    Composed by Alan Cohen.
    Belwin-Mills Publishers.

Kaddish: Elegy
    Composed by Srul Irving Glick.
    Toronto Jewish Congress.

2. Chamber Orchestra

Lament: In Memory of the Warsaw Ghetto
    Composed by Abraham W. Binder.
    Belwin-Mills Publishers.

3. String Ensemble

The Diary of Anne Frank (themes from a TV program)
    Composed by Emanuel Vardi.
    String ensemble with optional flute and oboe.
    Marks Music Publishers.

Elegy
    Composed by Samuel Adler.
    Theodore Presser Publishers.

Elegy
    Composed by Robert Starer.
    String Ensemble.
    MCA Publishers.

Revolt in the Warsaw Ghetto
    Composed by Eda Rapaport.
    Fleischer Collection in Philadelphia.

Threnody
    Composed by Alan Schulman.
    C. F. Peters/Alexander Broude Publishers.

4. String Quartet

Prakludium, for String Quartet
    Composed by Viktor Kohn (martyred at Terezin).
    Available from Joza Karas.

String Quartet, No. 8
    "Dedicated to the Martyrs of the Holocaust."
    Composed by Dmitri Shostakovich.
    G. Schirmer Publishers.

5. String Solo

Elegy
    Composed by Tzvi Avni.
    Cello solo.
    Israel Music Institute.

Elegy
    Composed by Mordecai Seter.
    Viola and piano.
    Israel Music Institute.

Kaddish
    Composed by Valdimir Dyck.
    Violin and piano.
    Salabert Publishers.

Yizkor: In Memoriam to the Holocaust Martyrs
    Composed by Oedoen Partos.
    Three versions: violin and piano; viola and piano; cello and piano.
    Israel Music Publishers.

6. Piano

Holocaust (themes from TV series)
> Composed by Morton Gould.
> Simplified piano in folio with background on TV series.
> G. Schirmer Publishers.

Piano Sonata
> Composed by Gideon Klein (martyred at Terezin).
> Available from Joza Karas.

7. Organ

Elegy and *In Memoriam*
> Composed by Herman Berlinski.
> Transcontinental Music/UAHC.

In Memoriam
> Composed by Herbert Fromm.
> Transcontinental Music/UAHC.

Lamentation and Kaddish
> Composed by Mario Castelnuovo-Tedesco.
> Leeds Music Publishers.

Prelude and Kaddish
> Composed by Abraham W. Binder.
> Transcontinental Music/UAHC.

Note: There are numerous arrangements of the traditional *Kaddish* and *El Mole Rachamim* chants for organ accompaniment.

8. Harp

Prayer
> Composed by Sergiu Natra.
> Harp solo.
> Israel Music Institute.

9. Wind

Elegy
> Composed by Mordecai Seter.
> Clarinet and piano.
> Israel Music Institute.

Requiem
> Composed by Mordecai Seter.
> Oboe and Piano.
> Israel Music Institute.

Sources

Belwin-Mills Publishers/Marks
   Music Publishers/MCA
   Publications
25 Deshon Drive
Melville, N.Y. 11746

Fleischer Collection of Music
% Music Department of Gratz
   College
10th Street and Tabor Road
Philadelphia, Pa. 19141

Institute of American Music
Rochester University—Music
   Department
% Eastman School of Music
26 Gibbs Street
Rochester, N.Y. 13004

Israel Music Institute
P. O. Box 11253
Tel Aviv, Israel

Israel Music Publishers
P. O. Box 6011
Tel Aviv, Israel

Joza Karas
212 Duncaster Road
Bloomfield, Conn. 06002

Leeds Music Publisher
225 West 57th Street
New York, N.Y. 10019

C. F. Peters Publishers
373 Park Avenue South
New York, N.Y. 10016

Theodore Presser Publishers
Presser Place
Bryn Mawr, Pa. 19010

Salabert Publishers
575 Madison Avenue
New York, N.Y. 10022

G. Schirmer Publishers
866 Third Avenue
New York, N.Y. 10022

Toronto Jewish Congress
150 Beverly Street
Toronto, Ont. M5T 1Y6
Canada

Transcontinental Music/UAHC
838 Fifth Avenue
New York, N.Y. 10021

5. Music and Choreography

I Never Saw Another Butterfly (song cycle with dance)
   Music: Peter Schlosser.
   Libretto: poetry by the children of Terezin.
   Choreography: Wendy Osserman.
   Soloists (male and female SATB), chamber orchestra, and dancers.
   Available from Wendy Osserman.

The Last Sabbath (a dance drama)
 "Dedicated to the Warsaw Ghetto and Its Survivors."
 Music: Charles Davidson.
 Libretto: Ray Smolover.
 Interpretive choreography.
 Narrator, soloists (male T and female S), chorus, organ or piano,
  and dancers.
 Available from Ray Smolover.

Three Interpretive Dances
 Choreographer: Pearl Lang.
  Kaddish
  Music: Lazar Weiner.
  Dancers—with voice (med.) and piano.
  Lamentations of Jeremiah
  Music: Sergiu Natra.
  Dancers—with voice (med.) and instrumental group.
  Seder Night
  Music: Krzysztof Penderecki
  Dancers—with instrumental group.
 Available from Pearl Lang.

Sources

Pearl Lang
% Education Department
92nd Street YM-YWHA
1395 Lexington Avenue
New York, N.Y. 10028

Wendy Osserman
204 West 81st Street
New York, N.Y. 10024

Ray Smolover
10 Crest Lane
Scarsdale, N.Y. 10530

6. Music for Media Presentations

The Final Ingredient (one-act opera)
 "A Concentration Camp Seder."
 Music: David Amram.
 Libretto: Reginald Rose.
 Male soloists; chorus and chamber orchestra.
 Video recording.
 ABC-TV Department of Religious Programs.

The Holocaust and the Resistance
 Film-strips of paintings by the artist Shimon Balitski.
 Narrator with music background (folksongs).
 Shimbal Studios Production.

The Music of Auschwitz
   "Story of the Auschwitz Orchestra."
   16-mm color film and ¾-in. video cassette.
   Narrator and music performance.
   World Jewish Congress.

Shatter the Myth: Resistance
   "Jewish Ghetto Fighters and Partisans."
   Film-strips with cassette.
   Narrator, with suitable music selections.
   With scripts and activity guide.
   Board of Jewish Education of Greater New York.

A Song for the Conqueror (radio script with suggested music)
   "Survivors sing their songs in day-to-day life in a Polish ghetto
      under the Nazis."
   Eternal Light program (Dec. 25, 1955).
   Jewish Theological Seminary of America.

Songs from the Ghetto
   Film-strips with LP companion recording.
   Music: 12 songs.
   Text: adapted in English, Yiddish, and Hebrew.
   Prepared by the Ghetto Fighters Museum in Israel.
   Vidport Productions.

Teach the Holocaust
   Film-strips with LP companion recording.
   Music: Charles Davidson.
   Text: "I Never Saw Another Butterfly"—poetry of the Terezin
      children.
   With teacher's guide.
   Ashbourne Publications.

Sources

ABC-TV
Department of Religious
   Programs
7 Lincoln Square
New York, N.Y. 10023

Ashbourne Publications
425 Ashbourne Road
Elkins Park, Pa. 19117

Board of Jewish Education
   of Greater New York
426 West 58th Street
New York, N.Y. 10019

Jewish Theological Seminary of
   America
3080 Broadway
New York, N.Y. 10027

Shimbal Studios Productions
P.O. Box 313
Flushing, N.Y. 11367

World Jewish Congress
1 Park Avenue
New York, N.Y. 10016

Vidport Productions
711 Third Avenue
New York, N.Y. 10017

7. Relevant Published Literature

A. Books

Bor, Josef. *The Terezin Requiem.* Translated from Czech by Edith Pargeter. New York: Knopf, 1963.

> A survivor of Terezin, Auschwitz, Birkenau, and Buchenwald, the author describes how 500 singers and instrumentalists rehearsed and performed the Verdi Requiem before Eichmann in 1944. All, including their devoted conductor, Raphael Schaechter, were sent to the gas chamber.

Fenelon, Fania (with Marcelle Routier). *Playing for Time.* Translated from French by Judith Landry. New York: Atheneum, 1977.

> A personal account of ordeals of musicians in concentration camps and their struggles to live or die with some dignity.

Gradenwitz, Peter. *The Music of Israel.* New York: Norton, 1949.

> Background on particular musicians in flight from Europe to Israel.

Holde, Artur. *Jews in Music.* New edition prepared by Irene Heskes. New York: Bloch, 1974.

> Includes information about music and musicians of the Holocaust era, including account of Holde's early escape.

Rabinovitch, Israel. *Of Jewish Music.* Translated from Yiddish by A. M. Klein. Montreal: Canadian Jewish Congress, 1952.

> Chapter 25, "In Memoriam," reflects upon Jewish musical life in Poland before and during the catastrophe.

Rothmueller, Aron Marko. *The Music of the Jews.* New York: Thomas Yoseloff, 1967.

> With some material on music of the Holocaust era.

Stein, Erwin (ed.). *Arnold Schoenberg's Letters.* Translated from German by Eithne Wilkins and Ernst Kaiser. New York: St. Martin's, 1965.

The composer's letters document rising Nazism in Germany up to 1933, with its growing malevolence toward music and musicians, as well as other arts.

Werner, Eric. *A Voice Still Heard.* University Park: Pennsylvania State University Press, 1976.

Scholarly study of the tradition dating back to Rhine Valley settlements in Roman times which flourished and spread throughout Europe, flowering magnificently until the eve of its annihilation because of the Holocaust.

B. Articles

Gradenwitz, Peter. "Jews in Austrian Music." In *The Jews of Austria,* pp. 17–24. London: Vallentine-Mitchell, 1967.

Heskes, Irene. "Music of the Holocaust Era." *UPTA Beacon* 2, no. 6 (Spring 1963): 3, 7.

———. "Music of the Holocaust Period." *Recall: Jewish Heritage* 3, no. 1 (1963): 34–38.

———. "Nazis Versus Jewish Musicians." *World Jewry* 3, no. 5 (May 1960): 18.

———. "Songs of the Martyrs." *Jewish Frontier* 28, no. 9 (September 1961): 45–46.

Nettl, Paul. "Music." In *The Jews of Czechoslovakia,* pp. 539–558. Philadelphia: Jewish Publication Society, 1968.

Newlin, Dika. "Arnold Schoenberg's Religious Music." *Reconstructionist* 19 (January 1959): 16–21.

Rubin, Ruth. "Yiddish Folksongs of World War II." *Jewish Quarterly,* Summer 1966, pp. 12–17; adapted chapter from *Voices of a People: The Story of Yiddish Folksong.* 2d. ed. New York: McGraw-Hill, 1973.

Note: Relevant information concerning music and musicians during the 1920s and 1930s in Europe, as well as accounts of those who found refuge in America and Israel, may be found in biographical works on Bruno Walter, Arnold Schoenberg, Artur Schnabel, Bronislaw Hubermann, Artur Rubinstein, Herbert Fromm, Darius Milhaud, Paul Ben-Haim, Curt Sachs, Eric Werner, Oedoen Partos, Uriah Boscovitch, Max Brod, Max Steiner, Nathaniel Shildkret, Erich Korngold, Otto Klemperer, Erich Leinsdorf, and Kurt Weill. In this country, emigré musicians have been prominently active not only in the classical music world but in the genres of theater, radio, film, and general popular entertainment. Any discussion of the development of musical life in the State of Israel of course includes the varied contributions of refugee musicians—composers, performers, impresarios, and music educators.

8. Relevant Traditional Jewish Liturgical Chants

A. Ashkenazic

Selections are rendered "parlando" in simple motival chants, or in performances of compositions based upon appropriate cantorial motifs.

Psalms: 118 *(Min Ha-metzar)*—"Out of my distress I called on the Lord."

130 *(Mi-ma-amakim)*—"Out of the depths I cried unto you, O Lord!"

23 *(Adoshem Ro-i)*—"The Lord is my Shepherd."

Prayer: El Mole Rachamim (chant for the deceased).

Hymn: Ani Ma-amin ("I believe [in the coming of the Messiah]").

Additional suggestion: High Holy Day motival chant of *Un'sane Tokef*, a tenth-century piyut (poetic text) ascribed to the martyred Rabbi Amnon of Mayence, as a strong affirmation of faith.

B. Sephardic

Psalms and *Hashcaboth* (memorial prayers)

Additional suggestion: The Rosh Hashana metrical piyut *Akedah*, chanted in Hebrew and Ladino; in this poignant hymn, Isaac asks to have his ashes brought back to his mother, Sarah.

Note: Texts of Holocaust poetry—suitable for musical settings—can be found in the Sephardic section of the Yeshiva University Library in New York. Recommended:

1. Four poems by Yehuda Hayim Perahia, describing the martyrdom of the Jews of Salonica in 1943.
2. "La Vida del Lager en Germania," a poem recounting the suffering of young girls deported to Auschwitz.
3. A poem by survivor Simeon Shalom Goz in tribute to his relatives who perished.

So this is the rule:
here today,
somewhere else tomorrow,
and in this coffin now
as in stiff wooden clothing
my speech
still moves into song.

—Abraham Sutzkever; Vilna, 1941
(English translation by Seymour
Mayne)

Section IV

Mobile or Traveling Exhibits and Resource Kits

by David Szonyi and Rena Septee Goldstein

What follows is an alphabetical list, by title, of mobile exhibits on the Holocaust. The names in parentheses are contact people for information about the exhibits. Rental fees are as of the spring 1981 and are subject to change.

We wish to acknowledge with thanks the section on "Mobile Exhibits" in Sharon Joseph (ed.), *The Holocaust: An Annotated Bibliography* (Montreal: Canadian Jewish Congress, 1980), pp. 30–31, which was our starting point and the basis for some of the information contained in this section. We also are grateful to the contact people listed, and in some cases to their staffs, for providing information. Any errors are of course our sole responsibility.

"The Anatomy of Nazism"
    Anti-Defamation League of B'nai B'rith
    823 United Nations Plaza
    New York, N.Y. 10017
    (212) 490-2525
    (Claire Silverman, Publications Department, or Linda Miller, Audio-Visual Department)

This kit includes a silent filmstrip, study booklets, and a teacher's kit. Emphasis is on the social, cultural, economic, and political workings of fascism in Nazi Germany.

Rental fee: kit must be purchased—filmstrip $10; class kit (sufficient for a class of thirty) $25; teacher's kit $9.

"Five Hundred Years of Jewish Life in Germany: The 15th Century to the Nazi Era"
  Leo Baeck Institute
  129 East 73rd Street
  New York, N.Y. 10021
  (212) 744-6400
  (Dr. Fred Grubel)

This exhibit comprises thirty-five 2' x 3' styrofoam panels. Each panel is a collage of a number of pictures which span the years from the fifteenth century through the Nazi era. The exhibit is adaptable to individual needs. A teacher's manual is available upon request.

Rental fee: negotiable.

"Gestapo: A Learning Experience About the Holocaust"
  Alternatives in Religious Education
  3945 South Oneida
  Denver, Col. 80237
  (303) 758-0954
  (Rikki Zwerin)

"Gestapo" is an educational kit designed to challenge the survival instincts of the students by having the participants "experience" the events of 1933–1945. As during the Holocaust, only those who are clever, wise, or lucky will "survive." A follow-up discussion can lead students into a consideration of their own values. The kit contains sufficient material for twenty people, grades 8 through adult.

Rental fee: kit must be purchased—$9.50 plus postage.

"The Holocaust, 1933–1945"
  Center for Studies on the Holocaust
  Anti-Defamation League of B'nai B'rith
  823 United Nations Plaza
  New York, N.Y. 10017
  (212) 490-2525

This exhibit includes twenty 23" x 29" black-and-white posters which cover pre-Holocaust life in Europe, the war, and the building of new lives in Israel. It includes a viewer's guide and display suggestions.

Rental fee: exhibit must be purchased—$10.

"Holocaust: An Environmental Sculpture by Vivienne Hermann"
Judah L. Magnes Memorial Museum
2911 Russell Street
Berkeley, Calif. 94705
(415) 849-2710
(Ted Greenberg, Registrar, or Seymour Fromer, Director)

This mobile sculpture by Vivienne Hermann, a survivor of the Holocaust, is composed of seven translucent wire and mesh figures inhabiting an environment that recalls, in the abstract, prisoners' barracks in the Nazi concentration camps. This sculpture is supplemented with a series of self-portrait reproductions by the artist which reflect her inner struggle and strength during her incarceration.

Rental fee: $500.

"Holocaust Education Program"
David Bergman
27319 Aberdeen Drive
Southfield, Mich. 48076
(313) 557-2440

This educational program resource kit consists of a filmstrip entitled *To Hell and Freedom*, a teacher's guide, a book written by Bergman entitled *Never Forget and Never Forgive*, and a cassette narration. The teacher's guide includes two questionnaires. One, to be filled out before the filmstrip is viewed and the book read, asks, "If you were the victim what would you have done and how would you have reacted?" The second one, to be filled out after the program is complete, asks, "Now that you were the victim, what did you do and how did you react?" The filmstrip may be ordered separately. Books may be purcased for an entire group.

Rental fee: negotiable.

"The Holocaust and Resistance."
American Federation of Jewish Fighters, Camp Inmates and Nazi
    Victims, Inc.
505 Fifth Avenue, 12th Floor
New York, N.Y. 10017
(212) 697-5670
(Eli Zborowski)

These thirty-three panels of photos provide an outline of Jewish history in Nazi Europe. They display the story of the rise of Hitler in 1933, Crystal Night, discriminatory laws, the first concentration camps, Nazi occupation and persecution, ghettos, deportation, death camps, resistance, partisans, and liberation.

Rental fee: exhibit must be purchased—$25.

"The Holocaust: A Study in Values"
Alternatives in Religious Education, Inc.
3945 South Oneida
Denver, Col. 80237
(Rikki Zwerin)

This kit, primarily for grade-eight students to adults, is a ten-hour course which is geared to a discussion of Jewish values. The basis of the course is a series of case studies of different types of individuals who lived through the Holocaust. The students are asked to evaluate these people based on Jewish values. Included in this kit are twenty student booklets and a teacher's manual.

Rental fee: for purchase only—$22.

"Human Rights and the Holocaust" by Lillian Dubsky
Educational Activities, Inc.
1937 Grand Avenue
Baldwin, N.Y. 11510
(800) 645-3739 (In New York State, call (516) 223-4666)
(Charlotte Gray Reiter)

In this unique resource kit series are eight true stories—four on cassette and four in book form—related by Holocaust survivors. All provide insight into the forces of hatred and prejudice, and the principles of human rights, heightened appreciation of the foundations of democracy, and awareness of the powers of propaganda. In addition to the books and tapes, this exhibit includes transparencies and a teacher's guide.

Rental fee: kit must be purchased—$24.95.

"Images of Polish Jewry, Art and Culture"
YIVO Institute for Jewish Research
1048 Fifth Avenue
New York, N.Y. 10028
(212) LE 5-6700
(Hannah Fryshdorf)

"Images of Polish Jewry," the basis for the film *Image Before My Eyes*, portrays Polish Jewry prior to World War II. This photographic record provides moving testimony to the richness and vitality of scholarship, literature, theater, cinema, and photography in the largest Jewish community in Europe before it was destroyed.

Rental fee: $500, exclusive of transportation costs.

"Kaddish: Memorial to the Six Million"
Spertus Museum of Judaica
618 South Michigan Avenue
Chicago, Ill. 60605
(312) 922-9012
(Arthur Feldman)

This exhibit consists of eight framed etchings/aquatints, 52½" x 32", by Maurice Lasansky. As a memorial, they speak to the future and attest to the ability of those who suffered to endure and to live through the remainder of the twentieth century. "Kaddish" was created in the hope that the mistakes of the past will not be repeated.

Rental fee: $150 for three-month period, insurance cost included; transportation charges additional.

"The Last Jews of Rădăuti"
Lawrence Salzmann
3607 Baring Street
Philadelphia, Pa. 19104
(215) EV 2-1410

These forty framed, captioned prints and other relevant materials relate to the end of Jewish *shtetl* life right before the Holocaust. In addition to the prints, the exhibit includes copies of Salzmann's "Last Jews of Rădăuti" portfolio, plus ten exhibition posters. Mr. Salzmann is available to lecture during the exhibit.

Rental fee: for one month period—$250 plus incoming shipping charges and insurance.

Mr. Salzmann's lecture fee is $200 plus expenses.

"The Living Witness: Art in the Concentration Camps and Ghettos"
Dr. Mary Costanza
737 Polp Road
Bryn Mawr, Pa. 19010
(215) 525-4878 or (215) 525-5593

This exhibit includes lithographs, drawings, and original works done by individuals who were inmates in the concentration camps and ghettos. Slide presentations which give a more expansive look at the artists' works are available with this exhibit. Three months' notice must be given prior to the requested exhibition date. Dr. Costanza travels with the exhibit and thus assumes the responsibility for its display.

Rental fee: available upon request.

"Why: The Holocaust from Munich to Dachau"
Gert Jacobson
8915 Datapoint, Apartment 37B
San Antonio, Tex. 78229
(512) 690-0790

These twenty drawings by Gert Jacobson depict Jewish life in Europe during World War II. Each painting is accompanied by a 5 x 7 card which gives a brief description of the scene which is portrayed. In addition, a twenty-five-minute color narrative of the Holocaust based on Mrs. Jacobson's paintings is available.

Rental fee: transportation and insurance charges only.

Note: The following three exhibits are available for exclusive use in Canada; they cannot be distributed to the United States. All are available from the Canadian Jewish Congress, 1590 Avenue Dr. Penfield, Montreal, Quebec H36 1C5. (514) 931-7531 (Rebecca Rosenberg).

"The Documentary Evidence"

This exhibit was assembled from information gathered at the United States National Archives. It comprises fourteen posters, 18" x 26", mounted on styrofoam, which show and explain actual German documents pertaining to the Final Solution.

Rental fee: transportation cost only.

"The Holocaust and Resistance"

This is a mounted photographic exhibit with an overview of the Holocaust and resistance efforts. The exhibit comprises sixteen panels, 39" x 39", and an additional sixteen panels, 39" x 19½".

Rental fee: transportation cost and insurance cost.

"The Holocaust and Resistance: An Outline of Jewish History in Nazi-Occupied Europe, 1933–1945"

This is the same exhibit as above, but mounted on smaller panels, making it appropriate for a smaller setting. It comprises seventeen panels, 22" x 23", and fifteen posters, 13" x 23".

Rental fee: transportation cost.

Section V

Holocaust Education and Commemoration Centers and Research Institutes and Archives

What follows is information on Holocaust education and commemoration centers in the United States and Canada, beginning with the U.S. Holocaust Memorial Council. (Although not a center, the Council is listed because of its national importance.) Some of the listings in this section were obtained from a list compiled by Isaiah Kuperstein of the Holocaust Center of Greater Pittsburgh. There follows a list of six research institutes and archives that are of particular importance to students of the Holocaust. Interested individuals might consult scholars and librarians in their area for other institutions in the United States, Canada, Europe, Israel, and elsewhere housing primary source material on the Holocaust. We would welcome additional information for a second edition of this work.

U.S. Holocaust Memorial Council
　　425 13th Street, N.W., Suite 832
　　Washington, D.C. 20004
　　202-724-0779
　　Elie Wiesel, Chairman
　　Dr. Seymour Siegel, Director
　　Micah Naftalin, Deputy Director
　　Marion Craig, Coordinator
　　Menachem Z. Rosensaft, Chairman, Second Generation Advisory
　　　　Committee

　　Established by President Carter, the U.S. Holocaust Memorial Council memorializes the six million Jews who were killed by the

Nazis, as well as the other victims of genocide in the twentieth century. It carries out the recommendations of the President's Commission on the Holocaust (its predecessor body) to establish: (1) a national Holocaust memorial and museum in Washington, D.C.; (2) an educational research foundation; and (3) a Citizens' Committee on Conscience to alert the public about possible future acts of genocide. It has organized national commemorations of the Holocaust, published a number of services, and sponsored, in November 1981, a conference on liberators of concentration camps.

1. Holocaust Education and Commemoration Centers and Organizations

Canadian Center for Studies of the Holocaust and Genocide
2787 Bathurst Street
Toronto, Ont. M6B 3A2
Canada
416-781-3571
Dr. Henry Fenigstein, Executive Director

The Canadian Center exists to (1) study, collect, research, and disseminate materials related to the Holocaust and other forms of genocide; (2) help organize commemoration programs and provide other services to survivors, their children and families, and to the community at large; (3) conduct lectures and seminars on a non-profit, nonsectarian, nonpolitical basis; (4) cooperate with other institutions and individuals sharing the Center's goals.

Center for Holocaust Awareness
2258 South Josephine Avenue
Denver, Col. 80208
303-753-2068
Dr. Irving Goldenberg, Director

The Center for Holocaust Awareness, which is affiliated with the Center for Judaic Studies at the University of Denver and serves the Denver and Colorado Rocky Mountain area, provides monthly programs of general interest with films and speakers for the public. It sponsors a Yom HaShoah awareness week in the spring, in conjunction with other organizations. It has special programs for particular groups, e.g., teacher workshops and an interfaith confer-ence, and a speaker's bureau for schools and religious organiza-tions. The Center also houses an oral history archive with both audio and video tapes from survivors and concentration camp liberators.

Center for Holocaust Studies at Brookdale College
  Newman Springs Road
  Lincraft, N.J. 07738
  201-842-1900
  Seymour Siegler, Director

The Center serves the general community by providing schools and other institutions with books and other publications, films, tapes, posters, curriculum guides, survivor testimonies, reports of conferences, and other resources on the Holocaust. It also coordinates speakers for schools and other institutions and groups. In addition, the Center offers an annual program of teacher-training workshops, lectures, seminars, discussion groups, and film series.

Center for Holocaust Studies, Documentation and Research
  1605 Avenue J
  Brooklyn, N.Y. 11230
  212-338-6494
  Dr. Yaffa Eliach, Director
  Stella Wieseltier, Assistant Director

The Center for Holocaust Studies was established by a group of dedicated individuals who understood the need to record oral testimonies of Holocaust survivors and to collect documents pertaining to the Holocaust. In addition to its oral history archives, the Center houses many documents, photographs, letters, artifacts, and memorabilia from the Nazi period. It also has developed a research library with a reference collection and an audio-visual department. Finally, the Center has organized a speakers' bureau, sponsors an excellent annual lecture series, and publishes a quarterly newsletter.

Center for Studies on the Holocaust
  Anti-Defamation League of B'nai B'rith
  823 United Nations Plaza
  New York, N.Y. 10017
  212-490-2525
  Theodore Freedman, Director
  Judith Muffs, Director of Research and Curriculum

The Center for Studies on the Holocaust is probably the leading source for "hands-on" material on the Holocaust, including books, films, and other audio-visual material, *The Record* (an educational tabloid on the Holocaust), and a poster exhibit. It also produces filmstrips and other teaching aids for junior and senior high school audiences, has organized a number of major international conferences on teaching the Holocaust, runs in-service teacher-training programs around the country, and publishes *The Holocaust in Books and Films* (1981).

Community Relations Committee (CRC) of the United Jewish Federation Greater San Diego
    5511 El Cajon Boulevard
    San Diego, Calif. 92115
    715-582-2483
    David Nussbaum, Director

The CRC serves as the coordinating body for the Jewish community in Holocaust educational efforts, working in cooperation with the Jewish Community Council, the New Life Club, the Bureau of Jewish Education, and the Anti-Defamation League. The Speakers Bureau of the CRC involves a number of Holocaust survivors as well as educators who, as a community service, offer their time and skills as speakers to classes in the city schools. Supplementing these speakers' efforts are the audio-visual materials that are available on a loan basis. Also available are pamphlets, soft-cover books, and other materials on the Holocaust, as well as referral services to national organizations concerned with Holocaust education.

Greater Framingham Jewish Federation—Holocaust Media Bank
    76 Salem End Road
    Framingham Center, Mass. 01701
    617-879-3301
    Carol Tannenbaum, Chairman and Coordinator

Established in 1971, the Holocaust Media Bank offers a number of basic resources, including a fifteen-week curriculum on the Holocaust (adopted from the curriculum *Facing History and Ourselves,* used in the Brookline, Mass., public school system and elsewhere), films, and a number of commemorative services.

Holocaust and Education Center of Central Florida
    851 North Maitland Ave.
    Maitland, Fla. 32751
    305-628-0555
    Tess Wise, Director

The Center provides educational programs for public schools. Its library includes films and tapes as well as books. The Center consults with local schools and offers a course at a local community college. With the help of a local college, it is recording the histories of Holocaust survivors and their children who live in the area. It also coordinates an interfaith dialogue and an interfaith mission to Israel. Finally, the Center organizes a Yom HaShoah program and provides scholars and speakers to commemorative events in central Florida.

Holocaust Center of Greater Pittsburgh
315 South Bellefield Avenue
Pittsburgh, Pa. 15213
412-621-6500
Isaiah Kuperstein, Director

The Center is helping the Community Day School and the Hillel Academy of Pittsburgh develop an integrated curriculum on the Holocaust, has assisted survivors and children of survivors in organizing groups, and coordinates commemoration programs in the Pittsburgh area. It also conducts teacher workshops to train qualified educators in the Holocaust, provides speakers for groups and classrooms, and has a documentation repository on the Holocaust. Currently it is planning the creation of a museum. Its library consists (as of the summer of 1981) of over 500 books, as well as films, filmstrips, slide-tape programs, photographs, poster exhibits, and video cassettes. It will be particularly active in Holocaust education in public and parochial schools.

Holocaust Library and Research Center of San Francisco
639 14th Avenue
San Francisco, Calif. 94118
415-751-6040
Lonny Darwin, Coordinator

The Library's collection of 6,000 books includes memorial books, photographs, and original documentation from the Holocaust. It provides a research facility for students from the secondary school to the graduate level, and it also is beginning to provide resources for local educational programs.

Holocaust Memorial Center
Jewish Community Center
6600 West Maple Road
West Bloomfield, Mich. 48033
313-661-1000
Rabbi Charles Rosenzveig, Executive Director

The Holocaust Memorial Center includes a memorial hall which displays visual material on the Holocaust, a library containing archives, books, films, and tapes, a chapel for daily memorial services, classrooms for visiting groups, a lecture hall, and a Hall of

Martyrdom containing the names of destroyed European Jewish communities. The Center has begun to develop and disseminate curriculum material, and otherwise serves as a resource center. It also coordinates Yom HaShoah and Week of Remembrance programs for the greater Detroit community.

Holocaust Resource Center
Jewish Welfare Federation of Greater Toledo
6505 Sylvania Avenue
Sylvania, Ohio 43650
419-885-4461
Irma Shainberg Sheon, Director
The Center contains books, current periodicals, video tapes, and other resources for those engaged in Holocaust education or commemoration. It has a lending library and works with public and parochial schools in the Toledo area, offering various teacher-training workshops and other resources. It has developed a Holocaust curriculum and has provided speakers on the Holocaust for local commemorative programs.

The Holocaust Studies Center
The Bronx High School of Science
  (see page 385)

Institute for Holocaust Studies
    Graduate Center of the City University of New York
    33 West 42nd Street
    New York, N.Y. 10036
    212-790-4395
    Randolph Braham, Director

The Institute offers a free public lecture series on the Holocaust that draws upon the extensive interdisciplinary faculty of the City University of New York with expertise in this area, as well as on survivors in the New York area. The Institute offers fellowships to CUNY in the $1,500–$3,000 range and counsels students in Holocaust studies. It hopes to establish a doctoral program in this area to train a new generation of scholars. It also offers a course on Holocaust education for secondary school teachers and curriculum developers. The Institute will publish several monographs a year as part of its plan to produce a comprehensive history of the Holocaust.

JIR—Holocaust Museum and Raoul Wallenberg Operation Truth and Brotherhood to Prevent Genocide Center
    1453 Levick Street
    Philadelphia, Pa. 19149
    215-535-4398
    Yaakov Riz, Founder and Director

This museum holds a collection of Holocaust memorabilia and neo-Nazi and anti-Semitic literature in America. The Center sponsors various community events, such as walkathons, to gain support. Mr. Riz, a Holocaust survivor, lectures on his experiences.

Martyrs' Memorial and Museum of the Holocaust
Jewish Federation Council of Greater Los Angeles
6505 Wilshire Boulevard
Los Angeles, Calif. 90045
213-852-1234, Ext. 3200
Judy Cowan, Curator

The Martyrs' Memorial Museum on the Holocaust was founded by survivors of the Holocaust, some of whom lead tours through the museum. Current projects include a newsletter, an oral history project, symposiums with speakers, and a slide presentation on Children of the Holocaust, which is part of the Children's Memorial. The museum is affiliated with the Peter M. Kahn Jewish Community Library, which is used as an educational library by teachers as well as by the Jewish Community, and also with a 700-member Second Generation group which holds an annual regional conference.

Memorial Center for Holocaust Studies
7060 Brookshire Drive
Dallas, Tex. 75230
214-363-8561 or 214-631-6740
Michael Jacobs, President

The Center includes a memorial room in which hangs an eternal light and a plaque with the Ten Commandments. Here, memorial lamps will be lit for the approximately eleven million people murdered by the Nazis; these people will also be commemorated by memorial plaques. Burnished in the stones of the floor will be the names of the concentration and death camps where millions perished. The Center's visual displays and archives will contain photographs, manuscripts, periodicals, clothing, and other articles which bear witness to the events of the Holocaust. Its library will contain extensive material for those interested in studying the Holocaust.

Memorial Committee for the Six Million Jewish Martyrs
260 South 15th Street
Philadelphia, Pa. 19102
Dorothy Freedman, Executive Secretary
215-545-8430

The Memorial Committee's primary concern is Holocaust education. Each year it sponsors a *Yizkor* (memorial) service for the martyrs of the Holocaust. The Committee also is involved with the Philadelphia Jewish Community Relations Council in sponsoring a full-day youth symposium for 400 students in the Philadelphia area. The symposium includes speakers, study seminars, and films on the Holocaust. In addition, the Committee holds an annual sale of books on the Holocaust.

Miami Holocaust Center
Greater Miami Jewish Federation
4200 Biscayne Boulevard
Miami, Fla. 33137
305-576-4000
Mark Pollick, Director

The Center contains a library and archive, as well as a multi-media educational resource center with cassettes, audio-visual materials, oral histories, artwork, and textbooks. It sponsors a public lecture series with outstanding scholars and authors, coordinates the annual Yom HaShoah commemoration in the Miami area, and organizes study missions, led by a survivor and a scholar, to Eastern Europe and Israel. In addition to providing educational resources for area schools, the Center offers a teacher-training program, and hopes to establish a museum on the Holocaust in the near future.

Montreal Holocaust Memorial Centre
Allied Jewish Community Services Building
5151 Côte Ste. Catherine Road
Montreal, P.Q., H3W 1M6
Canada
514-735-3541
Steven Cummings, Chairman
Janet Blatter, Curator

The Montreal Holocaust Memorial Centre was established to introduce the Greater Montreal community to the many issues and emotions raised by the Holocaust. In addition to its compelling permanent exhibit, the Centre has temporary exhibits, a library, lectures, audio-visual programs, and symposia. A catalyst for Holocaust curriculum development, it is particularly dedicated to community programming. Its exhibits and material about the Centre are in both English and French.

National Conference of Christians and Jews
  43 West 57th Street
  New York, N.Y. 10019
  212-688-7530
  Elliot Wright, Executive Vice-President and Director of Program-
    ming

Established in the late 1920s to foster greater Christian-Jewish
understanding, the NCCJ has played a pioneering role in encouraging the observance of—and preparing liturgy and other resource
material for—the Week of Remembrance of the Holocaust. It also
sponsors an annual scholars' conference on "The Church Struggle
and the Holocaust" and co-sponsors numerous conferences on the
Holocaust in the United States and Canada. NCCJ's publications
include: (1) *A Holocaust Memorial Service for Christians: A Resource for Christian Pastors Planning Services of Remembrance;*
(2) *Christians Confront the Holocaust—A Collection of Sermons
Preached by Christian Ministers;* (3) *The Miracle of Denmark: A
Christian Celebration of the Rescue of Danish Jews;* (4) *The Holocaust: Ideology, Bureaucracy and Genocide* (Henry Friedlander
and Sybil Milton, eds.); (5) *Human Response to the Holocaust:
Perpetrators and Victims, Bystanders and Resisters* (Michael Ryan,
ed.).

National Holocaust Remembrance Committee
  Canadian Jewish Committee
  1590 Avenue Dr. Penfield
  Montreal, P.Q. H3W 1H2
  Canada
  514-931-7531
  Rebecca Rosenberg, Director

The Committee coordinates Holocaust education and commemoration programs throughout Canada, serving as a central clearing
house which provides books, films, and poster exhibits to interested organizations. It also has published an annotated bibliography and audio-visual catalogue, put together a Yom HaShoah
programming kit as well as teaching kits on Raoul Wallenberg,
Janusz Korczak, and the Warsaw Ghetto Revolt, and produced a
Holocaust programming guide for summer camps. As the Canadian
representative of Yad Vashem, the Committee collects evidence
pertaining to "Righteous Gentiles" and is involved in presenting a
Righteous Gentile Award to individuals who risked their lives to
save Jews during the Holocaust. The Committee also publishes
Remembrance, a newsletter.

National Institute on the Holocaust
    P.O. Box 2147
    Philadelphia, Pa. 19103
    215-787-1753
    Dr. Franklin H. Littell, Chairman
    Marcia Sacks Littell, Director

The Institute provides ideas and resources to a wide variety of
educators and programmers in need of bibliographies, curriculum
ideas, or other basic resource material for teaching and studying
the Holocaust. It co-sponsors an annual conference on the Holocaust in Philadelphia, and organizes an annual seminar trip to
Eastern Europe and Israel. In addition, the Institute has published,
among other works, *Course Syllabi on the Holocaust* and a *Manual
of Liturgies and Sermons on the Holocaust.*

New York City Commission on the Holocaust
    111 West 40th Street
    New York, N.Y. 10018
    212-221-1514
    Dr. David Blumenthal, Director

The New York City Holocaust Memorial Commission, whose members are appointed by the mayor, proposes to construct a "living
memorial" of the Holocaust. The New York Holocaust Center will
house a multi-media exhibition area and study center. Included
will be a section of "the miracle of survival," which will depict
how individuals managed to survive such inhuman treatment. A
special archive of personal recollections, as well as testimony of
New York City's Holocaust survivors, is proposed for the library
and archive. A memorial sculpture will be erected in front of the
Holocaust Center: within will be an area for prayer and meditation.
Other objectives of the New York City Commission on the Holocaust include development and refinement of Holocaust studies in
New York City schools, community outreach regarding Holocaust
study and commemoration, and work with other leading American, Israeli, and European Holocaust education and commemoration centers on projects of common interest.

Philadelphia Coordinating Council on the Holocaust
    1520 Locust Street, Fifth Floor
    Philadelphia, Pa. 19102
    215-545-8430
    Raela Sharen, Coordinator

Working in cooperation with the Pennsylvania State Department of Education, the Council is concerned with Holocaust curricula on both the secondary school and the college levels. It organizes teacher-training sessions for area colleges and provides consultation services to schools, and to those organizing conferences. The Center is compiling a library of historical accounts, memoirs, and literature on Nazism and the Holocaust.

Ramapo College Resource Center for Holocaust and Genocide Studies
Mahwah, N.J. 07430
201-825-0550 and 201-825-8200, Ext. 564
Dr. Joseph Rudavsky, Acting Director
Dr. Ernest Simon, Educational Director
Mrs. Elaine Prosnitz, Administrative Assistant

The main purpose of the Center is to serve the community through a series of seminars and courses, mainly at Ramapo College. The Center includes a library, as well as multi-media resources, which are open to the public. It responds to requests for information, audio-visual aids, speakers, and programs. The Center also assists teachers in developing curricula, and helps community leaders in sponsoring Holocaust-related events and lectures.

St. Louis Center for Holocaust Studies
611 Olive Street, Suite 1711
St. Louis, Mo. 63101
314-621-8120
Dr. Warren Green, Director

The St. Louis Center for Holocaust Studies concentrates its efforts in three major areas: the establishment of a resource center, curriculum development, and community-wide programming. The Center's library includes a series of existing Holocaust curricula, books, monographs, and films which can be rented. It has developed, under the leadership of Professor Fred Stopsky, a Holocaust curriculum, provides in-service training at Catholic and other schools, and otherwise advises teachers. Finally, the Center has organized workshops, lectures, and art exhibits, as well as coordinated Yom HaShoah and Week of Remembrance commemorations in the St. Louis area.

Simon Wiesenthal Center for Holocaust Studies
9760 West Pico Boulevard
Los Angeles, Calif. 90035
213-553-9036/553-4478
Dr. Gerald Margolis, Director

The Simon Wiesenthal Center, named after the dedicated "Nazi hunter," is a unique educational complex dedicated to the belief that through public education, an atrocity of the magnitude of the Holocaust will never happen again. Its museum and multi-media complex use sophisticated audio-visual techniques and varied graphics, along with more traditional means, to convey the story of the Holocaust. It has played the leading role in Holocaust education in the western United States, particularly through lectures in schools, campaigns calling for justice against suspected Nazis, public programs and commemorations. The Wiesenthal Center also has an extensive oral history program, a faculty seminar on the Holocaust, and a large, active, Second Generation group. Its multi-media film *Genocide* was released in early 1982. Beginning in late 1983, it has published an annual journal of Holocaust studies.

Southeastern Florida Holocaust Memorial Center, Inc.
  Bay Vista Campus
  Florida International University
  151st Street and Biscayne Boulevard
  North Miami, Fl. 33181
  305-940-5690
  Susan R. Weitz, Executive Director

The Southeastern Florida Holocaust Memorial Center was established by the presidents of eight colleges and universities located in southeastern Florida to educate the community at large about the Holocaust so that such genocidal acts will never happen again. It does so mainly by recording oral, visual, and written testimonies of survivors, as well as liberators and those who hid Jews.

Standing Committee on the Holocaust
  950 West 41st Avenue
  Vancouver, B.C. V52 2N7
  Canada
  604-261-8101
  Graham Forst, Director

The Standing Committee is a national organization affiliated with the Canadian Jewish Congress. Its primary concern is the organization of an annual symposium each May involving 1,000 public school teachers and students. It also offers teacher-training workshops and otherwise provides resources to teachers in the Vancouver area. In addition, the Standing Committee's oral history project records eyewitness accounts of both Jews and non-Jews. The Standing Committee also provides speakers for Crystal Night, Yom

HaShoah, and Week of Remembrance programs in local synagogues and churches.

State Historical Society of Wisconsin Documentation Project
816 State Street
Madison, Wis. 53706
608-262-7304
Richard A. Erney, Director
Sara Leuchter, Archivist

The purpose of the Documentation Project is to collect information about individuals and communities in Wisconsin which were directly affected by the Holocaust. The Project's archives contain written records, microfilms, and cassette tapes from interviews. In the spring of 1983, the State Historical Study published a 200-page guide to survivors in Wisconsin, as part of its *Guide to Wisconsin Jewish Archives*.

Tauber Institute
Brandeis University
Waltham, Mass. 02254
617-647-2385
Dr. Bernard Wasserstein, Director

The Tauber Institute was established in 1980 to explore, within the context of modern history, the causes, nature, and consequences of the crisis of European society in the second quarter of the twentieth century, with a special focus on the Holocaust. It plans to develop the considerable library resources necessary for a major research enterprise. It also organizes a large number of guest lectures and symposia, bringing together scholars from throughout the world, and offers grants for research. Under the Brandeis University Press imprint, it will publish a monograph series, the first volume of which is Gerhard Weinberg's *A World in the Balance: Behind the Scenes of World War II*.

Witness to the Holocaust
Center for Research in Social Change
Emory University
Atlanta, Ga. 30322
404-329-7525
Dr. David Blumenthal, Director
Jack Boozer, Acting Director

The Center for Research in Social Change attempts to collect testimonies from liberators and other witnesses who were not victims of the Holocaust. To date the Center has over 100 taped interviews and 93 written interviews based on a questionnaire. In addition to collecting testimonies, the Center also reproduces authentic documents that were printed at the time of liberation, sponsors lectures, and produces a series of television programs. The Center has sixteen thirty-minute programs of interviews with witnesses.

ZACHOR: The Holocaust Resource Center
National Jewish Resource Center
250 West 57th Street
New York, N.Y. 10107
212-582-6116
Dr. Irving Greenberg, Director

ZACHOR disseminates information on the Holocaust to interested scholars and laypeople through its publication, SHOAH: A Review of Holocaust Studies and Commemoration, by commissioning and disseminating a series of "trigger films" on the Holocaust, by sponsoring or co-sponsoring conferences on the Holocaust for scholars and other educators, and by serving as a consultant on Holocaust memorials and programs throughout the country. With the help of two grants from the National Endowment for the Humanities, ZACHOR has assessed five public high school Holocaust curricula, and has produced this Guide. It also sponsors a Holocaust Studies Faculty Seminar and a Task Force on Holocaust Liturgy. In November 1979, ZACHOR sponsored the First International Conference on Children of Holocaust Survivors.

2. Research Institutes and Archives

American Jewish Historical Society
2 Thorton Road
Waltham, Mass. 02154
617-891-8110
Dr. Bernard Wax, Director
Nathan Kaginoff, Librarian

The American Jewish Historical Society collects, catalogues, displays, and publishes material on the history of the Jews in the United States, serves as an information center for questions relating to American Jewry, sponsors lectures and houses exhibitions, and has an excellent library of films and other audio-visual materials. The Society has a large collection of manuscripts and printed material relating to America and the Holocaust, including material on America's reaction to the Holocaust and on American efforts on behalf of the victims and refugees. AJHS publishes American Jewish History (quarterly) and a newsletter.

Leo Baeck Institute
    129 East 73rd Street
    New York, N.Y. 10021
    212-744-6400
    Max Grunewald, President
    Dr. Fred Grubel, Secretary
    Dr. Sybil Milton, Archivist
    Fred Bogin, Librarian

The Leo Baeck Institute engages in historical research on, as well as the presentation and publication of work relating to, German-speaking Jewry. It houses an extensive library and archives, often displays photographs, paintings, and documents of German Jewry during the modern period, hosts a monthly faculty seminar, and sponsors an annual memorial lecture on some aspect of modern Jewish history in the German-speaking lands. The *LBI Year Book* is an excellent source for scholarly work in the field. The LBI also publishes a newsletter, its annual memorial lecture, and a series of scholarly monographs, most of which are in German.

National Archives and Records Service
    Eighth Street and Pennsylvania Avenue, N.W.
    Washington, D.C. 20408
    202-523-3134
    Dr. Robert M. Warner, Archivist of the United States
    Dr. Edward Weldon, Deputy Archivist of the United States

    Modern Military Branch, Military Archives
    Same address as above
    202-523-3340
    Dr. Robert Wolf, Director

The National Archives holds over 30,000 rolls of microfilm reproducing captured German records from the Nazi period, including documents from: (1) the German Foreign Office, 1933–45; (2) the Reich Chancellories, 1933–45; (3) several offices of the Nazi party, including the SS; (4) a name index of Jews whose nationality was annulled by the Nazi regime and documentation concerning Jews in the Berlin Documentation Center; (5) the Reich Ministry of Public Enlightenment and Propaganda, 1936–44; (6) the Reich Ministry of Economics and Reich Ministry for Armaments and War Production; (7) the German embassies; (8) military records, including 1,450 rolls on the German Armed Forces High Command; (9) party records, including over 732 rolls on the Nazi party, 549 on Nazi cultural and research institutes, 543 on the Reich Leader of the SS and German police, and 680 rolls of miscellaneous SS records; (10) the Document Series—Interrogation Records assembled by the Office of the Chief of Counsel for War Crimes 1945–49 (Nuremberg Trials); (11) records of U.S. Army Commands, 1942–45; (12) collection of Hungarian political and military records, 1909–45, and (13) Italian military records, 1935–43, papers of Count Ciano, and personal papers of Benito Mussolini, together with some official records of the Italian Foreign Office and the Ministry of Culture, 1922–44.

Notes:
A. Except for privileged material ("R" rolls), specific rolls or entire series may be purchased at $15 per roll, advance remittance, from the Cashier, National Archives, General Services Administration, Washington, D.C. 20408. (Checks should be payable to the General Services Administration.)
B. Students and scholars may wish to consult the following reference works to help them use this material:
   1. *A Catalog of Files and Microfilms of the German Foreign Ministry Archives 1920–45* (Stanford, Calif., 4 vols., 1962–72)
   2. *List of Archival References to Material from the German Foreign Ministry Archives Filmed Under Grant from the Old Dominion Foundation* (Washington: American Historical Association Committee for the Study of War Documents, 1958)
   3. *Captured German Records Filmed at Berlin—Finding Aid* (Microfilm [in National Archives] T580, roll 999)
   4. *Captured German Documents Filmed at Berlin—Finding Aid* ("Nebraska" series) (Microfilm [in National Archives] T611, roll 1)
   5. *Guides to German Records Microfilmed at Alexandria, Virginia, Nos. 1–77* (identified as "GG" in each of the individual series)
   6. *Guide to the Collection of Hungarian Political and Military Records, 1909–1945* (Washington: National Archives, 1972)
   7. *Mussolini Collection—Finding Aid* (Microfilm [In National Archives] T586)

National Holocaust Remembrance Committee
   Canadian Jewish Congress
   1590 Avenue Dr. Penfield
   Montreal, P.Q. H3G 1C5
   Canada
   514-931-7531
   Rebecca Rosenberg, Executive Director
   Abba Beer, National Chairman

The National Holocaust Remembrance Committee is a major resource for films and program material for Canada, and for the Montreal area in particular. It also sponsors public programs and Holocaust commemorations. Among its publications are *The Holocaust: An Annotated Bibliography*.

William Wiener Oral History Library
American Jewish Committee
165 East 56th Street
New York, N.Y. 10022
212-751-4000
Irma Krent, Director

The Oral History Library is mandated to record American-Jewish experiences of the twentieth century. Several years ago, the Library received a grant from the National Endowment for the Humanities to complete a project on Holocaust survivors. Subsequently, 250 survivors and children of survivors were interviewed. Special emphasis was placed on the survivors' adaptation to life in America. These interviews were taped and transcribed. Fifty of these tapes were used as the basis of *Voices from the Holocaust*, a book published in 1981 by the New American Library for the AJC.

YIVO Institute for Jewish Research
1048 Fifth Avenue
New York, N.Y. 10028
212-535-6700
Morris Laub, Chairman
Samuel Norich, Executive Director
Marek Web, Archivist
Dina Abramowicz, Head Librarian

YIVO engages in social and humanistic research focusing on Eastern European Jewish history up to, and including, the Holocaust. Its very extensive library and archives, which include over 30,000 photographs, serve as an information center for organizations, local institutes, information media, and individual scholars and laypeople. YIVO has also published several books, put together the exhibit "Image Before My Eyes" (on Polish-Jewish life before the Holocaust), as well as the superb documentary film of the same title. It organizes one or two major conferences each year on Jewish life before the Holocaust. YIVO's publications include *Yedios fun YIVO—News of YIVO, Yidishe Shprach, YIVO Annual of Jewish Social Science,* and *YIVO Bletter.*

Section VI

Holocaust Memorials and Landmarks in the United States and Canada*

by Bernard Postal

In Judaism, Christianity, and Islam, burial places are marked by stone monuments. For most of the six million, there are no markers; we usually do not know where the victims were buried.

There will soon be a national monument to the victims of the Holocaust in Washington, and a number of cities—including New Haven, Connecticut, and Charlotte, North Carolina—have also erected such monuments.

For a guide to memorials in Europe, see In Everlasting Remembrance, published by the American Jewish Congress (15 East 84th Street, New York, N.Y. 10028). In Israel, Yad Vashem and the Kibbutz of the Ghetto Fighters (Kibbutz Lohamei Haghettaot) serve simultaneously as memorials, museums, and archives on the Holocaust.

—Judith Hershlag Muffs

The following list was included in some form in volumes 2 and 3 of American Jewish Landmarks (Fleet Press Publication Corp.) of which the late Bernard Postal was the author. I have done my best to update this list, and would be grateful to receive information for new listings, or revisions of existing ones.

—DMS

ALABAMA

Florence

Temple B'nai Israel of the Tri-Cities Jewish Congregation, 201 Hawthorne Street, has an etched glass memorial of the Nazi Holocaust in the door connecting the sanctuary and the library.

Mobile

Congregation Ahavas Chesed, 1717 Dauphin Street, has a unique hand-carved mahogany bas-relief sculpture memorial to the six million martyrs of the Nazi Holocaust. Designed by John Shaw, a non-Jew, it was carved by Abner Smiles of Pascagoula, Mississippi, a survivor of a death camp.

ARIZONA

Tucson

Congregation Anshe Israel, 5550 East 5th Street, has a mosaic mural dedicated to the six million victims of the Holocaust.

Jewish Community Center, 102 North Plumer, has in its lobby a twenty-four-foot mosaic mural depicting figures in the Warsaw Ghetto Uprising, as a memorial to the Holocaust's six million victims.

CALIFORNIA

Berkeley

In the Judah Magnes Memorial Museum, 2911 Russell Street, is a sculpture called "In Memoriam," a seven-foot-high design made by Hungarian-born Marika Somogyi. The sculpture contains three figures joined together arm-in-arm, hovering over fragments of broken glass. Enveloping these elements and forming the foundation of the work is a black plastic shape resembling a shroud. In this room, known as the Holocaust Room, are memorabilia from the Hitler era.

Beverly Hills

A curved brick wall of the Harrison Chapel of Temple Emanuel, 300 North Clark Drive, has on it a permanent memorial to the Jewish victims of the Nazi Holocaust, making the temple the only synagogue in the Los Angeles area to provide the community with an outdoor shrine to the Holocaust. The sculpture, donated by Nicolai Joffe, was designed and created by Dr. Eric May, a native of England, who was twice wounded in Israel's War of Liberation.

Expressed symbolically by upraised arms, with the Hebrew words exhorting to "Remember and Never Forget," the semi-bas-relief is made of cut, bent, and welded oxidized steel rising to a height of four feet six inches. The words "Do Not Forget" contain six Hebrew letters symbolizing the six million. The complete quotation was taken from an Israeli Haggadah produced by survivors of the Holocaust and yields the number seven which, when added to the number six, equals thirteen, the number of millions of Jews left in the world after the Holocaust. The *gematria* (the numerical equivalent of the letters), eighteen, represents the word for "life," *chai.*

Colma

Salem Memorial Park, in the section owned by San Francisco's Congregation B'nai Emunah, has a simple memorial to the six million martyrs of the Nazi Holocaust. The marble cenotaph contains the names of those martyrs who lie in unknown graves and whose relatives survived and settled in San Francisco.

Fullerton

The Holocaust Archives, housed in the library of California State University, is a collection of letters, documents, diaries, poetry, music, and mementoes of the Nazi concentration camps, as well as taped interviews with death camp survivors, collected by the Department of Religious Studies and by scholars and researchers.

Long Beach

Temple Israel, 3538 East 3rd Street, has a memorial to the victims of the Nazi Holocaust in the form of a group of six figures, each representing one million Jewish martyrs. Fashioned from sprayed bronze on carved foam, each figure is created by two Hebrew letters—*Shin-Shin*—forming the Hebrew word *shesh* ("six").

Temple Sinai, 2605 East 7th Street, has within it a plain shroudlike memorial named "Lest We Forget," with six bronze candle holders, each of which represents one million martyrs of the Nazi Holocaust. The memorial was dedicated by Mr. and Mrs. Paul Lewis of Dallas, Texas, in 1960.

Los Angeles

Martyrs Memorial for Jewish Federation-Council, on the twelfth floor of the Jewish Community Building, 6505 Wilshire Boulevard, is the official Yad Vashem memorial in Los Angeles and is thus aimed at furthering the goals of Israel's official Holocaust memorial. The memorial has a moving structure with an arched opening leading to a passage consisting of four models of trains with slots and plexiglass in the side walls. The passage simulates the infamous cattle cars used to transport Jews to the extermination camps. Lights behind the walls illuminate the names of martyred loved ones and the European communities where Jewish life was destroyed.

From the passage, the visitor enters a crypt in the shape of a rotunda. On a marble floor with brown discs are engraved the names of concentration camps. A marble sarcophagus, located above a pit, symbolizes a grave. In the rear, suspended from a chrome-plated arch, hangs a yellow, six-cornered star, intertwined with rusty barbed-wire.

The crypt leads into a chapel intended for services, lectures, or solitary contemplation. Inside are original statements from Nazi henchmen, stamps, envelopes, letters, Nazi insignia, swords, guns, and numerous original declarations from survivors and photographs of concentration camps.

Mount Sinai Memorial Park, 5950 Forest Lawn Drive, has a Warsaw Ghetto Memorial consisting of six figures carved out of redwood by the sculptor Bernard Zakheim. Set on a knoll, the six sculptures represent "Jew with Torah," "Woman Warrior," "Genocide," "For Our and Your Liberty," "Martyrdom," and "I Don't Want to Get Involved."

Temple Beth Am, 1039 South La Cienega, has in its sanctuary a heroic memorial wall dedicated to the martyred six million. Designed and built by Israeli artist Perli Pelzig, the wall is a mosaic of the horror of the camps. In the patio of the synagogue is Max Strassburger's memorial to the Jews massacred at Babi Yar, near Kiev, in September 1941.

Temple Israel of Hollywood, 7300 Hollywood Boulevard, has in the patio of the Broidy Wing of the Joseph H. Corwin Library, a black marble marker on which is inscribed a verse from Yevgeny Yevtushenko's poem "Babi Yar." The patio is named "Babi Yar Plaza," and is dedicated to the memory of the Russian Jews who were killed by the Nazis in the Babi Yar ravine outside Kiev on September 29–30, 1941.

The Hebrew Union College–Jewish Institute of Religion, 3077 University Mall, has the Skirball Museum, which houses approximately one hundred ceremonial objects rescued from among the thousands confiscated by the Nazis during World War II.

Simon Wiesenthal Center for Holocaust Studies at Yeshiva University in Los Angeles, 9760 West Pico Boulevard, is named for the famous Vienna-based hunter and exposer of Nazis, and is aimed at studying, interpreting, and sensitizing the public to the Holocaust. The center has five major sections—a library, commemoration hall in memory of the six million, lecture area, multi-media complex planned for the center's second phase of development, and a ten-foot brass Star of David in the form of a broken yet soaring rocket, symbolizing the renewed spiritual and physical forces within the Jewish people.

Other displays depict the rise and fall of Nazism, European Jewry's quiet heroism and refusal to accept defeat, the ninety-two people most responsible for conceiving and administering the Final Solution, and recent events that involve the denial of human rights.

Oakland

Jewish Community Center of the Greater East Bay, 3245 Sheffield Avenue, has a memorial to the six million erected on the southwest corner of Willow and Grand Avenues. It was built by the No. 593 Post of the Jewish War Veternans.

San Diego

Beth Jacob Congregation, 4855 College Avenue, has a memorial of the Holocaust just outside the sanctuary. It consists of a rugged opening in the wall with barbed wire connecting both sides of the opening. In back of the wire is a grim picture of a concentration camp. The designer of the synagogue is Bill Lewis, a former Mormon bishop.

Jewish Community Center, 4070 54th Street, has a small garden named the Memorial to the Six Million. It is a large bronze sculpture from which cascades of water flow into a reflecting pool. The memorial was a gift of the New Life Club.

Sholom Memorial Park, 13017 North Lopez Cloyon Road, has a Chapel of the Eternal Light dedicated as a memorial to the martyrs of the Holocaust.

San Francisco

Congregation Beth Shalom, 301 14th Avenue, has among its traces of Jewish history ten stained-glass windows depicting the Holocaust.

Holocaust Library and Research Center, 601 14th Avenue, has a collection of some 5,000 books about the Holocaust in Yiddish, Hebrew, Czech, Slovak, English, Polish, German, Hungarian, French, Dutch, Italian, and Serbo-Croatian, as well as a collection of hundreds of documents.

COLORADO

Denver

Babi Yar Park, a twenty-seven-acre park created at East Parker Road at Havana by the city and county of Denver and the Babi Yar Park Foundation at a cost of over $250,000, is said to be the first memorial to the more than 33,000 Russian Jews massacred by the Nazis at Babi Yar, outside Kiev, in 1941. A path to the right leads to the Grove of Remembrance, a formal planting of one hundred flowering crab apple trees, each tree symbolizing 330 Jews who perished at Babi Yar ravine. The earth to the east and north of the grove has been raised to an elevation that encloses the park. The flowering trees are intended to symbolize the beginning of life.

The path to the west from the grove leads to a rough granite stone. Walking around it enables visitors to see the ravine and the bridge that crosses it. The six-foot-wide bridge has no openings other than two-handled horizontal slits at mid-span. The symbolism of the bridge reminds one of the cattle cars, the imprisonment, closed vans, and camps without escape. At the opposite end of the bridge, hewn into the flat face of the rough stones, is a vertical polished strip that reflects the image of people as they approach. The remaining three points of the star are marked by granite stones at the convergence of paths cut into the grass.

At the entrance to the Hillel Academy, 430 South Hudson Street, stands the Memorial to the Six Million, a four-sided column topped by the eternal flames, with inscriptions in English and Yiddish, and one of the Psalms in Hebrew.

A one-third cross-section of the menorah is recreated in a large outdoor menorah that has a memorial to the six million victims of the Holocaust. It is a marble monument topped by six flames, a 1975 gift of Mr. and Mrs. Paul Lewis of Dallas, to the Jewish Community Center at 4800 E. Alameda.

Pueblo

In the Mineral Palace Park is a grove of trees and flowers planted by the Pueblo Jewish Community as a memorial of the Holocaust. The memorial carries the vow: "To our future generations, this must never happen again."

CONNECTICUT

New Haven

In a portion of Edgewood Park known as Holocaust Square stands the New Haven Memorial to the Six Million, said to be the first built on public land and with contributions raised from both the non-Jewish and Jewish communities. Designed by Gustav Franziani, a non-Jewish architect, and built by George Skolnick, who donated his services, the Holocaust Square is shaped like a huge Star of David, on the perimeters of which is barbed wire. Fifty trees are planted in the interstices of the Mogen David; each tree has the name of a concentration camp on it. The square is covered with cobblestones, reminiscent of the Jewish *shtetl* (a small, predominantly Jewish town) in Europe.

West Hartford

A Menorah Monument stands on the outdoor grounds of the United Synagogues Greater Hartford, dedicated by David Chase in honor of his parents and millions of other victims of the Holocaust. The memorial is a ten by eight foot monument in the form of a Mogen David.

DELAWARE

Wilmington

In Freedom Plaza, between the City-County Building and the State Office Building in the 800 block of French Street, in the midst of Wilmington's busiest section, stands the Memorial to the Holocaust. Financed with private funds, the memorial was designed by sculptor Elbert Weinberg and stands on city land. The sculpture consists of life-size bronze figures—a man, a woman, a mother and child, and three fifteen-foot, irregularly-shaped concrete columns on which are etched the names of a dozen concentration camps.

Three columns symbolize the inhumanity of man, the cold, cruel, and barbaric mentality of the Nazis, and—in the figure of the mother holding a child over her head—a glimmer of hope for the survivors and the world at large. The names of the concentration camps are arranged in a circle so that the Holocaust victims seem trapped and crushed by the enclosing columns.

DISTRICT OF COLUMBIA

Adas Israel Congregation, 2850 Quebec Street, N.W., has a plain memorial to the six million victims of the Nazi Holocaust, dedicated in 1963 by Paul and Leah Lewis of Dallas, Texas. A six-pronged giant menorah is in honor of the martyrs.

National Archives, Pennsylvania and Constitution Avenues, between 7th and 9th Streets, N.W., contains a broad array of Nazi papers and articles—originals and copies—documenting the persecution of the Jews up to and including the Holocaust. A 1979 exhibit of these materials showed a deathbook from Mauthausen concentration camp; a report from a mobile command unit operating in German-occupied Russia, reporting the shooting of 33,771 Jews at Babi Yar in 1941; an invoice from the Pest Control showing receipt of Zyklon B cyanide gas to be used for "disinfection and extermination" at Auschwitz concentration camp; minutes of the Berlin Wannsee Conference on January 20, 1942 at which the Nazi mass killing of Jews was approved; and the report of Jürgen Stroop, SS and police leader in Warsaw, declaring the successful suppression of the Jewish uprising in the Warsaw Ghetto and the destruction of the area.

FLORIDA

Bay Vista Campus—Florida International University

Southeastern Florida Holocaust Memorial Center, on Bay Vista Campus of Florida International University, exists to memorialize the victims of the Holocaust through oral history and education. The center gathers, collects, and records oral, visual, and written testimony of survivors, liberators, and resisters of the Holocaust. The center works with eight colleges and universities in southeast Florida.

Miami

The Martyrs Memorial, a granite monument at the main parkway entrance to Lakeside Memorial Park, Northwest 25th Street and 103rd Avenue, was erected in 1960 in memory of the victims of the Holocaust.

Miami Beach

A memorial monument to the six million victims of the Holocaust stands in front of the Beth Israel Congregation at 770 40th Street.

Pompano Beach

A memorial to the victims of the Holocaust is located in the Minyonaire Chapel of Temple Sholom, 132 Southeast 11th Avenue. It was underwritten by Mr. and Mrs. Motek Messer, whose entire families were victims of the Holocaust.

GEORGIA

Atlanta

The Goodfriend Collection of Holocaust Literature, in the Emory University Library, 1364 Clifton Road, N.E., was established by Ahavath Achim Synagogue in honor of its cantor, Isaac Goodfriend.

The Memorial Monument, erected at the Greenwood Cemetery, Jewish section, 1173 Cascade Avenue, S.W., is a starkly majestic stone tombstone that invites the public in, and yet achieves the privacy and holiness required by those mourning loved ones whose graves do not exist. It is topped by six huge candlesticks, honoring the memory of the six million victims of the Holocaust. A small casket containing the ashes of some of the unknown martyrs who died at Auschwitz is buried at the foot of the monument. The inscription on the front wall, in Hebrew, English, and Yiddish, is taken from the Book of Genesis: "The voice of the blood of thy brother crieth out to me from the ground." The architect is Benjamin Hirsch of the Hemschech Organization of Survivors of Nazism, the group which, along with the Atlanta Jewish Welfare Federation, erected the monument in 1965.

ILLINOIS

Champaign

Yad Vashem at Sinai Temple, 3104 West Windsor Road, has installed in the Ezra Lewin Lounge, as one enters the building, a bas-relief composed of three copper panels, each about six feet high and thirty to thirty-two inches wide. The first panel depicts flames, a partially destroyed Mogen David, underneath which is a line in Hebrew and English from an Israeli poem, the original of which is in Yad Vashem in Jerusalem. Below this is part of a swastika, against which are hands of various sizes and contours pushing against it, as though trying to lift an awful burden.

The second panel also depicts flames on the bottom of the wall. Below is shown the interior of a crematorium, on which are inscribed the first words of the *Kaddish** and six candles. The third panel, which takes up the rest of the wall, shows the flames dying away and the statement: "Dedicated to the Jews who died in the Nazi Holocaust, 1939–1945." On the oven door are the names of the death camps. The entire sculpture, which is the work of Charles Clement, is the gift of Mr.

---

*Kaddish—Hebrew memorial prayer for the dead.

and Mrs. Leon Bankier (two survivors) and their children, in memory of the Bankiers' parents and families.

Chicago

Anshe Emet Synagogue, 3760 North Pine Grove, has the Martyrs Memorial Sculpture, dedicated in 1968 by Mr. and Mrs. Paul Lewis of Dallas, Texas. It is a simple monument with an excerpt from Jeremiah 8:23, recalling the need to "weep day and night for the slain of my people."

Spertus College, 612 South Michigan Avenue, houses the Bernard and Rochelle Zell Holocaust Memorial as a permanent installation. The museum presents, through artifacts, literature, photographs, and an audio-visual component, the world of the Holocaust. The six pillars at the entrance record the names of the Holocaust victims whose families live in the Chicago community. As a permanent record, Pages of Testimony (information about victims of the Holocaust) are sent to the Yad Vashem Archives in Jerusalem. The museum also contains a permanent display of Holocaust photographs, diaries, documents, letters, and memorabilia.

Palatine

Memorial to the Six Million, at Sharon Memorial Park, rises eighty feet into the sky. A ten-foot gold-leafed flame, set in a lamp, is at the peak of the *Migdal Hazikaron* (Tower of Remembrance).

Skokie

Dr. Janusz Korczak Memorial, 3800 Church Street, and Dr. Korczak Terrace, is an Eternal Light dedicated in 1972 by the Village of Skokie and the Dr. Janusz Korczak B'nai B'rith Lodge in memory of the Jewish physician and educator who headed a Jewish orphanage in Warsaw and went to his death with 292 orphans during the Nazi occupation of Poland. Dr. Korczak, whose real name was Henryk Goldszmit, died at the age of sixty-three. About fifty percent of the population of Skokie consists of Holocaust survivors.

INDIANA

Indianopolis

Memorial to the Six Million, located in B'nai Torah Cemetery, is a tall marble black monument erected in 1949 by local survivors of the Nazi Holocaust. Sealed in the base of the monument is a parchment on which are listed the names of martyred relatives of Indianapolis survivors.

KENTUCKY

Fort Knox

A memorial light in tribute to the six million Jews who perished in the Nazi Holocaust is in the Eleventh Avenue Chapel of Fort Knox. The light, which has six branches in mounting flames, symbolizing the martyrs, is believed to be the first Holocaust memorial in a U.S. military installation.

LOUISIANA

New Orleans

The Howard Tilton Library of Tulane University contains a collection of many major monographs dealing with the period of the Third Reich. It was a gift of the Anti-Defamation League and the head of the Tulane University Library.

MARYLAND

Baltimore

The Holocaust Memorial, erected at Water, Gay, and Lombard Streets by the Baltimore Jewish Council, at a cost of over $300,000, is located on an acre of ground in the new downtown part of the city. It was dedicated November 2, 1980, and stands on a square block which formerly belonged to the Community College of Baltimore, Inner Harbor Campus. The college leased the land to the city, which in turn gave the Baltimore Jewish Council permission to build the Memorial. It was designed by Donald Kann and Arthur Valk.

The Memorial represents the intrusion of a cold, dark, brutal force into a pleasantly natural and warmly inviting setting—symbolizing perhaps the intrusion of the Nazi machine into the serene lives of its unsuspecting victims. The brutal force is represented by two giant, buff-colored, concrete, cantilevered monoliths, each seventy-five feet long and eighteen feet high. They form a frame over the concrete plaza which is the formal approach to the inscription of 172 words. One walks under the two monoliths, which skim the top of one's head, and then into the open spaces of the park. The engraved dedication to the six million Jewish victims of the Holocaust is constantly bathed in light. The south side of the park is marked by six rows of six trees, which bloom early in the spring. The inside of the Memorial serves as a sanctuary for ceremonies marking Yom HaShoah and the Warsaw Ghetto Uprising.

Aaron H. Leibtag Resource Center in the Board of Jewish Education Building, 5800 Park Heights Avenue, contains artifacts, documents, and other resources, and is the scene of occasional exhibits on the Holocaust.

A memorial in the shape of a Star of David stands in the reception of the HIAS office at 5750 Park Heights Avenue as a monument to the Holocaust. Weighing 278 pounds and sponsored by the New Americans Club, the star stands at the apex of beams radiating to scrolls on either side, one bearing the inscription in English, "In memory of the 6,000,000 of our people who perished under the Nazis," and the other engraved with quotations in Hebrew from Lamentations.

In the lobby of Ner Israel Rabbinical College, 400 Mount Wilson Lane, is a simple scroll memorializing the victims of the Holocaust. Dedicated in 1978 by Paul and Leah Lewis of Dallas, Texas, it contains a cut-off Star of David and a memorial declaration to recall the victims of the Holocaust.

Bethesda

In the Ark of Congregation Beth El of Montgomery County, 8215 Old Georgetown Road, is a Torah Scroll that was a gift of the Jewish community of West Germany's state of Württemberg in memory of Dr. Otto Hirsch of Stuttgart. Dr. Hirsch was president of the Central Organization of Germany Jews until his deportation to the Mauthausen concentration camp, where he died in 1941. His son, Hans George Hirsch, a member of the congregation, selected the Torah.

Chevy Chase

In the front lobby of Ohr Kodesh Congregation, 8402 Freyman Drive, is a memorial to the relatives of congregation members who died in the Holocaust.

Olney Memorial Gardens

The Holocaust Memorial, designed by Philip Ratner, was erected in the Judean Memorial Gardens in the Maryland suburbs in 1981. The sculpture contains seventeen figures, representing many different ages—including men, women, and children—all of whom are linked arm-in-arm to form a Star of David. The outer perimeter of figures face upward in prayer and questioning. The inner group stands with heads bowed, also in prayer. Facing into a park, the farthest point of the star forms the prow of a ship. The base of the ship represents an eternal flame, a symbol both of destruction and hope. In the prow are a man and woman symbolizing Noah's ark, as well as the exodus of Jewish refugees from Nazi Europe.

Randallstown

The Memorial to Holocaust Victims, a nine-foot marble shaft on which is inscribed in Hebrew the "Eleventh Commandment," "Thou Shalt Not Forget," was erected in 1964 in the Randallstown Cemetery. The shaft is topped by a Star of David, below which are the words: "In memory of the six million victims of tyranny in Europe and to those who fell in the defense of human dignity and freedom, 1938–1945." The memorial was sponsored by a group of Germans.

Silver Spring

A unique outdoor memorial to the victims of the Holocaust stands in the form of an elaborate garden-patio and two massive sculptured tablets symbolic of the Ten Commandments outside Temple Israel, 420 University Boulevard East.

MASSACHUSETTS

Randolph

Holocaust Memorial Courtyard, at Temple Beth Am, 871 North Main Street, has an atrium on the second floor consisting of an eighteen-foot by five-foot mosaic depicting the plight of the Jews during the Nazi era, and an eight-ton Star of David with an eternal flame. There is also a small museum housing Holocaust artifacts.

Swampscott

In the sanctuary of Temple Israel, 837 Humphrey Street, there is a memorial wall commemorating the victims of the Holocaust. Made up of bronze and wood, the wall portrays, in three parts, the agony of Holocaust victims, the suvivors' vow of "Never Again," and the hope for tomorrow.

Waltham

The Holocaust monument, next to the Berlin Chapel, which serves the three major faiths represented on the Brandeis University campus, is a statue of Job, cast in bronze from the original which stands at Yad

Vashem in Jerusalem. Both statues are the work of the sculptor Nathan Rapaport. Six feet high, the statue was commissioned and sponsored by the New Americans of Boston, a group of Holocaust survivors. Ashes from the Treblinka concentration camp are interred at the base of the statue.

The Tauber Institute of Brandeis University is engaged both in research and in teaching in the following areas: nationalism and racism in modern Europe, European Jewish history since the Enlightenment, refugee problems, and the roots and development of Nazism, fascism, and anti-Semitism. The resources of the Institute are available to members of Brandeis University and to accredited visitors drawn from the academic community. The Institute was established under the terms of a gift to Brandeis University by Dr. Laszlo N. Tauber in honor of Dr. Tauber's parents, and is dedicated to the memory of the victims of Nazi persecution.

MICHIGAN

Clinton Township

Holocaust Monument, in the Workmen's Circle Cemetery, 14 Mile Road and Gratiot, is a six-angled structure. One angle displays a triangle which was a symbol of the concentration camps. Another has corners with a yellow Star of David indicating the emblem intended as a mark of shame for Jews, but which has been worn proudly by those who defied the Nazi murders. As a background, six tall evergreens pay tribute to resistance fighters. A chimney depicts the sad recollection of the Jews' suffering. The word Yizkor ("remember") is prominently shown.

Lake Orion

War Crimes Museum, 2369 Joslyn, in the Kinsington Antique Village, exhibits artifacts, photographs, and letters from concentration camp inmates and Stars of David from Jews' concentration camp uniforms, all intended to remind Americans of the evils of the Nazi regime.

Livonia

Memorial to Holocaust Victims, at the entrance to Beth El Memorial Park, 28120 West McNichols, is a curved marble monument inside of which there is an eternal light. Inscribed on the monument are these words: "To the sacred memory of the 6,000,000 men, women and children, pious, good and innocent, who gave their lives for the sanctification of God's name and whose unforgettable story is part of the saga of our people."

Royal Oak

The Memorial to Holocaust Victims, a nine-foot-tall monument of bronze in Oakview Cemetery, 1032 North Main, was dedicated in 1972 by Congregation B'nai Moshe. The monument depicts a family rising from the debris and ashes of concentration camps, surrounded by menorahlike arms that extend upward to signify hope for the future. The sculpture is mounted on a granite block on which are inscribed the names of relatives of B'nai Moshe members who perished in the Holocaust.

West Bloomfield

The Holocaust Memorial Center, a wing adjacent to the main entrance of the Jewish Community Center of Metropolitan Detroit, 6600 West Maple Street, has an exhibition area and concourse, library and resource center, lecture and conference rooms, and a memorial garden. The Memorial Center is part of the Jewish Community Center, but it functions as an independent agency. It has a full museum containing Holocaust artifacts, archives, books, films, and taped oral histories.

MINNESOTA

Minneapolis

Temple Israel, 2324 Emerson Avenue South, has in its gallery a simple memorial to the six million victims of the Holocaust.

MISSISSIPPI

Meridian

In the courtyard of Temple Beth Israel, 5718 14th Place, is a small gravestone-type marker which reads "Am I my brother's keeper?" and "In Memoriam, Six Million Jews, 1933–1945."

MISSOURI

Kansas City

The Holocaust Memorial, which stands in front of the main entrance to the Jewish Community Center, 8201 Holmes Road, was dedicated in 1973 by the Center's New Americans Club. Made of pure aluminum, and standing 10 feet high, 9¾ feet wide, and 2 feet deep, the monument features sculptured human figures and is welded in bas-relief. One side of the memorial portrays the Warsaw Ghetto Uprising. The opposite side recalls the Exodus from Egypt and King David and his lyre. A menorah is depicted on a side facet. Former President Harry S. Truman was the principal speaker at the dedication.

St. Louis

St. Louis Center for Holocaust Studies, housed in the Jewish Community Centers Association, 10957 Schuetz Road, organizes a full-time educational program developed by the St. Louis Holocaust Steering Committee of the Jewish Federation. Its director, Dr. Warren P. Green, and staff provide educational and other resources to both the Jewish and the general community, particularly the public and parochial school systems, and organize an annual community-wide Yom HaShoah program.

In front of the St. Louis Rabbinical Association, 7400 Olive Street, is a cemetery created in 1942 for deceased refugees. It contains nearly 200 graves.

NEBRASKA

Omaha

The Holocaust Memorial, standing on the wall of the Omaha Jewish Community Center, 333 South 32nd Street, is a large marble plaque representing the six million victims of the Holocaust. It was given by Mr. and Mrs. Paul Lewis of Dallas.

NEVADA

Las Vegas

The Gertrude Sperling Resource Library for Holocaust Studies, housed in the Las Vegas Jewish Federation, 846 East Sahara Avenue, serves as a resource center for the State of Nevada for materials on the Holocaust. It includes an audio-visual unit.

NEW JERSEY

Cherry Hill

The Holocaust memorial, standing in Camden County Park on Cooper River Parkway opposite Temple Emanuel, consists of an impressive high granite base on top of which sits a twenty-seven-foot-high stainless steel rendering of a memorial flame. A focal point for community observances, it stands on land given by the Camden County Park Commission, to which the memorial was donated.

Clifton

Memorial to the Six Million stands in King Solomon Memorial Park, Dwas Lane and Alwood Road.

Deans

The Holocaust Memorial, in the Washington Cemetery, honors the long list of martyrs killed by the Nazis in Hungary—particularly in Ungvár, capital of Ruthenia. It was erected in 1976 by the Association of Jews from Ushorod and vicinity. A tall monument with Yiddish inscriptions on all four sides, the memorial gives the names of individuals from the Ushorod area who were killed at Auschwitz and other concentration camps.

Fair Lawn

The Holocaust Sculpture, standing in the lobby of the Fair Lawn Jewish Center, 1010 Norma Avenue, shows a survivor of the Holocaust surrounded by barbed wire and flames. He is holding aloft a torn, battered Torah scroll. The wall inscription from Psalm 30 emphasizes the theme "Tears may linger for a night, but joy will come with the dawn." The sculpture is the work of Nathan Rapaport, who created the Warsaw Ghetto Memorial and the Yad Vashem Memorial in Jerusalem. It was commissioned by the Lorch and Loeb families in memory of Sandy Lorch.

Hackensack

The Holocaust Memorial Plaque, at the corner of Court and Main Streets, was erected by the United Jewish Committee's CRC Holocaust Committee.

Irvington

There is a Holocaust Memorial in Congregation B'nai Israel, 1706 Nye Avenue.

Mahwah

The Resource Center for Holocaust and Genocide Studies is part of Ramapo College, and is sponsored by the College and the United Jewish Community of Bergen County.

Metuchen

A Holocaust Memorial, a sculpture by Linda Gissen, stands in the lobby of Temple Neve Shalom, 250 Grove Avenue. Flowing upward, the sculpture is illuminated by six memorial candles to form the Hebrew word *Zachor*, "Remember." It uses a mixture of steel, copper, and brass along with strands of barbed wire, all of which are welded together.

North Bergen

A Holocaust memorial stands in the main entrance of Temple Beth-El, 7501 Hudson Avenue. It consists of a table and eternal light.

Perth Amboy

A Yad Vashem memorial light near the ark in Congregation Beth Mordecai, 224 High Street, perpetuates the memory of the victims of the Holocaust.

Pleasantville

A Holocaust Memorial in Rodef Sholom Cemetery is a large, three-paneled stone bearing the names of Holocaust victims who were immediate relatives of Holocaust survivors living in Atlantic City, and who belonged to the Club of New Americans, which erected the memorial.

Trenton

A Holocaust Memorial stands in the Bellevue Avenue wall of the Lewis Auditorium of Congregation Adath Israel, 715 Bellevue Avenue. The memorial is an aluminum sculpture affixed to a bronze plaque on which there is a couplet in Hebrew and English from one of Abraham Shlonsky's poems.

Union

In the Eastern Union County YM-YWHA on Green Lane, there are on display the Holocaust memorial designs chosen from those submitted by some 1,200 artists and craftsmen from New Jersey for a portable memorial to the Holocaust. Four noted judges will select the three finalists from which a winner will be chosen. The designs include poetry, drawings, photographs, and oils. The contest was sponsored by the Jewish Federation of Central New Jersey.

Ventnor

The Holocaust Memorial, standing in the lobby of Congregation Beth Judah, 6725 Ventnor Avenue, is a black and bronze menorah memorializing the six million victims of the Holocaust. It is an eight by ten foot menorah, one-third of which is missing, to indicate the loss of one-third of the Jewish population. The menorah was donated by Paul and Leah Lewis of Dallas.

Vineland

In the lobby of Beth Israel Congregation, 1915 Park Avenue, stands a Holocaust Memorial dedicated to "Jewish Martyrdom and Resistance" in the form of a wall-relief. It depicts concentration camps, a burning ghetto, and fleeing Jews. The central figure is of a Jew with four hands which engage in rescue, hold a revolver, lift a Torah and hold a garment (perhaps a *tallit*)* which has a yellow star on top of it. In the cavity of his heart is a crematorium out of which protrude two feet.

There is also a symbol of the burning and fighting ghetto. On top one sees the Jewish flag, and figures representing the remnants of the Warsaw Ghetto Uprising throwing Molotov cocktails at a German tank. The flames of the ghetto ascend heavenward, and within the sun is written *Zachor* ("Remember") in Hebrew. The figure in front of the ghetto is emaciated and in an oversized coat; on the extreme left are shown fighting partisans. Eighteen feet long and eleven feet high, it is the work of Dennis and Sansea Sparling.

Wayne

The Holocaust Study Center stands in the Goldman Judaica Library of the North Jersey YM-YWHA. Created in memory of Sri Orland, the memorial is a steel sculpture which is lit annually on Holocaust Remembrance Day.

NEW YORK

Albany

The Holocaust Memorial, at the front entrance of the Jewish Community Center of Albany, 340 Whitehall Road, is an impressionistic sculpture by Nathan Rapaport which is based on the theme of the Burning Bush. It also is a memorial to Anita L. Winter, whose generous gift to the Center made the Memorial possible.

---

*Tallit—prayer shawl.

Amherst

A memorial to the victims of the Holocaust stands in the courtyard of the suburban building of the Buffalo Jewish Center at 2600 North Forest Road. The abstract sculpture, resting on a sixteen-foot-high center post, is designed in the form of a book with movable pages inscribed with quotations and thoughts of the survivors.

Binghamton

The Margolis Holocaust Collection of books, documents, and other materials relating to the death of the six million martyrs, is housed in the State University of New York, Binghamton. The collection was assembled by the late Mrs. Belle Margolis, who lost thirty-two close relatives in the Holocaust.

The Star of David, cast as a Holocaust Memorial, is formed by the pillars of Temple Israel's monument on Deerfield Place.

Brooklyn

The Center of Holocaust Studies, 1609 Avenue J, has tapes of interviews, slides, movies, diaries, letters, posters, photographs, and clothing relating to the Holocaust. Designed to encourage the use of Holocaust materials and to provide lecturers on the subject, the museum is located in the Yeshiva of Flatbush. It was created by Dr. Yaffa Eliach, professor of Judaic studies at Brooklyn College and a survivor of the Holocaust.

East Midwood Jewish Center, 1625 Ocean Avenue, contains a tablet honoring the memory of the six million martyrs of the Holocaust. The tablet, measuring 8½ by 20 feet, is made of Italian marble. At its base, six lamps burn continually. It was a gift of Mr. and Mrs. Paul Lewis of Dallas.

The Progressive Synagogue, 1395 Ocean Avenue, has a stained glass window which memorializes the six million Jewish victims of the Holocaust. Designed by A. Raymond Katz, the design incorporates figures representing concentration camp survivors, the Nazi crematoria, and chimneys topped by the four freedoms in Hebrew.

Buffalo

The Monument to Holocaust Victims stands in Pine Hill Cemetery and is the resting place for the remains of the Jews cremated in the Nazi death camps.

East Meadow

The Children's Remembrance of the Holocaust, erected in November 1979, at Eisenhower Park in East Meadow, contains a memorial from the children of New York recalling the one million Jewish children killed in the Nazi Holocaust. It was erected by the New York City Board of Jewish Education, the Jewish National Fund, and the World Zionist Organization, in cooperation with the Long Island Committee for Soviet Jewry and the Jewish War Veterans.

Affixed to the block above the lake in Eisenhower Park are the words, "a living remembrance to the Six Million Jews." Originally dedicated in 1968 by Temple Beth El, Bellmore; Bellmore Jewish Center; Merrick Jewish Center; Congregation B'nai Israel, Freeport; South Baldwin Jewish Center; and the Wantagh Jewish Center, it was rededicated in 1973 on the thirtieth anniversary of the Warsaw Ghetto Uprising.

East Rockaway

A Holocaust Memorial stands in the main lobby of the Hewlett–East Rockaway Jewish Center, depicting the Burning Bush with six pointed flames symbolizing the six million martyrs of the Holocaust. The flames are of various sizes to symbolize children, adults, and the elderly. The contorted shapes recall the torturous experiences of these victims.

Farmingdale

Holocaust Memorial at Farmingdale Jewish Center, 425 Fulton Street, consists of a darkened corridor, lit only by *yahrzeit** candles, each of which represents approximately twenty-five Nazi concentration camps.

The monument to the martyrs of the Globoker Ghetto, erected by the Globoker Benevolent Society, an eighty-eight-year-old Jewish *Landsmanschaft*,† stands in Section 3, Block 14, of the New Montefiore Cemetery, Farmingdale. Only 250 of Globoker's 7,000 Jews escaped the 1944 Nazi roundups in this Polish town.

Radom's War Victims, erected by the Radomer Mutual Culture Center, Inc. on its plot in New Montefiore Cemetery, Farmingdale, memoralizes its Holocaust martyrs. In 1963, the society published *The Book of Radom: The Story of a Jewish Community in Poland Destroyed by the Nazis*.

---

*yahrzeit—memorial.
†Landsmanschaft—organization of Jews from the same town or area in Europe.

Great Neck

Temple Beth El, 5 Old Mill Road, has a stark white *bimah** wall and ark created by sculptress Louise Nevelson, on which a white flame memorializes the six million Jewish victims of the Holocaust. The abstract sculpture, consisting of white boxes of wood that break up light and shadow, is fifty-five feet wide and fifteen feet high, and includes a design for the ark and an Eternal Light.

Jericho

A permanent Holocaust memorial has been created in the Solomon Schechter Day School of Nassau County, Barbara Lane. Attached to one brick wall are candleholders holding six memorial candles.

Monticello

The Remembrance Shrine of the Holocaust is situated in a small two-room building behind the residence of Mr. and Mrs. Joseph Merfeld, 12 Osborne Street. It was built by the Merfelds, who donated it to the local Hadassah. One of the rooms has six steps at the entrance, six lights on its porch, and six small trees in an adjacent garden—all referring to the six million victims of the Holocaust. Another is a small museum on the Holocaust erected by the Merfelds, who were survivors.

New Rochelle

The Wall of Martyrs, a monumental bronze sculpture by Louise Kaish, in Beth El Synagogue, Northfield Road at North Avenue, is a symbolic representation of Jewish martyrdom throughout the ages, including the Holocaust. It hangs in the Hall of Martyrs and was endowed by Mr. and Mrs. Harry Platt.

New York City (Manhattan)

Anti-Defamation League of B'nai B'rith, 345 East 46th Street, includes on one of its walls, "Monument to the Holocaust," a series of bas-reliefs made possible by support from Mr. and Mrs. Moshe Deitcher and Mr. and Mrs. William Troy.

The Cathedral Church of Saint John the Divine, 1047 Amsterdam Avenue, has an Auschwitz memorial figure said to be the first Holocaust memorial to be installed in a Christian house of worship in the United States. It is a life-sized bronze sculpture by Elliot Offner of the

---

*bimah—synagogue podium.

prone skeletal figure of a death camp inmate agonizingly reaching skyward. It will be prominently displayed in the crossing under the dome of the Cathdral, the seat of the New York Episcopal diocese, as "a reminder to congregants and thousands of visitors from every part of the world, of the tragic consequences of religious and racial bigotry."

The Memorial to the One Million Jewish Children who perished in the Holocaust is affixed to the facade of the new school building of the Park Avenue Synagogue, 87th Street and Madison Avenue. The two large sculptures are the work of Israeli artist Nathan Rapaport. The lower one shows Dr. Janusz Korczak, a Jewish physician and author who cared for hundreds of Jewish orphans in the Warsaw Ghetto, as he accompanies his charges to a Nazi death camp. Above this are three Israeli citizens who are aided by angels in returning the Jewish menorah to Jerusalem, symbolizing the restoration of the Jewish people to Israel. The sculpture was a gift of Mr. and Mrs. Leon Jolson. (Mr. Jolson lived through the Warsaw Ghetto Uprising.)

The Raoul Wallenberg Playground, West 189th Street and Amsterdam Avenue, memorializes the Swedish diplomat who disappeared from Budapest at the end of World War II, after helping save thousands of Hungarian Jews from the Nazi Holocaust. He is reported to have been arrested by the Soviets and is said to have been incarcerated in a Soviet prison in Siberia for more than thirty years.

The Workmen's Circle National Headquarters, 45 East 33rd Street, has a small monument by Nathan Rapaport, who sculpted the Warsaw Ghetto Uprising Memorial. The 7½ foot sculpture resembles this well-known memorial.

North Woodmere

The Holocaust Museum in Congregation Ohr Torah, 410 Hungry Harbor Road, houses artifacts of concentration camps, including items that were worn or used by camp inmates.

Roslyn Heights

A junior chapel dedicated to the memory of Anne Frank, the celebrated diarist and Jewish martyr from Amsterdam, stands in Temple Sinai, 425 Roslyn Road.

Yonkers

A memorial to the victims of the Holocaust stands on an exterior wall of the Midchester Jewish Center, 236 Grandview Boulevard. A huge bronze menorah, designed as a memorial to the six million who died in the Holocaust, it is a gift from Mr. and Mrs. Fred Silberman.

NORTH CAROLINA

Chapel Hill

In the Judge John J. Parker Collection, University Library, University of North Carolina, is an excellent collection of briefs, documents, exhibits, and transcripts from the Nuremberg war crime trials of November 1945 to October 1946. Parker was one of the judges who tried many of the leading Nazis responsible for implementing the Holocaust.

OHIO

Akron

The Workmen's Circle Cemetery, on Swartz Road, off South Main Street, has a monument with an inscription in English and Yiddish to the martyred six million.

Bedford Heights

The memorial to the Holocaust martyrs in Zion Memorial Park, Route 8, was erected by Kol Israel Foundation of Cleveland, which was formed by survivors of the Holocaust. Buried under the monument are ashes of victims who originally were buried after the war in the cemeteries of four death camps. The memorial is a tall marble slab with the names of martyrs and of concentration camps inscribed on the front and back, respectively.

Columbus

The chapel for daily services of Beth Jacob Congregation, 1223 College Avenue, has six walls to commemorate the martyrdom of six million Jews in the Nazi Holocaust.

Agudas Achim Synagogue, 1568 East Broadway (Bexley), has in its atrium Alfred Tiber's sculpture entitled "Remembrance," a bronze memorial to the martyrs of the Holocaust. It depicts the paths, guard towers, barbed wire, and crematoria of a concentration camp, and a helmeted Nazi soldier herding the victims toward the camp gates. Among the group of figures, a man rises holding aloft the flag of Israel. On the base are carved the names of all the death camps and, from an Emma Lazarus poem, the words, "The spirit is not dead, proclaim the word. Where lay the dead bones of a host of armed men, stand by! I open your graves, my people, saith the Lord, and I shall place you living in your land."

PENNSYLVANIA

Easton

The Memorial to Victims of the Holocaust, on the grounds of the Temple of Peace, 15th and Northhampton Streets, is a 140-foot bronze abstract statue consisting of a group of jagged, limblike forms, with a large hole cut through the center to convey a feeling of pain. Dedicated in 1962, it has a simple inscription in front of the base: "We must not forget." The space around the memorial is filled with plantings and a couple of stone benches as a memorial to Kurt Menkel, a survivor of the Holocaust who was responsible for the monument. The monument is the work of Hans D. Rawinsky, who was a refugee.

Philadelphia

In the Gratz College Library at 10th Street and Tabor Road is the Holocaust Oral History Project, developed by the Memorial Committee for the Six Million Jewish Martyrs and initiated by Nora Levin, professor of modern history at the College. It began with the recording of tapes by survivors who lectured in Professor Levin's class, and then spread citywide as the only major oral history collection on the Holocaust in Philadelphia. The indexed tapes are now being made available for free to the public.

Holocaust artifacts in the Wynnfield home of Arnold Shay is one of the largest private collections of artifacts from the concentration camps. It includes a child's banjo with a parchment body made from desecrated Torah scrolls, prisoners' uniforms, the death's-head visored hats, boots, jackets, guns, SS death's-head caps, and other items.

The Martyrs Monument, 16th Street and Benjamin Franklin Parkway, is an eighteen-foot bronze statue that memorializes the victims of the Holocaust. Erected in 1964, the statue is the work of Nathan Rapaport, the sculptor of the Warsaw Ghetto Uprising Monument in Warsaw and of the memorial at Yad Vashem in Jerusalem. A gift to the city of Philadelphia from the Association of Jewish New Americans and the Federation of Jewish Agencies of Greater Philadelphia, the monument portrays a dying mother lying amid flames, a writhing child upholding the Scroll of the Torah, a patriarchal figure with arms upraised in a gesture of priestly blessing, and several arms wielding daggers. These figures are framed by a blazing menorah and enveloped by a fiery bush.

At the bases, on the two sides, are dedications in Hebrew, Yiddish and English.

The Jewish Identity Center, 1453 Levick Street, has in its basement a Holocaust Museum, built and maintained by Yaakov Riz, a survivor of Auschwitz. In the museum are photographs and copies of books, exhibits, documents, and other reminders of the six millon Jews who perished in the Nazi Holocaust.

The National Institute on the Holocaust, 1616 Walnut Street, Suite 802, is directed by the noted Christian scholar on the Holocaust, Franklin Littell. It publishes a number of resource works, sponsors several conferences, and organizes an annual seminar trip to Eastern Europe.

Temple Sholom, Large Street and Roosevelt Boulevard, has a memorial to the victims of the Holocaust. It includes two oil paintings and a six-lighted candelabrum which burns continually. Located in the foyer of the Hyman S. Driban Auditorium, the paintings are by Miriam Brown Fine.

Pittsburgh

The Holocaust Memorial Commission and Holocaust Center, the community's living memorial to those who died in the Nazi Holocaust, has temporary offices and the beginnings of a museum in the United Jewish Federation building, 234 McKee Place. While plans are being developed for the recommended Holocaust Center site in the Jewish Community Center, Isaiah Kuperstein, its Director, is coordinating lectures, films, exhibits, Yom HaShoah observances, oral histories, and a whole range of special events built around the lessons of the Holocaust.

SOUTH CAROLINA

Charleston

A Holocaust Memorial, a plaque honoring the memory of the six million Jewish victims of the Holocaust who died in World War II, is in the garden of the Jewish Community Center, 1645 Milbrook Avenue. It was erected by the Kalushiner Society.

TENNESSEE

Memphis

A Holocaust Memorial stands on the grounds of the Jewish Community Center, 6560 Poplar. A gift of Mr. and Mrs. Paul Lewis of Dallas, the seventeen-foot marble memorial has the names of seven concentration camps on the front. At the top are six perpetual lamps—one for each million Jews killed by the Nazis. At the base is a simple appeal to remember the Holocaust and its victims.

TEXAS

Dallas

Garden of Memories, also known as The Lewis Park, has a twenty-four-foot monument to the Nazi Holocaust, designed in hexagonal form (each side symbolizing one million Jews who perished) in the new park of the Dallas Jewish Community Center, 7900 North Haven Road. It was built by Mr. and Mrs. Paul Lewis in Dallas, who have established many Holocaust memorials in synagogues and centers in various parts of the country. The monument contains a bronze structure entitled "The Last March."

The entire monument is surrounded by a fountain of water and is lit up. In front of the park is a plaza on which the granite monument stands. The front has a brief description of the Holocaust. Above the concentration camp names is the bronze sculpture by Nathan Rapaport. The top of the monument houses six lamps burning continually.

On the right side of the monument is a statement of gratitude to all of the Allied nations that liberated the survivors, as well as a tribute to the people of Denmark who rescued the Jews of that country. On the same side is a tribute to the five million non-Jews who shared the tragic fate of the Jews. On the left side of the memorial is listed the number of Jews lost in each country.

The lobby of Congregation Shearith Israel, 9401 Douglas, has what is said to be the first Holocaust memorial erected in the United States. In 1956, Paul Lewis of Dallas provided a monument consisting of a long marble wall in front of which are six lamps burning continually as a tribute to the six million Jewish martyrs.

Temple Shalom, Hilcrest and Alpha Roads, has on a marble wall in a corridor a combined memorial to the six million Jewish victims of the Nazi Holocaust and to the people of Denmark who risked their lives to save Danish Jewry during the Nazi occupation of that country. The memorial was provided by Paul Lewis.

Houston

Congregation Beth Yeshurun, 4525 Beechnut, has in its front hall a large memorial to the Holocaust victims, a gift of Paul Lewis. Affixed to a brick wall on the interior is a marble plaque with a reproduction of the sculpture "The Last March," the large-scale original of which stands in the plaza in front of the Dallas Jewish Community Center. Under the reproduction are the words "For these I weep," from the Book of Lamentations 1:16. Below are six lights burning continually, and a brief description of the Holocaust.

United Orthodox Synagogues, 4221 S. Braeswood, has a glass sculpture memorial to the victims of the Holocaust. The sculpture, which was created by the noted artist Herman Perlman, depicts six towering candles and a dove flying over the remnants of the Jewish people.

San Antonio

Congregation Agudas Achim, 1201 Donaldson Avenue, has a marble memorial to the victims of the Holocaust erected by Paul Lewis. At the bottom are six forms for candles, each representing a million of the six million Jewish victims.

VIRGINIA

Richmond

Congregation Beth Ahabah, 1117 West Franklin Street, has the cornerstone of the synagogue in the small town of Stolzenau, Germany, dedicated in Richmond in 1979. It was rescued by a Nazi who had helped set fire to the synagogue during Kristallnacht in 1938, when the Nazis burned scores of synagogues. The Nazi left word with the mayor of the town that when he and his wife were dead, the cornerstone was to be given to a Jewish organization. Eric Lipman, a citizen of Richmond who comes from Stolzenau, where his family settled in the eighteenth century, arranged to obtain the stone.

The Holocaust Memorial, erected by the New Americans Jewish Club in 1956, is dedicated to the Jewish victims of the Holocaust. It stands in the Emek Sholom Section of the Forest Lawn Cemetery.

WASHINGTON

Mercer Island

A Holocaust Memorial stands on the grounds of the Jewish Community Center of Seattle, 3801 East Mercer Way. The twelve-foot-high sculpture in bronze by Gizel Berman includes the words, "Thou shalt not forget."

Tacoma

In the lobby of Temple Beth El, 5975 South 12th Street, are two carved panels, one of which is a memorial prayer for the six million Jews killed in the Nazi Holocaust, and which includes the words from the martyrology section of the Yom Kippur liturgy. Joined to this panel is another inscribed with a passage from the prophet Joel.

The two panels are connected at the bases by pictures drawn by a child in a concentration camp, which were found after the war. The drawings show the railroad cars going to the death camps, as seen through the mind and expressed by the hand of a little child.

The two panels and the two inscriptions are also linked by the figures at the top of the panel, which speak of the Holocaust and the hatred it involved, as well as the continuity of life after the great destruction.

WYOMING

Cheyenne

Congregation Mount Sinai, 2610 Pioneer Avenue, has a central stained bank of windows depicting the Holocaust, called the "Martyrs Window," in its sanctuary. It was funded by public subscription. In the design are depicted German bombers, the German eagle, and a factory, a menorah, the Star of David, a blue-and-white flag, and the words "Memorial to the 6 Million Martyrs. May their memory never fade."

CANADA

Lantier, Quebec

The Holocaust Memorial, erected by B'nai Brith in the Zentner Memorial Park, is a stark, twenty-foot granite structure, with six squared columns and inscriptions in English, French, Hebrew, and Yiddish.

Montreal, Quebec

The Montreal Holocaust Memorial is located on the lower level of the Allied Jewish Community Services' Cummings House, 5151 Côte Sainte Catherine Road, and covers 1,800 square feet of space. Its emphasis is on education. One of its three main sections is a permanent exhibit of artifacts and graphics detailing the events of the Holocaust. A second is devoted to rotating exhibits and public programs. The third area provides Montreal with a center for documentation and audiovisual material on the Holocaust for meetings and scholarly programs. (Located in the same building is the headquarters of the National Holocaust Remembrance Committee of the Canadian Jewish Congress.)

In the sanctuary is a corridor with the names of concentration camps and *shtetls*.* In the center is a sealed urn containing the ashes from a crematorium in a Nazi camp; it is mounted on a remnant of a column from a destroyed synagogue in Warsaw. This column and urn, which are under an eternal lamp and on a pedestal, take the form of a Star of David.

Ottawa, Ontario

The Holocaust Memorial is a torch-shaped granite monument erected in 1978 by the Ottawa Jewish Community Council. It stands in the open sector at the Jewish Community Cemetery on Highway 31, the site of the annual communal memorial service. Made of gray rock of ages, it is shaped like a Star of David, and stands eleven feet from its concrete base to the top of the flame. The bottom base is hexagonal, carries the Hebrew word "Remembrance," the number six million and the dates 1933–1945.

Shtetl—an Eastern European village, a good part of whose population is Jewish.

Section VII

An Introduction to High School Holocaust Curricula

by Mary T. Glynn

Webster's Dictionary offers two definitions of "holocaust": (1) burnt offering, and (2) complete destruction of animals or people by fire. But contemporary history and literature offer a whole raft of different definitions: the Jewish catastrophe, Hitler's Final Solution, genocide, the unthinkable, the Inferno, the incomparable crime, the European tragedy, the most tragic page in Jewish history, the greatest barbarity, the most diabolical scheme ever wrought by man, and the war against the Jews.

Because of the scope of the subject, and the unique horror and brutality of its content, high school educators may perhaps be forgiven for waiting forty years before attempting to incorporate this area of human history into the curriculum. The event is so large, so unsettling, so subversive to many of the institutions, both national and cultural, in which we have invested so much, that the fact that we have begun to address it at all speaks somewhat well for the educational establishment. With regard to the Holocaust, educators find themselves in the difficult position of facing a phenomenon too big to ignore, too alive to bury, and too "hot" to handle. Because professional integrity demands it, high school teachers, administrators, and curriculum developers have recently begun pilot units and experimental courses on the Holocaust, usually as part of the social studies curriculum.

In many ways, the Holocaust has proved to be like a mountain whose true dimensions we can only see as we retreat from it. (If it is too close, we cannot assess its shape, size, or configuration.) As time passes and we get some distance from the period of the Second World War, we can see that the Holocaust dwarfs all of the other events of that catastrophic time. It casts shadows not only on history and sociology, but also on psychology, religion, and government. There is not a segment of our national, political, or cultural life that in some way does not fall under the shadow of this unspeakable event. But unlike other historical phenomena, distance does not grant us detachment. Forty years later, the Holocaust is still very much alive. It is not only an integral part of the lives of the survivors who are still among us bearing its indelible scars, it also pervades the human—and more particularly, the academic—conscience. Thus, more and more scholars from various disciplines have begun studying the Holocaust, analyzing its various aspects and mining it for the essential lessons we must learn.

Fundamentally, the study of the Holocaust is subversive: in its light, everyone is found wanting. Not one of our major institutions—national, cultural, ethnic, religious, or educational—lived up to its stated aims and long traditions when faced with the challenges posed by this barbarous event. To teach young people the weaknesses and failures of our most cherished institutions is a difficult task at best, and one made more difficult by the pluralistic nature of our society and by the unique relationship of church and state in the United States. And once the preparatory work has been done, the question keeps surfacing: How do we organize the concepts so that high school students can analyze, interpret, and eventually relate this material to their lives and to their own world?

While the Holocaust is one of those chapters in history which we have a moral responsibility to explore and raise questions about, a case can also be made that it is a chapter with a unique importance or, as Henry Feingold notes, a "special historical valence."

There is perhaps a link between the Holocaust and the threat of nuclear annihilation. The mind-set that conceived the Holocaust, the bureaucratic and technological apparatus that carried it out, the human ability to bifurcate consciousness so that life went on as normal for most people while atrocities were public knowledge—all exist today and have the potential to produce a nuclear catastrophe.

Teaching adolescents about the Holocaust also is increasingly seen as vital to their understanding of the nature of prejudice, as well as of the totalitarian and genocidal realities of the twentieth century. The President's Commission on the Holocaust has emphasized that "the study of the Holocaust [should] become a part of the curriculum in every school system throughout the country." Indeed, it should have a privileged place in that curriculum. As more and more school districts attempt to respond to this recommendation, all involved—scholars, educators, and concerned laypeople—must squarely confront the difficult issue of what the next generation should learn about the causes, history, immediate impact, and resonances of the Holocaust, and how best to teach it.

Although teachers of social studies and other disciplines are not involved in teaching values per se, there are certain behavioral patterns that they consider desirable in their students. Consciously or not, most teachers seek to instill in their students respect for human life, for learning, and for individual differences among students, as well as the constant need to question and to seek answers. All of these objectives are central to the teaching of this controversial and often unsettling material. Although progress toward these objectives cannot be easily measured, particularly since responses to material on the Holocaust may be slow in coming or be hidden, obtaining them will be among the most important goals behind this kind of instruction. While specific objectives differ from curriculum to curriculum, some common ones are:

1. To explore the period of the Holocaust and the many interpretations of it.
2. To assist students in probing the complexities of human behavior under stress.
3. To organize the materials and concepts of the Holocaust so that the students might apply the material to their own lives and time.
4. To provide students with decision-making tools by presenting diverse interpretations of moral and ethical issues arising out of the Holocaust.
5. To help students develop skills in communicating ideas and responses to the material presented, including skills in writing, discussion, and development of hypotheses and projects of their own choice.
6. To measure the change in students' attitudes and comprehension through the use of an evaluative technique.

Two general objectives in such teaching are to help the present generation learn from the barbarism and become aware of the possibility of its recurrence in the future, and to help them appreciate the Jews of Europe, and other victims of the Holocaust, as fellow human creatures whose suffering requires compassion, understanding, and empathy.

To date, there has been no systematic effort to study the dissemination of information about the Holocaust to teenagers. To assess what students *should* learn, what they *can* learn, and what they actually *do* learn requires careful scrutiny. The ZACHOR-sponsored Holocaust Curricula Assessment Project, which was carried out under a grant from the National Endowment for the Humanities, attempted to address these issues by examining the organization, instruction, and effects of courses on the Holocaust taught in four school districts with

extensive experience in Holocaust education. The curricula were those
of the Philadelphia school district, entitled *The Holocaust: A Teacher
Resource;* of the New York City Board of Education, entitled *The
Holocaust: A Study of Genocide;* of the Brookline, Massachusetts,
school system, entitled *Facing History and Ourselves;* and of the Great
Neck, New York, public schools, entitled *Social Studies Holocaust
Curriculum.*

The focus of the study was to understand the objectives, nature, and
effects of each of these curricula in its own terms, as well as to develop
general hypotheses about secondary Holocaust education. As a first
step, a national advisory board composed of educators, historians,
philosophers, and social scientists identified critical factors to be
addressed through a series of comparative case studies. These included:

1. *Variation of pedagogic situation,* such as differences in the scope
   and context of individual curricula; how they were conceived,
   developed, and implemented; differences among teachers' backgrounds, training, and experiences; differences among students'
   backgrounds and educational experiences.
2. *Variation of instructional process,* such as differences in the
   content and treatment of issues; differences in level of sophistica-
   tion and developers' pedagogic approaches; variations in teaching
   methods and styles of classroom interaction.
3. *Variation of effects on students,* such as the appropriateness of
   different kinds of materials for various ages and grade-levels of
   students; what students learn about the Holocaust and the historical and moral dilemmas engendered by it, both cognitively and
   emotionally.

During the spring and fall of 1980, the ZACHOR research team
conducted interviews with educators, teachers, and laypeople to collect information about these factors. Through small-group interviews
and individual questionnaires, the team examined what students learn
from studying the Holocaust. By conducting four parallel studies, it
developed comparable profiles of Holocaust instruction in each school
and, in turn, reported on the general implications of each for the
overall issue of Holocaust education.

One general conclusion our study reached was the vital importance
of some kind of teacher training in preparation for presenting a unit or
course on the Holocaust.

What follow are synopses of two of the four curricula—those of Great
Neck, New York, and Brookline, Massachusetts. (The final page of this
section lists other cities and two states whose boards of education or

school systems have developed their own curricula.) The final ZA-CHOR report, *American Youth and the Holocaust: A Study of Four Major Curricula*, is available from ZACHOR: The Holocaust Resource Center, 250 West 57th Street, Suite 216, New York, N.Y. 10107.

Curriculum 1

Facing History and Ourselves (Brookline, Mass.)

Origin and Target Audience

Facing History and Ourselves was developed in 1976 by Margot Stern Strom and William Parsons, two social studies teachers who felt strongly that a course on the Holocaust should become part of the junior high curriculum, and who found none available.* They worked with other teachers, administrators, college professors, and a child psychiatrist. Their curriculum went through many drafts.

The detailed unit they designed was initially intended for the eighth-grade social studies program, and lasts from eight to ten weeks. Ultimately, parts of it were adapted for high school history, English, law, and art classes.

Given the abundance of materials and activities, teachers can select materials appropriate to the academic level and interests of individual students.

---

*The curriculum is available from Ms. Margot Stern Strom, Program Director, *Facing History and Ourselves*, 25 Kennard Road, Brookline, Mass. 02146, Telephone 617-734-1111, ext. 335.

Teacher Training

Strom and Parsons also received a U.S. Department of Education grant to begin two types of teacher-training workshops, which came to involve not only social studies educators, but also art, science, and English teachers, as well as library and guidance personnel. Week-long summer workshops introduced teachers to a wide variety of materials for Holocaust education, while in-service programs during the school year provided teachers with an opportunity to share experiences and insights.

Rationale

In this course, students are shown how even a human catastrophe such as the Holocaust involves a series of individual and group choices. In turn, as they are presented with conflicting viewpoints, the students are forced to make their own moral and legal judgments on such specific issues as stereotyping and prejudice, the obligations of citizenship, and obedience to authority. The exercises which accompany each lesson force students to think about their daily lives and the consequences of their actions.

Course of Study

The program is divided into eleven chapters extending over eight sections. (A bibliography and filmography comprise a basic resource unit.) The individual chapters are composed largely of excerpts taken from memoirs, historical documents, and interpretations of the Holocaust. The teacher is provided with questions to challenge students to understand and to respond to the material. Follow-up activities are provided to help students develop a deeper understanding of the underlying concepts they have studied.

The eleven chapters are:

1. *An Introduction*. The class explores why adults and school systems have avoided discussing the Holocaust in the past. Activities are suggested to help students become comfortable with probing controversial issues. The teacher is instructed to provide the students with brief working definitions of key terms. The definitions will be filled out in greater detail as the students acquire additional information. Finally, the suggestion is offered that students keep journals, which may be shared with the class, the teacher, or kept private.

2. *Society and the Individual*. This chapter helps the students appreciate their role in society and to realize how various aspects of

society affect people. This leads the students to discuss the theme of the entire unit, "Facing Ourselves," and to investigate the whole area of decision-making. Teaching procedures are provided for using a prose selection by Kurt Vonnegut, for discussing several films, and for other activities to elicit greater student civic awareness and sensitivity.

3. *Individual Decisions Can Alter the Course of Human Development.* The students observe how groups of people all over the earth develop their cultures differently. Some groups evolve into a technological society more rapidly than others. The existence of less-developed groups could be threatened by more developed ones. Individuals have arisen at times in different cultures who try to impress their ideas on the whole population. The chapter serves as an introduction to the next four units, which examine Hitler's grand design.

4. *A Case Study in Prejudice and Discrimination: Anti-Semitism.* Students deepen their understanding of the concept of prejudice. They are shown how it leads to discrimination and, ultimately, to overt actions against a person. Through rumor and stereotyping, this prejudice is extended from individuals to a group, which becomes the scapegoat of the larger society. The students examine anti-Semitic remarks in the Gospels and in letters of Civil War generals.

5. *German History: World War I to World War II.* This chapter serves as a background for understanding the Holocaust in light of the political history of Germany from 1871 to 1939. Emphasis is placed on the periods following World War I and on Hitler's rise to power. Students learn that many complex but not inevitable factors contributed to Hitler's rise. The readings include excerpts from historical documents which help students understand the plight of the German people in the interwar period.

6. *Nazi Philosophy and Policy.* The first of the four themes in this chapter analyzes the roots of National Socialism by quoting several historians. The Nazi philosophy arose from a variety of sources, many of which the students may find contradictory. The students learn that the Nazi racial theory ranked and stereotyped all human beings, leading to acts of violence against those ranked lower. The Night of Broken Glass (the national pogrom of November 9–10, 1938) is examined as an example of what happens when this theory is put into practice. The concept of Nazi totalitarianism is taught by quoting sources and examining various German oaths. The final section introduces the students to the concept of the right of the German people to "living space" (*Lebensraum*).

7. *Preparing for Obedience.* The students learn that Hitler depended on obedience to implement his grand plan for a new order. The response was largely blind obedience, conformity, and passivity. The film *The Hangman* is viewed to illustrate the point. The teacher exposes the students to Kohlberg's stages of moral development. The chapter provides many excerpts from material on the training of Nazi youth, which helps them see people in conflict with themselves and with society. The students explore, through art and literature, the role propaganda played in shaping the German mentality toward specific beliefs. The readings which conclude the chapter focus upon the education and socialization of people growing up during the Nazi period.

8. *Victims of Tyranny.* The students learn that the uniqueness of the Holocaust stems from the Nazi use of the tools of modern technology— the bureaucracy of a modern nation with the cooperation of citizens, army, and industry—to commit mass murder. The students begin to learn about expulsions, resettlements, transports, ghettos, labor camps, and crematoria. They come to appreciate that an understanding of the Holocaust depends on who tells the story and on how it is told. The ghettos are studied by viewing and studying the film *The Warsaw Ghetto*. Several readings help the students to appreciate the knowledge, or lack of knowledge, German citizens had about the exterminations. First-hand accounts of life in the camps are provided. The chapter concludes with a lengthy discussion of why non-Jews should be concerned about the Holocaust.

9. *Human Behavior in Extreme Situations.* In the previous chapter, the horrors of the camps were exposed. However, students must make an imaginative leap to actually understand the terrible realities. The harsh events of the Holocaust sharply limited moral choice. The question of the Jewish resistance to the Holocaust is examined in great detail. The second and third sections of this chapter detail how individuals, German and non-German, attempted to aid the Jews. The efforts of the United States and Denmark are singled out to show what some nations did to help the Jews.

10. *Judgment.* In this chapter, the students learn about the war crimes trials, and read testimony of the perpetrators and victims. The readings and testimonies excerpted from the Nuremberg trials stimulate discussion about the perpetrators' motivations and reasoning. The students are again faced with the basic issues of human behavior and morality in situations of ultimate stress and danger.

11. *Facing Today and the Future*. The final chapter is divided into three sections. The first part is addressed to the teacher and helps him or her evaluate what students have learned and what changes in attitudes have occurred. The second section challenges the students to examine the Holocaust through the eyes of an artist. Various monuments and tributes to the victims of the Holocaust are studied. The final section directly relates the issue of the Holocaust to contemporary parallels by examining relevant news stories.

Summary

This is basically a textbook on the Holocaust geared toward individual students. Very few plans and directions are given to the teacher on how to use its wealth of materials. The teacher who just picks up the manual will find no list of learning objectives for each of the eleven chapters (perhaps this is due to the authors' insistence on the importance of the teacher's participation in an in-service program before using the material).

It is significant that the material is divided into chapters and not into lesson plans. In a few cases, discussion questions and exercises are provided for the many readings. However, most material is merely presented without an explanation of how it should be used. The exceptions to this are the fine aids provided for viewing films and the chapter "Preparing for Obedience," which has excellent teaching suggestions. Comments of teachers and students who have used the curriculum are included, but these are of only limited value to the development of a teaching strategy.

Curriculum 2

Social Studies Holocaust Curriculum (Great Neck, New York)

Origin and Target Audience

This curriculum was initiated in 1978 by Erica Merems, a social studies teacher at North Junior High School.* When she approached the school administrator to do work on Holocaust education, he arranged for released time and substitute service for Ms. Merems and four other teachers to develop a curriculum. The curriculum they produced, which was refined during a summer workshop offered to other teachers, became a required unit in the ninth-grade social studies classes; it has since been adapted for both of Great Neck's high schools.

Teacher Training

An intensive in-service training program is offered, in which a large proportion of the staff participates.

Rationale

The unit is offered to help students become better citizens by understanding such issues as the importance of an active citizenry in combating tyranny and hatred, the dangers of modern technology, and the nature of genocide as a "crime against humanity."

---

*The curriculum is available from Dr. Samuel Polatnik, Assistant Superintendent of Instruction, 345 Lakeville Road, Great Neck, N.Y. 11020.

Course of Study

The program is divided into eight sections. The first chapter, which is in large part addressed to the teacher, is an introduction to the study of the Holocaust, and stages the background for such a program. The purposes of the course are outlined in chapters two and three on "Needs and Assessment" and "Unit Objectives."

The fourth chapter lists fifty-three concepts to be learned. The fifth, "Outline of Understandings and Content," presents in outline form ten units on the Holocaust. These units include:

1. Nazi Anti-Semitism.
2. Period 1, 1933–1939: The Attempted Destruction of German Jewry.
3. The Pre–World War II Response of the Western World to the Nazi Treatment of German Jewry.
4. Pre–World War II Response of Eastern Europe to Nazi Behavior.
5. Period 2, 1939–1941: The Years of Nazi Conquest.
6. Period 3, 1941–1945: The Implementation of the Final Solution to the Jewish Question.
7. Jewish Resistance to the Nazis.
8. The Response of the Allies to the Nazi Murder of the Jews.
9. The Impact of the Holocaust on the Jews.
10. The Impact of the Nazi Rule on Other Peoples of Europe.

This outline organizes a great deal of factual material and serves as a resource for the teacher.

In the fifth chapter, six major teacher themes, which are the actual teaching units, are presented. Each theme is divided into three parts: statement of theme, suggested readings relating to it, and student activities to deepen the understanding of the theme and readings. All of this information is presented in outline form. The six themes are:

1. The Importance of Studying the Holocaust.
2. Historical Prologue.
3. Perpetrators and Victim.
4. The World Reaction.
5. The Aftermath.
6. Application to Today's World.

The sixth and by far the largest section consists of the appendices, which comprise 150 pages of the 186-page curriculum and contain readings. The five preceding chapters allude to specific selections in the appendices, but these selections do not specify particular learning objectives.

Sections seven through eight consist of, respectively, a two-page bibliography of secondary sources and a quarter-page list of audio-visual aids. The most recent work in the bibliography is dated 1975.

Summary

A unique feature of this curriculum is the listing of ten objectives: that students—

1. Realize that man's inhumanity to man can surface at any period in history when moral and ethical standards are allowed to deteriorate.
2. Give meaning, structure, and immediacy to what they may perceive as only one more distant historical event.
3. Perceive that genocide is a threat to all humanity, and that a program of genocide invariably results in the destruction of a rich heritage of traditions and contributions of a people.
4. Be aware that anti-Semitism has had a long history and is still present in the world today.
5. Understand the relationship between the Nazi Holocaust and the establishment of the State of Israel.
6. Gain insight into the difficulty of maintaining human dignity under the dehumanizing policy followed by the Nazis.
7. Appreciate the physical and moral courage of those who fought back against overwhelming odds.
8. Understand that individuals seek different ways of survival.
9. Be aware of the potentially destructive implications of modern technology and of the imperative that responsible men determine and control technology for the benefit of mankind.
10. Become active citizens, for in a democracy, the citizens must be responsible for controlling the activities of government.

While ten objectives help the teacher place the teaching of the Holocaust in a specific perspective, the six teaching units described above are not very detailed: the themes might be expressed more specifically and related more directly to the Outline of Understandings and Content mentioned above.

Some Other Localities Offering Curricula on the Holocaust

Among other cities and states which have developed curricula and resource guides on the Holocaust are:

1. *Baltimore:* "The Holocaust"—a required three-week unit for the eighth and eleventh grades as part of U.S. history courses.
2. *Bellmore-Merrick, New York:* Holocaust unit for tenth-grade social studies course.
3. *Chicago:* "Man's Inhumanity to Man," a curriculum now being field-tested.
4. *Great Barrington, Massachusetts:* "Society on Trial," a four- to seven-week unit for ninth-grade required world history course (*The Holocaust Years: Society on Trial,* Bantam, 1978).
5. *State of Georgia:* "Teaching About Prejudice: The Holocaust as a Case Study" (for secondary schools).
6. *Hewlett-Woodmere, New York:* "The Destruction of Europe's Jews: A Case Study of Modern Inhumanity."
7. *Los Angeles:* "The Holocaust: An Instruction Guide for Secondary Schools."
8. *State of New Jersey:** "The Holocaust and Genocide: A Search for Conscience," for grades nine to twelve; two-volume Anthology and Teachers Guide.
9. *New York City:* "The Holocaust: A Study of Genocide: two- to five-week, nine-week, and eighteen-week units for the secondary school.
10. *Philadelphia:* "The Holocaust: A Teacher Resource": adaptable for grades seven to twelve; now part of the Philadelphia social studies curriculum—used most extensively in grade nine.
11. *Southfield, Michigan:* "The Struggle for Human Dignity": draft curriculum for secondary schools.

---

*Available from Department of Curriculum Research, Anti-Defamation League of B'nai B'rith, 823 United Nations Plaza, New York, N.Y. 10017.

Section VIII
Teacher Development

by Judith Muffs and David Szonyi

Because many high school and college teachers have a very limited knowledge of the Holocaust, it is important that school districts have some kind of teacher-development program. We recommend courses of a more intensive and extensive nature, those that thoroughly familiarize the teacher with the roots, unfolding (from both a German and a Jewish perspective), and implications of the Holocaust, while also introducing him or her to some pedagogic "how-to's." The course should be long enough so that the teacher has time to absorb the material and to formulate his or her own questions.

When this is not possible, the very least that should be offered in the way of teacher development is two sessions—one before and one during the time that a unit on the Holocaust is taught. The latter session allows teachers to share insights, problems, and questions that arise in the classroom.

All teacher training workshops should:

- *Display* posters, examples of student work (e.g., drawings and poetry) and other work.
- *Distribute* a basic kit of materials, including sample guides to teaching the Holocaust.
- *Demonstrate* approches and techniques that have worked for others and that teachers can replicate in their classrooms.
- *Discuss* the feelings and questions teachers have in dealing with such an intellectually demanding and emotionally draining subject.
- *Show* films, slides, posters, and other visual material.
- *Suggest* specific books and articles.
- *Stress* the importance of teachers becoming as knowledgeable about the Holocaust as possible.

A number of universities have offered special summer workshops on the Holocaust. Two we find worthy of note were offered by Northwestern University (Evanston, Ill.) and Yeshiva University (New York City). For the past several years, a particularly fine teacher-development program has been offered by the Eisner Institute of Holocaust Studies at the City University of New York Graduate Center. In addition, a particularly demanding but high-quality program is the summer seminar on the Holocaust offered in English at Yad Vashem in Jerusalem.

West Chester State College near Philadelphia also has developed a certification program on Holocaust education. To receive a certificate, a teacher has to complete six courses: "Twentieth Century Germany," "The Jew in History," "Ethics and Morality," "The Holocaust," "Holocaust Literature," and "Workshop on the Holocaust." The courses are taught by faculty members from the history, English, philosophy, and social sciences departments.

An easy and inexpensive way for teachers to reach their colleagues is through the National Council for the Social Sciences (NCSS) or the National Education Association (NEA), and to make presentations on Holocaust curricula at these organizations' regional and national conferences.

What follow are three examples of teacher-development programs:

- An eight-week in-service course offered by the Los Angeles Unified School District.
- "Teaching About Genocide and the Nazi Holocaust," a similar course taught in Chicago.
- A report on a brainstorming session held as part of an in-service teacher training program in Oceanside, New York.

We have also included "Getting Started," a questionnaire developed by Phillip Kaufman of Bernardsville, New Jersey. Teachers might want to use such a questionnaire to gauge their students' knowledge at the beginning, in the middle, and at the end of a unit on the Holocaust.

1. Teaching About an Infringement of Human Rights: The Holocaust
Los Angeles Unified School District

Why we must teach about it.

How we might teach about it.

An in-service course for Los Angeles teachers, developed in response to the expressed interest of teachers and their requests for guidance in presenting the subject accurately and appropriately

Included in the course:

- Background for a Holocaust
- Historical counterparts
- Mechanics of the Nazi genocide program
- Implications for today in a multi-racial society
- Values for the student
- Relevant films, publications and teaching materials

EIGHT MEETINGS, THURSDAY AFTERNOONS, 4 TO 6
ONE UNIT OF IN-SERVICE CREDIT

This course was developed in consultation with the Anti-Defamation League of B'nai B'rith.

Los Angeles Unified School District Staff Development Point Project Course Outline

1. COURSE TITLE: Teaching About an Infringement of Human Rights: The Holocaust

2. NO. OF SALARY POINTS: 1

3. DESCRIPTION OF COURSE:

    A study of past and present abuses of human rights with emphasis upon the Nazi Holocaust, and recommended methodologies for introducing content to secondary school students.

4. COURSE OBJECTIVES:

    a. To suggest to teachers the focusing and affirmation of human rights that can be derived from such a study, and how it can foster positive attitudes toward other cultures and people.

    b. To analyze positive human values—sense of justice, compassion, human responsibility, perspective, moral stamina—that can be strengthened by this study.

    c. To provide specific and accurate information about the Holocaust that will enable the teacher to present the event effectively and accurately, thereby replacing ignorance and indifference with concern that such an event never happen again.

    d. To help the teacher select appropriate materials and strategies that will make the Holocaust meaningful to students and will assist them in confronting value conflicts and decision-making today.

e. To assist participants in acquiring techniques and in developing insights that will enable them to deal with the special aspects of teaching this subject.

f. To bring to a practical and usable point for teachers the body of material that has been accumulating about the Holocaust.

5. COURSE OUTLINE:

There will be eight two-hour sessions. During each session there will be opportunity for examination of texts, evaluation of materials (including films and filmstrips) and discussion of methods.

1st Session

Importance of teaching about the Holocaust:

Recent increase of interest and concern; need for its inclusion in history; value of knowledge of Holocaust in combatting ignorance, prejudice, crimes of genocide; distribution of material and bibliographies; discussion of outside preparation and assignments.

2nd Session

Background for a Holocaust:

Related instances in history; major events in the history of the Jewish people; development of Jewish culture in Eastern Europe; rise of Nazism in Germany.

3rd Session

Human prejudice, anti-Semitism, and mechanics of the Final Solution:

Holocaust as prime example of race prejudice; mechanics of Nazi genocide program; euthanasia, development of psychological techniques; resistance; world responses to the Holocaust; centers and memorials today; historical counterparts of genocide.

4th Session

Methods and materials for teaching:

Prepared courses and teaching plans; application of studies and proposals to date; questions of appropriate length for study; reading assignments, activities for students.

5th Session

Continuation of Session 4:

> Review of readings, films and filmstrips, music, maps, tapes, photographs. (*Note:* Some of these materials will be presented at appropriate times in other sessions.)

6th Session

Special problems in teaching the Holocaust and human value judgments:

> Success in teaching seen in how students can relate to the Holocaust; questions of internalization, emotional response, teaching to Jewish and to other cultural groups, use of eyewitnesses and survivors, etc.

7th Session

Reports by participants on outside preparation assignment:

> Careful examination and discussion of curriculum units prepared by class as main course assignment; material to be exchanged among class members.

8th Session

Implications for today, and values of teaching about the Holocaust:

> Discussion of philosophic, religious, social and psychological implications of the Holocaust and other instances of genocide; participants will be asked to share their own feelings and involvements. Reevaluation: What is the value of teaching about the Holocaust?

6. OUTSIDE PREPARATION AND STUDY REQUIREMENTS:

> Teachers, probably working in teams, will be asked to select the achievement level and number of teaching sessions to be devoted to the subject, and to prepare a study-unit appropriate for inclusion in the social science, history, or literature curriculum. This preparation will require the review of books, films, and other material. One class session will center on examining and discussing these units. There will be required reading of at least one bibliography item on the history of the Holocaust, and other assigned readings and/or viewing of films and filmstrips.

2. Teaching About Genocide and the Nazi Holocaust

Chicago Board of Education

An in-service course for Chicago Board of Education teachers, developed by the Anti-Defamation League of B'nai B'rith and the Spertus College of Judaica. It is designed as a project-oriented workshop.

Course Coordinators—Dean Nathaniel Stampfer, Spertus College; Mr. Alan Katchen, Anti-Defamation League; and Mr. Leonard Rubin, Chicago Board of Education.

Course Objectives:

a. To analyze the problem of genocide in history—"the deliberate and systematic extermination of an ethnic or national group." Analogies to the Holocaust will be sought in the past and present genocidal experiences of other minority peoples, and the implications of this universal problem for contemporary man.

b. To provide specific and accurate information about the Holocaust that will enable the teacher to present the event effectively and accurately, thereby replacing ignorance and indifference with concern that such an event never happens again.

c. To analyze what the Holocaust reveals about man's nature, his behavior, and positive human values—sense of justice, compassion, human responsibility, perspective, moral stamina.

d. To demonstrate to the teacher the most effective ways to integrate a Holocaust study unit into the social studies curriculum.

e. To introduce teachers to the large and growing body of material and extraordinary resources available for the study of the Holocaust in the Chicago area.

f. To help the teacher select appropriate materials, strategies, and techniques that will make the Holocaust meaningful to students and will assist them in confronting value conflicts and decision-making today.

g. To assist participants to develop a Holocaust study unit of their own for classroom use.

1st Session

Dr. Elliot Lefkowitz, Spertus College, and staff.

Why Teach About the Holocaust?

Recent increase of interest and concern; need for its inclusion in history; value of knowledge of Holocaust in combatting ignorance, prejudice, crimes of genocide.

Distribution of material and bibliographies; discussion of outside preparation and assignments.

Background for a Holocaust:

> Understanding European and World History after the First World War; the roots of Hitlerism and the Nazi Movement; how and why the Nazi movement succeeded in Germany and throughout most of Europe; the role of Hitler: what should be known of his personality and techniques; the concept of the New Order and its ultimate aims of destroying the foundations of Western Civilization.

> The Nazi attack against minority rights; and the development of the Jewish minority's culture in Eastern Europe.

2nd Session

Dr. Elliot Lefkowitz and staff.

How the Holocaust took place; Human prejudice, anti-Semitism, and mechanics of the Final Solution.

> Holocaust as prime example of race prejudice; the mechanism of human extinction; the central role of human extinction in the Nazi plan; examples of specific countries, cities, population groups; the utilization of slave labor, human experimentation, torture, and ultimate extermination; resistance, world responses to the Holocaust; centers and memorials today.

A guided tour of the Spertus College Museum, featuring "Image Before My Eyes;" a photographic history of Jewish Life in Poland, 1864–1939; and especially its Zell Exhibit Hall on the Holocaust. Mr. Arthur Feldman, Director of the Museum, will conduct the tour.

3rd Session

Genocide:

A panel of outstanding educators will discuss historical counterparts of the Nazi genocide. The objective of this comparative analysis will be to understand the implications of this universal problem for contemporary man.

Professor Arthur Zilversmit, Department of History, Lake Forest College, Moderator; Dr. Elliot Lefkowitz, Spertus College; Mr. Louis Sigalos, Principal, Peabody Elementary; and Mr. Sam S. Ozaki, Principal, Taft High School.

Discussion of Assignments.

4th Session

Moral implications of the Holocaust for today, and value of teaching about it.

Dean Nathaniel Stampfer, Moderator
Professor Andre Lacoque
Rabbi Joel Eckstein
Father John Pawlikowski

A distinguished panel will discuss the philosophic, religious, social, and psychological implications of the Holocaust and other instances of genocide. Classroom participants will be asked to share their own feelings and involvements.

Discussion of Assignments.

5th Session

Mrs. Ann Nick, Mrs. Ursula Bennett, Mr. Alan Katchen, and Mr. Leonard Rubin
Methods, resources, and materials for teaching:

> Review of readings, films and filmstrips, music, maps, tapes, photographs. (Note: Some of these materials will be presented at appropriate times in other sessions.)

> With the films such as *Night and Fog*, *Genocide*, *Warsaw Ghetto*, and *Joseph Schultz* we will assign individual teachers the task of conducting a model discussion as they would in the classroom.

> Students will be taken on a guided tour of the Spertus Library, with its outstanding collection of Holocaust sources. Mr. Richard Marcus, Director of the Asher Library at Spertus, will conduct the tour.

6th Session

Mrs. Ann Nick, Mrs. Ursula Bennett, Mr. Alan Katchen and Mr. Leonard Rubin

Methods, resources, and materials for teaching:

Review of prepared courses and teaching plans to date. Different interpretations of the Holocaust—and implications for the curriculum and the classroom teacher.

Basic techniques of teaching the Holocaust: simulations, role-playing, use of eyewitnesses and survivors, coping with emotional response, etc.

How to integrate a Holocaust unit into the social studies curriculum—world and U.S. history.

Questions of appropriate length for study, reading assignments, activities for students.

Reports by participants on outside project assignment.

Careful examination and discussion of curriculum units prepared by class as main course assignment. Material to be exchanged among class members.

OUTSIDE PREPARATION AND STUDY REQUIREMENTS:

Teachers, probably working in teams, will be asked to select the achievement level and number of teaching sessions to be devoted to the subject, and to prepare a study unit appropriate for inclusion in the social studies curriculum. This preparation will require the review of books, films, and other material. One class session will center on examining and discussing these units. There will be required reading of at least one bibliography item on the history of the Holocaust, and other assigned readings and/or viewing of films and filmstrips.

The Text:

All members of the class will be required to read *Never to Forget: The Jews of the Holocaust,* by Milton Meltzer.

INSTRUCTIONAL MATERIALS AND RESOURCES:

HISTORY AND THE NAZI REGIME:

Dawidowicz, Lucy S. *The War Against the Jews, 1933–1945.* New York: Holt, Rinehart & Winston, 1975 (paperback, Bantam).

Flender, Harold. *Rescue in Denmark.* New York: Simon & Schuster, 1963.

Hilberg, Raul. *The Destruction of the European Jews.* New York: Quadrangle, 1961.

Meltzer, Milton. *Never to Forget: The Jews of the Holocaust.* New York: Harper & Row, 1976.

Morse, Arthur D. *While Six Million Died: A Chronicle of American Apathy.* New York: Random House, 1967.

Pilch, Judah. *The Jewish Catastrophe in Europe.* New York: American Association for Jewish Education, 1968.

Schoenberner, Gerhard. *The Yellow Star.* New York: Bantam, 1972.

Shabbetai, K. *As Sheep to the Slaughter?* New York: World Federation of Bergen-Belsen Survivors, 1963.

ANTHOLOGIES:

Friedlander, Albert. *Out of the Whirlwind.* New York: Union of American Hebrew Congregations, 1968.

Glatstein, Jacob; Knox, Israel; and Margolis, Samuel. *Anthology of Holocaust Literature.* New York: Atheneum, 1975.

Korman, Gerd. *Hunter and Hunted.* New York: Delta, 1973.

PERSONAL ACCOUNTS:

Flinker, Moshe. *Young Moshe's Diary.* Jerusalem: Yad Vashem, 1965.

Gray, Martin. *For Those I Loved.* Boston: Little, Brown and Co., 1972.

Meed, Vladka. *On Both Sides of the Wall.* Israel: Lohamei Haghettaot, 1973.

Senesh, Hannah. *Hannah Senesh: Her Life and Diary.* London: Vallentine-Mitchell, 1971.

Sereny, Gitta. *Into That Darkness: From Mercy Killing to Mass Murder.* New York: McGraw-Hill, 1974.

Wiesel, Elie. *Night.* New York: Avon, 1960 (orig. ed., France, 1958).

HISTORICAL NOVELS:

Kuznetsov, Anatoli. *Babi Yar.* New York: Simon & Schuster (Pocket Books), 1971.

Schwarz-Bart, André. *The Last of the Just.* New York: Atheneum, 1960.

THE SEARCH FOR MEANING:

Berkovits, Eliezer. *Faith After the Holocaust.* New York: Ktav, 1973.

Des Pres, Terrence. *The Survivor.* New York: Oxford University Press, 1976.

Frankl, Viktor. *Man's Search for Meaning.* Boston: Beacon Press, 1959.

Greenberg, Irving. *Confronting the Holocaust and Israel.* New York: UJA Study Conference, 1975.

Pawel, Ernst. *Writings of the Nazi Holocaust.* New York: Anti-Defamation League of B'nai B'rith.

Wiesel, Elie. *One Generation After.* New York: Random House, 1965.

PEDAGOGICAL MATERIALS:

Friedlander, Henry. *On the Holocaust: Critique of the Treatment of the Holocaust in History Textbooks.* New York: Anti-Defamation League of B'nai B'rith, 1972.

———. *Teaching and Commemorating the Holocaust.* New York: American Association for Jewish Education, 1974.

———. "Teaching the Holocaust to Children." In *The Second Jewish Catalogue.* Philadelphia: Jewish Publication Society of America, 1974.

Nick, Ann L. *Teachers' Guide to the Holocaust.* New York: Anti-Defamation League of B'nai B'rith, 1977.

Roskies, Diane K. *Teaching the Holocaust to Children.* New York: Ktav, 1975.

3. A "Brainstorming" Session

From Mel Cooperman, ADL Regional Director.

Subject: Oceanside In-Service Course

We asked the participants in the course to submit teaching ideas relevant to their own specialties.

Two of them are music teachers. One dealt with what its author called "the Nazi murder of art," the other took the theme of the music of the Jewish resistance. They are both meant for concurrent social studies units on the Nazi era.

A teacher of speech pathology talked about her experience in the course, as she could relate it to the process of "mainstreaming" the handicapped into regular school buildings and classes. The existence of antipathy toward handicapped youngsters by both students and parents, she observed, is a problem of prejudice. Therefore, she intends to use materials on Nazi treatment of the mentally ill and physically handicapped in the process of sensitization.

A first-grade teacher presented her idea of how children's art could be used. Her approach is as follows:

> It is everybody's wish to be liked by other people. Some people dislike other people for different reasons. One reason is that the other person has done something which was hurtful. Another is simply because the other person is very different. Here is a picture drawn by a child. What kind of place does this seem to be? Did these children do anything to be put in a place like this? What kind of people would put children in a place like this? What does this tell you about how we should treat people who are different from ourselves?

One science teacher presented an interdisciplinary approach to the concepts of genetics and race. Another discussed the moral dimensions of applied science as related to the Holocaust.

Teachers who attended the course for their own information, but who did not, at first, see any relation to their specialties, gained insight into new dimensions of teaching. If for no other reason than that, the course was a success.

While the major thrust of a conference/workshop may be for educators, occasionally there is opportunity or there is a need to open part of the program to the community.

One Example: Conference for Teachers on the Holocaust—New Bedford, Massachusetts: A two-pronged program aimed at teachers and the general community. ADL's Community Consultant wrote:

> On Thursday evening the Boston cast of *Shadows in the Night* (a play about the Holocaust) was presented to approximately 225 people, who paid $1 admission. The play was presented at the local high school and comments were very favorable. Many in the audience wept at the moving depiction of events in the Warsaw Ghetto as interpreted by the young proteges of Elie Wiesel.
>
> The next day we hosted a day-long teachers' conference for New Bedford teachers and teachers from three local suburban systems: Dartmouth, Fairhaven, New Bedford—plus the archdiocese of New Bedford. The superintendents released all of the teachers in English and Social Studies for the entire day. Well over 350 educators attended.
>
> Program topics included: The Holocaust in Theological Per-

spective—A Panel Discussion with Catholic, Protestant and Jewish Clergy and Workshops; The Holocaust in History; in Literature; and a Model Curriculum.

4. Getting Started

Philip Kaufman, Gill/St. Bernards, Bernardsville, N.J.

This "survey" is extensive—not really meant to be easily tabulated or to yield statistical or tangible data. It's much more a teaching tool and discussion starter. I use it on the first day of the course with the "kids"—to assess their ignorance, let them see what's coming up and whet their appetites. I've used it very successfully with groups of adults to run discussion-teaching sessions. The kids have used this (or ones like it) to survey—or really interview—neighbors, friends, others here at school, etc., once they've learned the answers for themselves. It's very rich and has worked well in a variety of ways.

Survey Questions:

1. (a) How many civilian Jews were killed by the Nazis? (b) What percentage of European Jews were killed by the Nazis?

2. (a) How many other civilians were killed by the Nazis? (b) Who were these other civilians whom the Nazis killed?

3. How many human beings died as a result of World War II?

4. How many Americans died as a result of World War II?

5. Was Hitler ever elected to office in Germany?

6. Was the Nazi party ever a strong force in free elections in Germany?

7. What was the position (legally, socially, economically) of a typical Jew in (a) Germany (b) Russia, before Hitler came to power?

8. Can you list some reasons why so many Germans accepted Hitler's rule so enthusiastically?

9. Why did England, France or other countries not stop Hitler's growing power in Europe before the outbreak of the war?

10. What do you think Hitler's major goal was? What motivated him, what was he most anxious to achieve?

11. What countries did most of Hitler's Jewish victims come from?

12. How were these Jews killed? Can you be specific: what intermediate steps were there between normal life and death before Hitler and the Nazis?

13. (a) Did the Jews know what was being done to them? (b) Did their countrymen make any effort to help them?

14. (a) Did they make any efforts to resist? (b) Did their fellow countrymen—non-Jews—know what was being done?

15. About how many Germans do you think were actively involved in deliberately killing innocent civilians? Were they all crazy or sick? Why did they do what they did?

16. Were all of these concentration camp guards and secret police agents guilty of crimes, in your opinion, or were they just soldiers doing their job in wartime?

17. What happened to Nazi officials and Jew-killers after the war?

18. Do you think alleged Nazi war criminals living in America today should be returned to the scene of the crimes to stand trial?

19. How would you feel if you found out that someone you know, who has always seemed perfectly nice and normal (a friend's parent or a store owner in your town, for example), was an active Nazi 35 years ago? Would your attitude toward him change?

20. Do you know of any things in Germany's history, culture, traditions, etc., that might explain why the Nazi system grew there? What kind of culture and traditions might provide fertile ground for a brutal, anti-human system like Nazism?

21. Do you think *Germany* as a culture and nation is to blame for Hitler and the incredible crimes committed under his rule? Or do you think the blame rests only with those who were specifically and actively involved with the crimes?

22. What is to be learned by studying what happened under the Nazis? Do you think there are lessons for all societies? . . . our society? . . . your own life and values?

23. Could Nazism, or something like it, ever happen in the United States? Has anything similar to it—even on a much smaller scale— ever happened here? Have you ever had personal experience with anything that seems similar to Nazism?

Section IX

Holocaust Survivor and Children-of-Survivor Groups

by Judith Muffs and David Szonyi

Until relatively recently, most survivors were silent witnesses. In some cases, even their children were told nothing of what they had experienced. In order that wounds could heal and new lives begin, memories and images of the Holocaust were pushed back.

Today, almost thirty-five years after the war, more and more survivors are beginning to speak out, to tell their stories, to share their hurts and their hopes. Increasingly, they want to be heard.

And children of survivors—both those who were told much about their parents' experiences and those who were told almost nothing—are beginning to speak out, to form groups, and to write of their experiences. In November 1979, they held an international conference sponsored by ZACHOR; a second, and far larger such gathering was held in May 1984, under the auspices of the International Network of Children of Jewish Holocaust Survivors. Both survivors and children of survivors participated in the World Gathering of Jewish Holocaust Survivors in Jerusalem (1981), and in a similar American Gathering (1983).

There are also thousands of other eyewitnesses of the Holocaust, particularly Allied soldiers who participated in liberating concentration camps, an experience none will forget. Oral histories of such liberators are being recorded at the Center for Holocaust Studies in Brooklyn and at Emory University in Atlanta. (See Section V for the addresses, phone numbers, and contact people at these centers.)

Immediately after the war, the Joint Distribution Committee and the United Nations Relief and Rehabilitation Association (UNRRA) sent hundreds of personnel to war-ravaged, refugee-filled Europe. Both organizations, which are located in New York, include among their records information about survivors interviewed.

To develop a roster of Holocaust survivors in your community, place notices in local papers and congregational bulletins. Some survivors may be willing to be speakers for educational or commemorative programs. Survivors and/or eyewitnesses also may wish to know one another, and a community project may offer them a means to do so. More and more children of survivors, in particular, feel the need to meet one another and openly to discuss their common backgrounds and concerns.

Using Survivors in the Classroom

Having survivors speak to students can be a moving and a valuable learning experience. However, both the survivor and the students should be well briefed, so that the survivor is utilized as a key witness, rather than as a substitute for a unit on the Holocaust. Thus, it probably is preferable that the survivor speak at the end of a unit, and that sufficient time be left for questions and answers.

The teacher should be sensitive to the fact that the survivor is not a professional lecturer, and that he or she probably speaks with an accent. What really matters, however, is the authenticity of the individual and his or her story.

The Atlanta Experience

Some forty metropolitan Atlanta high schools have taught substantive units on the Holocaust. Frequently, these units include, at the request of the teacher, a speaker on the Holocaust, "someone who actually experienced the tragedy."

Survivors generally are asked to go into the classroom to *culminate* the learning process. Before they come, the students have explored such questions as: How could such a tragedy have taken place in the twentieth century? Why the Jews? What is the historical background—both Jewish and German—to the Holocaust? What is anti-Semitism? What does the Holocaust reveal about man's nature? The students also view several films on the Holocaust.

The speaker who is most in demand was a prisoner in Buchenwald, as well as in Auschwitz-Birkenau, from the age of fourteen until he was liberated. Word of his special appeal travels from school to school. He is known in the Atlanta area as a soccer player, and has an enthusiastic spirit, as well as a look of vitality that belies his age. He agreed to be video-taped in his first classroom appearance, after which several individuals interested in Holocaust education critiqued his presentation and developed guidelines for others to use in the future.

Some student reactions to his presentation:

- "We realize how hard it was for you to discuss your experiences, and help teenagers understand. I admire your courage."

- "I now understand how prejudices affect the world . . ."

- "Before our study and your talk with us, the horrors of Germany had been just numbers."

- "I am glad someone like you will take the time to let the younger generation know about the evils of the past. I know such things can return and the people who experienced them might not be around to do something about it. It will be up to us."

1. Survivor Groups

The following, compiled by Samuel Mozes and David Sznoyi, is a list of names, addresses, and, where available, phone numbers and contact persons for Holocaust survivor groups in the United States and Canada. For certain cities where there is no formal group, we have listed a key contact person. Additional information on survivor groups should be sent to:

American Gathering of Jewish
Holocaust Survivors
122 West 30th Street
New York, N.Y. 10001

A. National and International Groups

American Federation of Jewish Fighters,
Camp Inmates and Nazi Victims
505 Fifth Avenue
New York, N.Y. 10017
212-697-5670
(Solomon Zynstein)

American Gathering of Jewish Holocaust Survivors
122 West 30th Street, Room 205
New York, N.Y. 10001
212-239-4230

Czech and Slovak Holocaust Survivors
61-11 Broadway
Woodside, N.Y. 11377
212-335-8953
(Martin Zapletal)

World Federation of Bergen-Belsen Associations
515 Park Avenue
New York, N.Y. 10022
212-PL2-3387
(Sam E. Bloch)

B. Local Groups in the United States

Arizona

Tucson Holocaust Survivors
8241 East Baker Place
Tucson, Ariz. 85710
602-885-5685
(William Spitzer)

California

American Congress of Jews from Poland and
    Survivors of Concentration Camps
6534 Moore Drive
Los Angeles, Calif. 90048
213-938-7881
(Benjamin Grey)

Council of Post-War Jewish Organizations, Survivors of the Holocaust
6205 Orange Street
Los Angeles, Calif. 90048
213-855-7071, 213-657-0063
(Irving Peters and Fred Diament)

Jewish Community Relations Council
870 Market Street
San Francisco, Calif. 94102
415-392-4500
(William Lowenberg or Naomi Lauter)

New Life Club
% Earl Schwarts
4803 Lorraine Drive
San Diego, Calif. 92115

Colorado

Club of New Americans
481 South Locust Street
Denver, Col. 80224
303-355-1179
(Bernard Sayone)

Florida

American Anti-Nazi Association of Greater Miami
MPO Box 011191
Miami, Fla. 33101
(Seymour Kaplowitz)

David Ben-Gurion Culture Club for the State of Florida
501 Three Islands Blvd. #501
Hollandale, Fla. 33009
305-458-2585
(Carl Rosenhoff)

David Schaechter
DNS Industries, Ltd.
5179 N.W. 151st Street
Miami Lakes, Fla. 33014

Holocaust Survivors Social Club of South Florida
66-98 Moonlit Drive
Del Ray Beach, Fla. 33446
305-499-0551
(Sam Desperak)

Ludwik Brodzki
2740 Northeast 33rd Street
Fort Lauderdale, Fla. 33306
305-776-0371

Georgia

Eternal Life–Hemshech Organization of Survivors from Nazism
3120 Boxwood Drive
Atlanta, Ga. 30345
404-355-5222
(Alexander Gross or Cantor Isaac Goodfriend)

Illinois

Holocaust Memorial Foundation of Illinois
P.O. Box 577
Northbrook, Ill. 60062

Sol Goldstein
7227 N. Hailan Avenue
Skokie, Ill. 60076
312-679-3400

B'nai B'rith Janusz
    Korczak Lodge
2812 Woodland Drive
Northbrook, Ill. 60603
312-564-1319 (h); 312-569-2634 (o)

Maryland

Chavra Ahava Chesed
3820 Coronado Road
Baltimore, Md. 21207
301-655-3515
(Gunther Stern)

Massachusetts

New Americans Association of Greater Boston
% Mrs. Celia Moneta
8 Elmswood Park
Quincy, Mass. 02170
617-471-4514
(Celia Moneta or Jacob Birnbaum)

Michigan

Shaarith Haplaytah
171-92 Shervilla Street
Southfield, Mich. 48075
313-559-3649
(Rabbi Charles Rosenzveig)

Missouri

New Americans Club
603 West 86th Terrace
Kansas City, Mo. 64114
816-363-6259
(Jack Igielnik)

Nebraska

Society of Survivors
% Jewish Community Center
333 South 132nd Street
Omaha, Neb. 68154
402-333-1303, 402-342-6655
(Sam Fried or Bella Eisenberg)

New Jersey

Lithuanian Jewish Survivors
62 Irwin Street
Springfield, N.J. 07081
201-379-2016 (h); 212-921-3878 (o)
(Dr. Nahum Gershwin)

Samuel Halpern
100 Woodbine Avenue
Woodbridge Township, N.J. 07001
201-351-0410 (h); 201-381-0410 (o)

Survivors of Theresienstadt
17 Rose Tree Terrace
Richfield, N.J. 07657
201-945-1675, 201-945-8015
(Paul Safirstein)

New York

New York City:

Cracow Society
65 West 36th Street
New York, New York 10018
212-279-4848
(Michael Kluger)

Federation of Former Jewish Underground Fighters
12 East 31st Street
New York, N.Y. 10016
212-684-7480
(Samuel Gruber)

Holocaust Survivors of Auschwitz
33 West 17th Street
New York, N.Y. 10011
212-675-4236
(Ernest Honig)

Jewish Nazi Victims of America
373 Fifth Avenue, 4th Floor
New York, N.Y. 10016
212-683-7245
(Rabbi Chaskel Besser)

Lodzer Society
64-21 Douglaston Parkway
Douglaston, N.Y. 11362
212-631-1999
(Max Temkin)

Piotrkow-Trybuwalski Relief Association and
    Nazi Victims in New York
% Ben Giladi
135-30 82nd Avenue
Kew Gardens, N.Y. 11435
212-263-8158

Survivors of the Riga Ghetto
P.O. Box 91
New York, N.Y. 10033
212-543-2655
(Lore Oppenheimer)

United Radomer Relief for the United States and Canada
45-20 217th Street
Bayside, N.Y. 11361
212-279-4848
(Alfred Lipson)

United Restitution Organization
570 Seventh Avenue
New York, N.Y. 10018
212-921-3864
(Simon Gutter)

Warsaw Ghetto Resistance Organization
871 Seventh Avenue
New York, N.Y. 10019
212-LO4-1065
(Benjamin Meed)

World Federation of Hungarian Jews
136 East 39th Street
New York, N.Y. 10016
212-725-1211
(Dr. Ervin Farkas)

Outside New York City:

Mordecai Anielewicz Organization
32 Zornow Drive
Rochester, N.Y. 14623
716-334-1267
(Simon Buckstein)

Ohio

Jewish Survivors from Nazism
1580 Summit Road
Cincinnati, Ohio 45237
513-761-5950
(Samuel Kaltman)

Kol Israel Foundation
14462 East Carroll Boulevard
Cleveland, Ohio 44118
216-382-7597
(Leon Bergrin)

Pennsylvania

Association of New Americans
11809 Audubon Avenue
Philadelphia, Pa. 19116
215-934-7296
(Irving Teitelbaum or Abe Shnaper)

Rhode Island

Holocaust Memorial Committee of Rhode Island
150 Benefit Street
Providence, R.I. 02903
401-831-1837
(Raymond Eichenbaum)

Tennessee

Memphis Holocaust Memorial Committee
5649 Rich Road
Memphis, Tenn. 38119
901-682-0103
(Leonid Saharovici)

Texas

Holocaust Survivors in Dallas
6408 Brookshire
Dallas, Tex. 75230
214-363-8516
(Michael Jacobs)

Survivors of the Holocaust
6 Gessner Road
Houston, Tex. 77024
(Siegmund and Ruth Izackson)

Washington, D.C. Area

Club Shalom
2077 Westview Drive
Silver Spring, Md. 20910
301-589-7252
(Abe Malnik)

Washington Holocaust Information Network
1416 Q Street
Washington, D.C. 20009
202-659-9640 (MM) or
301-681-7211 (JF)
(Joel Fried or Marc Masurovsky)

Wisconsin

New American Club
4153 North 91st Street
Milwaukee, Wis. 53222
414-464-3738 (h); 414-332-2389 (o)
(Israel Walnerman)

C. Canada

British Columbia

Canadian Jewish Congress
950 West 41st Street
Vancouver, B.C. VSZ 2N7
604-261-8101
(Morris Saltzman)

Dr. Robert Krell
2255 Westbrook Mall
University Campus
Vancouver, B.C. VGT 2A1
604-228-7299

Quebec

Bergen-Belsen Survivors Association
2117 Scott Street
St. Laurent, P.Q.

National Holocaust Remembrance Committee,
    Canadian Jewish Congress
1590 Avenue Drive
Montreal, P.Q. H36 IC5
514-737-7707
(Aba Beer)

Ontario

Bergen-Belsen Survivors Association
352 Brooke Avenue
Toronto, Ont. MSM 2L3
(David Goldsilver)

Holocaust Remembrance Committee, Canadian Jewish Congress
150 Beverly Street
Toronto, Ont. M5T 1Y6
416-977-3811
(Ruth Resnick)

2. Children-of-Survivor Groups in the U.S.

The following is a list of children of Holocaust survivor groups—or key
resource people associated with them—by state. The names in parentheses are contact people. Groups preceded by an asterisk are affiliated
with the main umbrella organization for the "second generation":

> International Network of Children of
>   Jewish Holocaust Survivors, Inc.
> 261 Madison Ave., Suite 1104
> New York, N.Y. 10016
> (Menachem Z. Rosensaft, Chairman)

ZACHOR would welcome information for an update of this list.

California

*Generation to Generation
Jewish Community Relations Council
870 Market Street, Suite 920
San Francisco, Calif. 94123
(Darlene Bosch)

Second Generation
6505 Wilshire Boulevard
Los Angeles, Calif. 90036
(Nina Klein or Miriam Scharf)

*Sons and Daughters of the 1939 Club
6425 Del Valle Drive
Los Angeles, Calif. 90048
(Julie Kohner)

Colorado

*Second Generation
315 Forest Street
Denver, Col. 80222
(Lorraine Miklin)

Florida

*Children of Survivors
1910 N.E. 210th Street
North Miami, Fla. 33179
(Rositta Kenigsberg)

Georgia

*Children of the Holocaust
185 Zeblin Road, N.E.
Atlanta, Ga. 30342
(Saba Silverman)

Illinois

*Association of Children of Holocaust Survivors
P.O. Box 25663
Chicago, Ill. 60625
(Esther Fink)

Indiana

*Second Generation of South Bend
104 North Conestoga Lane
South Bend, Ind. 46617
(Romana Strochlitz Primus)

Kansas

*Chevrah of the Second Generation
9605 W. 98th Street
Overland Park, Kans. 66212 (Kansas City area)
(Rosemary Nochlin or Robin Moss)

Maryland

Second Generation—Children of Holocaust Survivors, Inc.
P.O. Box 20913
Baltimore, Md. 21209
(Sara Kaplan)

Massachusetts

*One Generation After
17 Commonwealth Avenue
Boston, Mass. 02116
(Ruth Bork)

Michigan

*Children of Holocaust Survivors in Michigan: CHAIM
23130 Webster
Oak Park, Mich. 48237
(Bernard Kent or Charles Silow)

Missouri

*St. Louis Second Generation
1324 Henriette Hills Drive
Creve Coeur, Mo. 63141
(Jim Bright)

New Jersey

*Second Generation of Central New Jersey
509 Laurie Lane
Aberdeen, N.J. 07747
(Mark Mandelbaum)

*Second Generation of New Jersey
1508 Timber Oaks Road
Edison, N.J. 08820
(Steven Weinberg)

*Second Generation of North Jersey
P.O. Box 1058
Teaneck, N.J. 07666
(Jeanette Friedman-Sieradski or Stephen Tencer)

New York
  New York City

Children of Survivors Group
Hillel CCNY
475 W. 140th Street
New York, N.Y. 10031
(Carmella Frisch)

Children of Survivors Group
Kings Bay YM-YWHA
3495 Nostrand Avenue
Brooklyn, N.Y. 11229
(Nancy M. Sargon)

The Generation After
2747 Throop Avenue
Bronx, N.Y. 10469
(Sheldon Ranz)

*Group Project for Holocaust Survivors and Their Families
60 Riverside Drive
New York, N.Y. 10023
(Eva Fogelman)

Piotrkov Association Second Generation
% Alex Rosenblum
1292 East 49th Street
Brooklyn, N.Y. 11234

*Second Generation: Children of Holocaust Survivors
350 Fifth Avenue, Suite 3508
New York, N.Y. 10118
(Shirley Eisner or Rebecca Knaster)

  New York State

*Generation to Generation
26 Warren Drive
Syosset, N.Y. 11803
(Flo Feinberg)

*Second Generation of Long Island
1322 Beech Street
Atlantic City, N.Y. 11509
(Sarah Ducorsky)

Second Generation of Syracuse
1220 Wescott Street
Syracuse, N.Y. 13210
(Evelyn Loeb or Barbara Eisenbud)

*Second Generation of Westchester
2 Easton Avenue
White Plains, N.Y. 10605
(Rena Berkowicz Borow)

*Utica Chapter of Children of Jewish Holocaust Survivors
22 Emerson Avenue
Utica, N.Y. 13501
(Judy Oster)

Ohio

*Children of Holocaust Survivors
2615 Clifton Avenue
Cincinnati, Ohio 45220
(Rabbi Abie Ingber)

*Second Generation Kol Israel
P.O. Box 24376
Lyndhurst, Ohio 44124
(Judy Deutchman or Helene Frum)

Pennsylvania

*Second Generation of Pittsburgh: The Legacy
6573 Rosemore Street
Pittsburgh, Pa. 15217
(Dr. Edie Naveh)

*Sons and Daughters of Holocaust Survivors
P.O. Box 1014
Bala Cynwyd, Pa. 19004
(Sylvia Perel)

Texas

*Second Generation of Holocaust Survivors of Dallas
c/o Jewish Community Center
7900 Northaven Road
Dallas, Tex. 75230
(Michael Schiff)

*Second Generation of Houston
9523 Wickenburg Drive
Houston, Tex. 77031
(Hedy Ganz)

Washington, D.C.

*The Generation After
P.O. Box 7478
Silver Spring, Md. 20907
(Leslie Ackman)

Wisconsin

*The Generation After
10415 North Sunflower Court
Meguon, Wis. 53902
(Sandy Hoffman)

Section X

Yom HaShoah and Day of Remembrance Services

The area of Holocaust liturgy is a very new one, and only a handful of appropriately sensitive and creative Jewish, Christian, and ecumenical services are available.

Reprinted below are two services prepared for the U.S. Holocaust Memorial Council, both entitled "A Holocaust Commemoration," one for a predominantly Jewish group, and the other for a predominantly Christian group. Both are reprinted with the permission of the Council, 425 13th Street, N.W., Washington, D.C. 20004.

Three other recommended services are:

1. *Night Words: A Midrash on the Holocaust*, by David Roskies (B'nai B'rith Hillel Foundations, 1640 Rhode Island Avenue, N.W., Washington, D.C. 20036, $1.00). *Night Words* is a remarkable participatory reading with thirty-six characters, using a variety of biblical and talmudic materials, a medieval chronicle, and literature from and about the Holocaust.
2. *A Christian Service in Memory of the Holocaust* (available from the Holocaust Remembrance Committee, Canadian Jewish Congress, 150 Beverly Street, Toronto, Ont. M5T 1Y6). This is a sensitive, thoughtful service with readings ranging from excerpts from the Gospel of Matthew to Philip Hallie's *Lest Innocent Blood Be Shed*.
3. *The Miracle of Denmark* (available from the National Conference of Christians and Jews, 43 West 57th Street, New York, N.Y. 10019). First performed in a Copenhagen synagogue in 1973, this service reenacts the Danish people's heroic 1943 rescue of almost all of the country's Jews, and includes a narrative recounting the rescue, a reading showing how Denmark was different, and "The New Hallel."

A Holocaust Commemoration for Days of Remembrance

For Communities, Synagogues, Centers and for Home Use

Edited by Irving Greenberg and David Roskies

1. Ideally, a commemoration should reach out with love and bring Jews of every background and religious or secular view together. A community gathering would be preferable to separate groups. In the Holocaust, there was no difference between religious and secular Jews, or between assimilated and committed Jews. The unity of Jewish destiny should be no less manifest or, at least, assumed in our remembrances. (Of course, we respect the right of every group or congregation to have their own service should that be their choice.)

2. Any liturgy of the Holocaust should avoid total affirmation or resolution. This tragedy is too devastating to be overcome lightly or swiftly. It poses radical questions to all of humanity and to all views. Neither should the mood be one of total defeat and despair. That would not do justice to those who remained faithful and human even in the moments of greatest agony or to the incredible model of renewal of life and of faith which survivors exemplified after the war.

3. This service recommends use of a film. This may appear to be unusual, especially in a synagogue liturgy setting. However, we believe that a ritual emerging after the Holocaust can speak out of the "secular" with a revelatory power that touches the deepest levels of reverence. And if the classic Jewish model of remembrance is reenactment, then documentary films, pictures and survivors' testimony is appropriate and moving. For this reason, also, an address or brief testimony by a survivor is recommended as part of this liturgy.

4. As we feel the inadequacy of words and fear the inability of conscious artistic response to express the inexpressible, we think that prayers preferably should be taken from the actual writings and testimony of those who went through the Holocaust who tried to tell us what and how to remember.

5. We conclude the service with the hallowed mourners' prayer—the Kaddish. (Service I offers a version written in light of the Holocaust by Aharon Zeitlin, a Yiddish poet.) There is a tradition that when a person dies without leaving immediate family, then the nearest living relative says the Kaddish. For millions in the Holocaust, the entire family with all its branches was wiped out. Therefore we—the living Jews—are the nearest living relatives. We believe it appropriate for the entire congregation to join in saying this Kaddish. For those who have religious or other reservations, however, we suggest that the entire

group stand together. Those who feel they should not say the Kaddish should stand silently and thus participate and speak in silence which, after all, may be the only authentic liturgical response to the Holocaust.

—David G. Roskies
Irving Greenberg
Editors

Commemoration Service

1. *Lighting of the Six Memorial Candles*

2. *Testimony: On Children and Parents*

We form a line, and under guard we go down to the ravine, to the huge open grave, in formations of fives. The fire is burning, the smoke stings our eyes and the smell chokes us. The fire crackles and sizzles. Some of the bodies in the fire have their hands extended. It looks as if they are pleading to be taken out. Many bodies are lying around with open mouths. Could they be trying to say "We are your own mothers, fathers, who raised you and took care of you. Now you are burning us." If they could have spoken, maybe they would have said this, but they are forbidden to talk too—they are guarded. Maybe they would forgive us. They know that we are being forced to do this by the same murderers that killed them. We are under their whips and machine guns. They would forgive us, they are our fathers and mothers, who if they knew it would help their children. But what should we do?[1]

Reader:

זיי זען׳ געווען די ערשטע אומצוקומען, די יידישע די קינדער, אלע זיי, דאָס רוב
אָן טאַטע־מאַמע. קינדער אויפגעגעסענע פון קעלט, פון הונגער און פון לייז.
משיחים הייליקע, געהייליקטע אין ליידן... אָ, זאָגט, פאַרוואָס די שטראָף?
פאַרוואָס אין אומקום־טעג די ערשטע צאָלן אים, דעם בייז, דעם עכסטן פרייז?

They, the children of Israel, were the first in doom and disaster;
most of them without father and mother, were consumed by frost,
starvation and lice, holy messiahs sanctified in pain.
Say then, how have these lambs sinned?
Why in days of doom are they the first victims of wickedness,
the first in the trap of evil are they! . . .

Congregation:

די ערשטע אומצוברענגען זען׳ געוועזן קינדער, יתומימלעך פאַרלאָזענע, עס הייסט
דאָס בעסטע אויף דער וועלט, דאָס שענסטע וואָס די ערד, די פינצטערע, פאַרמאָגט!
אָ, פון די עלנטסטע יתומימלעך און קינדערהיימען וואָלט געוואָקסן אונדז אַ טרייסט,
פון די אומעטיקסטע, שטומע פנימלעך, די חושכדיקע,
וואָלט געטאָגט אונדז, וואָלט געטאָגט!

The first one to be destroyed were the children, little orphans,
abandoned upon the face of the earth;
they who were the best in the world, the acme of grace on the dark
   earth!
Oh, tender orphans!
From them, the bereaved of the world
in a house of shelter we drew consolation;
from the mournful faces, mute and dark,
we said the light of day will yet break upon us! . . .

זיי זען' געווען די ערשטע, די גענומענע צום טויט, די ערשטע אויף דער פור,
מען האָט געוואָרפן אין די וועגענער די גרויסע זיי, ווי הויפנס מיסט, ווי מיסט –
און אוועקגעפירט זיי, אויסגעהרגעט זיי, פֿאַרניכט זיי, ס'איז קיין שפור
פון זיי, פון מיינע בעסטע, ניט געבליבן מער !
אָך ווי איז מיר און ווינד איז מיר און וויסט !

The first were they detained for death,
the first into the wagons of slaughter;
they were thrown into the wagons, the huge wagons,
like heaps of refuse, like the ashes of the earth—
and they transported them, killed them, exterminated them
without remnant or remembrance . . .
The best of my children were all wiped out!
Oh woe unto me—Doom and Desolation![2]

Reader:

Today the ghetto knows a different fear.
Close in its grip. Death wields an icy scythe
An evil sickness spreads a terror in its wake.
The victims of its shadow weep and writhe

Today a father's heartbeat tells his fright
And mothers bend their heads into their hands
Now children choke and die with typhus here.
A bitter tax is taken from their bands.

My heart still beats inside my breast while friends depart for other
   worlds.

Perhaps it's better—who can say?—Than watching this, to die today?

Congregation:

No, no, my God, we want to live! Not watch our numbers melt away.
We want to have a better world, we want to work—we must not die![3]

Reader:

וויין ניט... איך האָב געזען אַ מיידעלע פון אַ יאָר פינף אין יענעם „פּ ו נ ק ט "‚

זי האָט אַ וויינענדיקן ברודערל‚ אַ קלענערן אַ סך פון איר‚ אַ ליידנדן געגערט...

זי האָט פאַרדאַרטע שטיקלעך ברויט אין אַ מאַרמעלאַד אַ שיטערן געטונקט

און קונציק אים אין מיילעכל אַרײַנגעשמוגלט... מיר איז געוזען באַשערט

צו זען עס‚ זען דער מאַמען‚ זען דער מאַמען דער פינפיעריקער

ווי זי שפּײַזט אים‚ אירע רייד

צו אים געהערט‚ מיין מאַמע‚ איינע אין דער וועלט‚ איז ניט דערפינדעריש אַזוי געוזען!

זי האָט אַ טרער אים אָפּגעוזישט מיט אַ געלעכטער‚ אַרײַנגערעדט אין אים אַ פרייד‚

ס'יידיש מיידעלע! שלום־עליכם האָט עס בעסער ניט געקענט‚ איך האָ'ב'ס געזען!

Do not cry . . .
At this station another girl I saw, about five years old;
She fed her younger brother and he cried, the little one, he was sick;
into a diluted bit of jam she dipped tiny crusts of bread,
and skillfully she inserted them into his mouth . . .
This my eyes were privileged to see!
To see this mother, a mother of five years feeding her child,
to hear her soothing words—
My own mother, the best in the world, had not invented such a ruse.
But this one wiped his tears with a smile,
injected joy into his heart—A little girl in Israel![4]

Congregation:

ד ע ר ס ו ד : מ ע נ ט ש

זאָג מיר נישט, אַז מענטש איז חיה.
קעגן מענטש איז חיה — מלאך.
בויט אַ חיה קרעמאַטאָריעס?
שלײַדערט זי אין פייער קינדער?
איז זי זיך מיט מאָרד מחיה?
זאָג מיר נישט, אַז מענטש איז חיה.

Do not tell me man is a beast. Compared to man, beast is—angel.
Do beasts build crematoria? Do they hurl children to fire?
Do they take pleasure in death? Do not tell me man is a beast.[5]

3. *Reflection: Meditation or Reading*

To sink is the easiest of matters; it is enough to carry out all the orders
one receives, to eat only the ration, to observe the discipline of the work
and the camp. Experience showed that only exceptionally could one
survive more than three months in this way. All the mussulmans who

finished in the gas chambers have the same story, or more exactly, have no story, they followed the slope down to the bottom, like streams that run down to the sea. On their entry into the camp, through basic incapacity, or by misfortune, or through some banal incident, they are overcome before they can adapt themselves, they are beaten by time, they do not begin to learn German, to disentangle the infernal knot of laws and prohibitions until their body is already in decay, and nothing can save them from selections or from death by exhaustion. Their life is short, but their number is endless, they the Musselmanner, the drowned, form the backbone of the camp, an anonymous mass, continually renewed and always identical . . .

They crowd my memory with their faceless presences, and if I could enclose all the evil of our time in one image, I would choose this image which is familiar to me an emaciated man, with head dropped and shoulders curved, on whose face and in whose eyes not a trace of a thought is to be seen.[6]

At the risk of offending, it must be emphasized that the victims suffered more, and more profoundly, from the indifference of the onlookers than from the brutality of the executioner. The cruelty of the enemy would have been incapable of breaking the prisoner; it was the silence of those he believed to be his friends—cruelty more cowardly, more subtle—which broke his heart.

There was no longer anyone on whom to count: even in the camps this became evident. "From now on we shall live in the wilderness, in the void blotted out of history." It was this conviction which poisoned the desire to live. If this is the world we were born into, why cling to it? If this is the human society we come from—and are now abandoned by—why seek to return?

At Auschwitz not only man died, but also the idea of man. To live in a world where there is nothing any more, where the executioner acts as god, as judge—many wanted no part of it. It was its own heart the world incinerated at Auschwitz.[7]

4. *Alternate: Film: "A Time to Remember" or "Night and Fog"*[8]

Alternate: Address by survivor or appropriate person about the Holocaust

The following song from the ghetto may be sung.

5. Response:

Reader:

Fire, brothers, fire!! The time may come,
God forbid, when the town with you together
Will go up in ashes and flame. Nothing will remain at all—
Just a blackened wall. And yet you look and stand
With folded hand—and look and stand
While our town burns

Congregation:

Fire, brothers, fire!! It all turns to you
If you love the town, take pails, put out the fire.
Quench it with your own blood too
Show what you can do, brothers—
Do not look and stand—with folded hand
Brothers, do not look and stand, when the town burns.[9]

"Though He slay me, yet I will hope."

All: Song of the Partisans/Sung in Yiddish

זאָג ניט קיינמאָל אַז דו גייסט דעם לעצטן וועג,
ווען הימלען בלייענע פאַרשטעלן בלויע טעג;
ווייל קומען וועט נאָך אונדזער אויסגעבענקטע שעה,
ס׳וועט אַ פויק טאָן אונדזער טראָט —
מיר זיינען דאָ!
פון גרינעם פּאַלמען־לאַנד ביזן לאַנד פון ווייסן שניי,
מיר קומען אָן מיט אונדזער פּיין, מיט אונדזער וויי,
און וווּ געפאַלן ס׳איז אַ שפּריץ פון אונדזער בלוט,
וועט אַ שפּראָץ טאָן אונדזער גבורה אונדזער מוט.

Do not say you walk your final road
Because leaden days hide blue skies
The time we long for will come near
Our cadence will sound out. We are here

From tropical lands to distant snow-covered plain
We come with our suffering and our pain
And where our blood spurted and fell
There our strength and power will grow and swell.[10]

(Sing)

אֲנִי מַאֲמִין בֶּאֱמוּנָה שְׁלֵמָה בְּבִיאַת הַמָּשִׁיחַ וְאַף עַל
פִּי שֶׁיִּתְמַהְמֵהַּ עִם כָּל־זֶה אֲחַכֶּה־לּוֹ בְּכָל־יוֹם שֶׁיָּבֹא:

Ani maamin, be'emunah shelaymah
B'viyat ha mashiach, b'viyat ha mashiach
Ani maamin
v'af al pi she-yiat ma-mayah
im kol zeh, ani maamin.

Still I believe, totally,
in the coming of the Messiah
I remain steadfast
Even though he is late
despite everything, I hope and trust.[11]

(Congregation rises)

Reader:

גערוויסט און געהייליקט זאל ווערן זיין נאמען
אויף דער וועלט, וואס ער האט לויט זיין רצון געשאפן,
און איינפירן זאל ער זיין מלכות דא אונטן
ביי אייער לעבן, אין אייערע טעג.
אין א נאענטער צייט
זאל ער זיין אויסלייזונג שיקן, א תיקון
צו געבן דעם לעבן דא אויף דער ערד,
און גאנץ זאלן ווערן זיין טראָן און זיין נאמען.
זאגט אָמן.

May His name be glorified and sanctified
In this world which He created as He willed.
May He establish His rule here below
By your lives, in your days
Soon.
May He send his liberation. His healing
To give life here on earth
And may His rule and His name be restored again
and say, Amen.

Congregation:

דער, וואָס שאַפט פרידן אין זיינע הייכן,
וועט ברענגען שלום דא, אין דער אונטנקייט,
און זאלן די אותיות פון זיין נאמען
האלטן אונדז, אונטערשטע, אין פארבונדנקייט
מיט ד ע ם ישראל, וואָס לעבט אויף יענער־זייט,
שפראצט ווי א בוים איבער אייביקע שטראָמען.
און ענטפערט: אמן.

He who makes peace in His heights
Will bring peace here below.
And may His qualities
Keep us, those below, in close bond
With that Israel which lives on the other side,
Which flourishes as a tree near eternal streams
And answer: Amen.[12]

6. *Chanting of El Moleh Rachamim*

Congregation Recites Kaddish

Notes

This commemoration service was prepared by the Holocaust Liturgy
Task Force of ZACHOR, a project of the National Jewish Resource
Center.

A more structured program, lasting about 1½ hours and requiring a
minimal amount of preparation, is *Night Words: A Midrash on the
Holocaust*, available from the B'nai Hillel Foundation, 1640 Rhode
Island Avenue, N.W., Washington, D.C. 20036. This is essentially a
group reading for at least thirty-six participants that combines literary,
documentary, and musical sources in an attempt to recast the standard
Jewish liturgy in the light of the Holocaust. *Night Words* is ideally
suited for havurot and adult study groups, but may also be "presented"
for the community at large. Copies should be distributed to all who
attend, and at least one day of preparation for the participants is
needed. *Night Words* is also a useful anthology from which to excerpt
responsive readings for synagogue use.

Further suggestions or information may be obtained from the:

> United States Holocaust Memorial Council
> 425 13th Street, N.W. Suite 832
> Washington, D.C. 20004

Traditional synagogues may hold regular daily services in conjunction with this program. It is suggested that the liturgy be done after the
regular service.

1. From Leon Wells, *The Janowska Road* (New York: Holocaust
   Library, 1980).
2. From Yitzhak Katzenelson, *The Song of the Slaughtered Jewish
   People*, sec. 6, "The First" (Israel: Beit Lohamei Hagettaot, 1979),
   pp. 40–42.

3. Hana Volakova, *I Never Saw Another Butterfly: Poems by the Children of Theresienstadt* (New York: McGraw Hill, 1964).
4. From Katzenelson, *Song*, p. 41.
5. Aharon Zeitlin, from *Lider fun Churbn un Lider fun Gloybn* (New York: Bergen-Belsen Association, 1967), I, p. 140.
6. From Primo Levi, *Survival in Auschwitz* (New York: Collier Books, 1961).
7. From Elie Wiesel, "A Plea for the Dead," in *Legends of Our Time* (New York: Holt, Rinehart & Winston, 1968).
8. The Film *A Time To Remember* uses documentary films and photographs to portray the Holocaust. It was produced by the Holocaust Educational Project for Zachor, the Holocaust Resource Center of the National Jewish Resource Center, 250 West 57th Street, New York, N.Y. 10107. It is available for purchase and can be used for adult education and classrooms. The film is powerful and particularly moving because its narration is excerpted from interviews with survivors. The scenes on the screen are, as it were, described by people who lived through them.
   Night and Fog uses documentary films and photographs to portray the Holocaust. It is a very powerful film. Some Jews object to using it on the grounds of its false universalization of the Holocaust. Nowhere does its narration say that the victims of the Holocaust were in fact Jews.
9. Mordecai Gebirtig, Es Brent "Fire!"
10. Partisans Hymn by Hirsh Glik (Vilna Ghetto).
11. Maimonides, *Thirteen Principles of Jewish Faith*, from Daily Prayer Book.
12. Aharon Zeitlin, "Kaddish," from Zeitlin, *Lider*, pp. 328–329.

A Holocaust Commemoration for Days of Remembrance

For Communities, Churches, Centers and for Home Use

Prepared by Dr. Harry James Cargas

Narrator

We come together for this memorial service to remember. Re-member means to bring certain events of the past together again, to make them whole in order that they may not be forgotten. We must make efforts not to let the great tragedy of the Holocaust slip from the mind of the world or to slip from our minds individually. For if the Holocaust is forgotten, the way will be paved for another, perhaps a final destruction of all humanity. The massacre of six million Jews must not be a prelude to a future disaster. Our attitude toward the Holocaust may well determine that of our children and of our children's children. What we do today (this evening), now, is of extreme importance.

We pay homage to the dead in what must be seen as momentous Christian tragedy. If Dr. Martin Luther King, Jr., was right when he insisted that racism is really a white people's problem, then we are correct in witnessing to the Holocaust as a Christian problem. It was in traditionally Christian nations that the murders took place. Many Christians died at the death camps of Auschwitz, Dora, Bergen-Belsen, and the rest, and we gather today (this evening) to re-member these non-Jewish dead as well. Yet many non-Jews were able to save themselves by espousing the Nazi cause. No Jew was allowed to do so. While Poles and Germans and French and others were victims of Hitler's policies, only the Jews were victims of victims, that is, only Jews were singled out for killing by Poles and Germans and French and others.

Think of it! How many people does it take to kill six million Jews and perhaps an equal number of non-Jews as well. Who even thought of the plan of trying to rid the world of every Jewish woman, man, and child? Who thought of ovens for human beings while living in nations committed to Jesus Christ, called the Prince of Peace? Who designed the ovens and the gas chambers? Who engineered them, bribed high government officials to gain the murderous contracts? Who operated the demonic facilities, repaired them when they broke down, studied their operations to make them more efficient? When Nazi troops conquered countries, and did not know which people were Jews and which were not, who pointed out the Jews to the invaders?

The question remains: How many people does it take to cooperate in such a large-scale slaughter?

And who among us can be certain that if we were in the wrong place at the wrong time, we too might cooperate with the forces of evil? Are we, in some way, doing exactly that by our subtle racism, our lack of interest in war torn nations around the world, our deliberate ignorance of genocide through starvation that some people are experiencing as we sit here, this very moment?

Let us beg the Lord God for forgiveness and make a firm purpose of amendment.

30 second meditation

1st Reader (a woman)

Written in Pencil in the Sealed Railway-Car
>   here in this carload
>   i am eve
>   with abel my son
>   if you see my other son
>   cain son of man
>   tell him i

—Dan Pagis

(translated from the Hebrew by Stephen Mitchell)

Narrator

The mother speaking in this poem did not have time to complete her thought. Death was too eager to take her. She went to her end like so many mothers and children without having a chance at life.

2nd Reader (a child)

These words were written by a young Jewish girl, imprisoned in a ghetto:

>   *The Garden*
>
>   A little garden.
>   Fragrant and full of roses.
>   The path is narrow
>   And a little boy walks along it.
>
>   A little boy, a sweet boy.
>   Like that growing blossom.
>   When the blossom comes to bloom,
>   The little boy will be no more.

—Franta Bass

Narrator

Over one million Jewish children under the age of twelve lost their lives in the Holocaust.

3rd Reader (a man)

And so a long line is formed in the front of the orphanage on Sliska Street. A long procession, children, small, tiny, rather precocious, emaciated, weak, shriveled and shrunk. They carry shabby packages, some have school-books, note-books under their arms. No one is crying.

Slowly they go down the steps, line up in rows, in perfect order and discipline, as usual. Their little eyes are turned towards the doctor.

They are strangely calm, they feel almost well. The doctor is going with them, so what do they have to be afraid of? They are not alone, they are not abandoned.

Dr. Janusz Korczak busies himself with the children with a sober earnestness. He buttons the coat of one child, ties up a package of another, or straightens the cap of a third. Then he wipes off a tear which is rolling down the thin little face of a child . . .

Then the procession starts out. It is starting out for a trip from which—everybody feels it—one never comes back. All these young, budding lives. . . . And all this is marching quietly and orderly to the place of their untimely doom.

The children are calm, but inwardly they must feel it, they must sense it intuitively. Otherwise how could you explain the deadly seriousness on their pale little faces? But they are marching quietly in orderly rows, calm and earnest, and at the head of them is Janusz Korczak.

All in unison

(or Narrator and congregation alternate stanzas)

Psalm 79

God, the pagans have invaded your heritage,
they have descrated your holy Temple;
they have left the corpses of your servants
to the birds of the air for food,
and the flesh of your devout to the beasts of the earth.

They have shed blood like water
throughout Jerusalem, not a gravedigger left!
we are now insulted by our neighbors,
butt and laughing-stock of all those around us.
How much longer will you be angry. Yahweh? For ever?
Is your jealousy to go on smouldering like a fire?

Pour out your anger on the pagans,
   who do not acknowledge you,
and on those kingdoms
   that do not call on your name,
for they have devoured Jacob
   and reduced his home to desolation.

Do not hold our ancestors' crimes against us,
in tenderness quickly intervene,
we can hardly be crushed lower,
help us. God our savior,
for the honor of your name.
Yahweh, blot out our sins,
rescue us for the sake of your name.

Why should the pagans ask, "Where is their God?"
May we soon see the pagans learning what vengeance
you exact for your servants blood shed here!
May the groans of the captive reach you,
by your mighty arm rescue those doomed to die!

Pay our neighbors sevenfold, strike to the heart
for the monstrous insult proferred to you Lord!
And we your people, the flock that you pasture,
　　giving you everlasting thanks,
　　will recite your praises for ever and ever.

　　　4th Reader (a woman)
　　　　　　　　O the Chimneys

　　　　　　　　O the chimneys
　　　　　　　　On the ingeniously devised habitations of death
　　　　　　　　When Israel's body drifted as smoke
　　　　　　　　Through the air—
　　　　　　　　Was welcomed by a star, a chimney sweep.
　　　　　　　　A star that turned black
　　　　　　　　Or was it a ray of sun?

　　　　　　　　Oh the Chimneys!
　　　　　　　　Freedomway for Jeremiah and Job's dust—
　　　　　　　　Who devised you and laid stone upon stone
　　　　　　　　The road for refugee of smoke?

　　　　　　　　O the habitations of death.
　　　　　　　　Invitingly appointed
　　　　　　　　For the host who used to be a guest—
　　　　　　　　O you fingers
　　　　　　　　Laying the threshold
　　　　　　　　Like a knife between life and death—

　　　　　　　　O you chimneys.
　　　　　　　　O you fingers
　　　　　　　　And Israel's body as smoke through the air!
　　　　　　　　　　　—Nelly Sachs, from *In the Habitations of Death*

5th Reader (a man)

As it began to grow light, the fire was lit in two of the pits in which about 2,500 dead bodies lay piled one on top of the other. Two hours later all that could be discerned in the white-hot flames were countless charred and scorched shapes, the blackish-phosphorescent hue a sign that they were in an advanced stage of cremation. At this point the fire had to be kept going from outside because the pyre which at first protruded about half a metre above the edge of the pit had, in the meantime, gone below this level. While in the crematorium ovens, once the corpses were thoroughly alight, it was possible to maintain a lasting red heat with the help of fans, in the pits the fire would burn only as long as the air could circulate freely in between the bodies. As the heap of bodies settled, no air was able to get in from outside. This meant that we stokers had constantly to pour oil or wood alcohol on the burning corpses, in addition to human fat, large quantities of which had collected and was boiling in the two collecting pans on either side of the pit. The sizzling fat was scooped out with buckets on a long curved rod and poured all over the pit causing flames to leap up amid much crackling and hissing. Dense smoke and fumes rose incessantly. The air reeked of oil, fat, benzol and burnt flesh.

—Filip Muller, Eyewitness Auschwitz

Narrator

Master of the universe, help us to bear in mind always our potential for evil. And strengthen us, our God, so that we may fulfill our potential for good instead.

6th Reader (a man)

One day when we came back from work, we saw three gallows rearing up in the assembly place, three black crows. Roll call SS all around us, machine guns trained the traditional ceremony. Three victims in chains—and one of them, the little servant, the sad-eyed angel.

The SS seemed more preoccupied, more disturbed than usual. To hang a young body in front of thousands of spectators was no light matter. The head of the camp read the verdict. All eyes were on the child. He was lividly pale, almost calm, biting his lips. The gallows threw its shadow over him.

This time the Lagerkapo refused to act as executioner. Three SS replaced him.

The three necks were placed at the same moment within the nooses.

"Long live liberty!" cried two adults.

But the child was silent.

"Where is God? Where is He?" someone behind me asked.

At a sign from the head of the camp, the three chairs tipped over.

Total silence through the camp. On the horizon the sun was setting.

"Bare your heads!" yelled the head of the camp. His voice was raucous. We were weeping.

"Cover your heads!"

Then the march past began. The two adults were no longer alive. Their tongues hung swollen, blue-tinged. But the third rope was still moving, being so light, the child was still alive.

For more than half an hour he stayed there, struggling between life and death, dying in slow agony under our eyes. And we had to look him full in the face. He was still alive when I passed in front of him. His tongue was still red, his eyes were not yet glazed.

Behind me, I heard the same man asking.

"Where is God now?"

And I heard a voice within me answer him.

"Where is He? Here He is—He is hanging here on this gallows . . ."

That night the soup tasted of corpses.

—Elie Wiesel, *Night*

7th Reader (a woman)

If as Christians we thought that Church and Synagogue no longer affected one another, everything would be lost. And where this separation between the community and the Jewish nation has been made complete, it is the Christian community which has suffered. The whole reality of the revelation of God is then secretly denied.

For in the person of the Jew there stands a witness before our eyes, the witness of God's covenant with Abraham, Isaac and Jacob and in that way with us all. Even one who does not understand Holy Scripture can see this reminder.

And don't you see, the remarkable theological importance, the extraordinary spiritual and sacred significance of the National Socialism that now lies behind us is that right from its roots it was anti-Semitic, that in this movement it was realized with a simply demonic clarity, that *the* enemy is the *Jew*. Yes, the enemy in this matter had to be a Jew. In this Jewish nation there really lives to this day the extraordinariness of the revelation of God.

When the Christian Church confesses Jesus Christ as Savior and the Servant of God for us, for all men, also for the mighty majority of those who have no direct connection with the People Israel, then it does not confess Him *although* He was a Jew.

No, we must strictly consider that Jesus Christ, in whom we believe, whom we Christians out of the heathen call our Savior and praise as the consummator of God's work on our behalf—He was *of necessity a Jew*. We cannot be blind to this fact; it belongs to the concrete reality of God's work and of his revelation.

The problem of Israel is, since the problem of Christ is inseparable from it, the problem of existence as such; the man who is ashamed of Israel is ashamed of Jesus Christ and therefore of his own existence.

The attack on Judah means the attack on the rock of the work and revelation of God, beside which work and which revelation there is no other.

—Karl Barth, *Dogmatics in Outline*

Homily

(A brief homily by a pastor is in order here. Perhaps two short talks would be appropriate, one by a Christian minister, one by a rabbi.)

Narrator

Holocaust survivor and author Elie Wiesel has said this.

If someone suffers and he keeps silent, it can be a good silence. If someone suffers and I keep silent, then it's a destructive silence. If we envisage literature and human destiny as endeavors by man to redeem himself, then we must admit the obsession, the overall dominating theme of responsibility, that we are responsible for one another. I am responsible for his or her suffering, for his or her destiny. If not, we are condemned by our solitude forever and it has no meaning. This solitude is a negative, destructive solitude, a self-destructive solitude.

—From *Harry James Cargas in Conversation with Elie Wiesel*

8th Reader

Indeed we may not remain silent in view of the horror of the Holocaust. And yet we must choose our words carefully. We must not oversentimentalize the tragedy, we must not treat it with irreverence. How, then, are we to speak out? Rabbi Irving Greenberg has given us this guide: "Let us offer, then, as a working principle the following. No statement, theological or otherwise, should be made that would not be credible in the presence of burning children."

Narrator

There are times also, for silence, silence in the face of the awesome proportions of the tragedy of the Holocaust. We arrive at such a time now, as we ask six Holocaust survivors from our community [or, if this is not possible, six diverse members of the community] to each light a candle, one candle to represent one million Jewish dead, the totality, when lit, to symbolize all those who died in the Holocaust.

When the candles are lit, the overhead lights will be extinguished for two minutes while we each offer our own prayers. When the electric lights are turned back on you may, of course, continue to pray, but when you do begin to leave, please do so quietly.

Lighting of the Candles

Lowering of the Lights (2 minutes)

Lights Back On

Dismissal

Section XI

Oral History With Holocaust Survivors

by Sara Leuchter

Oral History: an Introduction

Oral history is primary source material which is collected by producing sound recordings of first-hand testimony of witnesses to historical events. It embodies the oral tradition by which knowledge of past events is handed down from one generation to the next, and augments the body of personal accounts, diaries, and journals which heretofore have been the most popular means of preserving life stories and historical events. The first organized oral history activity began in 1948, under the direction of Professor Allan Nevins of Columbia University. With the development of the portable cassette recorder in the mid-1960s, oral history experienced a tremendous surge in popularity.

Oral history is a powerful research tool. A narrator's personal experiences and emotions may have a profound impact on the listener. However, the method has its limitations: memory loses its sharpness, personal events may become exaggerated, perceptions change. Dates, places, and names which are recalled may not be corroborated by books. Yet despite these limitations, oral history is a valuable methodology which allows participation by a great number of people, most of whom might not otherwise put their remembrances into writing.

Since December 1979, I have been involved with a statewide oral history and photographic documentation project concerned with Jewish survivors of the Holocaust who settled in Wisconsin after the war. To date, my colleague, Jean Loeb Lettofsky, and I have conducted twenty-four interviews totaling 160 hours of tape, and have collected more than 1,000 photographs. The material will be part of the perma-

nent collection at the Wisconsin Jewish Archives, a special section of
the State Historical Society of Wisconsin.

In 1974, after listening to an interview with a survivor now residing
in Green Bay, archivists at the Society decided to undertake a year-long
project to record the testimony of survivors with a variety of backgrounds and experiences. A $39,000 grant from the Wisconsin Humani-
ties Committee, together with matching funds from the State Historical
Society and more than $11,000 in private contributions, made the
project possible. After the first year, additional funds were raised from
private sources for the publication of a guide to both the oral histories
and photographic documentation.

TEN KEY QUESTIONS

Oral history projects must be governed by professional standards. It is
not enough for the interviewer merely to place a microphone in front of
an individual and request that he/she talk about historical events.
Rather, interviewers, particularly those working on a large-scale project, should spend a great deal of time planning and organizing interviews. According to Dale Treleven, State Oral Historian at the State
Historical Society of Wisconsin, there are ten essential questions which
must be addressed before the first interview can be conducted:

1. What Are the Objectives of the Project?

Should the project be designed to record an unlimited number of
spontaneous, unstructured reminiscences, or should its primary objective be to collect substantive historical data that augment and complement other forms of documentation?

2. Who Will Be Interviewed, and How Is This to be Decided?

Should the project focus on one particular kind of survivor (from one
particular experience or of a certain age or place), or should it be
designed to include survivors of varied experiences, backgrounds, and
places of origin? A small committee which relies on the input of several
people who may not necessarily have personal "favorites," might be
formed to resolve this and related questions.

3. Will Enough Time Be Available to the Interviewer(s) to Prepare for the Taped Discussion?

The quality of the information obtained from an interviewee is inte-
grally related to the interviewer's background and knowledge of the
subject matter. If the project is to have certain historical standards,
background research is essential.

4. Who Will Conduct the Interviews?

Will it be one researcher, or a team which will share the research, the interviewing, and the processing of tapes? If there is a team, a coordinator should be responsible for scheduling and maintaining equipment, monitoring quality, and performing routine administrative tasks.

5. How Will the Interviews Be Conducted?

High-quality interviews result from sound procedures, as well as from clear project objectives. An unrecorded, preliminary interview is helpful in building rapport, completing personal-background questionnaires, explaining the necessity for a legal-agreement form, and finding a noise-free place to conduct the taping.

6. What Kind of Equipment and Supplies Should Be Used?

Because of cost considerations, most oral history interviewers use a cassette recorder, together with a reasonably good brand of tape and a reliable external microphone. Sixty-minute cassette tapes (30 minutes per side) should always be used, and whenever possible, an electric power cord should be substituted for battery power. Good maintenance of recording equipment is essential to ensure high-quality sound recordings; a $10 demagnetizer and a few dollars worth of isopropyl alcohol and cotton swabs will be sufficient for the routine demagnetizing and cleaning of the recorder after each ten or fifteen hours of use.

7. How Will the Taped Interviews Be Qualitatively Evaluated?

There are two main criteria for qualitative evaluation: the quality of the sound recording itself (absence of extraneous noise), and the nature of specificity and the information on the tape.

8. What Happens After an Interview Is Completed?

A master tape of each cassette containing a field interview should be copied onto good-quality open-reel tape, since cassette tapes are unsuited to long-term preservation. Subsequently, an index should be prepared of the contents of each side of each tape, and a uniform method used to measure segments. These might include a recorder's digital counter, which gives a crude approximation of elapsed time; a stop-watch, which is more accurate; or the State Historical Society of Wisconsin's TAPE System, described at length later in this chapter. The original tapes should never be used until a master tape is prepared. The latter is used only to generate additional copies, when needed, and should be stored under conditions of relatively stable temperature and humidity.

9. Who Owns the Tapes (and Indexes, Transcripts, etc.)?

Property and use rights to a sound recording are vested in those whose voices are heard on the recording. The rights to a one-on-one oral history interview, therefore, are held jointly by the interviewer and the interviewee. Both parties must sign legal-agreement forms in order to transfer tape rights to the organization sponsoring the oral history project. An original of this form is kept on file by the sponsoring agency.

10. What Products May Result from the Tapes of an Oral History Project?

The basic product is a package containing the interview tapes, indexes, and ideally, brief interviewers' introductions which provide future users with additional information about each interviewee, and general impressions of the interview sessions. An index serves as an approximate location guide to the content of each side of each tape; users will be able to locate and transcribe portions of discussion for a publication, or make copies of specific portions of the tape for use in preparing a tape/slide presentation or film.

The Planning Phase

The most important step in conducting an oral history project is the initial planning phase, during which it must be decided whom to interview, who will conduct the interviews, and how much money will be available for the storage of the tapes and the preparation of finding aids.

After the goals of the project have been established, efforts should be focused on locating possible interviewees. In most cases, Holocaust survivors will be known to such community-resource people as rabbis, social workers, and senior-citizen program planners. It is imperative that project personnel approach community-resource people with a brief outline that explains the nature of the project, so that resource people can, without trepidation, refer possible interviewees. A show of support for the project by respected individuals in the community may help the interviewer gain entry to certain survivors.

In order to reach a wide audience, the project personnel may wish to run a small news release in local newspapers which describes the project and asks interested persons to contact the staff. The press release should instruct potential interviewees to call collect, if necessary. Also, staff members should not underestimate the value of the "grapevine," which provides a unique method of informing survivors about the project.

One of the most important issues the interviewer must confront is the potential interviewee's suspicion. Many survivors are hesitant to grant interviews if they feel there is some chance that their experiences (and suffering) will mean monetary reward for someone else. The staff should emphasize the research value of the tapes and reiterate that the project is a nonprofit venture. Project staff may choose to mention the increase in anti-Semitic incidents in this country and abroad, and to suggest that the tapes may serve as a deterrent to such acts. Also, many survivors are not aware of the so-called revisionists who claim that the Holocaust never happened, and that allusions to it are merely a Zionist plot to gather sympathy for Israel. Given the sensitive nature of the subject, a survivor may feel more comfortable conducting an interview with someone who is Jewish. Since the topic of anti-Semitism and, in some causes, anti-Gentile feelings will arise naturally in the course of the interview, the survivor may feel less inhibited discussing such matters with someone of the same religion. In addition, a Jewish interviewer may be more familiar with Yiddish expressions, Jewish customs and ceremonies, and certain terms mentioned in the interview which may require follow-up questions. However, a positive interview can be conducted by a non-Jewish interviewer, but he/she should be aware that the survivor may decline to participate upon learning of the difference in religion. Interviewees need to be thoroughly convinced of the interviewer's sensitivity toward the actual events of the Holocaust.

After the project staff has identified possible interviewees, it should send them introductory letters. These letters, which may be brief, should contain the name of the community-resource person who suggested the survivor, the purpose of the project, and the final repository of the tapes. They should also indicate that a follow-up telephone call will be placed to the survivor to determine his/her reaction to the project, and to answer any questions concerning it.

The follow-up telephone call, which provides the first personal contact between the potential interviewer and the potential interviewee, should make the survivor feel comfortable. The interviewer should be careful not to "push" the survivor into agreeing to be interviewed. Sometimes a gentle coaxing will assuage the survivor's fears so that he/she will consent to the preliminary interview. The staff should be prepared for a fair number of negative responses, most of which have nothing to do with the objectives of the project. Many survivors have never spoken to anyone about their experiences, least of all an outsider; some will decline for health reasons. While initially there may be a dearth of individuals willing to participate in an oral history project, potential interviewees will "surface" once the project is under way and other interviews have spoken favorably about it.

The Preliminary Interview and Questionnaire

Once the project's goals have been established, the staff should prepare a preliminary questionnaire to be completed by both interviewer and interviewee during the initial interview. This questionnaire will serve as a skeletal outline of questions, based on the interviewee's experiences. Questions should focus on genealogical history (date and place of birth, names of parents and their dates/places of birth); school attendance; religious education and family religious life; the subject's experience during the Holocaust, including relevant places, names, dates, and circumstances surrounding liberation; contact with surviving family members after the war; immigration to the United States (or to another country, if the survivor did not come immediately to this country); places of residence and employment to the present date; and pertinent information on the interviewee's spouse and children.

The preliminary interview should run at least 1½–2 hours in length. The interviewer should attempt to limit the responses of the survivor to relevant information, to ensure that he/she does not relate a fascinating story which should be saved for the tape-recorder. (More often than not, the first telling of a story is its best.) Should this happen, the interviewer should make a note to ask the survivor to relate the story in a pertinent place during the taped interview.

The preliminary interview also serves to familiarize the survivor with the legal-agreement form. The interviewer might show the agreement to the survivor and suggest that both of them sign release rights. The interviewer should demonstrate that he/she has no hesitation about relinquishing rights to the interview, which may help alleviate the potential interviewee's suspicion of how the tapes will be used.

Once the preliminary questionnaire has been completed, the interviewer should do some basic research in order to prepare good, detailed questions. For example, if the survivor is a Ukrainian Jew who fought with the partisans, the interviewer might read the chapters on Ukrainian partisan units in Reuben Ainsztein's *Jewish Resistance in Nazi-Occupied Europe*. If the survivor is a Dutch Jew who was "underground," Dr. J. Presser's work, *The Destruction of the Dutch Jews*, will provide the researcher with dates of important edicts and deportations, which could become focal points of the interview.

Family-related questions are among the best ways to put the interviewee at ease and to alleviate his/her discomfort with the tape-recorder. They should focus on memories of the interviewee's parents, grandparents, and siblings, as well as descriptions of his/her home, closest friends, and religious upbringing. It is advisable to keep the interview chronological in nature, both to facilitate the survivor's ability to remember events and to provide the interviewer with a clear, historical framework.

Of course, the purpose of the project will influence specific questions. The Wisconsin State Historical Society oral history project was concerned as much with resettlement in Wisconsin as with pre-Holocaust and Holocaust experiences. The questions about the Wisconsin experience dealt with the survivor's role in the community, how he/she was accepted into the community, and how he/she felt today as part of it. We also included a series of "control" questions which probed the attitudes of the survivor toward such matters as intermarriage, the *Holocaust* television special, and reasons for participating in the oral history project. Among other matters, we sought information on:

1. Family Background: interviewee's date/place of birth; names of parents—their dates/places of birth; names of grandparents—their dates/places of birth
   a. any special recollections of grandparents
   b. description of parents
   c. parents' occupations

2. Siblings: names; their dates/places of birth; recollections of them

3. Other family members in interviewee's town or area

4. Family and/or close friends in the United States prior to the war and contact with them

5. Prewar home and immediate community surroundings

6. Prewar religious life:
   a. synagogue attendance
   b. traditions in the home
   c. religious school attenance

7. Prewar education:
   a. extent
   b. curriculum
   c. cultural activities

8. Family political involvement and social activities (clubs, etc.) before the war

9. Prewar incidents of anti-Semitism

10. Identification with surrounding community:
    a. languages spoken
    b. sense of patriotism or loyalty to national culture

11. Sense of a "gathering storm" in Europe
    a. awareness of Hitler and the Nazis
    b. family and personal reactions to the German menace
    c. reactions to Hitler's threats against the Jews

12. Memory of the outbreak of World War II (Sept. 1, 1939)
    At this point, questions were formulated according to the individual's experiences from the outbreak of the war until he/she left for the United States.

13. Postwar contact with family members in Europe

14. Contact with family/friends in the United States after the war

15. Decision to leave Europe
    a. reasons for leaving
    b. procedure for emigration
    c. how trip was made

16. Trip to United States (date, duration)
    a. feelings upon seeing Statue of Liberty
    b. relatives or others who metinterviewee

17. Life before coming to Wisconsin

18. Arrival in Wisconsin: individuals meeting interviewee

19. Help from Jewish community:
    a. problems of new immigrant
    b. anti-Semitism
    c. jobs for family members
    d. special acts of kindness
    Here establish what individual did from arrival in Wisconsin until the present, including jobs and residences.

20. Interviewee's family:
    a. spouse—name, date/place of birth, how met, occupation, date of marriage
    b. children—names, dates/places of birth, present activities

21. Religious life
    a. synagogue attendance
    b. traditions in the home
    c. children's Hebrew school education

Control Questions

22. How much do your children know about your experiences?

23. Do you see yourself as a more concerned parent than others? Why or why not?

24. Describe your contact with American-born Jews.

25. What kinds of things do you like to read?

26. What was your reaction to the *Holocaust* television program?

27. Where have you traveled in Wisconsin?

28. How do you feel about the high percentage of ethnic Germans in Wisconsin?

29. How do you feel you have contributed to the Wisconsin community?

30. What do you see as the most important issues facing America today?

31. Why do you feel it is important to participate in an oral history project on the Holocaust?

Interview Approaches

Although most of the questions are prepared before the interview, the interviewer should be prepared to ask additional questions according to the line of discussion. Often, the interviewee will mention an experience that was previously unknown to the interviewer, requiring the interviewer to think quickly in order to elicit stimulating discussion.

A complete interview often requires three or more visits to the survivor. Each interview should last no longer than three hours. The tape-recorder should remain on, except when the interviewer is changing tapes or when there are unexpected interruptions, such as the telephone or doorbell. (If the discussion becomes too emotionally charged, the interviewer should use his/her judgment about whether or not to turn off the machine.)

Responses should not be interrupted; the interviewee should be allowed to answer a question completely before another is asked. The survivor should be allowed sufficient time to think about a response, and should be reassured that pauses are natural in an individual's train of thought, and that tapes are inexpensive.

The interviewer should probe with "how" and "why" questions, as opposed to "yes" and "no" questions. He/she should elicit the opinions and feelings of the survivor on myriad subjects. If the survivor's recollection of events disagrees with the facts, the question might be rephrased without challenging the interviewee's veracity. If the interview digresses or rambles, the interviewer should make every effort to return to the prepared line of questioning. In concluding the interview, he/she should ask a wrap-up question which permits the interviewee to reveal any important memories or reflections which were missed.

Given the uniquely sensitive nature of Holocaust-related interviewing, many questions cannot and should not be asked because they deeply invade an individual's privacy. In the Wisconsin oral history project, we wanted to approach the interviewee as historians, not as psychologists. We vowed never to push an interviewee if he/she felt uncomfortable about a certain line of questioning. Thus, if it appeared that our questioning might place a burden of guilt upon the interviewee, we were careful not to probe too deeply concerning his/her method of survival.

Before we began the project, we realized the potential harm of dredging up old and painful memories. A psychologist assured us that while the taping might be painful to the survivor, it would not trigger a psychological crisis. We also were told that because survivors have lived with their memories for a long time, they usually have learned to deal with them, so that recounting them is not traumatic.

Materials, Seating, Timing, Tape Preparation

The interviewer should prepare a checklist of materials to bring to the interview, including a tape-recorder (we used a Sony 110), at least five 60-minute cassette tapes, interview questions, legal-agreement forms, and an extension cord. When the interviewer arrives for the first session, he/she should explain to the survivor exactly how the machinery is set up, to make it appear less intimidating.

The best seating arrangement occurs when the two participants face one another, with the tape-recorder and the microphone between them on a coffee table. The microphone should be placed on a telephone book to absorb vibrations from the table. This seating arrangement makes it possible for the interviewer to view the tape-counter and recording-level indicator, and also facilitates direct eye contact, which is important for successful interviewing. The interviewer and survivor may wish to agree upon an "end-of-tape-is-approaching" cue, thus ensuring that the discussion is not interrupted during a crucial point.

The tape should be fast-forwarded for about half a minute to allow for the interviewer's brief introduction, which is added after the interview is completed. The interview should terminate about 30 digits (by the recorder counter) from the end of the tape. To avoid confusion about used tapes, the interviewer should mark each side of the tape immediately after recording, and should include the interviewee's name, the place and date of the interview, and the tape number.

The Legal Agreement

At the end of each interview session, the legal-agreement form should be signed by both interviewer and interviewee. Both parties receive a copy of the agreement, the original of which is filed with the sponsoring organization. I suggest an agreement for an unrestricted interview (all parts open to the public), although some survivors may request restricting access to some parts of the tape, which can be done for a certain period of time.

The following is part of the legal agreement used by the State Historical Society of Wisconsin:

> I, [interviewee], hereby give, grant, assign and transfer, forever, to the State Historical Society of Wisconsin, as a donation, all my rights, title and interest in and to the recorded conversation made by me and [interviewer] on [day, month, year], and any written summaries or copies thereof and any documentation accompanying the recordings, for use by said State Historical Society in any lawful way including publication, except for the conditions specified below, if any.

The places for the interviewer's and interviewee's names may be interchanged, depending on who is signing the form.

The "Tape System"

A finding aid to tapes (a system for quickly locating pertinent segments) will facilitate their future use. The State Historical Society of Wisconsin recently developed the TAPE System, which is an alternative to the traditional procedure of preparing typewritten transcriptions and which has proved to be time- and cost-saving.

Equipment for the TAPE System is minimal: two standard (monaural) cassette recorders and an open-reel tape-recorder. A master tape of each interview is created on the open-reel machine from the cassette tape and from a second cassette containing a prerecorded time-signal (the time-signal consists of a voice announcing the elapsed time at five-second intervals).

An individual prepares a written abstract of the interview using a standard cassette transcribing machine or a monaural cassette recorder (preferably one with a foot pedal). The abstract summarizes the interview and indicates, on the basis of the time signal, the elapsed time. For example, a discussion of religious education may occur on Tape 1, Side 2, between the time signals 10 minutes and 15 seconds through 14 minutes. The abstract would summarize the discussion in several sentences and specify in the margin, 10:14—14:00. The TAPE System thus enables tape users to locate quickly those parts of the tape they wish to hear. A good abstract includes an index, which enables researchers to locate names, proper hours, dates, and other historical references. If a researcher is interested in locating the discussion on religious education, for example, the index will indicate that it appears on 1:2, 10:15 (Tape 1, Side 2, 10 minutes and 15 seconds on the time-signal). If the researcher wants to listen to the actual interview to learn more, he/she can fast-forward the tape until the time-signal 10:15, and then switch off the time-signal channel to listen uninterrupted to the interview. The abstract should begin with an introduction to the interview, which includes background on the project, on the interviewee, and on the taping session(s), as well as a brief analysis of the interview's special strengths and weaknesses. The introduction also might provide instructions on how to use the abstract and index efficiently to retrieve information or to locate a certain segment of the tape.

Use of the TAPE System alleviates the problem of unclear or obscure references in transcripts, which sometimes force researchers to return to the original tape. For example, Sylvia Rothschild, in her recent work, *Voices from the Holocaust*, describes the recurring misspellings and misunderstood phrases which she encountered in transcripts from the William E. Wiener Oral History Library of the American Jewish Committee. An obvious word such as Holocaust, she noted, appeared as "holy cust," and names of Jewish customs were often unintelligible.

After processing more than 300 hours of interviews, the Wisconsin State Historical Society has found that the average processing time per hour of taped interview is around 10 hours, less than half the time reported for professionally prepared transcripts. In addition, time/cost analysis has demonstrated that the TAPE System affords a reduction of more than 50 percent. Most important, it encourages the researcher to listen to the actual interview, and to regard the tapes, not the transcriptions, as the primary historical resource.

The Limits of Time

The most crucial aspect of planning an oral history project on Holocaust survivors is time. Oral history depends on first-hand testimony of witnesses. Within a few years, the number of Holocaust survivors will greatly decline. It is thus imperative that planning for oral history projects to record their testimony begin immediately. Let us not waste the tremendous wealth of human resources which could help prevent future acts of genocide.

Bibliography

Baum, Willa K. *Oral History for the Local Historical Society.* 2d ed. rev. Nashville, 1974.
    Available for $3.00 from the American Association for State and Local History, 1315 Eighth Ave. South, Nashville, Tenn. 37203.
————. *Transcribing and Editing Oral History.* Nashville, 1977.
    Available for $6.75 from the American Association for State and Local History (see address above).
Davis, Cullom, et al. *From Tape to Type: An Oral History Manual and Workbook.* Chicago, 1977.
    Available for $8.95 from the American Library Association, 90 East Huron St., Chicago, Ill. 60611.
Hoopes, James. *Oral History: An Introduction for Students.*
    Available for $5.00 from the University of North Carolina Press, Chapel Hill, N.C. 27514.
Ives, Edward D. *The Tape-Recorded Interview: A Manual for Field Workers in Folklore and Oral History.* Knoxville: University of Tennessee Press, 1980.

Section XII

Obtaining Speakers on the Holocaust

What follows is a list of speaker bureaus, or organizations making available speakers. Interested individuals should call for information on specific names and fees. Names are mentioned for informational purposes only and should not be construed as an endorsement. "Visiting lecturer" refers to someone who lives in Europe or Israel and is in the United States periodically.

B'nai B'rith Lecture Bureau
    823 United Nations Plaza
    New York, N.Y. 10017
    212-490-1170
    Ruth Wheat, Director

    The B'nai B'rith Lecture Bureau's speakers on the Holocaust include Lucy Dawidowicz, Emil Fackenheim, and Raul Hilberg, as well as visiting lecturers Aharon Appelfeld and Beate Klarsfeld.

The Holocaust Studies Center
The Bronx H.S. of Science
    75 West 205th Street   Bx 10463
    212-796-2421
    Mr. Stuart S. Elenko, Director

    This resource now seven years old contains over 1400 books, 44% of which are out of print and rare to very rare, and, a collection of Holocaust display materials which are considered one of the finest such collections in the nation. Included in this extraordinary collection are original Nuremberg Trial Documents, papers, and, photos, Warsaw Ghetto Photos, Unique Posters, Concentration

Camp pictures and documents, uniforms, and other important Holocaust related materials. This resource is now well along in producing the first Holocaust Data Base Program in the nation.

Visiting hours are by appointment only and community groups will be given tours upon appointment. Speakers are also provided upon request.

International Network of Children of Jewish Holocaust Survivors
211 Madison Avenue, Suite 1104
New York, N.Y. 10016
516-295-0670
Syd Mandelbaum, Secretary

The Network, which is in touch with, and sometimes coordinates activities among, the Second Generation groups listed in Section IX, can provide speakers who are children of survivors.

JWB Lecture Bureau
15 East 26th Street
New York, N.Y. 10010
212-532-4949
Steven L. Bayer, Director

The JWB Lecture Bureau handles arrangements for such lecturers as Irving Greenberg, Yuri Suhl, and Richard L. Rubenstein, as well as visiting lecturer Tuviah Friedman.

National Conference of Christians and Jews
43 West 57th Street
New York, N.Y. 10019
212-688-7530
Donald McEvoy, Director of Program Development

The NCCJ is in touch with many clergypeople, academicians, and other individuals who speak on the Holocaust. It has regional offices or chapters in over seventy-five American cities.

National Institute on the Holocaust
P.O. Box 2147
Philadelphia, Pa. 19103
215-787-1753
Dr. Franklin Littell, Chairman

In addition to Dr. Littell, a frequent and popular lecturer on the Holocaust, the National Institute is in touch with many individuals in the Philadelphia area and beyond who are knowledgeable about the Holocaust.

Simon Wiesenthal Center for Holocaust Studies
9760 West Pico Boulevard
Los Angeles, Calif. 90035
213-553-9030/553-4478
Dr. Gerald Margolis, Director

The Simon Wiesenthal Center is the leading resource for obtaining speakers on the Holocaust in the western half of the United States. It houses survivors and Second Generation groups, and works with academicians in the Los Angeles area who specialize in the Holocaust.

U.S. Conference of Catholic Bishops
1312 Massachusetts Avenue, N.W.
Washington, D.C. 20005
202-659-6857
Dr. Eugene Fisher, Secretariat for Catholic-Jewish Relations

Dr. Fisher, besides frequently speaking on various aspects of Catholic-Jewish relations, including the Holocaust, recommends other qualified speakers for Holocaust programs or commemorations.

ZACHOR: The Holocaust Resource Center
250 West 57th Street, Room 215
New York, N.Y. 10107
212-582-6116
Dr. Irving Greenberg, President

Through its Faculty Seminar and other activities, ZACHOR is in contact with many of the leading academic and other speakers on the Holocaust, particularly those in the New York City metropolitan area.

Others whom interested individuals might contact for information about speakers include:

1. The directors of the other Holocaust education and commemoration centers listed in this *Guide*.

2. The staff of Jewish federations and community relations councils, as well as the national and local offices of the American Jewish Congress, American Jewish Committee, and Anti-Defamation League of B'nai B'rith. (A list of national and key local Jewish organizations can be found in the annual *American Jewish Yearbook*, Philadelphia: Jewish Publication Society.)

3. Local academicians who teach courses on the Holocaust, as well as clergypeople, survivors, children of survivors, and liberators.

Section XIII

Funding for Holocaust-Related Research and Programming

There are only a very limited number of foundations funding Holocaust-related programming. Of the four with which I am most familiar, which are listed below, only the first deals largely with programming; the other three largely—though by no means exclusively—fund scholarly, evaluative, and bibliographical works.

Individuals planning community-wide Holocaust conferences, commemorations and other programs might also seek financial support from:

1. Local chapters of the Anti-Defamation League and National Conference of Christians and Jews.

2. The local Jewish federation or Community Relations Council, as well as the Catholic Diocese and various Protestant bodies.

3. Local private foundations and corporate public affairs programs.

4. Advertisements in a published memorial book.

5. Special events which might themselves be related to Holocaust education, e.g., the showing of a benefit film.

Holocaust Survivor Memorial Foundation
  350 Fifth Avenue, Suite 3508
  New York, N.Y. 10118
  212-594-8765

Contact: Jack P. Eisner, President and Founder
Shirley Eisner, Director

Illinois branch:
Holocaust Memorial Foundation of Illinois
P.O. Box 574
Northbrook, Ill. 60022
312-595-2095

Erna I. Gans, President

The Holocaust Survivor Memorial Foundation was established in 1979. Its purposes are to educate the general public about the historical events and lessons of the Holocaust by acting as a grant-giving organization, and by operating as an organization which sponsors programs on the Holocaust, particularly in the areas of the mass media and the arts.

In one recent year, the Foundation supported over twenty special Holocaust projects, ranging from artistic exhibits to research, publications, and lecture series. The grants ranged from $500 to $30,000.

Applications for grants are accepted and reviewed four times annually. In addition to filling out an application, which can be received by contacting the Foundation, those seeking funding must submit a statement of purpose, a description of the project, a suggested phase of implementation, and a project budget and timetable. The Foundation reviews the applications based on appropriateness, importance, usefulness, feasibility, originality, competence of persons involved, and soundness of budget.

For the appropriate forms, contact the Foundation at the address and phone number listed above.

Memorial Foundation for Jewish Culture
15 East 26th Street
New York, N.Y. 10010
212-679-4074

Contact: Dr. Jerry Hochbaum

The Memorial Foundation for Jewish Culture was established in 1964. Its purpose is to support doctoral scholarships, fellowships, and institutional grants in the area of Judaica, including the Holocaust.

Institutional proposals must be submitted by September 30th, and individual proposals by November 30th, for funding in the following year.

National Endowment for the Humanities
Old Post Office
1100 Pennsylvania Avenue
Washington, D.C. 20506
202-724-0386

Contact: John Lippincott, Public Affairs

The NEH was established by Congress in 1965 to financially support individuals and nonprofit institutions and organizations involved in humanitarian projects. There presently exist five Endowment divisions: Education Programs, Fellowships and Seminars, General Programs, Research Programs, and State Programs. In addition, the Endowment funds studies and surveys relating to important areas of humanistic activity.

In one recent year, the NEH financially supported ten Holocaust projects. Included were the Holocaust education curriculum for young people, a documentary film to accompany the art exhibit "Danzig, 1939," and an international bibliographical dictionary of Central European emigrés, 1933–1945. The grants ranged from $1,066 to $135,779.

To apply for a grant, one should contact the Public Affairs office at the NEH for the appropriate application form. There are different forms for each division, and application date deadlines vary, depending on the division. Each year, the NEH publishes an "Overview of Endowment Programs."

Once an application is received, it is reviewed by the appointed panelists and, in certain instances, by outside specialists. If the proposal passes through this stage, it is reviewed by the National Council on the Humanities. Final funding action is determined by the NEH chairman.

Additional information regarding the application procedure may be obtained by writing to the NEH.

A significant number of State Humanities Councils also have funded programs, conferences, research and memorials on the Holocaust. The addresses and phone numbers of the fifty state Councils, and that of the District of Columbia and Puerto Rico, are listed at the end of this section.

National Foundation for Jewish Culture
122 East 42nd Street
New York, N.Y. 10017
212-490-2280

Contact: Dr. Abraham Atik

The National Foundation for Jewish Culture was established in 1960 to create a broader understanding of the field of Jewish culture in America. One aspect of the Foundation is to act as a grant-giving body solely for doctoral dissertation candidates who are preparing research in a field related to Jewish studies.

Applicants must be citizens of the United States. They must be able to submit, along with the application, completed transcripts, Graduate Record Examination verbal scores, a dissertation prospectus, and three recommendations. Applicants must also show evidence of a plan leading to a career in Jewish life and proficiency in a language related to their area of study.

The grants range from $1,000 to $5,500, depending on individual requirements. Applications must be received by December 31st for the following academic year.

For additional information, contact the Foundation at the address and phone number listed above.

State Humanities Councils

Alabama

Committee for the Humanities in
  Alabama
Box 700
Birmingham-Southern College
Birmingham, Ala. 35204
(205) 324-1314

Alaska

Alaska Humanities Forum
429 D Street, Room 211
Loussac Sogn Building
Anchorage, Alaska 99501
(907) 272-5341

Arizona

Arizona Humanities Council
112 North Central Avenue,
  Suite 304
Phoenix, Ariz. 85004
(602) 257-0335

Arkansas

Arkansas Endowment for
  the Humanities
University Tower Building
12th & University, Suite 1019
Little Rock, Ark. 72204
(501) 663-3451

California

California Council for
  the Humanities
312 Sutter Street, Suite 601
San Francisco, Calif. 94108
(415) 391-1474

Colorado

Colorado Humanities Program
855 Broadway
Boulder, Col. 80302
(303) 442-7298

Connecticut

Connecticut Humanities Council
195 Church Street
Wesleyan Station
Middletown, Conn. 06457
(203) 347-6888

Delaware

Delaware Humanities Forum
2600 Pennsylvania Avenue
Wilmington, Del. 19806
(302) 738-8491

District of Columbia

D.C. Community
  Humanities Council
1341 G Street, N.W., Suite 620
Washington, D.C. 20005
(202) 347-1732

Florida

Florida Endowment for
  the Humanities
LET 360
University of South Florida
Tampa, Fla. 33620
(813) 974-4094

Georgia

Committee for the Humanities
  in Georgia
1589 Clifton Road, N.E.
Emory University
Atlanta, Ga. 30322
(404) 329-7500

Hawaii

Hawaii Committee for
  the Humanities
2615 South King Street, Suite 211
Honolulu, Hi. 96826
(808) 947-5891

Idaho

Association for the Humanities in
  Idaho
1403 West Franklin Street
Boise, Ida. 83702
(208) 345-5346

Illinois

Illinois Humanities Council
201 West Springfield Avenue,
  Suite 205
Champaign, Ill. 61820
(217) 333-7611

Indiana

Indiana Committee for
  the Humanities
4200 Northwestern Avenue
Indianapolis, Ind. 46205
(317) 925-5316

Iowa

Iowa Board for Public Programs
  in the Humanities
Oakdale Campus
University of Iowa
Iowa City, Iowa 52242
(319) 353-6754

Kansas

Kansas Committee for
  the Humanities
112 West Sixth Street, Suite 509
Topeka, Kan. 66603
(913) 357-0359

Kentucky

Kentucky Humanities Council
Ligon House
University of Kentucky
Lexington, Ky. 40508
(606) 258-5932

Louisiana

Louisiana Committee for
   the Humanities
4426 South Robertson
New Orleans, La. 70115
(504) 865-9404

Maine

Maine Council for the
   Humanities and Public Policy
P.O. Box 7202
Portland, Me. 04112
(207) 773-5051

Maryland

The Maryland Committee for
   the Humanities
330 North Charles Street,
   Room 306
Baltimore, Md. 21202
(301) 837-1938

Massachusetts

Massachusetts Foundation for the
   Humanities and Public Policy
237-E Whitmore Administration
   Building
University of Massachusetts
Amherst, Mass. 01003
(413) 545-1936

Michigan

Michigan Council for
   the Humanities
Nisbet Building, Suite 30
Michigan State University
East Lansing, Mich. 48824
(517) 355-0160

Minnesota

Minnesota Humanities
   Commission
Metro Square, Suite 282
St. Paul, Minn. 55101
(612) 224-5739

Mississippi

Mississippi Committee for
   the Humanities
3825 Ridgewood Road, Room 111
Jackson, Miss. 39211
(601) 982-6752

Missouri

Missouri State Committee for
   the Humanities
Loberg Building, Suite 202
1145 Dorsett Road
St. Louis, Mo. 63043
(314) 889-5940

Montana

Montana Committee for
   the Humanities
P.O. Box 8036
Hellgate Station
Missoula, Mont. 59807
(406) 243-6022

Nebraska

Nebraska Committee for
   the Humanities
Cooper Plaza, Suite 405
211 North 12th Street
Lincoln, Neb. 68508
(308) 234-2110

Nevada

Nevada Humanities Committee
P.O. Box 8065
Reno, Nev. 89507
(702) 784-6587

New Hampshire

New Hampshire Council for
the Humanities
112 South State Street
Concord, N.H. 03301
(603) 224-4071

New Jersey

New Jersey Committee for
the Humanities
Rutgers, The State University
CN 5062
New Brunswick, N.J. 08903
(201) 932-7726

New Mexico

New Mexico Humanities Council
1895 Roma N.E.
University of New Mexico
Albuquerque, N. Mex. 87131
(505) 277-3705 (Albuquerque)
(505) 646-1945 (La Cruces)

New York

New York Council for
the Humanities
33 West 42nd Street
New York, N.Y. 10036
(212) 354-3040

North Carolina

North Carolina
Humanities Committee
112 Foust Building
University of North
Carolina—Greensboro
Greensboro, N.C. 27412
(919) 379-5325

North Dakota

North Dakota Committee for the
Humanities and Public Issues
Box 2191
Bismarck, N. Dak. 58501
(701) 663-1948

Ohio

The Ohio Program in
the Humanities
760 Pleasant Ridge Avenue
Columbus, Ohio 43209
(614) 236-6879

Oklahoma

Oklahoma Humanities
Committee
Executive Terrace Building
2809 Northwest Expressway,
Suite 500
Oklahoma City, Okla. 73112
(405) 840-1721

Oregon

Oregon Committee for
the Humanities
418 S.W. Washington, Room 410
Portland, Oreg. 97201
(503) 241-0543

Pennsylvania

Public Committee for the
Humanities in Pennsylvania
401 North Broad Street
Philadelphia, Pa. 19108
(215) 925-1005

Puerto Rico

Fundación Puertorriquena de las
Humanidades
Box 4307
Old San Juan, P.R. 00904
(809) 723-2087

Rhode Island

Rhode Island Committee for
  the Humanities
86 Weybosset Street, Room 307
Providence, R.I. 02903
(401) 521-6150

South Carolina

South Carolina Committee for
  the Humanities
17 Calendar Court
Columbia, S.C. 29206
(803) 799-1704

South Dakota

South Dakota Committee on
  the Humanities
University Station, Box 35
Brookings, S. Dak. 57006
(605) 688-4823

Tennessee

Tennessee Committee for
  the Humanities
1001 18th Avenue South
Nashville, Tenn. 37212
(615) 320-7001

Texas

Texas Committee for
  the Humanities
1604 Nueces
Austin, Tex. 78701
(512) 473-8585

Utah

Utah Endowment for
  the Humanities
10 West Broadway
Broadway Building, Suite 900
Salt Lake City, Utah 84101
(801) 531-7868

Vermont

Vermont Council on the
  Humanities and Public Issues
Grant House, P.O. Box 58
Hyde Park, Vt. 05655
(812) 888-5060

Virginia

Virginia Foundation for the
  Humanities and Public Policy
One-B West Range
University of Virginia
Charlottesville, Va. 22903
(804) 924-3296

Washington

Washington Commission for
  the Humanities
Olympia, Wash. 98505
(206) 866-6510

West Virginia

Humanities Foundation
  of West Virginia
Box 204
Institute, W. Va. 25112
(304) 768-8869

Wisconsin

Wisconsin Humanities
  Committee
716 Langdon Street
Madison, Wis. 53706
(608) 262-0706

Wyoming

Wyoming Council for
  the Humanities
Box 3274, University Station
Laramie, Wyo. 82701
(307) 766-6496